Disputatio

An International Transdisciplinary Journal
of the Late Middle Ages

Disputatio 5:
Medieval Forms of Argument: Disputation and Debate

2002

*While this volume was in preparation, all those connected to *Disputatio* were saddened to hear of the death, on April 1st 2001, of Leslie W. Workman, who has been a steadfast supporter of *Disputatio* and a member of *Disputatio*'s editorial advisory board since 1996. Leslie Workman's main scholarly achievement consists in having established medievalism, i.e., the study of the reception of medieval culture in post-medieval times, as an academic field. This achievement has been recognized in the volume *Medievalism in the Modern World. Essays in Honour of Leslie Workman* (Turnhout, 1998), edited by Richard Utz and Tom Shippey. "Studies in Medievalism," the organization he founded, is alive and well, organizing annual conferences and publishing conference proceedings, *The Year's Work in Medievalism,* and the journal, *Studies in Medievalism.*

Disputatio

An International Transdisciplinary Journal
of the Late Middle Ages

Disputatio 5:
Medieval Forms of Argument: Disputation and Debate

Edited by Georgiana Donavin, Carol Poster, and Richard Utz

Wipf and Stock Publishers
Eugene, Oregon 2002

Wipf and Stock Publishers
150 West Broadway
Eugene, Oregon 97401

Printed in the United States of America

ISBN: 1-57910-916-0

Acknowledgements

We would like to thank our editorial board, Dr. Jeffrey Copeland, Head, Department of English Language and Literature, University of Northern Iowa, and the University of Northern Iowa Graduate College for their continued support. We would also like to thank Jack Clifford for his production work on the journal. Our greatest thanks are owed to the English Department (and especially Dr. Hunt Hawkins, Chair) and the College of Arts and Sciences of Florida State University for sponsoring the journal.

Disputatio

Volume 5 Spring 2002

The Issue of Theological Style in Late Medieval Disputations **1**
Mishtooni Bose

Order in Obligational Disputations **23**
Tomas Ekenberg

Albert the Great and Pagan Ethics: His Elaboration of Aristotle's Reflections on the Scientific Character of Ethics **41**
Jörn Müller

Joseph Albo, der Messias und die Disputation von Tortosa **53**
Sina Rauschenbach

Talk is Cheap: Political Discourse in Malory's *Morte Darthur* **67**
Cory Rushton

"Pinning Him to the Wall": The Poetics of Self-Destruction in the Court of Juan II* **87**
Gregory S. Hutcheson

The Love Debate Tradition in the Reception of Gower's *Confessio Amantis* in the Iberian Peninsula **103**
Francisco Javier Grande Quejigo and Bernardo Santano Moreno

The European *Querelle des* femmes **127**
Gisela Bock and Margarete Zimmermann

Muslime und Christen im *Grafen Rudolf* und in der *Kreuzfahrt Landgra Ludwigs des Frommen von Thüringen*: Zu Toleranz und Religiösem Disput zur Zeit der Kreuzzüge **157**
Maria Dorninger

La réception en langue vulgaire du "De falconibus" d'Albert le Grand **189**
An Smets

The Issue of Theological Style in Late Medieval Disputations

Mishtooni Bose

In November 1499, Erasmus recounted in a letter to John Sixtin an informal but heated theological disputation which had recently taken place over dinner at an Oxford college. Erasmus was careful to note the seating arrangements at this occasion, over which John Colet presided, and dryly drew attention to the way in which they seemed to have been designed so as to procure an even balance between the representatives of theology and the secular arts: 'ille Theologus, cui nos quidem laeuum latus clausimus, ne poeta conuiuio deesset. Ex aduerso Philippus, ne non adesset iuris peritus' ('in order to make sure that the feast had its poet, I sat next to the theologian, on the left flank, with Philip opposite, to ensure the presence of a lawyer'). The disputation, which began almost immediately, concerned the nature of Cain's sin. Colet, whom Erasmus initially presented as 'the defender and champion of the ancient theology' ('veteris illius theologiae vindex atque assertor'), maintained that Cain's sin was that of excessive self-reliance, as shown in his ploughing the earth instead of pasturing his sheep, which Abel did 'in contentment with things that grew of themselves' ('sponte nascentibus contentus'). Erasmus and the unnamed theologian took issue with Colet and they contended separately against their adversary, 'the theologian using syllogistic logic while I employed the methods of rhetoric' ('Theologus ille syllogismis, ego rhetoriis').[1] Notwithstanding the considerable disputative resources at their command, Erasmus and his scholarly ally were unable to win the argument from Colet.

This is a brief but carefully crafted vignette, and the degree of subsequent reflection prompted by the necessity of interpreting the event for Sixtin has clearly led Erasmus to give a self-consciously ambivalent colouring to the episode. The account is compelling for the way in which it captures for the reader a moment of apparently courteous, instinctive and unselfish collaboration between the disputative methods of the theologian and the poet, but it is also imbued in the retelling with the suggestion of latent tensions between the vocations represented at the dinner table. Erasmus concludes his account of the disputation, which he deemed too serious for a bout of table talk, by casting himself in a festive role, saying that he 'decided to play my part, that is, the part of a poet' ('tum ego meis, hoc est poetae, partibus functurus'). The spontaneity of the respectful collaboration between theology and rhetoric gives way to notably stereotypical self-presentation on Erasmus's part. Insistent on characterising himself in a manner calculated to evoke the emerging contest of cultures between rhetoric and dialectic, he rapidly retreats from the tantalising possibilities of reciprocity between the two arts, whose disputative resources had only a few moments previously been martialled against the inspired Colet.

The modern scholar, familiar with the contours of late medieval debates between scholastics and humanists, and in particular with those portions of the debates devoted to invective, the trading of *ad hominem* insults and the ritual denigrations of professional competence, may find this account valuable for its suggestion of a brief rapprochement between the practitioners of the arts of dialectic and rhetoric. Professional self-consciousness has led Erasmus to dramatise his Oxford disputation in ultimately oppositional terms, and it is impossible to know whether the disputation against Colet was really conducted with such courtesy and decorum, but, whatever the relationship between the narrative and actual events, Erasmus's version raises further questions about the extent to which he was committed to acknowledging that rhetoric and syllogistic, the techniques with which poetry and theology were most closely identified, could be viewed as complementary rather than conflicting modes of argument. A later and notably eirenic depiction by Erasmus of the use of dialectic in medieval theology gives further grounds for this line of inquiry. Nearly thirty years after his impromptu Oxford disputation, Erasmus offered a more considered acknowledgement of the fact that the different argumentative methods used by successive generations of theologians could be viewed as having been put to similar uses. This awareness is articulated in a brief history of medieval theology in which a shared commitment to disputation against heretics is seen as uniting the literary genres used by the Church Fathers and those honed by their successors, the scholastic theologians. The short history of disputative theology was not without its own rhetorical purpose: sustained attacks from his academic critics had led Erasmus to include in the tenth edition of the *Colloquia* a defence of the genre's pedagogic utility. In attempting to solicit support for his choice of literary form and to defend the gravity of his purpose, Erasmus constructed a history of disputation which is notable for its emphasis on the continuity, rather than the conflicts, between successive generations of theologians:

> Aliis aliae sunt dotes et alios alia capiunt, milleque modis homines trahuntur ad pietatem ... Adversus haereticos turbam intendit Hilarius, argutatur Augustinus, Hieronymus dialogis pugnat, Prudentius vario metri genere dimicat, Thomas et Scotus dialectices ac philosophiae praesidiis pugnat. Simile studium omnium, sed dissimilis singulorum ratio. Non reprehendit diversitas, quae scopum eundem petit.[2]

> [There is diversity of gifts and tastes; men are drawn to godliness by a thousand means ... Hilary thunders against heretics, Augustine disputes, Jerome contends in dialogues, Prudentius wars in various forms of verse, Thomas and Scotus fight with the help of dialectic and philosophy. All have the same purpose but each uses a different method. Variety is not condemned so long as the same goal is sought.] [3]

In evaluating scholastic theology in this uncontentious way, Erasmus acknowledges that different theological styles might be required by different circumstances and that the apparent stylistic discontinuity between the genres of ancient and medieval theology should not be allowed to obscure their common purpose: the defence, explication and elaboration of faith. Moreover, the narrative suggests that alternatives between disputative methods are essentially alternatives between *rhetorical* methods, the superficial diversity of theological styles underscored by a shared commitment to apologetic. Thus, Erasmus is able to align his own methods both with the disputations of the Church Fathers and with the dialectical engagements of Aquinas and Scotus (significantly letting pass the opportunity to indulge a sideswipe at the latter in particular). Within the terms established by this narrative, Scotus is depicted as continuing the work of the Fathers, rather than as a wilfully obscurantist and anti-charismatic figure.

Erasmus suggests that, when they are regarded principally as defences of the faith, even the scholastic exercises of Aquinas and Scotus may be viewed as performing persuasive as much as demonstrative functions. His consideration of the medieval church's diverse responses to heresy suggests, therefore, that in the face of such challenges, theologians must retain a keen awareness of the extent to which their professional requires mastery in techniques which could conventionally be regarded as aspects of the art of rhetoric. Far from dismantling the authority of the scholastic theologians, Erasmus was here contributing to the late-medieval discussion of a topic which had been of considerable concern to them: the extent to which the style of theology should be explicitly argumentative. This subject had once featured very prominently in the prologues to some of the most influential and widely-known commentaries on the *Sentences* of Peter Lombard, but declined in prominence during the fourteenth century, as a later generation of theologians subordinated discussion of explicitly rhetorical issues to questions pertaining to epistemology and metaphysics.[4] This did not absolutely preclude consideration of theological style, however, and, as will be discussed below, the subject returned to prominence in the late fifteenth- and early sixteenth-century literary debates through which the institutional culture of scholasticism was vehement criticised. Possibly the most self-reflexive of these debates was the long-running disputation concerning the legitimacy, charisma and moral vigour of disputative theology itself, and involvement in this debate obliged disputants to revisit the subject of theological style in explicitly rhetorical terms, which were in some cases similar to those used by the twelfth- and thirteenth-century commentators.

In a recent assessment of current scholarship concerning the methodological differences between humanists and scholastics, Charles G. Nauert has spoken of 'a yawning chasm between two antithetical conceptions of proper intellectual method' and conjures up the bleak picture of a fundamental lack of communication between the adherents of either approach.[5] In an attempt to modify this view of the relationship between the two cultures, this article will further the study of that relationship by examining an issue which, for some time, had the potential to resolve the impasse that Nauert describes. As has been seen, Erasmus's brief discussion of medieval theology is notable for the way in which it allies the achievements of scholastic and patristic theology, the urgent demands of self-defence having obliged him, in this particular narrative, to emphasise continuities in intellectual history. It would seem, therefore, that discussion of theological style in this period could, on occasion, challenge the assumption of absolute discontinuity not only between the persuasive and the demonstrative functions of theological discourse but also, and consequently, between the aims and methods of different generations of theologians. The argument from continuity had, however, been given a yet more distinctive inflection by a defendant of scholastic culture, Jacob Wimpheling, the Strasbourg theologian and contemporary of Erasmus who has featured with some prominence in recent discussions of this period and whose arguments this article will consider in some detail. Wimpheling's alertness to stylistic and historical continuity enabled him to give sustained consideration to an understanding of the scholastic past to which Erasmus was only fitfully committed. His defence of scholasticism accordingly involved an attempt to provoke awareness of the rhetorical finesse and commitment of the schoolmen and to argue that the incorporation of disputative rhetoric in patristic writings and in the scriptures themselves legitimated the overtly argumentative style of later academic theology and validated it as an essential tool in the defence of faith.

II

In order that the debate concerning theological style be accurately situated in the context of the critique of scholastic culture, it is first necessary to draw some distinctions between several closely related strands of that critique. The general contours of the debates between scholastics and humanists have been widely rehearsed and require little in the way of extended discussion here.[6] The chief concern of the present argument is to emphasise the distinction between medieval logic (a tool of analysis) and disputation (a cultural practice). Although these distinguishing characteristics of scholastic culture are sometimes conflated in anti-scholastic polemic, it is important to distinguish between the art of logic on one hand and, on the other, the practice of disputation. Although academic disputations were certainly seen as having been governed by rules concerning *obligationes* which were the province of medieval logic, disputation was also a pedagogic instrument which, as has been suggested above, could be regarded as having affiliations with rhetoric.[7]

An important strand of the anti-scholastic critique was devoted to consideration of semantic analysis, and originated in fourteenth-century criticisms concerning the analytic limitations of logic.[8] As developed later in the writings of Jean Gerson, for example, this strand of the critique took the form of a concern with the adequacy or otherwise of scholastic logic as a tool of analysis for the interpretation of scriptural statements.[9] The development of this strand of criticism ran parallel chronologically and thematically with the broader critiques of scholastic logic advanced by others, such as Lorenzo Valla, Thomas More and Juan Luis Vives. Nevertheless, despite the relative familiarity of modern scholars with the evolution of criticisms concerning scholastic culture and practices, it is still insufficiently emphasised that the comparative (and hardly ubiquitous) decline in prestige of scholastic logic as an analytical tool was not automatically accompanied by a decline in the prestige of the disputation *per se* as a vehicle for analytical inquiry within academic institutions and beyond, particularly in view of the fact that cultural developments as diverse as the revaluation of the Platonic dialogue and the Reformation debates were to give the genre a new lease of life. The writings of Italian humanists in the fifteenth century, for example, show a profound awareness of what a 'good' disputation might seek to achieve as a means of leading the mind towards truth, and their experiments with the genre reaffirm its continuing intellectual fertility.[10] The Italian perspective on this subject reinforces an appreciation of the heterogeneity of attitudes to disputation in the late Middle Ages, among which Northern disaffection was not necessarily the predominant element.[11]

The development of medieval logic and the development of the oral and literary genres of scholasticism, which included disputation, ran along parallel lines that should not be confused. What it has become possible to speak of under the collective heading of 'scholastic method' is really a coalescence between two kinds of writing with different origins. The origin of the *quaestio*, as Erasmus tacitly acknowledges in his potted history of disputation, extends as far back as patristic literature and the *quaestiones* of Augustine, for example.[12] These early questions provided influential models of the way in which literary criticism could proceed through the identification and exploration of textual cruces. The development of the literary *quaestio* was not necessarily dependent on the gradual absorption of the writings of Aristotle into university curricula during the early medieval period. The scholastic article and *quaestio* are structured in such a way as to reconcile apparently contradictory arguments or authorities and, like their cognate oral genre, the *disputatio*, they have a history independent from that of the academic interpretation of the Organon. As John Marenbon writes, 'the procedure [which Aristotle's *Topics*] describes bears little resemblance to that of the *quaestio*. A *quaestio* is designed to reconcile texts which appear contradictory; the elenchic debate described in the *Topics* has nothing to do with texts nor does it aim at the resolution of any problem'.[13] This impetus towards formal resolution may be seen in the literary forms of quodlibetal questions which had originally been 'staged' over two days. With the opening questions on the first day and the determinations on the next, masters were left with the task of synthesising the previous day's material in what another scholar significantly describes as an apparently logical manner. It has been asserted that these determinations were essentially 'artificial' ('factice'), constructed to give coherent resolution to the problems disputed.[14] Furthermore, it has also been pointed out that the wording of determinations was also flexible: Godfrey of Fontaines, for example, begins the determination to one section of his fourth quodlibet by explicitly opting for probable conjecture over the language of demonstrative resolution.[15]

Nevertheless, even if the argument for the 'parallel histories' of medieval disputation and logic is accepted, it is also necessary to establish in what sense medieval scholastic could be regarded as a persuasive discourse. It has been argued that Aquinas was aware that 'there is always a rhetorical element in teaching', but the question as to what is denoted by 'rhetoric' in such a context requires further consideration.[16] There has been some reluctance on the part of modern scholars to treat scholastic methods of argument as having rhetorical dimensions, and it is not difficult to see why an attempt to speak of, for example, thirteenth-century scholastic literature in terms of its persuasiveness could arouse some unease. It might be thought that arguments in support of the view of scholastic theology as a kind of rhetoric might be difficult to form, and might court accusations of a historical thinking, since it is comparatively difficult to catch the schoolmen in the act of reflecting on the philosophy and the rhetoric of their own literary methods.

Evidently, too general a use of the term 'rhetoric' in this context proves less than helpful, since it is a term which schoolmen are, on the whole, markedly reluctant to use in any context. Nevertheless, recent scholars have sought in different ways to show that the interpretative techniques of scholasticism were imbued with more than merely vestigially rhetorical considerations, and that the schoolmen used a coalescence between the structural categories of classical rhetoric and the Aristotelian notions of 'causes' as a means of organising their commentaries on authoritative texts.[17] Both Bonaventure and Aquinas make frequent references to the works of Cicero: for example, in the *Summa Contra Gentiles*, Aquinas makes use of Cicero's *Partitiones oratoriae*, a work that specifically addresses the structural rather than the affective dimensions of rhetoric, and it is an interest in varieties of argumentative structure and *dispositio*, as much as in the resources of scriptural tropes, which gives the scholastic engagement with rhetoric its distinctive character.[18] As will be discussed briefly below, the keen appreciation on Aquinas's part of the persuasive value and efficacy of structural oppositions also appears as an important principle underpinning the style of argumentation chosen for the *Summa Contra Gentiles*.

Some of the schoolmen's most illuminating comments on the literary implications of their techniques of argumentation appear in a discussion which frequently occurs in *Sentences*-commentaries and which is apparently far removed from the subject of rhetoric. This concerns the basis on which arguments ('rationes') may be used in theology. In the *Sentences*-commentary of St. Bonaventure, the author defines the 'modus procedendi' of his commentary as 'perscrutatorius, et inquisitivus', an argumentative style clearly designed to imitate the ratiocinative processes of a mind in search of understanding. The ratiocinative or analytical style of systematic theology uses arguments 'in three ways, according to three kinds of people. For some are the adversaries of faith; others are infirm in faith; others are perfect' ('Modus enim ratiocinativus sive inquisitivus valet ad fidei promotionem, et hoc tripliciter secundum tria genera hominum. Quidam enim sunt fidei adversarii, quidam sunt in fide infirmi, quidam vero perfecti').[19] This perception of differences between the argumentative purposes of theology, whether redargutive, pedagogic or consolatory, is also a recognition that the art requires a variety of persuasive strategies.

Aquinas's defence of an obtrusively rational rather than a viciously rationalised faith obliged him to frame comparable arguments for the legitimacy of natural reasoning which have the same rhetorical implications as do those of Bonaventure. In the ninth question of his fourth quodlibet, he asks 'whether a master, in determining theological questions, is more obliged to use reason, or authority'.[20] It might seem, he argues, that theology, whose first principles are the articles of faith, should be taught by means of authority alone. In opposition to this view, however, he cites St. Paul's letter to Titus (I:9), in which Paul urges the early Christians to argue against those who speak against the faith. Aquinas concludes that a learned disciple should be prepared to answer his critics, 'but those who contradict [the faith] are better won over by arguments than by authorities' ('contradicentes melius revincuntur rationibus quam auctoritatibus'). In his response to the question, Aquinas identifies two purposes to the academic disputation. The first is for the removal of doubts, and in such kinds of disputation it is of great value to use authorities respected by one's opponents. The Jews, for example, accept the authority of the Old Testament; the Manichees do not accept this, but will accept that of the New Testament; with schismatics, the matter is easier to resolve, since they accept the authority of both. There is, moreover, a further kind of disputation, which is called 'magistral'. This takes place in schools, 'not for the removal of error, but for the instruction of those attending, that they might be led towards the understanding of the truth which the master intends'. In this case, it is necessary to support the truth with original arguments which will make known not merely what the truth is, but how it works. If authorities alone are used, the student will know what constitutes 'truth', but will have acquired it parrot fashion, in a manner devoid of any valuable knowledge or understanding ('sciencia vel intellectus'). The syllogistic discourse of natural reason forces the student's mind to adopt the requisite mental postures in order fully to grasp the truth. It could certainly be argued that a degree of artifice is at work here. Aquinas is showing that a master has choices as to what form the magistral determination will take, and that such a choice must be based on recognition of the fact that alternative methods exist for leading the mind towards truth, in accordance with the character and experience, or otherwise, of the audience. This requires looking beyond the internal coherence of a science to the demands of those attempting to master it, and requires the use of a pedagogically appropriate and effective method of procedure rather than one whose course has been inflexibly pre-determined in accordance with the internal structure of the subject. The skilful teacher has to command similar selective and skills as those of the orator. This dimension of scholastic method is also at work in St. Bonaventure's discussion of the strategic use of different kinds of syllogisms in his commentary on the fourth book of the *Sentences*, in which he draws a distinction between the 'ostensive syllogism ('syllogismus ostensivus'), which leads directly to the truth, and which may be used with those who are 'tractable and pliable ('tractabiles et pliabiles'), and the syllogism 'per impossibile', which confronts less malleable opponents with a *reductio ad absurdum*.[21] There is a clear recognition here that choices between modes of communication are to a large extent determined by the character of the intended audience. Bonaventure manages to convey a sense that the syllogism was not merely an inert tool of argument, but an instrument of reasoning which, by virtue of the variety of its forms, could be adapted to the particular needs of different kinds of men. Once again, the formal and apparently inscrutable apparatus of scholasticism tells an incomplete story: Bonaventure on occasion reveals a degree of sensitivity towards different styles of utterance that is distinctly pragmatic.

Such pragmatism is taken much further in Aquinas's *Summa Contra Gentiles*. In the ninth chapter, Aquinas discusses the work's 'order and mode of procedure' ('ordo et modo procedendi'). He argues that divine truth is twofold: it is beyond the powers of human reason to grasp this in its purest manifestation, but it is possible to address those aspects of that truth which are accessible to human cognition, 'which relates to the knowledge of divine things in different ways'.[22] Aquinas describes his mode of procedure by saying that he will first put forward arguments using both demonstrative and probable reasons, some of which will be taken from the writings of the philosophers and the fathers, so that the truth may be reinforced and a possible adversary defeated. Secondly, he will attempt to make manifest those truths that exceed the capacities of human reason. Although these truths may not be demonstrated 'from within', since their internal structure is not open to human investigation, Aquinas will attempt to make them manifest by starting with an attempt to unpick the arguments of his adversaries. This will be achieved with the help not of demonstrative science but of 'probable reasons and authorities' ('rationibus probabilibus et auctoritatibus').[23]

Nevertheless, although the thirteenth-century schoolmen exhibited an awareness of the pragmatics of teaching and disputation which could legitimately be called 'rhetorical', this phase of scholastic self-consciousness gradually declined. In a quasi-mimetic process, the disappearance from *Sentences*-commentary prologues of discussions concerning theological style accompanied a general slackening of the rigid structure of the scholastic article familiar from Aquinas's works, as later prologues to commentaries on the *Sentences* reflected the interests of subsequent generations of theologians in questions of epistemology and metaphysics.[24] Thus, in fourteenth-century *Sentences* commentaries, the standard discussion as to whether or not theology is a *scientia* remained, but the consequent and explicitly *literary* question concerning the legitimacy of its literary form (*forma tractandi*), which had been a matter of some concern to earlier theologians such as Alexander of Hales, St. Bonaventure and Thomas Aquinas, became less and less explicitly a part of discussions of this topic. Nevertheless, concerns with epistemology and metaphysics did not entirely banish the question of literary form but recast it in terms very different from those used by Bonaventure and Aquinas.

The progress, and indeed the transformation of this question in late medieval theological disputations may be appreciated through the comparison and contrast of two commentaries on the *Sentences* written nearly a hundred years apart. The first is the work of the Dominican, Johannes Capreolus, whose commentary on the first book of the *Sentences* was completed in 1409.[25] Capreolus was engaged in a defence of Aquinas and his text makes heavy use of quotations from his master, in addition to permitting a fair representation of objections from the Franciscan commentator Petrus Aureolus and the Augustinian Gregory of Rimini, and also from Henry of Ghent and Durandus of St. Pourçain, all of whom had reached fundamentally different conclusions regarding the status and aims of theology. Capreolus's commentary is useful, therefore, both as a compendium of thirteenth- and fourteenth-century views on this group of questions and as a revealing witness to the survival and reinterpretation of those questions in the fifteenth century. Its title in the printed edition used here - 'Quaestiones ... ad Scholasticum certamen egregie disputatae' - reinforces the sense of Capreolus's having staged a disputation between himself and the fourteenth-century theologians in the interests of developing Aquinas's arguments and equipping them with new resources.[26]

In the prologue, Capreolus rehearsed the formulaic questions as to whether or not theology was a science, whether it was speculative or practical and the way in which, as an academic discipline, it related to its subject matter. In attempting to defend the theories of Aquinas to a new generation of theologians, he was obliged to engage in 'disputations' with some formidable fourteenth-century opponents. The arguments which Capreolus selects from Gregory of Rimini, for example, show that he had managed to weave into his criticisms of Aquinas's belief in theological science a revealing series of arguments which undermined theology's claim to be regarded as a demonstrative discipline. He had argued that theological discourse could not be regarded as a 'demonstration' of truths, for, if this were the case, the well-disposed infidel would be forced, by the operation of his natural powers, to assent to the conclusions of theology. Rather, theological argument rested on the power of authorities.

In responding, Capreolus offered a subtle appreciation of the extent to which theological discourse could be regarded as 'quasi-demonstrative'. He began by enlarging on the sense in which theology could not strictly be called a science. Quoting Aquinas verbatim, he nevertheless drew on arguments which emphasised the persuasive components in theological discourse. He quoted Aquinas as having argued that the arguments which are drawn from the writings of the saints in order to defend the faith 'are not demonstrative, but have a certain persuasive quality' ('non sunt demonstrativae, sed persuasiones quaedam') in order to show that what is proposed in faith is not impossible; alternatively, they proceed from the principles of faith, namely, from the authorities of sacred scripture.[27]

When answering Gregory's argument that the Bible does not proceed in the manner of a scientific demonstration, Capreolus granted this initial premise, but proceeded to argue that the saints had constructed arguments, which operate like the principles of a science, on the basis of scriptural evidence, and that theology proceeds from these principles by arguing against heretics. In this way, although the theology transmitted through the canon of holy scripture did not use an explicitly syllogistic style ('stilus syllogisticus'), nevertheless, in the works of later theologians it had been treated in the style of a science ('modo scientifico') and of an art ('modo artis'), that is, as a body of knowledge capable of systematic explication. Moreover, this mode of argument had been anticipated in the scriptures, as when St. Paul confirmed his statements in accordance with the evidence of the Old Testament, and Christ disputed with the Jews, urging them to 'Search the scriptures'.[28]

Petrus Aureolus had also argued that the articles of faith were not the first principles of theology, but rather its conclusions, which it was the duty of theologians to defend and 'declare'. Nevertheless, Thomas and other theologians had framed questions concerning the articles of faith and had treated them as the raw materials of disputation (‘ad eas dissolvendum, declarandum, & concludendum’) as, for example, when the Trinity was called into question.[29] This objection also had important implications for the nature of theological style, as Capreolus's response made clear. He granted that no science proceeds towards the demonstrative proof of its own principles; but nothing, he argued, forbade a science from making its principles manifest by means of similitudes (‘per aliquas similitudines’) and from defending them against detractors, or from showing that opposed arguments may be refuted. This was the reason for which Thomas and other doctors formed questions concerning the articles of faith and these were the grounds on which Capreolus justified a theology structured in such a manner as to imitate the inductive path of human ratiocination, using such principles as its starting-points, rather than treating them as a set of pre-determined conclusions towards the confirmation of which all theological discourse was to be aimed in a strictly deductive manner. Theological discourse might not be precisely and absolutely demonstrative but, he maintained, it could still be legitimately 'argumentative'.[30] Capreolus's significant concession clarified the Thomist understanding of the purpose behind the logical appearance of academic theology: it was intended to serve a multiplicity of discursive functions from the plainly redargutive to the 'making manifest' of doctrinal truths. Capreolus also acknowledged that it was necessary to use different kinds of material in disputations, depending on the nature of the disputants. In certain contexts, for example, as in disputations with heretics, it was possible to use the authorities of sacred scripture. If, on the other hand, it was not possible to find common ground with the disputant, whence arguments respected by both sides might be used, it was necessary to rely on the assumption that, since faith was grounded in infallible truth, it was impossible to demonstrate the contrary, since arguments brought against the faith were *solubilia*, capable of refutation, rather than negative demonstrations.[31]

At the root of the disagreement between Capreolus, Aureolus and Gregory lay fundamentally opposed interpretations of the function of the rhetoric of disputation in theology. In many ways, the disputation staged by Capreolus anticipated the contours of much ensuing debate in the fifteenth and early sixteenth centuries concerning the legitimacy of disputative theology, not least in the different and often contrasting uses to which patristic literature was put by the participants. Significantly, Capreolus's invocation of a *Christus dialecticus* and a *Paulus dialecticus* was in the tradition of defences of disputative theology whose origins could be found in patristic literature, and to which St. Augustine had made notable contributions.[32] Aureolus, likewise, had invoked Augustine's authority when arguing that the articles of faith should be treated as conclusions, rather than as the starting-point for dialectical activity. Capreolus devotes a considerable amount of space to the recapitulation of Aureolus's arguments. In *Contra Faustum*, Aureolus had argued, Augustine had set out to prove a particular article of faith, namely that Christ had become incarnate of the Virgin Mary. This example was taken by Aureolus to prove that theological arguments did not take the articles of faith as their starting-points, but argued towards the confirmation of those articles which in effect were being treated as pre-determined conclusions. According to Aureolus, Augustine had insisted in the *De Trinitate* and elsewhere that the proper purpose of theology was to generate, defend and nourish faith, but Aureolus believed that this could not be achieved unless the discourse of the theologian was directed towards the defence of the articles of faith, that is, unless theological argumentation was fundamentally deductive.[33] Capreolus, on the other hand, simply denied that Augustine had in mind an exclusively 'declarative, or defensive' theology. Augustine's legacy in this respect was, therefore, notably ambiguous, with either side in the disputation being able to call upon his authority for support. The reception and contestation of St. Augustine's authority is, therefore, a significant sub-text of the late medieval dispute concerning the rhetoric of theology.[34] Was he to be identified with a legitimately disputative theology, or with an affective theology whose literary modes were essentially confirmatory rather than analytical?

III

One indication of the directions taken by the controversy concerning theological style at the close of the medieval period is given by the discussion of the topic in the second example, Paulus Cortesius's commentary on the *Sentences*. In his prefatory remarks to Beatus Rhenanus, included in the 1513 edition of this commentary, Conrad Peutinger invokes Cicero in support of his argument that eloquence has value as an explanatory method which would be of help to theologians[35] and fulsomely praises the eloquence of Cortesius, whose ability succinctly to marshal the differing opinions of theologians he particularly admires.[36] This is followed by a long epistle from Cortesius himself to Pope Julius II which defends the use of eloquence in theological discourse but in terms which do not permit recognition of the persuasive character of scholastic discourse. First printed in Rome in 1504, only five years after Erasmus's Oxford disputation, the commentary is all too redolent of the climate of opposition between poets and theologians and, although its defence of the role of natural eloquence is subtle and discriminating, the position adopted by Cortesius is ultimately more adversarial than conciliatory, with traditional theologians depicted as in need of persuasion in order to recognise the benefits of eloquence to their profession. If anything, this is a reclamation of theology for rhetoric, rather than an assertion of the intrinsically persuasive qualities of much theological disputation: the balance has shifted in favour of *elocutio* and to the disadvantage of *dispositio*. A greater contrast with Capreolus's commentary cannot be imagined, and Cortesius' commentary, which likewise rehearses Thomist and counter-Thomist positions in its opening *distinctio*, shows the extent to which the terms of the debate concerning theological style had been transformed in the intervening century.[37]

The heterogeneity of late medieval positions regarding theological style may be demonstrated, however, by a treatise entitled *De ortu, progressu et fructu sacrae theologiae*, which pursues an argument very different from that of Cortesius and explicitly revives the discussion of theological style in an idiom which could have been recognisable to the thirteenth-century theologians who pioneered the development of the topic. In the seventh chapter of the treatise, entitled 'De modo tractandi in progressu sacrae scripturae', the author, whom Erika Rummel identifies as Jacob Wimpheling, identifies two ways in which theology may be said to teach.[38] The first method is characterised as being that of 'an art and a science', and a barrage of adjectives asserting its analytical and disputative character follows, with the style being described as 'perscrutatorius: ratiocinativus: & per rationes ad fidei defensionem, adversariorum confutationem, infirmorum confirmationem, & perfectorum in theologicis delectatorius: disputativus: inquisitivus & probativus …'.[39] This is the kind of obtrusively disputative theological discourse which is used among professional academics, and the author goes on to cite Augustine's *De Trinitate* in support of this mode of argument, to the effect that arguments should be used in defence of the faith against 'chatterers' ('garrulos') and those who are more enthusiastic than discriminating ('elatiores magis quam capaciores'). The second method, which is affective rather than disputative, reflects the duty that theology owes to simple faith, and takes cognisance of the fact that human affections are drawn to what is good and deterred from what is bad in a variety of ways. Theological discourse ought, therefore, to incorporate a variety of methods in order to achieve its aims of teaching and nourishing the faithful. Thus, the extensive rhetorical repertoire of scripture may be defended on the grounds that the various modes which it employs, whether narrative, preceptive, prohibitive, exhortative, and so on, are really components of a single authentic and authoritative style.

Wimpheling's even-handed portrayal of theological style, in which the disputative and the affective elements collaborate and reinforce each other, recalls the terms of earlier medieval theology which argued for the legitimacy of a disputative component to theology. In particular, in the passage discussed above, he attributes to disputative theology the same set of purposes that had been identified by Bonaventure, specifically the refutation of adversaries, the strengthening of faith in those whose believe is infirm and the delectation of those whose belief is strong. Wimpheling has achieved a certain prominence in modern discussions of the institutional contexts in which the debates between scholastic and humanist cultures were conducted.[40] He is a complex character whom it is difficult to claim for either side of the debate: Nauert identifies him as a humanist, and Rummel draws attention to some anti-scholastic sentiments in his correspondence and elsewhere, but the difficulty of classification in this case indicates, if anything, the inadequacy of the categories themselves, particularly in the case of such a prolific writer.[41] Wimpheling's contribution to the debates was not, moreover, conducted solely by means of authorship, for he was also a prolific editor and, while several of his editorial choices show the esteem in which he held preaching and contemplation, one in particular reveals the profundity of his understanding of the implicitly rhetorical awareness at work in the exegetical writings of earlier generations of schoolmen.[42] This is his edition of the influential *Compendium Biblie Totius* by Petrus Aureolus (1319), and it contains prefatory remarks in which he defends his choice of text on the grounds that Aureolus knew the writings of Cicero and St. Augustine and other sources congenial to potential critics of such a volume and was therefore a good example of an academic whose eclectic tastes complicated the stereotypes peddled by the critics of scholasticism.[43] Significantly, Wimpheling's prefatory epistle was addressed to Johann Eck, a theologian at Ingolstadt, where Wimpheling's best-known adversary, Jacob Locher, had been involved in a further phase of the controversy.[44]

Wimpheling's presentation of Aureolus shows his understanding that the editing of such a text afforded the opportunity to present what amounted to an alternative version of scholastic theology which emphasised its more rhetorically-sensitive aspects. It could be argued that Wimpheling's characterisation of Aureolus as a sensitive reader of the classics is simply a Procrustean attempt to mollify potential and actual critics, but Aureolus's exegesis serves Wimpheling's purposes quite plausibly. In a manner typical of an early fourteenth-century exegete, he divides the books of the Bible according to their stylistic modes, whether prophetic, poetic, disputative or historical, the generic categories thereby providing an interpretative matrix which serves as the foundation for exegesis, and which reflects the variety of ways in which sacred doctrine is accommodated to human understanding. Thus, the Pentateuch falls within the 'political and legislative' category, books such as Joshua, Judges and the books of Kings within the category of 'history', and Isaiah and Jeremiah within the 'prophetic' genre. Job and Ecclesiastes are characterised as 'dialectical and disputative' books.

Aureolus's rhetorical approach is also applied to the New Testament, most compellingly in the case of St. Mark's Gospel, which, as the work of an Evangelist, falls formally within the 'testimonial and affirmative' category. Aureolus's teaching concentrates on the way in which the structure of the text is a series of proof adduced in favour of one conclusion: 'haec est conclusio quam marcus in evangelio suo intendit: hominem Jesum esse et fuisse virtuosissimum dominum et imperatorem ac regem omnium' ('this is the conclusion which Mark intends in his Gospel: that Jesus is a man, *and* was the most virtuous Lord, ruler and king of all' [my emphasis]).[45] The most significant element in Aureolus's analysis of Mark is his perception that the text is structured so as to reinforce a syllogism concerning the divinity and humanity of Christ. As part of his reconstruction of the propositional element in the syllogism, Aureolus first lists the many characteristics proved by the events in Mark's narrative to be associated with Christ: his virtue and power extend to all spirits, created and uncreated; he also has it within his power to cure the sick and to forgive sins. The 'assumption' of the syllogism is the statement that a man capable of all these things must be the most righteous kind and Lord of all. The man who was called Jesus fulfilled all these conditions; thus, it follows in conclusion that he is the Lord of all. Mark proves this conclusion, Aureolus declares, by narrating Christ's deeds in such a way as to produce a syllogism of this kind.[46] The fusion between Mark's doctrinal and rhetorical purposes is not uncovered in a single statement, or series of statements; the interpretation of the narrative is cumulative, its conclusion proved by implications which must be drawn out by the reader in the way intimated by Aureolus's guidance. This is far from logic-chopping of the kind lampooned in humanist polemics. Aureolus shows instead that the syllogism can be deployed less esoterically as a rhetorical tool. Wimpheling's editorial remarks could therefore be seen as a justifiable attempt to find common ground with his opponents, rather than asserting the essential incommensurability of their methods with those which he was defending, or relying on claims of absolute superiority for the traditional methods which, as he takes pains to argue, have much in common with the literary tastes of his opponents.

Acknowledgement of the scriptural authors' investment in the rhetoric of disputation served as the basis for Wimpheling's own defence of scholastic style in a pamphlet explicitly designed to refute the arguments in favour of poetry that had been advanced by Jacob Locher. He insisted on a proper recognition of the dialectical qualities inherent not only in the Old Testament and in St. Paul's writings, but also in the exchanges between Christ and his disciples. The first authority whom Wimpheling invokes in chapter seven is 'the blessed Augustine', and later on he employs the *Soliloquia, De Doctrina Christiana* and *De Utilitate Credendi* in support of the argument that a theological style which incorporates questions and answers is a valuable road to truth. He notes that 'Luke the evangelist alludes to this mode of disputing ('hunc disceptandi modum'), from the characters of the Hebrews arguing *pro* and *contra* in response to the question put to them by Christ concerning the baptism of John'.[47] The text itself, Luke 20: 1-8, which Wimpheling does not discuss in detail, offers a prolonged and explicit use of techniques which the attacks of humanists were in the process of undermining. Christ is approached by the chief priests and scribes, who ask him by what authority he preaches the gospel. Instead of answering them directly, he responds with a question of his own, asking them if John's power of baptism was granted by heaven or by men. This confronts them with a dilemma, for, as they reveal when they confer among themselves, if they say it came from heaven, Christ will accuse them of not having believed John. If they say it was from men, they will be stoned by the people, who are convinced that John is a prophet. Facing an impasse, they admit that they cannot answer his question. He responds by saying that he, too, is unable to answer theirs. Christ has confronted the priests and scribes with a dilemma not unlike that infamous target of much humanist polemic, the 'crocodile'. He is here depicted using an argumentative tactic which Wimpheling's readers would have been able to identify as an *insolubilium*, albeit strikingly *avant la lettre*.[48]

The dialectical habits of Christ, St. Augustine and St. Paul, therefore, are called by Wimpheling in defence of traditional theological style. St. Paul, he writes, 'used this kind of question in many places in his Epistle to the Romans'.[49] Nor is the language of the prophets lacking in logical clarity and valid arguments. Wimpheling adduces as evidence of this the following extract from the first chapter of Malachi: 'the son honours his father; and the servant his lord ... if, therefore, I am a father, where is my honour? And, if I am a lord, where is the fear?'.[50] Wimpheling proceeds tartly to suggest that, were Locher's nose not blocked with the catarrh of ignorance, he would sense in these words of the prophet a beautiful 'locus' or dialectical topic. There is here a 'hidden' syllogism, and Locher would sense a hypothesis here and a strong dialectical argument ('the son honours his father; I am a father; I should be honoured'). 'If the triumphant Aristotle, who says that opposites placed next to each other appear more clearly, is insufficient, let Christ vanquish [Locher]', Wimpheling adds, the phrase from Aristotle's *Rhetoric* (1418b4) clarifying the extent to which scholastic argumentation may be identified as an artful deployment of the rhetorical *dispositio*. Wimpheling links Locher with Lorenzo Valla as an exemplar of the new contempt for authorities such as Isidore of Seville, who claimed that 'it is better to confer than to read. For conferring together ('collatio') creates docility ['teachableness']'. Returning to Augustine, lest Locher think that he had been reduced to drawing on unimpressive authorities, Wimpheling cites the opening book of *De civitate dei*, in which it is claimed that 'reasons and similitudes should be used against the chatterers for the defence of the faith' and, continuing to make use of Augustine's authority, Wimpheling borrows his argument to the effect that 'there is nothing so true that it might not become more true if chewed over in a disputation', for, in this process, 'two people dispute, object, respond, reply ... ('disceptant: obijciunt:respondent: replicant') and at last ... arrive at the truth. These exercises cannot be suitably accomplished without enthymemes and syllogisms...'.[51]

Wimpheling still firmly believes in the scholastic disputation as a vehicle for discovering the truth, rather than solely for teaching or for exciting admiration. It would be impossible, he maintains, to resist either heretics or infidels without philosophy and the benefits of dialectic. The consequence of this is that 'all well founded and solidly understood theology has its need of dialectical links and connections'. Wimpheling praises the 'industrious and most wise' Fathers, defiantly adding that 'today, whether among the Parisians, and in many German gymnasia, or in the most holy, venerable orders of the mendicants (at least in two), they avidly read those questions: they elucidate and dispute them ...'[52] The last example is a particularly vivid vignette of the re-enactment of disputes whereby textual *quaestiones* were brought to life.

Wimpheling's pamphlet is hardly free of the polemical sclerosis that increasingly marked the exhanges between the advocates of humanism and scholasticism, and it would be difficult to argue for its arguments having exerted great influence in subsequent phases of the debate, but it is, nonetheless, important for the distinctiveness and resourcefulness of the views expressed, which keep alive the sense expressed in the works of the schoolmen themselves that the relationship between demonstration and persuasion was often subtle and determined by context. Scholarship on Wimpheling, in the form of the works cited here, has tended to emanate from those concerned chiefly with the early modern period, but to the medievalist he offers an appreciation of the scholastic command of rhetorical finesse which is particularly instructive. His arguments are also important in view of the fact that, like the exchange between Capreolus and the opponents of Aquinas, they involved him in a contesting of the patristic legacy, an important strand throughout the debate in which he and others were engaged. It is, as is well known, a debate in which Erasmus also vigorously participated. While recent scholarship has drawn attention to the way in which Erasmus forged a relationship between his published persona and that of St. Jerome, it has long been noted that a similar relationship existed between the humanist and his other mentor, St. Augustine.[53] In 1529, Erasmus produced an edition of the doctor's complete works. Throughout his biographical introduction to the works, Erasmus attempts to claim Augustine for the side of what might be termed the practice of 'good' disputation. When enumerating Augustine's duties and achievements, he includes disputation as part of the natural armoury of one who combats heresy. In his description of Augustine's life, however, Erasmus carefully balances the claims of *sciencia* and *caritas*:

> There are those who delight in frivolous disputations ('argutiis') … There are those who subtly teach the things that are necessary ('subtiliter doceant necessaria'), but do not bring it about so that what is understood is loved. Again, there are those who excite people to the study of piety, but do not sweep those whom they have excited with their teaching off their feet ('excitatos doctrina non provehunt'). Unless you love what you have understood, you will understand in vain …[54]

Erasmus proceeds to show how Augustine, while maturing in faith, managed to preserve the equilibrium between these two extremes of the Christian life. He depicts him as intent on the investigation of the truth and as an acute disputant, but also as one who was interested not in learning for its own sake but in erudition as a means of promoting a good life. In such a way, Augustine could be incorporated into an implicit 'grand narrative' of theological style in which the most important role of disputation was in engagements with heretics. The examples discussed throughout this article have suggested the extent to which late medieval discussions of theological style were indebted to different appropriations of scriptural and patristic literature, and to different constructions of the history of theology, and of disputation in particular. It is a line of inquiry which is hardly exhausted, and which should inform future study of the uses of the past that informed the literary sensibilities and strategies of both the humanists and the scholastics.

University of Southampton

Notes

1. *Opus epistolarum* 1:268; *Correspondence*, 230. The college in which the disputation took place has been most plausibly identified as Magdalen.

2. Desiderius Erasmus, 'De utilitate colloquiorum', first included in the tenth edition of the *Colloquia* (Basle: Johannes Froben, 1526); here taken from *ASD* I.iii: 749.

3. *The Colloquies of Erasmus*, 633. Unless otherwise indicated, all further translations of Latin sources are my own.

4. On notions of theology as a science during this period, see Chenu, *La théologie comme science*; Köpf, *Die Anfänge der theologischen Wissenschaftstheorie*; On discussions of literary form in scholastic texts, see Minnis, *Medieval theory of authorship*, 118-147; Minnis and Scott, 197-276.

5. Nauert, 433.

6. The secondary literature on the development of the humanist critique of scholastic techniques is extensive. The most comprehensive recent account is Rummel (1995) which has an excellent bibliography on the subject. See also Jardine, 'Lorenzo Valla', Evans, Levi, Oberman, Perreiah, O'Rourke Boyle and Lawn.

7. This is not to avoid the thorny matter of the relationship between logic and dialectic in the late medieval period. The fluidity with which the terms *logica* and *dialectica* were used throughout the medieval period had the effect of turning dialectic into the 'Alsace-Lorraine' of the late-medieval trivium, sharing and on occasion contesting territory with both logic and rhetoric. The situation is complicated further with the emergence of the 'rhetoricised' dialectic of Agricola, on which see Mack (1993). For a general overview of the shifting medieval perceptions concerning the relations of dialectic with its sister-arts, see Michaud-Quantin, Ashworth (22) and McKeon. On the use of logic in disputation, see Angelelli, and on *obligationes*, see Stump and Spade, 'Obligations'.

8. For discussion of the academic context, see Courtenay, 'Force of words'.

9. 'De Duplici Logica'. *Oeuvres* 3:57-63.

10. See Gilbert.

11. Gilbert notes that 'the intellectual situation in Italy at the beginning of the fifteenth century differs significantly from the conditions that prevailed later at the University of Paris when Erasmus and Vives developed their lifelong aversion for dialectic'. Noticing that passages dealing with the utility of logic and disputation occur very frequently in the humanist dialogue, Gilbert suspects of Bruni's *Ad Petrum Histrum Dialogus* that 'the initial concern of these talks in Florence … was to promote the cause of serious yet relatively informal disputation' (204). For further discussion of the relation between the Italian dialogue and dialectic, see Cox.

12. On the origins of the *quaestio*, see Lawn, Bardy, Marenbon 10-1, 27-34; Bazan 21.

13. Marenbon, 13.

14. Glorieux (1925), 42, 45.

15. 'Sed nihil hoc determinando sed probabiliter coniecturando' (quodlibet 4, q. 3), quoted by J.F. Wippel in *Les questions disputées*, 92.

16. Otto Bird, 148.

17. Minnis; Minnis and Scott; Copeland, particularly 63-86.

18. For discussion of this aspect of the *Summa Contra Gentiles*, see Allard. See also Aquinas's 'De commendatione et partitione sacrae scripturae', in *Opuscula theologica* 1:435-439.

19. St. Bonaventure, *Commentarium in Primum Librum Sententiarum*, prol. Q2: *Opera* 1:11.

20. *Quaestiones Quodlibetales*, quod. 4.q.9. a.3. (83).

21. *Commentarium In IV Sententiarum.*, dist. xviii, pars ii. art. unicus, q.i. *Opera* 4: 485a.

22. *Liber de veritate Catholicae Fidei* … cap.9 (51).

23. The awareness that properly nuanced critical attention to the structure and purpose of the *Summa Contra Gentiles* requires the use of a sophisticated rhetorical taxonomy has informed some of the most stimulating recent scholarship on this text: see Jordan, Hibbs.

24. The changing emphasis in theology during this period is commented on briefly by Courtenay, *Schools and scholars*, 190-2.

25. On Capreolus, see Grabmann.

26. Capreolus (1588-89).

27. Capreolus 10. Capreolus was quoting from the *Summa Theologiae* 2a2ae. q.1 ar.5 ad.2.

28. Capreolus 11.

29. Ibid., 6.

30. Ibid., 11.

31. Ibid.

32. Pépin, especially 223-7.

33. Capreolus, 6.

34. The contest over Augustine's ambiguous legacy is alluded to briefly by Rummel 116-118.

35. *In Sententias*, a1^{r}.

36. Ibid., a6^{r}.

37. Ibid., b2^{v}-4^{r}.

38. For the attribution to Wimpheling, see Rummel 203.

39. *De ortu,* 165^{v}.

40. Rummel, 75-77, 79-80; Overfield, especially 81-86, 192-207; Bené, 'L'humanisme de J. Wimfeling', Heath 22-24.

41. Nauert 429; Rummel 67, 227-228. See also Overfield 207.

42. For further examples of Wimpheling's editorial choices, see his editions of the *Speculum anime* (1507) and *Modus predicandi* (1513).

43. *Compendium*, ai^{r}.

44. On this controversy, see Rummel 70 and Overfield 185-202. On Eck, see Heath, 55-59.

45. *Compendium*, m3^{r}.

46. Ibid.

47. *Contra turpem* bii^r. Overfield identifies the original place of publication as Nuremberg, and notes that it was issued by the Weissenberg firm (202).

48. For further discussions of medieval insolubilia, see Ashworth (1972).

49. *Contra Turpem*, bii^r.

50. Ibid. The reference is to Malachi 1:6.

51. Ibid.

52. Ibid.

53· On Erasmus and Jerome, see Jardine (1993). On Augustine, see Bené, *Erasme et Saint Augustin.*

54. D. Aurelii Augustini Hipponensis Episcopi Omnium Operum Primus Tomus, 7.

Works Cited

Primary

Aureolus, Petrus OFM. *Compendium Biblie Totius*, ed. Jacob Wimpheling. Strasbourg, 1514.

Aquinas, Thomas. *Opuscula Theologica.* Ed. P. Mandonnet. Rome: Marietti 1954. 1.

—. *Quaestiones Quodlibetales.* Ed. R. Spiazzi. Turin and Rome: Marietti, 1949.

—. *Liber de veritate catholicae fidei contra errores infidelium (Summa Contra Gentiles).* Turin and Rome: Marietti, 1961.

Capreolus, Johannes O.P. *In Libros Sententiarum Amplissimae Quaestiones Pro tutela Doctrinae S. Thomae ad Scholasticum certamen egregis disputatae* Venice, 1588-9.

Bonaventure, St. *Opera Omnia* . 10 vols. Quaracchi:Collegium S. Bonaventurae, 1882-1902.

Cortesius, Paulus. *In Sententias.* Basle, 1513.

Erasmus, Desiderius. *Opus Epistolarum*, ed. P.S. Allen. 12 vols. Oxford: Clarendon Press, 1906-1958. 1.

—.*Opera Omnia Desiderii Erasmi Roterodami recognita et adnotatione critica instructa notisque illustrata* (Amsterdam: North-Holland Publishing Co., 1969-) = ASD. 1.iii.

—. *The correspondence of Erasmus* 1-141, 1484-1500, trans. R.A.B. Mynors and D.F.S. Thomson, annot. Wallace K. Ferguson. Toronto and Buffalo: University of Toronto Press, 1974. *Collected Works of Erasmus* 1.

—. *The Colloquies of Erasmus*, trans. and annot. Craig R. Thompson. Toronto, Buffalo and London: University of Toronto Press, 1997. 2. *Collected Works of Erasmus* 40.

—, ed. *D. Aurelii Augustini Hipponensis Episcopi Omnium Operum Primus Tomus*. Basle, 1529.

Gerson, Jean. *Oeuvres* ed. P. Glorieux. Paris and New York: Desclée, 1962. 3: 57-63.

Wimpheling, Jacob. *Contra Turpem Libellum Philomusi Defensio Theologicae Scholasticae & Neotericorum.* n.p., n.d.

—. (attr.) *De ortu, progressu et fructu sacra theologiae. Farrago Miscellaneorum Conradi Wimpinae*. Cologne, 1531.

—, ed. *Speculum anime seu soliloquium Heinrici de Hassia.* Strasbourg, 1507.

—, ed. *Modus predicandi subtilis & compendiosus Stephani Hoest.* Strasbourg, 1513.

Secondary

Allard, G-H. 'Le "Contre Gentiles" et le Modèle Rhétorique'. *Laval philosophique et théologique* 30 (1974): 237-250.

Angelelli, I. 'The techniques of disputation in the history of logic'. *Journal of Philosophy* 67 (1970): 800-815.

Ashworth, E.J. *Language and logic in the post-medieval period.* Dordrecht and Boston: Reidel, 1974.

—. 'The Treatment of Semantic Paradoxes from 1400 to 1700'. *Notre Dame Journal of Formal Logic* 13 (1972): 34-37.

Bardy, G. 'La littérature patristique des quaestiones et responsiones sur l'écriture sainte'. *Revue Biblique* 41 (1932): 210ff., 314ff., 515ff.; 42 (1933): 14ff., 211ff., 328ff.

Bazan, B.C. 'Les questions disputées'. *Les questions disputées et les questions quodlibétiques dans les facultés de théologie, de droit et de médecine.* eds. B.C. Bazan, J.F. Wippel, G. Fransen and D. Jacquart. Typologie des sources du moyen âge occidental, 44-5. Turnhout: Brepols, 1988.

Bené, Charles. 'L'humanisme de J. Wimpfeling'. *Acta Conventus Neo-Latini Lovaniensis.* Proceedings of the First International Congress of neo-Latin studies, Louvain, 1971 eds. J. Ijsewijn and E. Kessler. Louvain: Louvain University Press, 1973): 77-84.

—. *Erasme et Saint Augustin.* Geneva: Droz, 1969. Travaux d'humanisme et Renaissance 103.

Bird, Otto. 'How to read an article of the *Summa*'. *New Scholasticism* 27 (1953): 129-159.

Chenu, Marie-Dominique OP. *La théologie comme science au xiiie siècle.* Third edition. Bibliothèque Thomiste 33. Paris: J. Vrin 1957.

Copeland, Rita. *Rhetoric, hermeneutics and translation in the middle ages: academic traditions and vernacular texts.* Cambridge: Cambridge University Press, 1991.

Courtenay, William. *Schools and scholars in fourteenth-century England.* Princeton, NJ: Princeton University Press, 1987.

—. 'Force of words and figures of speech: the crisis over *virtus sermonis* in the fourteenth century'. *Franciscan Studies* 44 (1984): 107-28.

Cox, Virginia. *The Renaissance Dialogue. Literary dialogue in its social and political contexts, Castiglione to Galileo.* Cambridge: Cambridge University Press, 1992.

Evans, G.R. 'Lorenzo Valla and the theologians'. *Journal of Theological Studies* 38 (1987): 436-441.

Gilbert, Neal W. 'The Early Italian Humanists and Disputation'. *Renaissance Studies in Honor of Hans Baron* eds. A. Molho and J. Tedeschi. DeKalb, Ill.: Northern Illinois University Press, 1971, 203-226.

Glorieux, P. *La littérature quodlibétique de 1260 à 1320.* Bibliothèque Thomiste 5. Kain: Le Saulchoir, 1925.

Grabmann, Martin. 'Johannes Capreolus O.P., der "Princeps Thomistarum", und seine Stellung in Geschichte der Thomistenschule'. *Mittelalterliches Geistesleben*, ed. Ludwig Ott. Munich: Max Hueber, 1956. 3: 370-410.

Heath, Terrence. 'Logical grammar, grammatical logic and humanism in three German universities'. *Studies in the Renaissance* 18 (1971): 9-64.

Hibbs, Thomas S. *Dialectic and narrative in Aquinas. An interpretation of the Summa Contra Gentiles.* Notre Dame and London: University of Notre Dame Press, 1995.

Jardine, Lisa. *Erasmus, man of letters. The construction of charisma in print.* Princeton, NJ: Princeton University press, 1993.

—. 'Lorenzo Valla and the intellectual origins of humanist dialectic'. *Journal of the History of Philosophy* 15 (1977): 143-164.

Jordan, Mark D. 'The protreptic structure of the Summa Contra Gentiles'. *Thomist* 50 (1986): 173-209.

Köpf, Ulrich. *Die Anfänge der theologischen Wissenschaftstheorie im 13. Jahrhundert*. Beiträge zur historischen Theologie 49. Tübingen: Mohr, 1974.

Lawn, Brian. *The rise and decline of the scholastic 'quaestio disputata'. With special emphasis on its use in the teaching of medicine and science*. Leiden, New York and Cologne: Brill, 1993.

Levi, A.H.T. 'The breakdown of scholasticism and the significance of evangelical humanism'. *The philosophical assessment of theology. Essays in honour of Frederick C. Copleston*, ed. Gerard J. Hughes. Tunbridge Wells: Search, 1987. 101-128.

Mack, Peter. *Renaissance Argument. Valla and Agricola in the traditions of rhetoric and dialectic*. Leiden, New York and Cologne: Brill, 1993.

McKeon, Richard. 'Rhetoric in the middle ages'. *Speculum* 17 (1942): 1-32.

Marenbon, John. *Later medieval philosophy 1150-1350. An introduction*. London: Routledge 1987. 1991.

Michaud-Quantin, P. 'L'emploi des termes *logica* et *dialectica* au moyen âge'. Artes libéraux et philosophie au moyen âge. Actes du quatrième congrès internationale de philosophie médiévale. Montréal: 1969. 855-862.

Minnis, A.J. *Medieval Theory of Authorship. Scholastic literary attitudes in the later middle ages*. Second edition. Aldershot: Wildwood House, 1988.

— and A.B. Scott, eds. *Medieval literary theory and criticism c. 1100-1375: the commentary tradition*. Revised edition. Oxford: Clarendon Press, 1991.

Nauert, Charles G. 'Humanism as Method. Roots of Conflict with the Scholastics', *Sixteenth-Century Journal* 29 (1998): 427-438.

Oberman, Heiko. 'Via antiqua and via moderna: late medieval prolegomena to early Reformation thought'. *From Ockham to Wyclif* eds. Anne Hudson and Michael Wilks. Studies in church history subsidia 5. Oxford: Blackwell, 1987. 445-463.

O'Rourke Boyle, Marjorie. 'Fools and Schools: Scholastic Dialectic, Humanist Rhetoric: from Anselm to Erasmus'. *Medievalia et Humanistica*. ns 13 (1985): 173-195.

Overfield, James. *Humanism and Scholasticism in Late Medieval Germany*. Princeton, NJ: Princeton University Press, 1984.

Pepin, Jean. *St. Augustin et la Dialectique*. The Saint Augustine Lecture 1972. Villanova, PA: Augustinian Institute, Villanova University, 1976.

Perreiah, Alan. 'Humanist critiques of scholastic dialectic'. *Sixteenth-Century Journal* 13 (1982): 3-22.

Rummel, Erika. *The Humanist-Scholastic Debate in the Renaissance and Reformation*. Cambridge, Mass. and London: Harvard University Press, 1995.

Stump, Eleonore and Paul Vincent Spade. 'Obligations'. *The Cambridge History of Later Medieval Philosophy* eds. Norman Kretzmann, Anthony Kenny and Jan Pinborg. Cambridge: Cambridge University Press, 1982. 315-341.

Order in Obligational Disputations

Tomas Ekenberg

Summary

In this paper I examine the phenomenon of order-dependence in obligational disputations. I am concerned with two medieval authors, Walter Burley and Richard Kilvington. In Burley's theory I especially concentrate on two of the 'useful' rules of *positio*, namely "one must pay special attention to the order" and "when a false contingent proposition is posited, one can prove any false proposition that is compossible with it". I argue that there is an intimate connection between these two rules in that they both express consequences of the notion of relevance inherent in the constitutional rules in connection with a false *positum*. Closely connected to the concept of order-dependence are the special kinds of inconsistencies that can be found in Burley's theory. I call these 'interdisputational' inconsistencies. Kilvington finds these consequences of Burley's theory unacceptable. According to Kilvington, there should be no inconsistencies and, consequently, no order-dependence. Regretfully, he does not present any explicit revision of the rules for obligational disputation in which his views are incorporated. Finally, I turn to the 'relativised' interpretation of Burley's theory, and more specifically the proposed purpose or meaning of the first useful rule. According to Paul Spade, Burley may be giving advice in saying "one must pay special attention to the order", referring to some preferred ordering of propositions. On my view, this interpretation is highly problematic. Burley's own explanation of the rule does not seem to support such an interpretation. Furthermore, the second of the two rules examined in this paper seems difficult to reconcile with the notion of a preferred order. If however, as I propose, the rules are simply seen as consequences of the constitutive rules, Burley's explanation is no problem and Kilvington's critique becomes clearly intelligible.

Introduction

Medieval treatises on obligational disputation concern a special kind of disputation, reminiscent of the Aristotelian dialectical arguments. The theories typically present a set of rules for a verbal exchange between two people, an opponent and a respondent. The opponent is to propose sentences, and the respondent is to reply to these sentences in accordance with the rules.

Modern discussions have primarily centered on the problem of how to interpret the disputational situation and obligational theory in general. As there is no evidence to support that these obligational disputations were actually performed, it is often supposed that obligational disputations were a 'convenient fiction.' Paul Spade has suggested that the theory of *obligationes* is in essence a theory of contrary-to-fact conditionals (counterfactuals). Mikko Yrjönsuuri claims obligations should rather be seen as a kind of thought experiment. Because the modern concept of counterfactuals is too narrow to capture the essential features of obligational theory, Henrik Lagerlund and Erik Olsson suggest that *obligationes* is a theory for belief revision. This can be seen as a refinement of Spade's interpretation, taking into consideration some of those aspects Spade's interpretation cannot account for. Common to all the foregoing positions is that they include the notion of *obligationes* as a technique for constructing consistent sets of sentences that may have some relation to the actual world. A different approach can be found in Eleonore Stump. On her view, *obligationes* is simply a technique for constructing paradoxes or sophismas.[1] These sophismas are typically disputations involving problematic references to the disputational context.[2]

In the present paper, I will be concerned with two medieval authors. The first is Walter Burley, whose *Treatise on Obligations* is among the best-known works in the genre.[3] The treatise contains a presentation of a set of rules along with a discussion. Burley's rules can be considered as standard for fourteenth century *obligationes*. The second author is Richard Kilvington.[4] In his treatise *Sophismata*, he formulates a critique of the standard rules of obligations.

A puzzling detail in Burley's theory is the fact that the order, in which the proposed sentences are put forward, can affect the outcome of the disputation. The prime aim of this paper is to clarify the connection between this peculiarity, the notion of relevance and the special kinds of inconsistencies that arise as a result of the rules. These connections are fundamental for the understanding of Burley's conception of obligational disputations. I will furthermore show how this yields a plausible interpretation of Kilvington's critique.

Background

Superficially, medieval obligational disputation can be seen as a highly technical and much stylized form of the dialectical disputation laid forth in Aristotle's *Topics*. In book VIII of the *Topics*, Aristotle describes the roles of the questioner and the answerer in such an argument:

> The business of the questioner is so to develop the argument as to make the answerer utter the most implausible of the necessary consequences of his thesis; while that of the answerer is to make it appear that it is not he who is responsible for the impossibility or paradox, but only his thesis. (159a15-24)

Aristotle identifies three types of dialectical discussion. The first type is arguments for the purpose of teaching and learning, the second is arguments conducted as competitions and the third is arguments for the sake of practice and experiment (159a25-39). Aristotle's primary concern is the third type, and his explicit aim is to stipulate rules for this kind of arguments. The starting-point of an Aristotelian argument is typically generally accepted or plausible views (*endoxa*), and the object of the argument is to examine or to test these views. The arguments culminate in a conclusion, in accordance to which the thesis is either accepted or rejected.

Included in the introduction of Walter Burley's *Treatise on Obligations*, dated around 1302, is a paraphrase on the passage in the *Topics*, quoted above:[5]

> The opponent's job is to use language in a way that makes the respondent grant impossible things that he need not grant because of the *positum*. The respondent's job, on the other hand, is to maintain the *positum* in such a way that any impossibility seems to follow not because of him but rather because of the *positum*. (Burley 0.01)

Aristotle's treatment of the dialectical disputation in the *Topics* is generally considered to be part of the origin of the obligational disputations discussed during the Middle Ages.[6] There is also another passage in Aristotle's *Organon* that is referred to in the medieval treatises on obligations. In part 13 of the *Prior Analytics* Aristotle says, "I use the terms 'to be possible' and 'the possible' of that which is not necessary but, being assumed, results in nothing impossible" (32a18-20). Together, these passages can be seen as a rough outline of the medieval conception of obligational disputation. In a disputational context, if a possible thesis is put forward, the disputation should not end in any contradictions. If it does, it must be the case that some logical error has been committed.

From an Aristotelian point of view, Walter Burley's work on disputations is probably most accurately described as pertaining to the second type, the contentious or competitive type of argument. This is made clear by the way in which he alters the wording of the description of the roles. In Aristotle, the role of the questioner (or "opponent" in medieval terminology) was to make the answerer accept the paradoxes inherent in or resulting from the thesis (or "*positum*"), whereas in Burley, the opponent is to make the respondent grant even "impossible things that he *need not grant*" (italics mine) because of the thesis.

It must be pointed out, however, that obligational disputation may well have been used as a teaching-instrument, although in a different way from the Aristotelian arguments.[7] In the medieval obligational disputations, interest has shifted towards the logical structure of disputation rather than the status of the thesis. Interest lies no longer primarily, or even at all, in examining whether what is generally held true is true. The thesis in an obligational disputation is often false. Instead, the focus is on the logical relationship between the thesis and the set of propositions put forward by the opponent, and the groundwork that in part determine this relationship, i.e. the rules governing the disputational situation.

Although disputes concerning obligational theory did indeed occur during the Middle Ages, one of which I will describe in the present paper, the rules of Walter Burley can in some sense be considered as standard and representative for fourteenth-century obligational theory.[8] One could say it is against the background of Burley's theory that various problems are discussed. I will therefore begin by outlining Walter Burley's theory of obligations.

Walter Burley's Obligations

An obligational disputation has two participants, an opponent and a respondent. Propositions are put forward by the opponent, and the respondent answers to each proposition by either granting, denying or saying that he is in doubt about it. The opponent's job is to get the respondent to contradict himself, while the respondent tries to stay consistent. The opponent has succeeded and the disputation is over if the respondent has answered badly, i.e. both granted and denied the same proposition. The respondent has succeeded if he has managed to get through the stipulated time-period without contradictions. Thus, there are two ways in which a disputation can end. Either the respondent has contradicted himself, which is sufficient to bring the disputation to an end, or the time is up and the phrase "The disputation is over" (*"Cedat tempus"*) is uttered, preferably by an impartial authority, a judge. After the disputation has ended it is to be determined whether the respondent has answered well.

In the beginning of his *Treatise on Obligations*, Burley makes some distinctions regarding the different species of obligations. The respondent can be obligated either to an act or a disposition. An act in this disputational sense may for example involve giving a certain answer to a specific proposition.

As for the obligations concerning dispositions, Burley divides them into those covering terms and those covering propositions. In the former, the obligation typically involves giving a new meaning to a term. For example, the respondent may be required to maintain that 'a man is a donkey.' In the latter, the respondent is required to maintain a proposition as either true, false or doubtful. In the species called *positio*, the respondent is obligated to grant a specific proposition, called the *positum*, should he be confronted with it. In *depositio* he is to deny, and in *dubitatio* he is to doubt the corresponding proposition.[9]

The species that is given the most attention by Burley is *positio*. This is also the one he uses as a prototype in the general description of obligational disputations in the introduction of his *Obligations*, quoted above. The disputation starts when a *positum* has been put forward.

> At the beginning of making a *positio*, we use the verb 'It is posited'; and at the end we use the expression 'The disputation is over' (*cedat tempus*). The respondent is obligated until 'The disputation is over' is said, unless the opponent and respondent agree otherwise. (Burley 3.04)

The proposition that is posited can be either possible or impossible. I will in this paper only be concerned with the first.[10] According to Burley there are two kinds of rules for the respondent in possible *positio*. First, there are constitutive rules. These rules constitute the practice of the art and concern what is posited and what is relevant and irrelevant, given the *positum*.

C1. Everything that is posited and put forward in the form of the *positum* during the time of *positio* must be granted.

C2. Everything that follows from the *positum* must be granted. Everything that follows from the *positum* either together with an already granted proposition (or propositions), or together with the opposite of a proposition (or the opposites of propositions) already correctly denied and known to be such, must be granted.

C3. Everything incompatible with the *positum* must be denied. Likewise, everything incompatible with the *positum* together with an already granted proposition (or propositions), or together with the opposite of a proposition (or the opposites of propositions) already correctly denied and known to be such, must be denied.

C4. If it is irrelevant, it must be responded to on the basis of its own quality; and this [means] on the basis of the quality it has relative to us. For example, if it is true [and] known to be true, it should be granted. If it is false [and] known to be false, it should be denied. If it is uncertain, one should respond by saying one is in doubt.[11]

In possible *positio*, an impossible proposition should not be admitted. The proposition that is posited may either be true or false. In any case, this proposition must be granted in accordance with rule C1.

A false *positum* is often accompanied by a proposition that makes definite the stipulated truth of the matter, the *casus*. This latter proposition can also be false. Together they form a kind of double hypothesis, e.g. "The truth of the matter is that Socrates is black; It is posited that Socrates is white".

The succeeding propositions can either be relevant or irrelevant. If the propositions are relevant they either follow or are incompatible. A proposition is incompatible if and only if its opposite, its negation, follows from the *positum*, or the *positum* together with one or more of the previously granted and denied propositions. A proposition that follows should be granted and an incompatible proposition should be denied, in accordance with rules C2 and C3.

> The rule concerning what follows and what is incompatible must be understood either conjointly or dividedly. But the rule concerning what is relevant must be understood only conjointly. For in order for something to be irrelevant, it needs to be irrelevant to the *positum*. And if some propositions are already granted, [what is irrelevant] must be irrelevant to the *positum* together with all the propositions that are granted. (3.32)

As soon as an irrelevant proposition has been granted or denied, it is no longer irrelevant, and should be treated as part of the body formed by the *positum* and all the previous propositions. It is in this sense that the rule is to be understood conjointly. The body of propositions, taken as a whole, determines the relevance and compatibility of future propositions.

In addition to the constitutive rules, Burley puts forward a set of rules that he characterizes as not constitutive, but useful:

U1. One must pay special attention to the order [of the propositions].
U2. During the time of the obligation one should not give a definite answer to a question requiring a distinction.
U3. Outside the time [of the disputation] the truth of the matter must be acknowledged.
U4. When a possible proposition has been posited, a proposition that is impossible *per se* must not be granted, and a proposition that is necessary *per se* must not be denied.
U5. When a possible proposition has been posited, it is not absurd to grant something impossible *per accidens*.
U6. When a false contingent proposition is posited, one can prove any false proposition that is compossible with it.
U7. When a false contingent proposition concerning the present has been posited, one must deny that it is the present instant.
U8. All responses must be directed at the same instant.
U9. When the *positum* is false, the proposition 'The *positum* is false' can be granted; and yet concerning what is posited one must never grant that it is false.[12]

These rules serve to clarify and complement the constitutive rules, and are more practical and specific in character. One could also say that these rules help the respondent avoid the most obvious traps in the hands of a cunning opponent.

For example, rule U2 aims at excluding a type of question as inappropriate that would otherwise soon bring the respondent into trouble.[13] Burley presents the following example: The stipulated truth of the matter is that Socrates alone is speaking, while it is posited that Socrates is silent. Then 'Some man is speaking' is proposed. The respondent will have to grant it, as it neither follows from nor is incompatible with the *positum*, and therefore is irrelevant and furthermore true in accordance with the initial, stipulated state of affairs. If the opponent then asks 'Who is this man (who is speaking)', the respondent will have to answer 'Socrates (is speaking)', which clearly contradicts the *positum*, and brings the disputation to an abrupt end. What Burley says is that the respondent should refuse to answer such a question. If instead of the question 'Who is this man who is speaking' the proposition 'Socrates is speaking' had been put forward, the respondent could simply have denied it as incompatible, without complication. In fact, the only questions the respondent should take into consideration are propositions that he can either grant, deny or say that he is in doubt about.

In order to avoid paradoxes based on the progress of time, the time in an obligational disputation is assumed to stand still in a sense. This property is expressed in rule U8. The respondent is to answer to the propositions as if they were all put forward at the same instant.

A complete discussion of the rules is beyond the scope of this paper.[14] Instead, I will now turn to the special problem of order and relevance. First, I will show how the problem manifests itself in Burley's theory, and then I will try to delineate Richard Kilvington's views on the problem.

Order and Relevance

The constitutive rules never require the respondent to grant a proposition that he is to deny at another stage in the same disputation.[15] The set of propositions representing the disputation will remain consistent in this sense on condition that the respondent is answering well. However, even Burley himself recognises a peculiarity here. In connection with the introduction of rule U1, 'One must pay special attention to the order', he writes:

> [A] proposition that is to be granted in one place is not to be granted in another place. Therefore, when some proposition is proposed, we should consider its order relative to propositions previously granted. (3.34)

Burley shows his point by means of an example of two disputations sharing the same *casus*, *positum* and propositions, differing only in the order of when the propositions are put forward. The *casus* states that the truth of the matter is that both Socrates and Plato are black. It is then posited that Socrates is white.

Positum: Socrates is white	
1. Socrates and Plato are alike (in color)	(granted: true and irrelevant)
2. Plato is white	(granted: follows)

Positum: Socrates is white	
1. Plato is white	(denied: false and irrelevant)
2. Socrates and Plato are alike (in color)	(denied: incompatible)

In this example, the proposition 'Plato is white' has both been granted and denied, albeit not in the same disputation. What is at issue here, therefore, is no inconsistency in the sense that a contradiction has occurred in a single disputation, but rather what I will call an interdisputational inconsistency. Furthermore, this is the stronger form of interdisputational inconsistency.

A second, weaker kind of interdisputational inconsistency is related to propositions that are in doubt for the respondent. This can be illustrated by the following example, where A and B are contingent sentences, neither of which implies the other. The truth or falsity of A is unknown and B is known to be false:

Positum: $A \vee B$	
1. A	(doubted: unknown and irrelevant)
2. B	(denied: false and irrelevant)
3. A	(granted: follows)

When A is proposed the first time, it is neither known to be true nor false. However, when it is introduced the second time, it follows from the *positum* and the opposite of B by means of disjunctive syllogism. If the opponent in a second disputation had initially proposed B instead of A, and after that A, the proposition A would never have been doubted. Therefore, as regards the two disputations, the respondent has granted in one what he has doubted in another.

An additional kind of inconsistency can also be found in the example above. The respondent has both doubted and granted, i.e. not been altogether consistent in his replies to, the same proposition in a single disputation. It must however be pointed out that this is not a form of interdisputational inconsistency, although it is intimately connected to the interdisputational inconsistency sketched above.[16]

Another peculiarity in Burley's theory is what is explicitly expressed in rule U6, namely that "when a false contingent proposition is posited, one can prove any false proposition that is compossible with it." In the following example, the truth of the matter is that the respondent is not in Rome, and that he is not a bishop (Burley 3.61).

Positum: You are in Rome
1. You are not in Rome or you are a bishop (granted: true and irrelevant)
2. You are a bishop (granted: follows)

The first proposition 'You are not in Rome or you are a bishop' does not follow from the *positum*. Neither does its opposite follow from the *positum*, or, in other words, it is not incompatible with the *positum*. Consequently it is to be considered irrelevant and answered to in accordance with the respondent's knowledge. In reality, the respondent is not in Rome and is not a bishop. The disjunction 'You are not in Rome or you are a bishop' is true against this background, and the respondent is obligated to grant the proposition. When 'You are a bishop' then is proposed, it follows from the *positum* and the granted disjunction by means of disjunctive syllogism, and the respondent has no choice but to grant it as sequentially relevant.

From an epistemic point of view, this is an example of duties in conflict. When the respondent is confronted with 'You are a bishop', a clash occurs between the respondent's duty to answer in accordance with his own knowledge and the *prima facie* duty to maintain the *positum* as true.

It is the granting of the disjunction that is the critical step. If A is the sentence 'You are in Rome' and B is the sentence 'You are a bishop', what happens is that the semantic background connected to the component "A" in the disjunction shifts from being something related to the knowledge of the respondent to being strictly determined by the *positum*. As the *positum* is contrary to fact, this will inevitably lead to a difference in truth-value before and after the granting of the disjunction.

Positum: A_P *Positum:* A_P
1 $\neg A_K \vee B$ $\Rightarrow$ The respondent grants 1 $\Rightarrow$ 1. $\neg A_P \vee B$

(2. B)

Evidently, the constitutive rules for *positio* do not allow for this compositional analysis. The disjunction is unconditionally to be seen as a semantic whole. The suggested compositional conception, if it were to make some other answer possible for the respondent, would require a revision either of the constitutive rules concerning what is relevant and irrelevant, or of the concept 'logical consequence' that is embedded in these rules, or of both. In other words, it is the notion of relevance that is the cause.

In his discussion on the matter Burley also offers two alternative formulations of the first sentence to be proposed:

1a. That you are in Rome and that you are a bishop are alike
1b. That you are in Rome and that you are a bishop are alike in truth or falsity

In the disputation in question, these propositions will produce the same result as the disjunction. They, however, differ in regard to the disjunction in that they predicate something of propositions rather than simply expressing a state of affairs. In (1a) the propositions are said either to share a likeness with regard to modal status, or to share a likeness with regard to truth-value.[17] The modes recognised by medieval logicians included truth and falsity together with necessity, contingency, possibility and impossibility. In (1b) the criterion of likeness is explicitly narrowed down to include only truth and falsity.

Like the disjunction, either one of the propositions (1a) and (1b) has to be considered irrelevant if it is proposed directly after the *positum*. As the respondent is in fact not in Rome and in fact not a bishop, the proposed likeness prevails and the proposition has to be granted. The proposition 'You are a bishop' then follows from the *positum* together with the proposition just granted.

The similarity of the examples belonging to rules U1 and U6 seem to expose an intimate link between the rules. The similarity can be accentuated by altering the order of the propositions of the latter example.

Positum: You are in Rome
1. You are a bishop (denied: false and irrelevant)
2. You are not in Rome or you are a bishop (denied: incompatible)

Evidently, this disputation could also have been used as an example in connection with rule U1. The suggested link between the rules is of course not surprising if both U1 and U6 are considered to be direct consequences of the constitutional rules. I will even argue that the consequence expressed by U1 is the same as the one expressed by U6.

In which obligational disputations does the order decide the outcome, in the manner indicated by rule U1?

A disputation, in which order decides the outcome, cannot consist of only relevant propositions, but at least one has to be evaluated as irrelevant. Suppose that, in two disputations sharing the same *casus, positum* and propositions, a particular subsequent proposition yields two different answers. It must then be the case that the proposition differed with respect to relevance. For if the proposition was relevant in both cases, it either followed from or was incompatible with the *positum*, or the *positum* together with previously granted and denied propositions, and was granted or denied accordingly. And if it was irrelevant in both cases, it was answered to in the same way in both cases, supposing the world and the respondent's knowledge of it did not change in the relevant respects. If a proposition is responded to in a different way when it is relevant than when it is irrelevant, a clash has occurred between the respondent's duty to answer in accordance with his knowledge and his duty to maintain the *positum* as true.

Furthermore, the *positum* in a disputation where order is of significance has to be false and known to be false. This will hold for cases where the posited proposition expresses a state of affairs which contradicts the respondent's knowledge. Alternatively, the *positum* can be introduced together with a *casus*, a stipulated actual state of affairs, with which the *positum* is incompatible.

If the *positum* were true, no clash could ever occur between the respondent's duty to answer on the basis of his knowledge and his duty to maintain the *positum*. Consequently, no propositions would be granted in one ordering that would not be granted in another. The set of propositions of the disputation would grow into something more and more like the set of propositions representing the respondent's knowledge, supposing this second set is consistent.

The following disputational properties can be identified as regards a disputation where the answers to the propositions depend on the order:

1. The *positum* is false
2. The respondent has answered to a proposition, which is not the *positum* or a consequence of the *positum* alone, in a different way than he would if he were to answer in accordance with his own knowledge. In other words, a clash has occurred between the respondent's duty to answer in accordance with his knowledge and the *prima facie* duty to maintain the *positum* as true.

It is easy to see that the second property is closely linked to the concept of interdisputational inconsistency, introduced above. If and only if a clash has occurred, a second disputation can be constructed, differing only in the order of the propositions, where some proposition yields a different reply.

The replies can be different in two ways. A proposition may have to be granted in one disputation and denied in the other. This is an example of the stronger form of interdisputational inconsistency. Alternatively, a proposition may have to be doubted in one disputation and either granted or denied in the other. This is the weaker form of interdisputational inconsistency.

According to rule U6 any false proposition that is compossible with the *positum* can be proved when the *positum* is false. To prove a false proposition is the same as producing a clash, forcing the respondent either to grant a proposition as sequentially relevant that he considers false, or to deny a proposition as incompatible that he considers true. This description holds for all disputations involving the stronger form of interdisputational inconsistency.

Consequently, if one were to imagine the set of all possible disputations, the set of disputations where false propositions are proved is a subset of the set of disputations where order determines the outcome.

The intimate relationship between rule U1 and U6 is due to the fact that they both express consequences of the notion of relevance in connection with a false *positum*.

In the next section, I will outline Richard Kilvington's views on obligational theory against the background of the foregoing discussion. By means of the concepts of relevance, order-dependence and interdisputational inconsistency, I aim to show precisely which features of Burley's theory Kilvington finds unacceptable.

Kilvington's Response

The work *Sophismata* by Richard Kilvington, written in the early 1320s, is a collection of sophismas, or logical problems, dealing with various topics in natural philosophy and epistemology. In sophisma 47 Kilvington formulates a critique on the standard rules of obligations. Regretfully, Kilvington does not give any systematic account on obligational theory. Instead he concentrates on two examples to which he attaches an elaborate and rather complicated set of replies and objections.

He begins by putting forward an example in which two incompatible propositions are proved on the basis of the same hypothesis: 'If the king is seated, you know that the king is seated, and if the king is not seated, you know that the king is not seated' (Sophisma 47 a-d). The hypothesis is to be seen as a *positum* in an obligational disputation. The hypothesis is furthermore to be considered contrary to fact. The truth of the matter is that the respondent is not at the same place as the king. He is therefore unable to determine whether the king is seated or not seated.

I. *Positum:* If the king is seated, you know that the king is seated, and if the king is not seated, you know that the king is not seated

1. You know that the king is seated or you know that the king is not seated *(granted: follows)*
2. You do not know that the king is not seated *(granted: true and irrelevant)*
3. You know that the king is seated *(granted: follows)*

II. *Positum:* If the king is seated, you know that the king is seated, and if the king is not seated, you know that the king is not seated

1. You know that the king is seated or you know that the king is not seated *(granted: follows)*
2. You do not know that the king is seated *(granted: true and irrelevant)*
3. You know that the king is not seated *(granted: follows)*

The disputations are conducted in accordance with Burley's rules. In the first disputation, the proposition 'You know that the king is seated or you know that the king is not seated' follows from the *positum* together with 'The king is seated or the king is not seated', which is trivially true. The proposed sentence 'You do not know that the king is not seated' must be considered irrelevant as it neither follows from, nor is incompatible with, the *positum* together with the disjunction that was just granted. It is furthermore true, and must therefore be granted. Next, 'You know that the king is seated' must be granted as sequentially relevant, as it follows from the disjunction together with the true and irrelevant proposition by means of disjunctive syllogism. In the second disputation, 'You do not know that the king is seated' is proposed. After this, 'You know that the king is not seated' must be granted.

The respondent has not granted and denied the same proposition in either of the disputations. Yet, it is clear that Kilvington does not accept the outcome. For him the two disputations, seen together, form a sophisma in need of a solution. According to Kilvington, a consequence of accepting this example as valid is that "two men who are equally obligated with regard to a single hypothesis would have to grant two contradictories in replying correctly" (S. 47 j).

From this we can conclude that there is at least one form of interdisputational inconsistency which Kilvington finds unacceptable, and this is the stronger form. The respondent has granted the proposition 'You know that the king is seated' in the first disputation, as following from the *positum* together with previously granted propositions. In the second disputation he has granted its opposite, i.e. 'You do not know that the king is seated', as true and irrelevant.

In order to solve the sophisma, Kilvington introduces another example, previously used by Burley. At the same time, he challenges Burley's rule U6. According to Kilvington, it is not the case that any false proposition compossible with the *positum* can be proved, when the *positum* is false.[18]

Positum: You are in Rome
1. 'You are in Rome' and 'You are a bishop' are alike (granted: true and irrelevant)
2. You are a bishop (granted: follows)

On Kilvington's view, granting the first proposition is the same as not taking the obligation of the *positum* seriously enough. If the respondent were actually in Rome, he would not grant the first proposition unless he was a bishop.

According to Kilvington, "a proposition following from what is true and the *positum* is as much to be granted as a proposition following from the *positum* and what has been granted, other things being equal" (S. 47 r). If the proposition 'You are a bishop' is considered true, as following from the *positum* together with a previously granted proposition, it should also be considered true when proposed directly after the *positum*. According to the standard rules of obligations, however, the proposition 'You are a bishop' is to be evaluated as false and irrelevant if it is introduced directly after the *positum*. Consequently, Kilvington does not accept the notion of relevance inherent in the standard rules of obligations, and more specifically the alleged irrelevance of the first proposition.

In addition to the foregoing argument he offers a second one, in which the standard notion of relevance is maintained. Even if the respondent has granted the proposed sentence "'You are in Rome' and 'You are a bishop' are alike", he does not have to grant the proposed sentence 'You are a bishop', according to this argument. This is because the former sentence is about propositions, while the latter is about a state of affairs (S. 47 s). The disputation in question could be given the following appearance:

Positum: You are in Rome
1. A and B are alike (granted: true and irrelevant)
2. You are a bishop (denied: false and irrelevant)

In the first proposition, A stands for the proposition 'You are in Rome' and B stands for the proposition 'You are a bishop'. From the *positum* 'You are in Rome' and the proposition 'A and B are alike' it does not follow that 'You are a bishop'. Therefore, the second proposition should be denied as false and irrelevant.

In order to make this second argument valid, Kilvington denies that the truth of a proposition should imply the occurrence of the expressed state of affairs. He also denies, conversely, that a state of affairs should imply the truth of the corresponding proposition (S. 47 t-z). For example, these two consequences are invalid, according to Kilvington: "This is true: 'You are in Rome'; therefore you are in Rome", and "you are in Rome; therefore this is true: 'You are in Rome'". Kilvington goes on to conclude that "[f]rom these considerations it is evident that it is in no way to be granted that you are a bishop on account of the positing of 'You are in Rome'" (S. 47 bb).

However, this second argument, depending on the relationship between propositions on one hand and states of affairs on the other, seems to be somewhat redundant.[19] As Kilvington moves towards the solution of the first problem, 'You know that the king is seated', it becomes clear that it is the first argument that he finds the most definitive. The proposition "'You are in Rome' and 'You are a bishop' are alike" should not be admitted by the respondent, although it is true and irrelevant according to the standard rules. The fact that a proposition is true and irrelevant does not mean it has to be granted, at least not if the term 'irrelevant' is taken to mean what is commonly meant by it, i.e. what is meant according to the standard rules of obligations (S. 47 cc). Therefore, the proposition "'You are in Rome' and 'You are a bishop' are alike" could well be denied, although it is true and irrelevant.

Similarly, as regards the first example, the proposition 'You know that the king is seated' is to be doubted by the respondent, although this is to be granted according to the standard rules. Kilvington bases his response on the following consideration:

The king is either seated or not seated. According to the *positum*, if the king is seated, we know that the king is seated, and conversely, if the king is not seated, we know that the king is not seated. As we do not know the present posture of the king, we have to doubt each one of the antecedents in the *positum*, 'The king is seated' and 'The king is not seated'. Since we doubt the antecedents, we must consequently also doubt the consequents. When 'You do not know that the king is not seated' is proposed to the respondent, he should therefore say that he is in doubt, although the proposition is to be considered true and irrelevant. After that, when 'You know that the king is seated' is proposed, he should respond by doubting this as well.

A peculiarity of the first example is that the propositions referring the respondent's knowledge, the consequents in the *positum*, appear to require a binary response. Either you know that the king is seated or you do not know that the king is seated. Intuitively, there does not seem to be any room for doubt. That you are in doubt whether you know or do not know that the king is seated seems close to nonsensical. To say that the propositions 'The king is seated' and 'The king is not seated' are in doubt seems to implicate the opposites of both consequents, i.e. 'You do not know that the king is seated' and 'You do not know that the king is not seated'. To this Kilvington responds by saying that to be forced to doubt a proposition does not necessarily mean that one is actually in doubt about it.

> [T]his does not follow: 'This proposition must be doubted by me; therefore, this proposition is not known by me'; for a proposition must be doubted on an occasion when it is known, and so it must sometimes be doubted when it is not known by me whether it is known. (S. 47 dd)

Evidently, this position is not compatible with Burley's theory of obligations. According to Burley's theory, a proposition that is irrelevant must be responded to on the basis of the respondent's knowledge only. According to Kilvington, the respondent should take both his knowledge and the *positum* into consideration when answering. An irrelevant proposition should be evaluated under the supposition that the *positum* is actually true. The epistemic clashes that are not directly caused by the *positum*, but occur only as a result of the notion of relevance in Burley's theory, should be ruled out. The exclusion of these kinds of clashes is the same as the exclusion of both forms of interdisputational inconsistency. Therefore, order will be of no significance.

The "Relativised"Interpretation

In his paper "Three Theories of *Obligationes*: Burley, Kilvington and Swyneshed on Counterfactual Reasoning", Paul Vincent Spade suggests that Burley may not have been entirely indifferent to the problem of interdisputational inconsistency ("Three theories" 17).[20] In formulating rule U1, "one must pay special attention to the order", Burley could be seen as giving advice rather than simply stating a consequence of the constitutional rules. Consequently, what Burley could be aiming at is some preferred ordering of propositions. Spade calls this the 'relativised' interpretation on Burley's theory.

In the same vein Henrik Lagerlund and Erik Olsson say that "[o]ne is under the impression that there is, according to Burley, one correct ordering and that one has to be careful not to deviate from that ordering, which raises the question which ordering Burley has in mind" (Section 3). However, Spade later in his paper admits that "there is no evidence whatever for this 'relativised' interpretation apart from the inconclusive observation that 'one must pay most attention to the order'. Not only is there no evidence in Burley himself, but as far as I have been able to determine, there is no evidence in any other author who held in effect the same theory before or after Burley." ("Three Theories" 18)

If the 'relativised' interpretation is adopted, rule U6 becomes somewhat peculiar. Rule U6 states that any false irrelevant proposition can be proved in case of a false *positum*. With the notion of a preferred order, this is definitely one of the things one would want to avoid. If the principle stated in rule U6 is correct, it seems to undermine the effort to attain a certain outcome. Consequently, if rule U1 is to function as a restriction in some way in Burley's theory, picking out some orderings as more preferable than others, it must be working on some different level than rule U6.

However, as I see it, there are two problems associated with this approach. First, as Henrik Lagerlund and Erik Olsson point out, it raises the question which ordering Burley has in mind. Secondly, the passage where Burley explains rule U1 becomes problematic:

> The reason for this rule is that a proposition that is to be granted in one place is not to be granted in another place. Therefore, *when some proposition is proposed, we should consider its order relative to propositions previously granted.* (Burley 3.34, italics mine)

Here Burley offers an alternative formulation of rule U1. The party referred to as "we" is the respondent, as he is the one to which the propositions are proposed. Consequently, rule U1 seems to be directed at the respondent. The respondent has no influence on the selection of propositions, and can therefore not affect the outcome of the disputation. Or, in other words, he is not in a position to see to it that some preferred order is attained.

On the other hand, if the rules in question are simply seen as consequences of the constitutive rules, the rules seem unproblematic. On this interpretation, the rules simply complement each other in stating a consequence of the relevance criterion inherent in the constitutive rules.

Finally, in order to make Kilvington clearly intelligible and to render his contribution a critique of the standard rules, I believe that one must assume that Burley is more or less comfortable with the interdisputational inconsistencies. Kilvington does not accept these inconsistencies, and his attack is primarily directed at the notion of relevance. It is not clear, however, if he meant his contribution to be a definite revision or more of a critique of the theory of obligations, as he does not offer an explicit alternative formulation of the rules.

University of Uppsala

Notes

1. The term "sophisma", in this nonderogatory medieval sense applied to various paradoxes used as starting-points for logical exercises and discussions in a disputational context.
2. For a summary of the recent discussions, see Yrjönsuuri, "Disputations".
3. Walter Burley, or Burleigh, (c. 1275 – after 1343). English philosopher and theologian who studied at Oxford and Paris. His works include several commentaries on Aristotle as well as a series of treatises on a variety of subjects, e.g. on forms, and on form and matter. His general attitude was that of a traditionalist and he was a realist as regards universals. He consequently opposed at least some of the views of Ockham and the "moderns" (i.e., the nominalists).
4. Richard Kilvington, (ca. 1300 - 1361). English philosopher and theologian. He taught at Oxford and knew Walter Burley personally. Besides the Sophismata, a treatise on various logical problems, he wrote three commentaries on Aristotle and one on Peter Lombard. Later in his life he was appointed dean of St. Paul's Cathedral in London. (Kilvington xvii-xxxiv)
5. The dating is from Kretzmann and Stump's introduction in Burley, "Obligations (Selections)".
6. See e.g. Stump 355 and Yrjönsuuri, "Aristotle's Topics" 61-68.
7. On the proposed role of obligational disputations in medieval education, see Perreiah 85-103.
8. See Stump 355 and Yrjönsuuri, *Obligationes* 16.
9. For a more thorough discussion on the species, see Yrjönsuuri *Obligationes* 40-43.
10. On impossible *positio*, see e.g. Knuuttila.
11. Burley 3.06, 3.14-3.16. The numbering has been added for the sake of clarity. Rule C4 is not put forward explicitly as a rule. It is however later in the work both treated like and referred to as one. Furthermore, in the discussion on *petitio*, another species of obligational disputation, the corresponding passage on irrelevant propositions takes the form of an explicit rule. See Burley 1988, 2.07.
12. The useful rules can be found in Burley 3.34, 3.35, 3.38, 3.40, 3.49, 3.61, 3.73, 3.84 and 3.89, respectively.
13. According to Yrjönsuuri rule U2 should read: "During the time of the obligation one should not give a definite answer to a doctrinal question". The dispute concerns whether in the original Latin text, the question is characterized as 'distinguibilis'or 'disciplinalis'. Yrjönsuuri argues in favour of 'disciplinalis', while Kretzmann and Stump, in their translation of Burley's text, chose 'distinguibilis'. See Yrjönsuuri, Obligationes 56.
14. For a thorough discussion, see Yrjöönsuuri, *Obligationes* 49-58.
15. C. L. Hamblin ascribes the formal property of semantic consistency to the rules: Hamblin 258-262. See also Yrjönsuuri, *Obligationes* 10-12, and Spade, "Three Theories" 7.
16. For a discussion on the different kinds of inconsistencies see Spade, "Three Theories" 7-9.
17. Modern scholars have interpreted the proposed 'likeness' of propositions in the medieval treatises in different ways. The 'likeness in truth-value' interpretation can for example be seen in Yrjönsuuri *Obligationes* 118. N. Kretzmann and B. E. Kretzmann choose the 'likeness in modal status' interpretation, see Kilvington 336.
18. Sophisma 47 q: "Thus I say – as regards a familiar example [...] -- that when 'You are in Rome' has been posited, it is not the case that anything false that is compossible with it can be proved, such as 'You are a bishop' and the like.".

19. Also, as Paul Spade notices, the argument can be sidestepped by using Burley's first choice for first proposition, 'You are not in Rome or you are a bishop' instead of "'You are in Rome' and 'You are a bishop' are alike". See Spade, "Three Theories" 21 (footnote 62).
20. See also Spade, "If Obligationes Were Counterfactuals" 182.

Works Cited

Aristotle. *The Complete Works of Aristotle.* Vol. 1-2. Ed. J. Barnes. Princeton: Princeton University Press, 1985.

Burley, Walter. "Obligations (Selections)." *The Cambridge Translations of Medieval Philosophical Texts.* Vol. 1. *Logic and the Philosophy of Language.* Ed. N. Kretzmann and E. Stump. Cambridge: Cambridge University Press, 1988: 369-412.

Hamblin, C. I. *Fallacies.* London: Methuen, 1970.

Kilvington, Richard, 1990. *The Sophismata of Richard Kilvington.* Trans. N. Kretzmann and B. E. Kretzmann. Oxford: Oxford University Press, 1990.

Knuuttila, Simo. "*Positio Impossibilis* in Medieval Discussions of the Trinity." *Vestigia, Imagines, Verba: Semiotics and logic in medieval theological texts (XIIth-XIVth century).* Ed. C. Marmo. Turnhout: Brepols, 1997: 277-288.

Lagerlund, Henrik and Olsson, Erik J. "Disputation and Change of Belief – Burley's theory of *obligationes* as a theory of belief revision." *Medieval Formal Logic.* Ed. M. Yrjönsuuri. *The New Synthese Historical Library.* Dordrecht: Kluwer Academic Publishers, 2001: 35-62.

Perreiah, Alan. "Logic Examinations in Padua, *circa* 1400." *History of Education* 13 (1984): 85-103.

Spade, Paul Vincent. "If *Obligationes* Were Counterfactuals." *Philosophical Topics* 20:2 (1992): 171-188.

—. "Three Theories of *Obligationes*: Burley, Kilvington and Swyneshed on Counterfactual Reasoning", *History and Philosophy of Logic* 3 (1982): 1-32.

Stump, Eleonore. "The Logic of Disputation in Walter Burley's Treatise on Obligations." *Synthese* 63 (1985): 335-374.

Yrjönsuuri, Mikko. "Aristotle's *Topics* and Medieval Obligational Disputations." *Synthese* 96 (1993): 59-82.

—. "Disputations, Obligations and Logical Coherence." *Theoria* 66 (2000): 205-223.

—. *Obligationes.* Helsinki: Acta Philosophica Fennica, 1994.

Albert the Great and Pagan Ethics: His Elaboration of Aristotle's Reflections on the Scientific Character of Ethics

Jörn Müller

This paper focuses on Albert's reflections on the scientific character of ethics as a philosophical discipline which can be found in his two commentaries on Aristotle's "Nicomachean Ethics".[1] My considerations are divided into five parts: first, the basic texts on which my interpretation is based will be introduced. In the second part, I will give a short sketch of Aristotle's treatment of ethics as a science. In the third and fourth part, I will try to show how Albert depicts ethics as a practical science in his commentaries. My concluding remarks in the final part concentrate on Albert's motives for his treatment of this subject and on its relevance to our present philosophical and ethical discussion.

I

Albert wrote two commentaries on Aristotle's "Nicomachean Ethics". One of these commentaries, "Super Ethica", was written between 1250 and 1252 at Cologne and has been highly acclaimed by contemporary scholars, especially after the completion of its critical edition in 1987.[2] It is the first Latin commentary on the whole of the "Nicomachean Ethics", which was completely translated into Latin by Robert Grosseteste, Bishop of Lincoln, around 1246/7,[3] and thus Albert's pioneering commentary represents a milestone in the intellectual history of the thirteenth century. On the other hand, Albert's second commentary, "Ethica", which was written in approximately 1262,[4] has received little attention among scholars up to now, not least because of the fact that we do not yet have a critical edition of this work.[5] I have attempted to remedy this unsatisfactory situation by presenting a critical edition of the first treatise of book I in my recently published dissertation thesis on Albert's philosophical ethics.[6] In this paper, the quotations from this treatise follow the text of my edition.

Another reason for the negligence of the second commentary is the fact that it is mainly composed as a paraphrase. Therefore, it is often very difficult to distinguish Albert's own statements from his reconstruction of the Aristotelian text. By contrast "Super Ethica" contains *quaestiones*, which are less ambiguous in this respect. In spite of the stylistic differences between these two works and the hermeneutic problems caused by them, they share an important feature: at the beginning of both commentaries, Albert discusses the scientific nature of ethics by depicting, among other issues, the nobility, subject, unity, method, character and aim of this discipline as well as its place in the philosophical canon in general. But first of all, he attempts to answer the question on which depends the entire idea of a practical science of ethics: how is a science of ethics possible at all?

II

This intriguing question, which even today arouses animated and subtle discussions among moral philosophers, is another legacy of Aristotle. But his treatment of the subject leaves some important questions unanswered. On the one hand, he develops a model of science which is characterised by two main features: scientific knowledge is based on deduction, and the principles or presuppositions of this deduction are necessarily true.[7] In consequence, scientific knowledge, at least according to Aristotle's considerations in the "Posterior Analytics", is at the same time deductive and categorical, that is: absolutely true. On the other hand, this ideal model of science obviously does not cover all branches of philosophical knowledge. In his ethics, Aristotle ascribes probability to ethical arguments rather than certainty because the subject matter of ethics does not permit absolute certainty. But he nevertheless depicts ethics as a science and concludes his treatment of this subject with the famous remark that "it is the mark of the trained mind never to expect more precision in the treatment of any subject than the nature of that subject permits."[8] This short sketch creates the impression that either the conception of science has to be understood in a wider sense than the one defined in the "Posterior Analytics", or that ethics, in spite of its philosophical importance, cannot be called a genuine branch of science. Therefore, at least one question necessarily arises for all subsequent readers of Aristotle's "Nicomachean Ethics": is a science (in the strict sense of the word) of ethics possible at all, which does justice to the specific subject matter of ethical inquiry?

III

In "Super Ethica", Albert defends the possibility of scientific ethics against two lines of argument:[9] the first objection stresses that the subject matter of ethics, moral habits, cannot meet the criteria which are demanded of a deductive science: necessity and universality. Human actions and the habits constituted by them are not necessary but subject to the freedom of will of the particular agent. Furthermore, moral habits obviously differ depending on the cultural context in which they prevail. Therefore morals are too changeable to make possible an exact science in the sense of the "Posterior Analytics". The second objection stresses the practical character of ethics, its claim to be relevant to human actions in general. But scientific knowledge is supposed to be theoretical knowledge, i.e. knowledge sought for its own sake and not for the sake of action. Thus the objections build up a kind of trap: if Albert proves that morals can be investigated in accordance with the standards of the "Posterior Analytics", he is at risk of undermining the practical character of ethics. But if he focuses on the practical side of ethics, it is difficult to maintain its scientific character. How does Albert pass the Scylla and Charybdis of these arguments?

He counters the first objection by pointing to an important distinction: we have to distinguish the surface appearance of morals from their underlying structures, which Albert describes as *rationes morum*.[10] This technical term is highly disputed in the literature on the subject, not least because of the numerous meanings of *ratio* in Latin.[11] In spite of this problem, Albert's discussion in later parts of "Super Ethica" and in other writings clarifies the intended meaning.[12] The *rationes morum* signify essential ontological structures, which can be expressed in a formal manner, for example by definitions. They stand for concepts which characterise the basic structure of individual beings and are a bridge between the underlying structure of reality and its cognition by the human mind. In a formal sense, which refers to all sciences, these are concepts like form, matter, property, genus or species. Looking at ethics in particular, concepts like happiness, virtues and their objects, means and impediments as well as classifiable circumstances of action will enter the scene. These concepts are closely intertwined with particular actions but they can be abstracted from their particular occurrence. Since they do not depend on the particular occurrence from which they are abstracted in their existence and characterisation, they fulfill the Aristotelian demand of necessity. Furthermore, Albert argues that it is possible to establish connections between these concepts which fulfill the criteria of deductive arguments. In his understanding, science ascribes specific differences and properties to an object on a necessary basis.[13] The aforementioned concepts are the basis for the establishment of these connections and thus make deductive arguments about morals possible.

In order to exemplify the meaning of this model we should have a look at the relationship between particular actions and virtues. Particular actions as such cannot be objects of science because they occur in infinite forms. But it is also possible to regard them as expressions of underlying virtues, as tokens of a certain type, and from this point of view a science of them is possible.[14] Virtues are definite and general enough to allow for definitions and necessary properties, which are the basis of deductive arguments. There are close parallels to this, stressed by Albert himself,[15] with his discussion of the question of whether a natural science is possible. In "Physica" he rejects the argument that the infinity of natural things does not allow for a natural science by pointing to their *species*.[16] The natural species, which express the *ratio rei*, possess the qualities necessary to function as objects of deductive science.

Much more would have to be said to show how Albert puts this model into practice in his commentaries,[17] especially how he links this conception with the precepts of natural law and the idea of a universal *medium virtutis*.[18] But for our present purpose it is sufficient to conclude that the basic universal concepts of morals, which underlie the real structure of actions as well as our cognition of them, make possible a deductive doctrine of ethics in the sense of the "Posterior Analytics".

But Albert still has to counter the second objection that a deductive system of ethics is irrelevant to human actions. He attempts to solve this problem by distinguishing two parts of ethics: *Ethica docens*, that is a teaching discipline of ethics, and *ethica utens*, applied ethics.[19] This distinction is not Albert's invention but had been used before him at Paris, e.g. in Ps-Peckham's commentary on the "Ethica nova" and "Ethica vetus".[20] Albert uses the distinction to show that ethics has a twofold aim in accordance with these two parts: while the teaching discipline aims at knowledge, the applied one is directed towards action.[21] This division of aims also has some methodological consequences. While the teaching part of ethics can use genuine syllogistic proofs, applied ethics relies on "persuasive arguments".[22] "Persuasive arguments" are, for instance, incomplete syllogisms and examples, i.e., arguments which are based on probable and not on necessary presuppositions.[23] In consequence, only the teaching discipline of ethics can fulfill the criteria of science in the strict sense of the word, while applied ethics cannot meet them. But applied ethics can be related to individual human actions, which is not the case for the teaching discipline.

Up to now, Albert seems to have avoided the pitfalls set up by the two objections. But an important link between his different lines of argument is obviously missing. Albert has shown that the teaching part of ethics is truly scientific and that the applied part is practical, but he still has to answer a fundamental question: how is ethics as a practical science possible? His distinction between the two parts of ethics has fundamentally put at risk the unity of the discipline of ethics as a whole. In order to find a solution which is in accordance with his findings up to the present point, he has to answer the following question: how is the teaching part of ethics connected with the applied one? Albert does not present a solution to this problem in "Super Ethica", but this gap can be filled by his treatment of the subject in "Ethica", to which I would like to turn now.

IV

In the first treatise of "Ethica", Albert raises a question similar to the opening question of "Super Ethica", but with a different emphasis: is a scientific treatment of virtue possible at all? This question is provoked by some arguments which are borrowed from Plato's "Menon"[24] and claim that the virtues can be neither taught nor learnt. The knowledge of virtue does not result from scientific arguments, based on necessary principles, but from practical self-awareness.[25] Albert refutes these objections with an argument resembling his treatment of this question in "Super Ethica": again, he distinguishes between the surface appearance and the underlying real and, in consequence, conceptual structure of morals. The virtues cannot be taught or learnt in a scientific manner as concrete actions in particular situations, but only insofar as they are regarded as substances (*secundum substantiam*) with inherent differences and properties which can be deductively demonstrated.[26] The virtues establish the conceptual scheme in which the scientific treatment of the subject becomes possible. Therefore, the knowledge of virtue is closely connected with scientific arguments and not simply a result of

self-awareness. Alberts names *genera*, *species*, *differentiae*, *propria*, *effectus* and *impedimenta* of virtues as central concepts in scientific reasoning about morals.[27] Thus, my reading of "Super Ethica" with regard to the meaning of *rationes morum* is confirmed by Albert's considerations in "Ethica".
Albert also takes up the distinction between a teaching and an applied part of ethics:

> (...) in omni scientia duo sunt: doctrina et usus. *Et* {*om. p*} doctrina est sicut informans et dirigens, usus autem sicut exsequens et faciens. *Et* {*om. p*} scientiam, quae est doctrina de re, vocant scientiam docentem, illam autem, quae est de usu, vocant *utentem* {virtutem *p*}.[28]

But this time Albert realises the need to bridge the gap between the theoretical and the practical part of ethics, between the teaching discipline and applied ethics. How can they form a practical science together? Albert's answer can be summarised as follows: both parts of ethics can be connected with actions, but on different levels. While the teaching discipline focuses on the overall aims of human action, applied ethics deliberates about the means which are necessary to achieve these goals.[29] Thus, the teaching part of ethics can obtain a guiding role for human practice without referring to particular actions. The applied part is connected with the particular exercise of virtue, but not in a so-called practicistic manner which simply jumps from ethical deliberation to action: in "Ethica", Albert explicitly emphasises that ethics in itself cannot cause the virtues and that its relation to particular actions can only be established by the virtues.[30] Furthermore, the applied part of ethics does not usurp the role of prudence as it is the case in Ps-Peckham.[31] Albert points at the necessity for prudence as an action-guiding principle which is responsible for the formation of concrete practical syllogisms.[32] Prudence is itself an indispensable link between the subject matters of *ethica docens* and *utens*, between the ethical universal and the circumstances of action.[33]

Therefore, the applied part of ethics does not replace but assist prudence by providing general outlines of action.[34] Performing this function it receives its central concepts and its guiding principles from the teaching discipline. Albert gives the following example to shed light on this connection: the development of virtues through the performance of virtuous acts is due to the deliberations of the *ethica utens* and the willingness to continue the action even under difficult circumstances, but the *ethica docens* maintains its influence on the whole process by delivering the universal principles which govern this virtue. Thus, the teaching discipline is also a cause of the development of virtue, but a distant one (*causa remota*). The *ethica utens* and the virtuous acts are "informed" by the conceptual scheme of the teaching discipline.[35]

Following this line of argument we can conclude that the *ethica docens* does not produce morality but reflects on its nature and its central universal principles and concepts. These reflections in themselves do not make human beings good, but by informing the *ethica utens* and the virtuous acts they help them to maximise their morality.[36] Thus, the *ethica docens* continues a central idea of Aristotle's ethics.[37] On the other hand, the reflections of the teaching discipline make possible syllogistic demonstrations about the principles and concepts of morality in accordance with the demands of the "Posterior Analytics". The relevance of ethics to human action is granted by the *ethica utens*, which takes into consideration the particular circumstances of action, but in a rather general manner.

In order to underpin these considerations, Albert explicitly reflects on the question of whether ethics as a whole is a theoretical or a practical discipline in "Ethica" I, 1, 4. The answer neatly sums up the main findings of the first treatise of "Ethica": as regards its scientific method, the teaching part of ethics can be called theoretical, but it is also practical insofar as the consideration of the principles of morals is directed towards action.[38] The teaching discipline, however, is not immediately related to action but needs the mediation of the applied part of ethics, which is in itself practical without being practicistic.[39] Therefore, both parts of ethics together constitute a branch of knowledge which is at the same time scientific as well as practical, in short: a practical science.

To sum up: in "Super Ethica", Albert proves that a science of ethics is possible by pointing out the difference between the surface appearance and the underlying structure of morals (*rationes morum*), which can be expressed by ethical concepts. In "Ethica", he spells out the connection between the two parts of ethics, *ethica docens* and *utens*, and thus proves that a practical science of ethics is possible. Therefore, we can speak of a complementary relationship between the two commentaries: the second commentary takes up the main findings of "Super Ethica" and extends the investigation, thereby solving problems which were not solved or even articulated in the first commentary. Other examples of this complementary character of the two prologues can be easily found: in "Ethica" (chapters 1 and 3), Albert for the first time discusses in a comprehensive manner the position of ethics among and its significance in comparison with the other philosophical disciplines, and he is more interested in weighing up arguments from different philosophical schools than in "Super Ethica". All this evidence indicates that we need a more thorough investigation of the rather neglected relationship between the two commentaries[40] and that "Ethica" should be more definitely taken into consideration for the reconstruction of Albert's philosophical ethics: only the combination of the two commentaries makes possible an adequate and coherent account of ethics as a practical science in Albert.

On the whole, Albert takes up Aristotle's conception of ethics as a practical science which is neither merely theoretical nor too practical, i.e. simply eradicating the gulf between action and the reflections of practical reason. But furthermore, Albert successfully answers some questions which were left open by Aristotle, especially in how far the ideal model of science of the "Posterior Analytics" can be integrated into ethical reflection without ignoring the special nature of morals. Certainly, his conception of ethics is not without problems which I cannot discuss here. But taking into consideration the historical situation which he had to face as the first Latin commentator on the complete "Nicomachean Ethics" it is certainly no exaggeration to call his attempt a major achievement.

V

Let me finally turn to Albert's motives for the treatment of this subject. His attempt to adjust ethics to the Aristotelian standards of science can be explained on different levels. On the one hand, the tendency to use the Aristotelian epistemology in different branches of knowledge dates back at least to the twelfth century and can be connected with the historical fact that most of Aristotle's works were translated into Latin during the twelfth and thirteenth centuries. These translations triggered a renewal of interest in Aristotle, well documented by the large number of commentaries in subsequent times as well as by the prohibitions of several Aristotelian writings in the first half of the thirteenth century.

On this explanatory level, Albert's occupation with Aristotle's ethics is a logical consequence of the academic trends of his times. When he had the complete translation of the "Nicomachean Ethics" in his hands, Albert was adventurous enough to enter unknown academic territory. I do not claim that this interpretation is false but it fails to answer some essential questions. Why does Albert not simply stick to Christian authorities like St. Augustine when he reflects on the right conduct of life? And why is he particularly interested in the scientific nature of ethics, indeed so interested that he even elaborates on the Aristotelian conception of ethics as a practical science?

In my opinion his interest in combining ethics with Aristotle's epistemology can be traced back to the fact that Christian ethics was to some degree challenged in his lifetime. Christianity was more and more faced with the rivalling religious and moral claims of the Jewish and especially the Arab world. In situations like these, the traditional moral authorities need justification based on criteria which are shared by the different participants of the discussion, as Abelard made clear in his "Dialogue between a philosopher, a Jew and a Christian".[41] And Aristotle's epistemology was a promising candidate for this role: it does not depend on transcendent or religious presuppositions, and it was widely understood in the Jewish and Arab world. Thus Albert's conception of ethics as a practical science can be interpreted as an attempt to gain steady ground for the rational justification of the Christian tradition of ethics in order to answer this challenge.

Like Albert, we have to face what Samuel Huntington has described as "The clash of civilizations," that is a historical situation characterised by the conflict of values between different cultural contexts. We have also gained insight into the formation of our own ethical thinking, as it has been described by moral philosophers like Alasdair MacIntyre.[42] But the task of justifying our values to different cultures with convincing arguments still largely remains to be fulfilled. Thus, Albert has set an example which we will have to follow in one way or another. This shows once more the relevance of medieval thinking to our present philosophical discussion.

University of Bonn

Notes

1. The following text is a modified version of a paper presented at the "International Medieval Congress", Leeds, 12-15 July 1999.

2. Albertus Magnus, *Super Ethica commentum et quaestiones*, Ed. Colon. 14/1 and 14/2, ed. W. Kübel, Münster 1968/1987. R.A. Gauthier / J.Y. Jolif, *L'Éthique à Nicomaque. Introduction, Traduction et Commentaire*, vol. 1, 1st ed., Louvain 1958, 79*, have praised "Super Ethica" even before the publication of its critical edition as "le meilleur, et de beaucoup, des innombrables commentaires que nous a légués le moyen âge."

3. Cf. D.A. Callus, "The Date of Grosseteste's Translations and Commentaries on Pseudo-Dionysius and the Nicomachean Ethics", *RThAM* 14 (1947), 186-210, here: 202-208.

4. The exact date of this commentary cannot be firmly established. In the relative chronology of Albert's works "Ethica" was written before his commentary on the "Metaphysics". J.A. Weisheipl, "The Life and Works of St. Albert the Great", in: id. (ed.), *Albertus Magnus and the Sciences. Commemorative Essays 1980*, Toronto 1980 (Studies and Texts, 49), 13-51, here: 39, assumes that Albert wrote "Ethica" during his stay with pope Urban IV at Viterbo and Orvieto, i.e. between August 1261 and February 1263. The date given in the text is based on the most recent inquiry into the chronology of Albert's writings by H. Anzulewicz, *De forma resultante in speculo. Die theologische Relevanz des Bildbegriffs und des Spiegelbildmodells in den Frühwerken des Albertus Magnus*, vol. 1, Münster 1999 (BGPhMA, N.F. 53/1), 16.

5. The uncritical editions by Jammy (t. 4[a], Lyon 1651) and Borgnet (t. 7, Paris 1891) are – as I found out in the course of my collation – almost identical with the printed version edited by Octavianus Scottus at Venice in 1520.

6. Cf. J. Müller, *Natürliche Moral und philosophische Ethik bei Albertus Magnus*, Münster 2001 (BGPhMA, N.F. 59), 325-358. This edition is based on the 23 manuscripts (20 manuscripts containing the whole work and 3 relevant fragments) described by W. Fauser, *Die Werke des Albertus Magnus in ihrer handschriftlichen Überlieferung. Teil 1: Die echten Werke*, Münster 1982 (Alberti Magni Opera Omnia, Tomus subsidiarius I), 174-178, n.1-23. Additionally, I have taken into account the manuscript Sion, Bibliothèque du Chapitre 109, which has been recently described by Ch. H. Lohr, *Aristotelica Helvetica. Catalogus codicum latinorum in bibliothecis confederationis Helveticae asservatorum quibus versiones expositionesque operum Aristotelis continentur*, Fribourg 1994 (Scrinium Friburgense, suppl. vol. 6), 273. The title "Ethica" is confirmed by the Incipits of 15 of the aforementioned manuscripts.

7. Cf. Aristotle, *Analyt. Post.* I 1-4, 71a 1 – 74a 3.

8. Aristotle, *Eth. Nic.* I 1, 1094b 23-25.

9. Cf. *Super Ethica*, prol., Ed. Colon. 14/1, p.1 v.56 – p.2 v.1.

10. "Ad primum in contrarium dicendum, quod si consideretur mos secundum id quod est, sic est a causa non necessaria et non cadit in demonstratione scientiae. Si autem consideretur secundum intentionem suam et rationem, sic rationes morum sunt necessariae, et de his potest esse scientia, sicut etiam ipsa generabilia et corruptibilia sunt a causis contingentibus, tamen de eis est scientia naturalis secundum rationes universales ipsorum." (loc. cit., p.2 v.11-19)

11. While M. Dreyer ("Ethik als Wissenschaft nach Albertus Magnus", in: J.A. Aertsen / A. Speer (eds.), *Was ist Philosophie im Mittelalter?* Berlin – New York 1998 (Miscellanea Mediaevalia, 26), 1017-1023) interprets *rationes* in a metaphysical sense and thinks that Albert wants to stress the metaphysical principles in which human action is embedded, H. P. F. Mercken ("Ethics as a Science in Albert the Great's First Commentary on the Nicomachean Ethics", in: D. Føllesdal et al. (eds.), *Knowledge and The Sciences in Medieval Philosophy,* Helsinki 1990 (Annals of the Finnish Society for Missiology and Ecumenics, 55), 251-260) identifies *rationes* with the intentions of human agents. Further discussions of Albert's conception of ethics as a science can be found in M.J. Tracey, *The Character of Aristotle's Nicomachean Teaching in Albert the Great's* Super Ethica commentum et quaestiones, Diss. phil., Notre Dame 1999, 66-135; G. Wieland, *Ethica – Scientia practica. Die Anfänge der philosophischen Ethik im 13. Jahrhundert,* Münster 1981 (BGPhMA, N.F. 21), 98-129; A.J. Celano, "The End of Practical Wisdom: Ethics as Science in the Thirteenth Century", *JHP* 33 (1995), 225-243; F. Bertelloni, "Regimen ipsius - regimen alterius. Individuum und Gesellschaft in den Quellen des Prologus zu *Super Ethica* des Albertus Magnus", in: J.A. Aertsen / A. Speer (eds.), *Individuum und Individualität im Mittelalter,* Berlin – New York 1996 (Miscellanea Mediaevalia, 24), 479-492; Th.W. Köhler, "Scientia perfecta. Zur Konzeption philosophischer Erschließung empirischer Gegenstandsbereiche im 13. Jahrhundert", in: J.A. Aertsen, / A. Speer (eds.): *Was ist Philosophie im Mittelalter?* Berlin – New York 1998 (Miscellanea Mediaevalia, 26), 749-755.

12. Cf. *Super Ethica,* l.6 lect.5, p.421 v.60-68: "Dicendum quod contingentia possunt dupliciter considerari: aut quantum ad esse, quod habent in materia subiecta variationi, et sic propter suum fluxum non habent certitudinem (...) Sed secundum rationem ipsorum certitudinem habere possunt, quia rationes mutabilium perpetuae sunt et necessariae, secundum quas de eis est scientia. (...) sic potest esse scientia universalis in generabilibus per rationes eorum quae sunt necessariae." This argument does not aim at the metaphysical causes of contingent things, as Albert clarifies loc. cit., v.85-88: "dicendum quod causae contingentium non contingentes sunt causae remotae (...) et in talibus causis res non cognoscuntur certitudinarie." Cf. loc. cit., l..7 lect.2, p.523 v.48-59. Furthermore, Albert argues several times for the possibility of natural science (*scientia naturalis*) by pointing to the disctinction between natural things as they are in their present state and their underlying ontological structure: Loc. cit., l.6 lect.5, p.427 v.56-64; *Physica,* l.1 tr.1 c.2, Ed. Colon. 4/1, p.4 v.1-41 and p.4 v.81 – p.5 v.19. This is important evidence for the understanding of the scientific character of ethics because Albert himself stresses the parallels between ethics and physics in this respect; cf. the quotation above, no. 10.

13. "Item, omne quod habet differentias et passiones, quae de illo probari possunt, habet scientiam, in qua determinantur; sed mores sunt huiusmodi; ergo de moribus potest esse scientia. Quod concedimus." (*Super Ethica,* prol., p.2 v.6-10) Cf. also Albert, *De sex princ.,* tr.1 c.1, Ed. Paris. 1, p.307a; *Metaph.,* l.1 tr.1 c.2, Ed. Colon. 16/1, p.3 v.64-68; *Politica,* l.1 c.1, Ed. Paris. 8, p.6b; *Sent.* I, d.1 a.1, Ed. Paris. 25, p.14b; loc. cit., a.2 p.16b.

14. Cf. the *expositio textus* in *Super Ethica*, l.1 lect.3, p.18 v.40-44: "Quaedam autem in civilibus sunt distributa in multa sicut virtus in species suas, et quantum ad hoc dicit: *universaliter*, quaedam vero in cognita ex multis sicut temperantia ex omnibus suis circumstantiis (...)" Cf. Tracey (see above, no. 11), p.88f., who also emphasises the relevance of the distinction between type and token to Albert's understanding of human actions.

15. Cf. above, no. 10.

16. Cf. Albert, *Physica*, l.1 tr.1 c.2, Ed. Colon. 4/1, p.4 v.42-55. Cf. *De gen. et corr.*, l.1 tr.1 c.1, Ed. Colon. 5/2, p.110 v.4-6: "(...) et sic de talibus [scl. generabilibus et corruptibilibus], non in numero acceptis, sed in rationibus talibus, esse scientiam et demonstrationes."

17. Cf. e.g. Albert's formalised investigation into felicity, where he discusses its genus and its differences: *Super Ethica*, l.1 lect.3, p.14 v.19-24; lect.7, p.31 v.22-30; lect.8, p.36 v.28-29.

18. "(...) universales rationes, quae cadunt in doctrina huius scientiae, sunt eaedem apud omnes secundum medium determinatum 'determinatione quoad nos'." (loc. cit., prol., p.2 v.30-33)

19. "Ad secundum dicendum, quod scientia morum potest considerari dupliciter, scilicet aut ut utens aut ut docens; unde quamvis ad usum scire non multum valeat, tamen ad doctrinam multum valet." (loc. cit., p.2 v.20-23)

20. Ps-Peckham, *In Ethicam novam et veterem*: "(...) verbi gratia loqui est de morali philosophia ut est speculans (...) vel inquantum est operans" (quoted from G. Wieland, "Ethica docens – ethica utens", in: W. Kluxen et al. (eds.), *Sprache und Erkenntnis im Mittelalter.* Berlin – New York 1981 (Miscellanea Mediaevalia, 13/2), 593-601, here: 596 no.13).

21. "Dicendum, quod dupliciter potest considerari scientia ista: secundum quod est docens, et sic finis est scire; vel secundum quod est utens, et sic finis est, ut boni fiamus." (*Super Ethica*, prol., p.4 v.16-19)

22. "Dicendum, quod modus huius, inquantum est utens, est persuasivus, inquantum est docens, est demonstrativus sicut cuiuslibet alterius scientiae." (loc. cit., p.4 v.37-39)

23. Cf. loc. cit., l.1 lect.2, p.11 v.11-17.

24. L. Gaul, *Alberts des Grossen Verhältnis zur Plato. Eine literarische und philosophiegeschichtliche Untersuchung*, Münster 1913 (BGPhMA, 12/1), 131, doubts that Albert took these arguments directly from Plato's dialogue.

25. Cf. *Ethica*, l.1 tr.1 c.2, Ed. Paris. 7, p.3a-b.

26. "(...) dicimus virtutem esse scibilium bonorum, si secundum substantiam et ea, quae substantiae insunt, consideretur: sic enim est quoddam ens particulare subiectum, cui passiones insunt et differentiae, quae per propria principia scibilium sibi probantur inesse. Si autem virtus accipiatur secundum esse, quod habet in virtuoso, sic bene concedimus quod quantum ad proxima principia non est discibilis" (loc. cit., p.4a). Again, Albert draws a parallel between ethics and natural science: Cf. loc. cit., c.3, p.8b: "(...) ea, quae nec stantia sunt nec ordinata in esse, rationem tamen habent stantem et ordinatam sicut omnia naturalia, quae omnia fluctuantia sunt et opinioni et non scientiae subiecta, (...) tamen de rationibus eorum est vera scientia. Ex forma enim et ratione non habent fluctuationem, sed ex materia, in qua sunt."

27. Cf. loc. cit., c.7, p.16a, together with: l.10 tr.1 c.1, p.599a-b.

28. Loc. cit., l.1 tr.1 c.2, p.4b. Here and in the following I have indicated in brackets where Borgnet's text (*p*) differs from my edition.

29. "Dupliciter enim stare dicitur {dicitur enim stare dupliciter *p*} scientia ad aliquid, scilicet sicut ad terminum operis vel sicut ad finem intentionis. Et scientia moralis docens, licet stet ad conclusionem vel ad medium, quod est causa vel signum, sicut ad terminum operis sui, quod est {sicut *p*} decursus syllogisticus, tamen non stat in ipso sicut in fine intentionis, quod {sed *p*} refertur ad opus, quod est operatio virtuosi. Haec solutio confirmatur per hoc, quod dicit Aristoteles in secundo Topicorum, quod una scientia est plurium velut amborum finium, unius tamquam finis, alterius tamquam eius, quod est ad finem." (loc. cit.)

30. "(...) talis scientia [scl. moralis] ab Aristotele non scientia sed potentia vocatur, quia sicut potentia est indeterminata inter esse et non esse, sic talis scientia est {*om. p*} inter facere vel {et *p*} non facere, cum tamen practica sit et in opere stare debeat [...] Unde deceptus est Socrates in hoc quod scientiae morali attribuit, quod attribuere {tribuere *p*} debuit virtuti secundum esse, quod habet in virtuoso" (loc. cit., c.3, p.10a). Cf. loc. cit., c.4, p.12a: "(...) scire, quod acquiritur scientia morali, non est nisi terminus considerationis moralis et non est terminus considerantis. Hoc {Hic *p*} enim non considerat, nisi ut referat ulterius ad opus, quod est finis intentionis eius." Therefore, Albert stresses that ethics is "valde debilis" (loc. cit., c.3, p.10b) with regard to human perfection.

31. Cf. Wieland (see above, no. 11), 112-114.

32. Cf. *Super Ethica*, l.6 lect.7, p.441 v.21-39

33. In "Ethica", Albert distinguishes two kinds of prudence which somehow mirror the distinction between *ethica docens* and *ethica utens*: l.6 tr.2 c.23, p.440a-b (corrected with ms. Erlangen, Universitätsbibliothek 263, fol. 157ra: "(...) propter quod oportet ambas habere in prudentia, scilicet universalium et singularium cognitionem {cognitiones *p*}, si perfecta debeat esse prudentia (...) Cum autem ambae sint in prudentia, una erit architectonica, hoc est princeps et ordinatrix {ordinativa *p*} alterius, altera autem ususalis et ordinata. Quae enim circa universalia est, theorica et architectonica est; quae vero circa singularia, usualis est et practica."

34. Cf. *Super Ethica*, l.3 lect.2, p.150 v.13-15: "(...) dicendum, quod moralis non est ponere omnes diversitates circumstantiarum, sed sufficit in generali determinare". Cf. also loc. cit., l.5 lect.12, p.364 v.6-9: "Dicendum, quod tractare particulariter omnes circumstantias pertinet ad rhetorem (...) Sed determinare de eis in universali pertinet ad ethicum." Cf. also loc. cit., l.1 lect.2, p.96 v.4-13. These passages echo to a certain degree Aristotle's conception of ethics as a "typos"-science which only provides the outlines of the subject matter; for this model in Aristotle cf. O. Höffe, *Praktische Philosophie. Das Modell des Aristoteles*, 2nd ed., Berlin 1996, 101-180.

35. "Et haec quidem scientia de virtute, licet non sit proximum principium virtutis secundum esse perfectum, tamen est principium primum et in {*om. p*} secundum, quod est proximum, et in tertium {intrinsecum *p*}, quod ipsius virtutis generativum est, quod est in difficilibus perseverare, sui regiminis et informationis habet influxum. Et sic virtutis primum et formale est principium, quod tamen in principiando {procedendo *p*} per velle et perseverare, cui {circa *p*} formam influit et regimen, efficitur proximum et immediatum. (...) Quia licet virtus non dependeat ad accepta secundum sui generationem in subiecto, tamen forma agentium ipsam in subiecto accipitur de scientia docente, quia velle et perseverare in difficilibus non generant virtutem nisi informata ratione recta, quam sapiens determinavit. Et sic scientia docens prima {principia *p*} forma est, cuius virtute velle et perseverare virtutem generant." (*Ethica*, l.1 tr.1 c.2, p.5b)

36. "(...) bene operari non potest esse sine virtute morali, virtus autem moralis non potest esse sine prudentia, quae instruitur per doctrinam de moribus, et ideo bene operari non potest esse sine doctrina morali, quamvis potest esse bona operatio." (*Super Ethica*, l.10 lect.17, p.778 v.1-6)

37. Cf. Höffe (see above, no. 34), 84-98, especially: 90: "Die Ethik, ein integrierender Teil des Polis-Lebens, will aus diesem Leben heraus auf es reflektieren, um durch die Reflexion das sittliche Leben in der Polis sittlicher zu machen. *Ethische Reflexion macht nicht gut; ethische Reflexion macht besser*."

38. "Et hoc modo bene concedimus quod moralis docens theorica est et moralis utens practica. In omnibus enim talibus theorica ad praxim {proximum *p*} ordinatur (...) Unde constat quod et finis intellectus et {*om. p*} finis affectus opus est, a quo fine tam docens quam utens scientia practica vocatur, large accipiendo practicam secundum quod practica dicitur rationes operabilium considerans." (*Ethica*, l.1 tr.1 c.4, p.12a-b)

39. Because of the aforementioned reasons I do not agree with the judgement by Wieland (see above, no. 11), 123 and 129, that Albert is guilty of a practicistic misunderstanding of ethics. Tracey (see above, no. 11), 104-109, offers an elaborate criticism of Wieland's position.

40. Explicit reflections on the relationship between the two commentaries are only available in J. Dunbabin, "The Two Commentaries of Albertus Magnus on the Nicomachean Ethics", *RThAM* 30 (1963), 232-250, and C. Vansteenkiste, "Das erste Buch der Nikomachischen Ethik bei Albertus Magnus", in: G. Meyer / A. Zimmermann (eds.), *Albertus Magnus. Doctor universalis: 1280 / 1980*, Mainz 1980 (Walberberger Studien. Philosophische Reihe, 6), 373-384.

41. Peter Abelard, *Dialogus inter Philosophum, Iudaeum et Christianum*, ed. R. Thomas, Stuttgart 1970.

42. After Virtue, 2nd ed., London 1985; Whose Justice? Which Rationality?, London 1988; Three Rival Versions of Moral Enquiry, Notre Dame 1990.

Joseph Albo, der Messias und die Disputation von Tortosa[1]

Sina Rauschenbach

English Summary

The paper deals with the Spanish rabbi and philosopher Joseph Albo (around 1380- 1444) and the different positions concerning the Messiah Albo takes in the Tortosa Disputation (1413-1414) as a representative of the Jewish community of Daroca and in his *Sefer ha-Ikkarim*, his *Book of Principles* (1425). In general Albo is known for excluding belief in the Messiah from the existential principles of Judaism. And it is in fact not only in the Latin protocolls of the Tortosa Disputation but also in the very first chapter of his book that Albo stresses that a Jew who doesn't believe in the arrival of the Messiah is no denier of the Torah. But it seems as if the exclusion of the belief in the Messiah from the existential principles of Judaism was just one position of the Spanish rabbi addressing those Jews who had become uncertain of their belief due to the Christian mission and the reprisals. Since it can be shown that there exists a second, fairly less well known position of Albo`s which can be described as the integration of the Messiah into the Anafim, the true (but not existential) doctrines of Judaism and which addresses all the other Jews, who have firmly remained in their belief *despite* Tortosa and *despite* the Christian mission. With regard to this second position Albo doesn`t depart as much from the position of Maimonides as it is generally considered.

Die Disputation, die zwischen 1413 und 1414 im spanischen Tortosa stattfand, gilt als eine der größten, längsten und folgenschwersten Disputationen des Mittelalters.[2] Ihr christlicher Protagonist war Josua Lorqui, Arzt und jüdischer Gelehrter aus Alcañiz, der 1412 unter dem Einfluß des Dominikaners Vicente Ferrer zum Christentum übergetreten war und sich seit seiner Konversion Jerónimo de Santa Fe nannte.[3] Mit seinem Traktat *Contra Iudaeos*[4] hatte Jerónimo die Unterstützung des um Anerkennung ringenden Gegenpapstes Benedikt XIII. gewonnen und schickte sich an, aus den jüdischen Quellen selbst zu beweisen, daß der Messias bereits erschienen sei. Ende 1412 wurden die führenden Rabbiner Aragoniens und Kastiliens für das kommende Jahr nach Tortosa geladen. Unter ihnen war als Gesandter der jüdischen Gemeinde zu Daroca[5] Joseph Albo, der in den Protokollen zu dieser Disputation zum ersten Mal erwähnt wird.

Die Disputation beginnt am 7. Februar 1413 im bischöflichen Palast zu Tortosa und endet nach 69 Sitzungen am 13. November 1414 im benachbarten San Mateo. Ihre Folgen für die jüdischen Gemeinden Kataloniens und Aragoniens sind verheerend. Benedikt XIII. berichtet in seiner Bulle *Etsi doctoris gentium* von mehr als 3000 Konversionen in Verbindung mit der Debatte.[6] Die lateinischen Protokolle erwähnen Taufen am Ende der 12., der 14. und der 22. Sitzung.[7] Zu den jüdischen Gemeinden, die sich in den Jahren nach der Disputation auflösen, zählt auch die Gemeinde zu Daroca.[8] Albo selbst verläßt Aragonien und zieht ins kastilische Soria. Dort schreibt er 1425 sein *Sefer ha-'iqqarim (Buch der Grundlehren).*[9]

Gegen Maimonides, der in seinem *Kommentar zur Mischna* (1167/ 68) die *'iqqarim* des Judentums auf dreizehn, unter ihnen der Glaube an den Messias, festgelegt hatte[10], definiert Albo die *'iqqarim* des göttlichen Gesetzes als diejenigen Bestandteile, ohne die das Gesetz nicht bestehen kann[11], und reduziert sie im Folgenden auf drei: die Existenz Gottes, die Offenbarung sowie Lohn und Strafe.[12] Aus diesen drei *'iqqarim* leitet Albo acht *shorashim*, Wurzeln, ab, von denen er schreibt, der Leugner eines *shoresh* sei demjenigen gleich, der einen *'iqqar* selbst leugne.[13] Der Glaube an den Messias findet sich nicht unter diesen *shorashim*. Er wird einer dritten Gruppe zugeordnet, die Albo als *'anafim*, Zweige, bezeichnet, und von denen er schreibt, sie seien Dogmen, die jeder Bekenner der Tora zu glauben hätte, die aber nicht existenziell für den Bestand derselben seien.[14]

These

Albo vertritt in seinem *Sefer ha-'iqqarim* im Hinblick auf den Messias zwei verschiedene Positionen, die sich an zwei verschiedene Gruppen von Lesern wenden. Die erste dieser Positionen ist die Herausnahme des Messias aus den Grundlehren des Judentums. Sie ist Bestandteil derselben Strategie, die Albo auch in Tortosa verfolgt, und wendet sich an alle Juden, die, verunsichert durch die dominikanische Mission, aus Zweifeln über einzelne Fragen wie diejenige des Messias Zweifel an ihrem Glauben insgesamt abgeleitet haben.

Die andere Position Albos ist die Eingliederung des Messias in die *'anafim*. Sie wendet sich an alle anderen Juden, die *trotz* Tortosa und *trotz* der dominikanischen Mission unerschütterlich an der Tora festhalten. Im Hinblick auf diese zweite Position entfernt sich Albo in seinem *Sefer ha-'iqqarim* nur unmerklich von der Linie seiner Vorgänger. In letzter Konsequenz bleibt auch im System Albos der Messias ein Dogma, das jeder Jude glauben muß, wenn er sich seines Anteils an der kommenden Welt sicher sein möchte.

Joseph Albo und die Disputation von Tortosa[15]

In den lateinischen Protokollen der Disputation wird Albo in neun Sitzungen namentlich erwähnt. Dies schließt nicht aus, daß weitere Äußerungen im Rahmen der Auseinandersetzung ebenfalls von Albo stammen, zumal in den Protokollen die Rabbiner größtenteils unpersönlich als „iudei" bezeichnet werden. Für eine Analyse der Rolle Albos in der Disputation müssen jedoch die wenigen Zeugnisse, die sicher über ihn erhalten sind, ausreichen.

Die erste Bemerkung, die von Albo hierbei in den Protokollen wiedergegeben wird, ist zugleich eine der eindrucksvollsten der gesamten Disputation. Am 9. Februar 1413, in der dritten Sitzung und der Debatte über die Bedeutung der 85 Jubeljahre in *Sanhedrin* 97b, fällt Albo „magna cum furia", mit großer

Wut, dem Papst mit der Bemerkung ins Wort: „Posito Messiam michi (sic) probari iam venisse, non putarem deterior esse iudeus."[16] Ob der Messias bereits erschienen sei oder nicht, sei für sein, Albos, Judentum nur von unter-geordneter Bedeutung.

Auch die zweite Äußerung Albos in den Protokollen bezieht sich auf die christologische Deutung der 85 Jubeljahre, und auch bei ihr ist es der Papst selbst, den Albo unterbricht. Aus der angeführten Stelle des Talmuds, so Albo, gehe ausschließlich hervor, daß die Welt *nicht weniger* als 85 Jubeljahre bestehe und daß der Messias im letzten Jubeljahr der Welt erscheine. Daß dieses letzte Jubeljahr der Welt gleichsam auch das 85. Jubeljahr sei, könne daraus keineswegs geschlossen werden. Damit aber sei *Sanhedrin* 97b ohne Beweis-kraft für die Frage nach dem Kommen des Messias.[17] Die anderen jüdischen Gesandten distanzieren sich noch in derselben Sitzung von beiden Äußerungen Albos[18] und bekräftigen diese Unterschiede zwischen ihrer eigenen und der Position Albos, die sie „keineswegs für gut befanden" („minime approbabant"), an späterer Stelle ein zweites Mal.[19]

In der achten Sitzung erklärt Albo zur Bedeutung des hebräischen Wortes *'ad* im Zusammenhang mit Gen 49, 10: „Nie weicht von Juda das Zepter, der Herrscherstab von seinen Füßen, bis (*'ad*) der kommt, dem er gehört, dem der Gehorsam der Völker gebührt"[20], die verschiedenen Auslegungen, die sich zu dieser Stelle im Talmud fänden, seien jede für sich mit Vorsicht zu genießen, da zu viele Möglichkeiten existierten und eindeutige Schlußfolgerungen nicht gezogen werden könnten.[21] Albo scheint auch weiterhin an der Diskussion von Gen 49, 10 Anteil gehabt zu haben, ohne daß seine Äußerungen allerdings in die Protokolle aufgenommen worden wären. In der neunten Sitzung nämlich distanziert sich Rabbi Mathias von ‚all dem, was Albo im Folgenden öffentlich gesagt hatte' („omnia que in proximo lapsa dieta [...] Rabi Juce Albo predixerat"), und erklärt es für nichtig.[22] Aus den Worten Mathias' kann geschlossen werden, daß es dieses Mal um die Bedeutung des Wortes *ceptrum*, Zepter, an derselben Stelle gegangen sein muß.

Danach sind von Albo keine weiteren Äußerungen bis zur Sommerpause verzeichnet. Zwischen dem 30. 8. 1413 und dem 29. 11. 1413 wird die Disputation unterbrochen. Erst in der 48. Sitzung, am 8. Januar 1414, meldet sich Albo wieder zu Wort. Während über den formalen Fortgang der Disputation beraten wird und nur drei Rabbiner, Ferrer, Mathias und Astruch, erklären, daß sie neue Argumente in die Disputation einzubringen hätten, plädiert Albo dafür, daß die übrigen Gesandten, die über keine neuen Argumente verfügten, aus ihrer Verpflichtung entlassen und nach Hause geschickt würden.[23] Da Albo selbst in den Protokollen kein ausdrückliches Interesse an der Fortsetzung der Disputation zeigt, ist wahrscheinlich, daß es sich bei seinem Plädoyer auch um ein Plädoyer in eigener Sache handelt. Das Plädoyer bleibt ungehört. Die Disputation wird von der 62. Sitzung an in San Mateo mit einer Auseinandersetzung über den Talmud und seine „innumerabiles errores et hereses“, seine „unzähligen Irrtümer und Häresien“, so ein Teil der christlichen Anklage, fortgesetzt.[24] In der 64. Sitzung ziehen sich die Gesandten mit einer Erklärung Rabbi Astruchs, in der sie sich auf ihre eigene Unwissenheit berufen, aus der Debatte zurück.[25] Nun ist es wiederum Albo, der sich diesem taktischen Rückzug verweigert. Zusammen mit Rabbi Ferrer distanziert er sich von den Worten Rabbi Astruchs und reicht statt dessen eine Schrift zur Verteidigung des Talmuds ein[26], die jedoch weder erhalten noch in den Protokollen zusammengefaßt ist. Auch von einer neuerlichen Erklärung Astruchs in der 67. Sitzung, die sich im Wortlaut allerdings nur geringfügig von derjenigen der 64. Sitzung unterscheidet, nehmen Albo und Ferrer noch Abstand.[27] Erst in der 68. Sitzung schließen sie sich den übrigen Gesandten an.[28]

Bei einer Zusammenstellung der in den Protokollen aufgeführten Äußerungen Albos fällt auf, daß alle von ihnen sich durch eine gewisse Ungeduld und Diskussionsmüdigkeit auszeichnen. Bereits in der dritten Sitzung sind die Einwürfe Albos „magna cum furia“ begleitet, wenig später heißt es: „Rabbi Iucef Albo prorupit in hec verba,“[29] Albo sei in diese Worte „eingefallen“. Beide Male ist es der Papst selbst, den Albo unterbricht. In drei von zehn erhaltenen Äußerungen geht Albo nicht auf den Diskussionsstoff ein, sondern versucht, die Diskussion insgesamt in Frage zu stellen. In der dritten Sitzung betont er, selbst wenn ihm bewiesen würde, daß der Messias bereits erschienen sei, wäre er dadurch kein schlechterer Jude. In der achten Sitzung erklärt er die von Jerónimo angeführten Dissonanzen innerhalb verschiedener Stellen des Talmuds für bedeutungslos und führt sie darauf zurück, daß die Christen mit der den Juden eigenen Art der Talmudauslegung nicht vertraut seien. In seiner zweiten Bemerkung in der achten Sitzung mahnt er zur Vorsicht, eine Bibel-stelle wie Gen 49, 10, die zu viel „Spielraum“ („ludus“) bei ihrer Auslegung lasse, für wichtige Beweise heranzuziehen.[30] Und in der 48. Sitzung spricht sich Albo direkt für die Entlassung der jüdischen Gesandten aus der Disputation aus.

Ob er den Messias als unwichtig für sein Judentum bezeichnet, die von Jerónimo angeführten Stellen als irrelevant herabstuft oder für eine Auflösung der gesamten Disputation plädiert, die Tendenz Albos an all diesen Stellen ist offensichtlich. Anstatt auf Details der christlichen Argumente einzugehen, versucht er, sich über die Debatte zu stellen und jene *unabhängig von ihren Ergebnissen* fragwürdig erscheinen zu lassen. Daß Albo mit dieser Tendenz in weiten Zügen der Disputation auf Seiten einer Minorität unter den Rabbinern, wenn nicht alleine steht, ist im Zusammenhang mit der konkreten Fragestellung dieser Arbeit von untergeordneter Bedeutung, sollte aber der Vollständigkeit halber bemerkt werden.

Der Messias in Albos *Sefer ha-'iqqarim*

In seinem *Sefer ha-'iqqarim* vertritt Albo im Hinblick auf den Messias zwei verschiedene Positionen.

1) Die Herausnahme des Messias aus den Grundlehren des Judentums

Sieht man von einigen einleitenden Worten ab, in denen Albo auf die Gefahr verweist, der sich derjenige aussetze, der über die Grundlehren seiner Religion Nachforschungen anstelle, so beginnt Albos *Sefer ha-'iqqarim* mit einem Kapitel über den Messias und dessen Herausnahme aus den *'iqqarim* des göttlichen Gesetzes. Albo zitiert an dieser Stelle Rabbi Hillel, der in *Sanhedrin* 99a die Meinung vertritt, die Israeliten hätten keinen Messias mehr zu erwarten, da dieser ihnen schon in Hiskija, dem König von Juda, erschienen sei. Aus der Tatsache, daß Hillel trotz dieser Äußerung nicht aus dem Verband der Israeliten geschieden sei, sondern im Gegenteil im Talmud den Titel eines Rabbiners trage, könne, so Albo, geschlossen werden, daß der Messias –im Gegensatz zu der von Maimonides bezogenen Position- keine Grundlehre der Tora sei. Daß es in derselben Gemara auf der anderen Seite heiße: „Der Herr verzeihe R. Hillel,"[31] bestätige aber, daß Hillel gesündigt habe. Für Albo ergibt sich die Schlußfolgerung: Jeder Jude ist verpflichtet, an den Messias zu glauben, wird aber nicht zum Häretiker, wenn er dies nicht tut.[32]

Indem Albo bereits im ersten Kapitel des ersten Abschnitts den Glauben an den Messias aus den *'iqqarim* des Judentums herausnimmt, ist es für ihn im Folgenden nicht mehr nötig, auf weitere Details im Zusammenhang mit dem Messias einzugehen. Wenn er dennoch am Ende des letzten Abschnitts, in den Kapiteln IV, 42 und IV, 44, noch einmal auf das Thema zurückkommt, so nur, um erneut die Sinnlosigkeit der christlich-jüdischen Auseinandersetzung über einzelne Stellen des Tanachs, unter ihnen Gen 49, 10, zu verdeutlichen. Die Art und Weise, wie Albo dies tut, soll im Folgenden dargestellt werden.

Bereits im ersten Abschnitt seines Buches unterscheidet Albo zwischen Geschichtswahrheiten (*nimshekhot*, wörtl.: Fortsetzungen) und Überlieferungen (*ha-qabbala ha-nimshekhet*, wörtl.: die sich fortsetzende Tradition). Hierbei sind Geschichtswahrheiten eine von vier Arten der Erkenntnis, deren Wahrheit grundsätzlich nicht erwiesen werden brauche.[33] Als Beispiel für eine Geschichtswahrheit nennt Albo die Tatsache, daß Rom, Jerusalem und Babylon in der Vergangenheit große bewohnte Staaten gewesen seien, obwohl dies in der Gegenwart nicht mehr der Fall sei.[34] In die Kategorie der Geschichtswahrheiten fällt, Albo zufolge, auch die Offenbarung.[35] Im Gegensatz zu den Geschichtswahrheiten sind die *Überlieferungen* Traditionen, die zuerst durch die Erfahrung, eine andere der vier Arten der Erkenntnis, gewonnen und im Anschluß vom Vater an den Sohn weitergegeben werden.[36] Zwar betont Albo, daß auch die Überlieferungen in ihrer Wahrheit nicht in Frage zu stellen seien, da ein Vater kein Interesse haben könne, seinen eigenen Sohn zu belügen,[37] es ist jedoch offensichtlich, daß sie gegenüber den authentischen Geschichtswahrheiten einen untergeordneten Stellenwert haben müssen.[38] Diesen Überlieferungen, den Traditionen, die vom Vater zum Sohn weitergegeben wurden, ordnet Albo nun im vierten Abschnitt noch eine zweite Tradition unter, die er *ausschließlich* als „Tradition“ (*qabbala*) bezeichnet.[39] Insgesamt existieren damit im System Albo drei Stufen von Tradierung: die Geschichtswahrheiten, die Überlieferungen und diese „einfache“ Tradition, wie ich sie im Folgenden nennen möchte.[40] Im Zusammenhang mit dem Messias sind es die letzten beiden Traditionen, die für Albo von Bedeutung sind.

Beide Traditionen, sowohl die Überlieferung als auch die „einfache“ Tradition, sind, so Albo, in ihrer *Autorität* für alle Juden verbindlich. Dennoch unterschieden sie sich hinsichtlich des Wahrheitsanspruchs ihrer Inhalte, der sich bei der „einfachen“ Tradition ausschließlich durch den Glauben, bei der Überlieferung historisch begründe.[41] Stütze sich nun, so Albo, der Glaube an den Messias alleine auf die „einfache“ Tradition, sei also keine Überlieferung, so bedeute dies, daß sich keine Stelle in den Prophetenbüchern finden ließe, die in *eindeutiger* Weise eine Aussage über den Messias treffe.[42] Der Glaube an den Messias wäre in diesem Falle ausschließlich von verschiedenen Auslegungen bestimmter Stellen des Tanachs durch verschiedene religiöse Autoritäten abhängig. Diese Auslegungen wären alle durch ihre Autorität bindend, nähmen sich allerdings, und hier liegt der entscheidende Punkt, hinsichtlich ihres Wahrheitsanspruchs nichts, da die Textgrundlage eine eindeutige Entscheidung, welche Autorität mit ihrer Auslegung recht behielte, nicht zulasse.

Albo verdeutlicht die Problematik am Beispiel von Gen 49, 10. Seit Onkelos, so Albo, sei es ein Teil der Tradition, diese Stelle auf den Messias zu beziehen. Damit sei offensichtlich, daß der Messias zu Onkelos’ Zeiten noch nicht erschienen sein könne. Ausgeschlossen werden könne aber nicht, daß der Messias *nach* Onkelos erschienen und aufgrund der Sünden Israels unerkannt geblieben sei.[43] Gen 49, 10 selbst lasse in dieser Hinsicht keine eindeutigen Aussagen zu. Albo folgert: Was aus der Bibel nicht eindeutig erkannt werden kann, kann auch aus der Tradition nicht eindeutig erkannt werden.[44] Dies bestätigt: Ist nicht nur Autorität, sondern auch Begründbarkeit gefragt, so eignen sich nur diejenigen Stellen des Tanachs, die in *eindeutiger* Weise eine Aussage treffen. Gen 49, 10 gehört diesen Stellen nicht an. Die Replik Albos auf die christliche Mission an dieser Stelle ist evident. Gen 49, 10 hat von jeher in der christlichen antijüdischen Polemik und damit auch in der Disputation in Tortosa einen hohen Stellenwert. Zitiert Albo auch, wenn er von der Vielzahl aller möglichen Auslegungen dieser Stelle spricht, nur rabbinische Quellen, nimmt er dennoch die christliche Exegese von diesen Möglichkeiten nicht aus. Vielmehr muß gefragt werden, ob Albo nicht nur um dieser christlichen Exegese willen alle anderen, jüdischen Quellen anführt. In jedem Falle aber wird auch die christliche *traditionelle* Auslegung von Gen 49, 10 nur zu einer von vielen möglichen, insgesamt jedoch *uneindeutigen, traditionellen* Aus-legungen und verliert damit in entscheidendem Maße an Aussagekraft, ohne auch nur explizit formuliert oder diskutiert werden zu müssen. Albo knüpft mit dieser Position unmittelbar an seine Haltung in Tortosa an.

Wie zu erwarten, erklärt er schließlich, die unterschiedlichen Deutungen von Gen 49, 10 seien für die Frage des Messias unbedeutend, da andere Stellen in den Prophetenbüchern existierten, die in *eindeutiger* Weise auf den Messias verwiesen.[45] Eine dieser Stellen sei Jes 59, 20 und 21, „Doch für Zion kommt er als Erlöser und für alle in Jakob, die umkehren von ihrer Sünde- Spruch des Herrn. Das ist der Bund, den ich mit ihnen schließe, spricht der Herr: Mein Geist, der auf dir ruht, soll nicht von dir weichen, und meine Worte, die ich dir in den Mund gelegt habe, sollen immer in deinem Mund bleiben und im Munde deiner Kinder und im Mund deiner Enkel, jetzt und in Ewigkeit – spricht der Herr.“[46] Durch sie, nicht durch Gen 49, 10, werde der Glaube an den Messias ein Teil der Überlieferung und damit begründbar.[47] Albo folgert: „Every adherent of the Law of Moses is obliged to believe in the coming of the Messiah, as we explained above. The Torah expressly commands us to believe the words of the prophet: ‚Unto him ye shall hearken.‘[48] But the prophets announced the coming of the Messiah, hence it is clear that any one who does not believe in the coming of the Messiah denies the words of the prophets and transgresses a mandatory precept.“[49] Wer nicht an den Messias glaubt, übertritt eine *miswa*, ein Gebot der Tora, indem er den Worten der Propheten kein Gehör schenkt. Derjenige aber, der eine *miswa* übertritt, ist, wie Albo bereits im ersten Abschnitt seines *Sefer ha-'iqqarim* erläutert hatte, wenn auch ein Sünder, so doch kein Leugner der *'iqqarim* des göttlichen Gesetzes, und gehört nicht zu denen, die ihres Anteils an der kommenden Welt verlustig gehen.[50]

2) Die Eingliederung des Messias in die *'anafim*

Es muß jedoch bemerkt werden, daß die Position, die Albo im Hinblick auf den Messias bezieht, nicht so eindeutig ist, wie dies zunächst scheinen mag. Albos Zuordnung des Glaubens an den Messias zu den *miswot* beschränkt sich auf die wenigen genannten Kapitel des *Sefer ha-'iqqarim*. In den übrigen Teilen des Buches ist der Messias ein *'anaf*, der sich aus dem *'iqqar* von Lohn und Strafe ableitet.[51] Und über die *'anafim* schreibt Albo, sie seien wahre Dogmen, die jeder Bekenner der Tora zu glauben hätte.[52] Kapitel I, 23 endet mit den umstrittenen Sätzen: „We did enumerate specially the six beliefs [i.e. die *'anafim*. S. R.] above mentioned, because they are accepted dogmas among our people necessary for the maintenance of the fundamental and derivative principles of the Torah. The fulfilment of the Torah is dependent upon them, though they are not essential principles, since the Law can exist without them, as we explained above. He who denies them is called a heretic, though he does not deny the Torah, and has no share in the world to come.“[53]

Wer einen *anaf* leugnet, hat keinen Anteil an der kommenden Welt. Weder ist von einem Ausscheiden aus dem speziellen Religionsverband die Rede noch – wie im Falle Rabbi Hillels- von einer Sünde. Unter den Kommentatoren von Albo hat dieser letzte Satz viel Verunsicherung hervorgerufen.[54] Es muß jedoch betont werden, daß es sich trotz des offensichtlichen Widerspruchs zum ersten Kapitel des ersten und zum 42. Kapitel des vierten Abschnitts bei der scharfen Formulierung Albos in Kapitel I, 23 in keiner Weise um eine ungewollte Äußerung zu handeln scheint.

Vielmehr scheint Albo bestrebt zu sein, die Frage nach dem Leugner des Messias mit den beiden entgegengesetzten Positionen offen zu halten und in letzter Instanz vom individuellen Fall abhängig zu machen. Am Beispiel der Auferstehung, eines anderen *'anaf* in Albos System, wird diese Strategie offensichtlich.

Albo zufolge kann derjenige, der die Auferstehung stellvertretend für Lohn und Strafe leugnet, keinen Anteil an der kommenden Welt haben. In Kapitel I, 10 zitiert Albo in Anlehnung an Maimonides *Sanhedrin* 90a: „Ganz Jisrael hat einen Anteil an der zukünftigen Welt [...] Folgende haben keinen Anteil an der zukünftigen Welt: Wer sagt, die Auferstehung der Toten befinde sich nicht in der Torah, (wer sagt,) die Torah sei nicht vom Himmel, und der Gottesleugner"[55]und erklärt, die drei Leugner an dieser Stelle bezeichneten die Leugner der drei *'iqqarim*.[56] Zwischen dem Leugner der Existenz Gottes aber, dem Epikuräer, und dem Leugner der Offenbarung steht nicht der Leugner von Lohn und Strafe, sondern der Leugner der Auferstehung der Toten. Damit ist eindeutig, daß derjenige, der die Auferstehung leugnet, an dieser Stelle mit demjenigen übereinstimmt, der Lohn und Strafe leugnet. Albo selbst erklärt: „This refers to the person who denies divine retribution, symbolized in resurrection of the dead, which is a divine act in relation to body and soul, and represents all kinds of retribution."[57] Er fährt jedoch fort: „The Rabbis indicate in their expressions that the term resurrection of the dead is used in a general and a particular sense. It may mean specifically the resurrection of the dead, and it may be used in a broader sense to denote the judgment.[58] Und in Kapitel I, 23 schließlich schreibt er über den Leugner der Auferstehung im speziellen Sinne: „As long as one believes in reward and punishment generally, whether corporeal, in this world, or spiritual, in the world to come, he does not deny a principle of the Law of Moses if he disbelieves in resurrection."[59] Derjenige also, der mit der Auferstehung nur den Lohn in der kommenden Welt leugne, sei kein Leugner. Nicht das Leugnen an sich, sondern die Art, wie geleugnet wird, scheint ausschlaggebend für die Bestrafung.

Dieser Gedanke nun läßt sich auf den Messias übertragen. Steht die Auferstehung nämlich für den jenseitigen Teil der Vergeltung, so steht der Messias für den diesseitigen und macht damit gleichermaßen nur die andere Seite des Problems aus.[60] Im Falle Rabbi Hillels muß sich ergeben: Wer den Glauben an den Messias stellvertretend für den anderen, diesseitigen Teil des Lohnes leugnet, ist kein Leugner, sondern ein Sünder. Wer aber den Glauben an den Messias stellvertretend für Lohn und Strafe generell leugnet, kann nicht weniger bestraft werden als derjenige, der die *Auferstehung* stellvertretend für Lohn und Strafe generell leugnet. In Kapitel I, 10 schreibt Albo explizit: „They [i.e. die Rabbiner S. R.] also make clear that the Messiah, which is a physical reward, represents all kinds of reward"[61]und bestätigt diese Position im letzten Satz von Kapitel I, 23: Der Leugner eines *'anaf* hat keinen Anteil an der kommenden Welt. Nicht *jeder* Leugner des Messias also kann sich der milden Bestrafung

Rabbi Hillels gewiß sein. Die Frage bleibt offen und abhängig vom individuellen Fall.

Ergebnisse

Joseph Albos *Sefer ha-'iqqarim* ist, wie nachgewiesen werden kann, weder eine ‚Zusammenfassung der jüdischen Positionen in Tortosa'[62] noch eine direkte Antwort auf die Disputation oder die Argumente in der Disputation. Dennoch kann das Buch nicht anders als im Zusammenhang mit der Disputation gelesen werden. Es ist für Juden geschrieben, die in ihrem Glauben schwankend geworden sind und einer Festigung bedürfen. Albo definiert die *'iqqarim* des göttlichen Gesetzes als diejenigen Lehren, ohne welche dieses Gesetz keinen Bestand haben kann. An erster Stelle aber, bevor Albo zu dieser Definition oder überhaupt zu inhaltlichen Fragen kommt, verweist er auf die Gefahr, die mit der Erforschung der *'iqqarim* verbunden sei. Es steht außer Frage, daß die Gefahr, von der Albo an dieser Stelle spricht, eine Gefahr ist, die nicht nur das Seelenheil des Einzelnen, sondern das Judentum überhaupt betrifft. Jede intellektuelle Auseinandersetzung muß die Gefahr in sich bergen, daß im Rahmen dieser Auseinandersetzung Unklarheiten entstehen. Jede Unklarheit über existenzielle Bestandteile einer Lehre aber muß die Lehre als Ganze in Frage stellen. Im Hinblick auf das Judentum bedeutet dies: Jede Verun-sicherung über die *'iqqarim* der Tora muß zu einer Verunsicherung über die Tora als Ganze führen. Jede Verunsicherung über die Tora als Ganze aber kann, wenn auch nicht zwangsläufig, gleichbedeutend sein mit einem ersten Schritt zur Aufgabe des Judentums und zur Konversion.

Es kann nicht wundern, daß Albo gerade den Messias, der einen Hauptbestandteil der dominikanischen Mission vor, in und nach Tortosa ausmacht, aus denjenigen Bestandteilen herauszunehmen bestrebt ist, die er als existenziell für die Tora beschrieben hat. Wie groß die Meinungsverschiedenheiten in Fragen des Messias selbst unter gläubigen Juden sein konnten, hatte Albo nicht zuletzt in der Disputation selbst in aller Deutlichkeit vor Augen geführt bekommen.[63] Neben dem Messias nimmt Albo ebenfalls zwei andere Punkte, die im Zentrum der christlichen antijüdischen Polemik stehen, aus den *'iqqarim* heraus und gliedert sie in die *'anafim* ein: die Unveränderlichkeit der Tora und die Stufe der Prophetie Moses'. Indem Albo alle diese Fragen für nicht mehr existenziell für das Judentum erklärt, macht er die Diskussion über sie nicht nur ungefährlich, sondern auch überflüssig. Bereits in Tortosa sind Albos Äußerungen von auffallender Unlust gezeichnet, auf die christlichen Argumente einzugehen. In seiner Herausnahme der kontroversesten Themen aus den *'iqqarim* des Judentums führt Albo diese Linie nach der Disputation fort.

Gleichzeitig legt eine andere Bemerkung Albos die Vermutung nahe, auch die Herausnahme des Messias aus den *'iqqarim* des Judentums könne mehr aus taktischen Erwägungen denn aus wahrer Überzeugung erfolgt sein. Die Bemerkung, auf die ich mich beziehe, macht Albo im dritten Abschnitt seines

Buches im Zusammenhang mit einem der beiden anderen erwähnten *'anafim*, der Überlegenheit Moses' über alle gewesenen und kommenden Propheten. Hier schreibt er: „Now it would seem [...] that the superiority of Moses as a prophet should be counted as a special and separate dogma of the Mosaic law, because it signifies the perpetuity of the latter."[64] Da aber ein Gegner Einwände erheben könne, sei es dennoch angemessen, die Überlegenheit Moses' eben *nicht* als *'iqqar*, sondern als *'anaf* einzustufen. Erklärt nun Albo selbst, er habe die Überlegenheit der Prophetie Moses' nur deshalb nicht in die *'iqqarim* des göttlichen Gesetzes aufgenommen, um damit möglichen Gegnern keine Argumente zu liefern, so muß zumindest gefragt werden, ob nicht auch seine Herausnahme des Messias aus den *'iqqarim* des Judentums ähnlich bewertet werden muß. In diesem Falle wäre Albos wirkliche Position nicht diejenige, die er im Hinblick auf Rabbi Hillel vertritt, sondern diejenige des letzten Satzes aus Kapitel I, 23: Der Leugner der *'anafim* hat keinen Anteil an der kommenden Welt.

Unabhängig von den möglichen Antworten auf diese Frage muß festgehalten werden, daß der Messias auch bei Albo ein Dogma bleibt, dessen Leugner zumindest *Gefahr läuft*, seinen Anteil an der kommenden Welt ebenso zu verlieren wie der Leugner eines *'iqqar* oder eines *shoresh*. In dogmatischer Hinsicht unterscheiden sich die *'anafim* im religionsphilosophischen System Albos nur noch geringfügig von den *'iqqarim* und *shorashim* des göttlichen Gesetzes. Die erste Bemerkung, mit der sich Albo in die Disputation von Tortosa einbringt, kann damit nur noch in Teilen für die Haltung stehen, die Albo in seinem *Sefer ha-'iqqarim* im Hinblick auf den Messias einnimmt. In Tortosa mußte Albo betonen, sein Judentum sei mit oder ohne den Messias dasselbe. In seinem *Sefer ha-'iqqarim* muß Albo eine Position beziehen, die nicht nur der allgemeinen Verunsicherung begegnet, sondern auch diejenigen Juden, die in der Tradition ihrer Väter ausharren, in ihrer Haltung bestätigt.

In Anlehnung an die erste Bemerkung Albos in der Disputation ließe sich diese Position folgendermaßen ausdrücken: „Posito Messiam mihi probari iam venisse, tamen non esset mihi causa revocandae religionis. Sed sine dubio deterior essem iudeus, cum Messias sit dogma quod credere neque vero quaerere debeo." – „Auch wenn mir bewiesen würde, daß der Messias bereits erschienen sei, hätte ich dennoch keinen Grund, meine Religion zu widerrufen. Ein schlechterer Jude wäre ich aber ohne Zweifel, denn der Messias ist ein *'anaf*, und ich habe ihn zu glauben, nicht zu hinterfragen."

Universität des Saarlandes, Saarbrücken

Notes

1. Der folgende Text geht auf einen Vortrag zurück, den ich im Mai 1999 auf der *31st Annual RMMRA Confererence* in Phoenix gehalten habe. Ihm liegen die Ergebnisse meiner bisher unveröffentlichten Dissertation über Joseph Albo zugrunde. Mein Dank gilt

der Freien Universität Berlin, die mir durch einen Reisekostenzuschuss die Teilnahme an der Konferenz ermöglicht hat.

2. Für Sekundärliteratur zu Tortosa vgl. v. a. Yitzhak Fritz Baer, *Die Disputation von Tortosa*, in: *Spanische Forschungen der Görresgesellschaft*, 1. Reihe: *Gesammelte Aufsätze zur Kulturgeschichte Spaniens* 3 (1931), S. 307- 336 und ders., *Historia de los Judíos en la España Cristiana* (EA Tel Aviv 1945) Madrid 1981, Repr. Barcelona 1998, S. 611- 684; Heinrich Graetz, *Geschichte der Juden von den ältesten Zeiten bis auf die Gegenwart*, Leipzig 1853- 75, Bd. VIII, S. 113- 124; Hyam Maccoby, *Judaism on Trial*, London 1982, Paperback Repr. 1996, S. 82- 101 und S. 168- 215; Antonio Pacios López, *La Disputa de Tortosa*, 2 Bde., Madrid 1957; Félix Pérez Aguado, *Un Congreso Cristiano-Rabbinico Celebrado en Tortosa*, in: *La Ciudad de Dios* 34 (1894), S. 29- 37; 180- 190; 584- 590; 35 (1894), S. 18- 26; 189- 200; 513- 522; 37 (1895), S. 35- 43; 197- 203; 401- 408; 38 (1895), S. 501- 511 und 39 (1896), S. 94- 113 und Adolf Posnanski, *Le Colloque de Tortose*, in: *REJ* 74 (1922), S. 17- 39; 160- 168; 75 (1922), S. 74- 88; 187- 204; 76 (1923), S. 37- 46.

3. Zu Josua Lorqui vgl. v. a. Baer, *Historia*, S. 570- 580; L. Landauer (Hg.), *Das Apologetische Schreiben des Josua Lorqui an den Abtrünnigen Don Salomon ha-Levi*, Antwerpen 1906; Moises Orfali, *El Tratado „De Iudaicis Erroribus ex Talmut" de Jerónimo de Santa Fe*, Madrid 1987, Pacios López, *La Disputa*, Bd. I, S. 40- 44, Posnanski, *Le Colloque de Tortose* und Joseph Rodríguez de Castro, *Biblioteca Española*, Madrid 1781, Repr. Hildesheim, New York 1977, Bd. I, S. 203- 227.

4. Zu den verschiedenen Manuskripten vgl. Orfali, *The Portuguese Edition (1565) of Hieronymus de Sancta Fide's Contra Iudaeos*, in: Ora Limor und Guy Stroumsa (Hg.), *Contra Iudaeos, Ancient and Medieval Polemics between Christians and Jews*, Tübingen 1996, S. 240, Anm. 7. Gedruckt wurde der Traktat -- zusammen mit einem zweiten Traktat Jerónimos gegen den Talmud -- erstmalig 1552 in Zürich unter dem Titel *Contra Iudaeos Hieronymi de Sancta Fide, Iudaei, Ad Christianismum conuersi, Libri duo: Quorum prior fidem & religionem eorum impugnat, Alter verum Talmuth.*

5. In der 48. Sitzung der Disputation wird Albo als „darocanus" bezeichnet. Vgl. hierzu Pacios López, *La Disputa*, Bd. II, S. 404.

6. Vgl. hierzu Pacios López, *La Disputa*, Bd. II, S. 598. Die Bulle Benedikts XIII. wurde in der 68. und der 69. Sitzung der Disputation verlesen und am 11. Mai 1415 in Valencia in Kraft gesetzt. Für den originalen Wortlaut der Bulle vgl. Pacios López, *La Disputa*, Bd. II, S. 597- 608 bzw. Ramón O'Callaghan, *Anales de Tortosa e Historia de la Santa Cinta*, Tortosa 1886-88, Bd. III, S. 76- 94 und S. 269- 282 (zweisprachig in Lateinisch und Kastilisch).

7. Vgl. zum Ende der 12. Sitzung Pacios López, *La Disputa*, Bd. II, S. 86, zum Ende der 14. Sitzung ebd., S. 102 sowie zum Ende der 22. Sitzung ebd., S. 151.

8. Vgl. hierzu Miguel Angel Motis Dolader, *Los Judíos en Aragón en la Edad Media*, Aragón 1990, S. 24.

9. Für Ausgaben siehe Joseph Albo, *Sefer ha-Ikkarim, Book of Principles*, hg. und übers. von Isaac Husik (zweisprachig), 4 Bde., 5 Bücher, Philadelphia 1929-30, 2. Auflage 1946 sowie Joseph Albo, *Sefer 'iqqarim, Buch Ikkarim, Grund- und Glaubenslehren der Mosaischen Religion*, übers. von Wolf Schlessinger und Ludwig Schlesinger, Einl. und Anm. Ludwig Schlesinger (EA Frankfurt a. M. 1838-44), 2. Auflage Berlin 1922. Da die deutsche Übersetzung von Schlesinger und Schlessinger offensichtliche Fehler gegenüber dem hebräischen Original enthält und modernen wissenschaftlichen Kriterien nicht

standhalten kann, zitiere ich aus der englischen Übersetzung von Husik. Für Sekundärliteratur zu Albo vgl. z. B. Samuel Back, *Joseph Albos Bedeutung in der Geschichte der jüdischen Religionsphilosophie*, Breslau 1869; Isaac Husik, *Introduction*, in: Albo, *Sefer ha-Ikkarim, Book of Principles*, Hg. Isaac Husik, Bd. I, , S. xv- xxviii; ders., *Joseph Albo the Last of the Mediaeval Jewish Philosophers*, in: *Proceedings of the American Academy for Jewish Research* 1 (1928-1930), Repr. New York 1966, S. 61- 72 und ders., *Joseph Albo*, in: *A History of Mediaeval Jewish Philosophy* (EA New York 1916), Philadelphia 1946, S. 406- 427, Menachem Kellner, *Joseph Albo's „Sefer ha-Ikkarim"*, in: *The Solomon Goldman Lectures* 6 (1993), S. 139- 149; Daniel J. Lasker, *Joseph Albo's Theory of Verification* (hebr.), in: *Da'at* 5 (1980), S. 5- 12; Ralph Lerner, *The Politic Art of Joseph Albo*, in: Friedrich Niewöhner und Louis Sturlese (Hg.), *Averroismus im Mittelalter und in der Renaissance*, Zürich 1994, S. 251- 268 sowie Aaron Tänzer, *Die Religionsphilosophie Joseph Albo's nach seinem Werke „Ikkarim" systematisch dargestellt und erläutert*, Preßburg 1896.

10. Vgl. zu den *'iqqarim* des Maimonides J. Holzer, *Zur Geschichte der Dogmenlehre in der jüdischen Religionsphilosophie des Mittelalters, Mose Maimunis Einleitung zu Chelek im arabischen Text und in der hebräischen Übersetzung*, Berlin 1901 sowie für die deutsche Übersetzung Johann Maier, *Zu Person und Werk des Mose ben Maimon*, in: Moses Maimonides, *Führer der Unschlüssigen*, Übers. und Komm. Adolf Weiss, 2. Auflage, Hg. Johann Maier, Hamburg 1972, Erstes Buch, S. XL- XLVIII.

11. Vgl. hierzu Albo, *Principles*, I, 3, S. 55.

12. Vgl. hierzu z. B. Albo, *Principles*, I, S. 38 sowie ebd. I, 4, S. 64 und I, 10, S. 96/ 97.

13. Vgl. hierzu Albo, *Principles*, I, 13, S. 121. Zu den *shorashim* allgemein vgl. Albo, *Principles*, I, 15, S. 129- 137.

14. Zu den *'anafim* vgl. Albo, *Principles*, I, 23, S. 181- 187.

15. Die folgende Analyse der Rolle Albos in Tortosa orientiert sich am Protokoll der päpstlichen Scribenten, das als einziges vollständiges Zeugnis dieser Disputation erhalten ist und 1957 von Antonio Pacios López in Madrid ediert und kommentiert wurde. Vgl. hierzu Anm. 2. Neben dem lateinischen Protokoll existiert ein hebräisches Protokoll der ersten fünf Sitzungen, das einer der geladenen Rabbiner, wahrscheinlich Bonastruch Desmaestre aus Gerona, verfaßte und an seine Gemeinde sandte. Für den Originaltext dieses hebräischen Protokolls vgl. Solomon Joachim Halberstamm, *Wikkuah Tortosa*, in: *Jeschurun* (Bamberg) 6 (1868), S. 45- 55. Bei dem Text, den Ibn Verga im 40. Kapitel seines *Schevet Jehuda* zitiert und der lange Zeit für ein zweites hebräisches Protokoll der Disputation gehalten wurde, handelt es sich, wie Jaume Riera i Sans sehr überzeugend nachgewiesen hat, um eine literarische Bearbeitung des ersten hebräischen Protokolls. Vgl. hierzu sowie für eine katalanische Übersetzung der beiden hebräischen Texte Riera i Sans, *La crònica en hebreu de la disputa de Tortosa*, Barcelona 1974. Für eine deutsche Übersetzung des Textes von Ibn Verga vgl. Salomo Ibn Verga, *Liber Schevet Jehuda*, übers. von M. Wiener, Hannover 1856, Repr. 1924, S. 134- 158.

16. Pacios López, *La Disputa*, Bd. II, S. 35.

17. Vgl. hierzu Pacios López, *La Disputa*, Bd. II, S. 36.

18. Vgl. hierzu Pacios López, *La Disputa*, Bd. II, S. 37.

19. Vgl. hierzu Pacios López, *La Disputa*, Bd. II, S. 51.

20. Die Bibel, Einheitsübersetzung, Stuttgart 1980, Lizenzausgabe Freiburg im Breisgau, S. 51

21. Vgl. hierzu Pacios López, *La Disputa*, Bd. II, S. 55/ 56.

22. Vgl. hierzu Pacios López, *La Disputa*, Bd. II, S. 57. Vermutlich handelt es sich bei „dieta" an dieser Stelle um einen Druckfehler. Ich übersetze: „dicta".

23. Vgl. hierzu Pacios López, *La Disputa*, Bd. II, S. 404.

24. Vgl. hierzu Pacios López, *La Disputa*, Bd. II, S. 561.

25. Vgl. zum Wortlaut dieser Erklärung Pacios López, *La Disputa*, Bd. II, S. 567.

26. Vgl. hierzu Pacios López, *La Disputa*, Bd. II, S. 568 und S. 574.

27. Vgl. hierzu Pacios López, *La Disputa*, Bd. II, S. 593.

28. Vgl. hierzu Pacios López, *La Disputa*, Bd. II, S. 595.

29. Pacios López, *La Disputa*, Bd. II, S. 36

30. Vgl. hierzu Anm. 21.

31. b. San 99a, in: *Der Babylonische Talmud* (Goldschmidt), Bd. IX, Berlin 1934, S. 74

32. Vgl. hierzu Albo, *Principles*, I, 1, S. 44- 48.

33. Zu den vier Arten der Erkenntnis vgl. Albo, *Principles*, I, 17, S. 147/ 148.

34. Vgl. hierzu Albo, *Principles*, I, 17, S. 147.

35. Vgl. hierzu Albo, *Principles*, I, 17, S. 151.

36. Vgl. hierzu Albos Erläuterungen zum dritten *'iqqar* von Lohn und Strafe, der -- eben im Gegensatz zur Offenbarung -- diesen Überlieferungen zugeordnet wird, in: Albo, *Principles*, I, 17, S. 152. Im vierten Abschnitt ist es die Erfahrung mit den Worten der Propheten, die den Überlieferungen zugrunde liegt. Vgl. hierzu Albo, *Principles*, IV, 44, S. 437- 439.

37. Vgl. hierzu z. B. Albo, *Principles*, IV, 44, S. 438.

38. Vgl. hierzu z. B. Albo, *Principles*, I, 20, S. 171 sowie Anm. 40.

39. Vgl. hierzu v. a. Albo, *Principles*, IV, 42, S. 421 sowie die Inhaltsangabe zu demselben Kapitel, in: Albo, *Principles*, I, S. 32. Aus Kapitel IV, 44 geht hervor, daß Albo die Prophetenbücher, die er an beiden Stellen der „Tradition" (*qabbala*) gegenüberstellt, als Teil der Überlieferungen auffaßt. Vgl. hierzu Albo, *Principles*, IV, 44, S. 437-439. Husik bezeichnet diese letzte Tradition als „rabbinic tradition". Vgl. hierzu ders., *Joseph Albo the Last of the Mediaeval Jewish Philosophers*, S. 66.

40. Aus den hebräischen Bezeichnungen geht der Stellenwert der Überlieferungen zwischen den Geschichtswahrheiten und der Tradition deutlich gervor, indem in „*ha-qabbala ha-nimshekhet*" gleichsam die „*nimshekhot*" und die „*qabbala*" miteinander verbunden werden. Gleichzeitig trennt Albo zwischen den Geschichtswahrheiten und den übrigen zwei Arten der Tradierung, indem er nur die letzten beiden als „Traditionen" bezeichnet. An einigen Stellen verwendet Albo „*qabbala*" auch als Oberbegriff für die beiden letzten Traditionen. Vgl. hierzu z. B. Albo, *Principles*, I, 14, S. 127.

41. Zum unterschiedlichen Wahrheitsanspruch der prophetischen Überlieferungen und der „einfachen" Tradition vgl. Albo, *Principles*, IV, 42, S. 423. Zur Autorität der Tradition allgemein vgl. Albo, *Principles*, III, 26, S. 251/252.

42. Vgl. hierzu Albo, *Principles*, IV, 42, S. 421.

43. Vgl. hierzu Albo, *Principles*, IV, 42, S. 423. Husik verweist zu Recht auf die Ähnlichkeit der Argumentation Albos an dieser Stelle zur christlichen antijüdischen Polemik seiner Zeit. Vgl. hierzu Husik, *Joseph Albo the Last of the Mediaeval Jewish Philosophers*, S. 66.

44. Vgl. hierzu Albo, *Principles*, IV, 42, S. 423.

45. Vgl. hierzu Albo, *Principles*, IV, 42, S. 424.

46. *Die Bibel*, Einheitübersetzung, Stuttgart 1980, Lizenzausgabe Freiburg im Breisgau, S. 864

47. Vgl. hierzu Albo, *Principles*, IV, 44, S. 439- 440.

48. Deut 18, 15

49. Albo, *Principles*, IV, 42, S. 413.

50. Albo erklärt mit diesem Unterschied zwischen dem Übertreter einer *miswa* und dem Leugner eines *'iqqar* nicht zuletzt die Tatsache, daß keine *miswa* zu den *'iqqarim* des göttlichen Gesetzes gezählt werden dürfe. Vgl. hierzu Albo, *Principles*, I, 14, S. 123/ 124. In Kapitel IV, 42 wiederholt Albo an zwei Stellen explizit, daß derjenige, der den Messias leugne, kein Leugner des göttlichen Gesetzes an sich sei. Vgl. hierzu Albo, *Principles*, IV, 42, S. 413 und S. 414.

51. Vgl. hierzu Albo, *Principles*, I, 23, S. 186.

52.Vgl. hierzu Albo, *Principles*, I, 23, S. 181.

53. Albo, *Principles*, I, 23, S. 187.

54. In seinem Kommentar *'Es shatul* (1618) erklärt Rabbi Gedalia Lipschütz zum letzten Satz von Kapitel I, 23, der Leugner eines *'anaf* gehöre, wenn er auch Ketzer genannt werde, nicht zu denjenigen, die keinen Anteil an der kommenden Welt hätten. Er werde nur deshalb Ketzer genannt, weil die *'anafim* den *'iqqarim* so ähnlich seien, daß auch derjenige, der sie leugne, wie der Leugner eines *'iqqar* bezeichnet werden müsse. Schlesinger und Schlessinger, die deutschen Übersetzer von Albo, scheinen sich an diesem oder einem ähnlichen Kommentar orientiert zu haben. Der letzte Satz von Kapitel I, 23 heißt bei ihnen: „Wer aber dieselben läugnet, wird Ketzer genannt, obschon er nicht zu jenen gehört, die das Gesetz läugnen und keinen Anteil am Jenseits haben." (Albo, *Buch Ikkarim*, S. 85). Es ist jedoch eindeutig, daß diese Übersetzung dem hebräischen Original nicht entspricht.

55. b. San 90a, in: *Der Babylonische Talmud* (Goldschmidt), Bd. IX, Berlin 1934, S. 27

56. Vgl. hierzu Albo, *Principles*, I, 10, S. 98- 100.

57. Albo, *Principles*, I, 10, S. 98

58. ebd.

59. Albo, *Principles*, I, 23, S. 185

60. Vgl. hierzu Albo, *Principles*, I, 10, S. 98.

61. Albo, *Principles*, I, 10, S. 98

62. Vgl. hierzu z. B. Haim Hillel ben Sasson, der über Tortosa schreibt: „The Sefer Ikkarim of Joseph Albo who participated in this disputation, is largely a summing up of the Jewish position taken there." (*Disputations and Polemics*, in: *EI*, Jerusalem 1971, Bd. VI, S. 92)

63. Baer schreibt: „Soweit eine innere Spaltung unter ihnen [i. e. den offiziellen Sprechern der Juden. S. R.] bestand, ist sie nicht in ihrem Verhältnis zur Hagada hervorgetreten, wie man bisher angenommen hat, sondern in ihrer Auffassung der Messianologie." (*Die Disputation von Tortosa*, S. 325)

64. Albo, *Principles*, III, 20, S. 189. Vgl. zu derselben Position auch ebd., III, 20, S. 191.

Talk is Cheap: Political Discourse in Malory's *Morte Darthur*

Cory Rushton

Thomas Malory, most critics now agree, lived a political life. Elizabeth Pochoda has written that Malory "could only understand his picture of the past as it functioned in the present, in his own culture," and consequently he wanted "the Arthurian story to correspond to the political theory of his day" (23). Malory's experience of Parliament and the workings of medieval government has rarely been examined directly in relation with his text, even though the general context of fifteenth-century England and the specifics of Malory's involvement in the Wars of the Roses have often been examined. Malory's specific political allegiance, Lancastrian or Yorkist, may always be a subject of the controversy, since his text both supports and simultaneously invalidates any particular theory. At the very least, his interest in matters of political language bolsters the critical consensus that Malory was a man with parliamentarian experience, a theory championed prominently in the work of Peter Field. We might come to some conclusions about Malory's political theory, the assumptions and beliefs he held concerning how England might best be governed, by examining his use of certain words that arise in political contexts: "counceyle," "langayge," and "parlemente." The art of political conversation, whether the counsel of a king's followers or a disputation between enemies, has a specific function in the *Morte Darthur*, and may point us towards a better understanding of Malory's motivations for composing the work.

Henry of Bracton was one of the first medieval political theorists to develop the importance of the royal council. He wrote that a king could make laws only if he had considerable participation from good councillors, who represented the continuity of the realm from monarch to monarch (Bracton II.305, Pochoda 46). This represented a shift from the old, regal style of rulership in which the king exercised full legal authority, a theory best represented by Policraticus (Pochoda 46). As Pochoda writes:

> From the time of Bracton when the king began to appear as an administrator of a public sphere rather than as a personal liege lord, the choice of a council, or limbs of the body politic, was of crucial importance. The strength of the state depended on the king's ability to attract the best councillors. (83)

Arthur is able to attract excellent councillors at the beginning of his reign: Merlin, for example, and knights such as Pellinore. The Round Table has long been considered an extension of Arthur's legal authority, the "limbs of the body politic," but the function of the Round Table knight according to critics often seems limited to killing giants and suppressing troublesome nobles. The Malorian knight of the Round Table has other functions, however, and foremost among these is the offering of counsel not only to Arthur (at the royal level) but to other knights (on a personal level). Stephen Knight has summarized the Malorian chivalric ideal as one in which "knights act alone, act well, and act for the communal good" unencumbered by the "armed 'affinities' which depended on a lord's patronage and which made his discipline entirely convergent with his self-interest" (113). Calling into question Knight's assertion that the "self- interest" of the nobility is not an important aspect of Malory's narrative, the affinities of the great knights become central to the dissolution of the Round Table. The "well-wyllars" whom both Gawain and Lancelot are said to attract are best described as traditional affinities, factions within Arthur's court which provide assistance and counsel to these powerful and charismatic figures who are themselves part of Arthur's own affinity. Lancelot and Gawain are both supported by their factions in situations where their "self-interest" is clearly not coincident with that of either Arthur or his realm. Gawain is a clear example: Arthur's primary counselor towards the end of the *Morte*, he is also counseled and supported by his own faction, composed of his brothers, cousins and other knights associated with his family. The council is not solely a royal phenomenon.

The concept of "counceyle" first appears prominently in the conflict with the rebellious kings led by Lot, when Arthur holds council with his allies Ban and Bors. The word is repeated three times in short succession:

> And than they wente unto counceyle, and with hem Gwenbaus, brothir unto kynge Ban and Bors, a wyse clerke; and thidir wente Ulphuns, Brastias and Merlion. And aftir they had [ben] in her counceyle they wente unto bedde. And on the morne they harde masse, and to dyner and so to theire counceyle, and made many argumentes what were beste to do. (16/9-13)

The overall impression is that of a round of political talks between allies, and although there are little specifics given, "counceyle" here seems to involve both debate and long hours. Furthermore, "counceyle" also refers to the advice (the "many argumentes") given in a "counceyle." This is the usage commonly associated with Merlin in the early books, where he is Arthur's chief counselor and accustomed to making long speeches, which are usually accepted by all as the right course of action by everyone involved. To choose one example of many, Merlin's advice following the battle against the eleven kings is to cease the slaughter; Ban and Bors pronounce the advice to be "trouthe" and Arthur proclaims that as Merlin says, "so shall hit be done" (24/33-25/16). "Counceyle" might also refer to smaller, more intimate councils between individual knights, such as Arthur's "counceyle" with Kay and Bedwere when he is about to secretly do battle with the Giant of Mont St. Michel (120/8-9).[1] Dinadan often acts as a counselor to both Tristram and Lancelot, and answers Lancelot's request for "counseyle" when Mark sends slanderous letters to Arthur detailing Guinevere's adultery; Dinadan's "counseyle" is to ignore Mark's villainy (381/38-44-382/1-

4). The absence, or sudden disappearance, of good counsel towards the end of Arthur's reign is an integral element in the Malorian vision (Radulescu 74). Merlin vanishes and Arthur is forced to rely upon merely mortal councillors, and Dinadan is killed on the Grail quest by those perennial ne'er-do-wells, Mordred and Aggravayne, an event which in itself seems to herald the beginning of the end (Hanks 159).

Plummer's comment that "counceyle" is a word "suggestive of judicious speech informed by thought" (161) is clearly inadequate to the many nuances it holds both in this scene and throughout the *Morte Darthur*; "counceyle" is not merely speech or advice, but also any plan hinging on that advice. The word "counceyle" is from the OF *cuncile* (itself derived from the Latin *concilium*), a convocation or assembly, sometimes but not always an assembly for consultation. As such, according to the OED, it became confused with the OF *counseil* (from the Latin *consilium*), an advisory body. Throughout Malory's text, variant spellings have little impact on the meaning of the word: "counceyle," "counseyle" and "counsel" are all interchangeable. Only in the sixteenth century are the two words "council" and "counsel" normalized into their modern usages.[2] All of the forms refer to political discussion, "debate" in a broader sense not necessarily restricted to conflict.

If the reader immediately recalls any specific Malorian council scene, it will likely be the council Arthur holds upon receiving the exorbitant demands of the Roman Emperor Lucius: "Then the kynge unto counsayle called his noble lordes and knyghtes, and within a towre there they assembled, the moste party of the knyghtes of the Rounde Table. Than the kynge commaunded hem of theire beste counceyle" (114/7-10). The resulting council is closely drawn from Malory's source, the *Alliterative Morte Arthure*, where the word "counsel" is also used. Arthur's request for advice is met with unanimity. Cador of Cornwall states that he is glad Lucius has demanded tribute "for now we shall have warre and worshyp" (114/11-13). Cador's fellow councillors follow the same speaking order as that of the poem and they all agree that war with the Romans is the most appropriate course of action. There is no dissent, only a series of vows concerning how many men each councillor will bring to the war effort; these vows are also soon fulfilled, forging a link between boast and action which is not so easily duplicated during the latter part of Arthur's reign. The Round Table in this passage, far from its modern reputation as a gathering held once a year to recount solitary adventures, is the king's main source of political advice, a body of men who should be consulted before military action is taken. That this unanimous council corresponds to the high point of Arthur's reign and culminates in the greatest extension of his political power only reinforces the message. Arthur's court will never again be so united on any given political issue.

Malory does make two significant changes to the account found in his alliterative source, both of which illuminate the political situation of both Arthur's court and a wider continental world: the first is an expansion of Lancelot's speech, and the second is the substitution of sir Bawdwyn for the sir Lot of Malory's source, made necessary by Lot's role in the rebellion against Arthur and his subsequent death. Lancelot's boast in the poem that he will knock the Emperor "stiffly fro his steed" despite his bodyguard of giants and Genoese (*AMA* 372-77) becomes a political statement in Malory: "'Though my londis marche nyghe thyne enemyes, yet shall I make myne avow aftir my power;" that vow is to bring "twenty thousand helmys in haubirkes" to the war effort (115/14-19). The rhetoric of the Malorian Lancelot, on the surface just another boast, effectively reminds both Arthur and the reader that his lands are threatened or (in some cases) under the control of mutual enemies. His efforts are not in vain: after the cessation of hostilities, Lancelot and Bors receive the "brode londis" that once belonged to their fathers from the hand of Arthur (145/23-29). It is an important intertextual moment in which Malory combines the Vulgate war against Claudas with the insular tradition of a continental campaign. Arthur's conquest of Europe ceases to be the arrogant quest of the *Alliterative Morte Arthure*, and becomes a manoeuver partially meant to strengthen the political position of his allies on the continent. Despite these two narrative differences, in both texts the councils arrive at the same unanimous decision, that Arthur and the Round Table will go to war with the Romans.

The word "counsel/council" also occurs in both Malory and the *Alliterative Morte Arthure* when Arthur seeks advice on the ordering of the realm in his absence during the Roman campaign. In the poem, Arthur chooses Mordred, himself a member of the king's council (648): "I set you here a soveraign, assent yif you likes" (644). Arthur is very much in control, desiring only nominal agreement from the gathering of "peeres of the rewm," called a "parlemente" by the poet (636- 37). The king also orders all English shipping to be commandeered for the war effort (632-33). Malory's Arthur also summons a "parlemente at Yorke" which gathers "unto counsayle" and where "they concluded shortly to areste all shyppes of this londe" and then choose two knights to rule in Arthur's absence, sir Bawdwyn and sir Constantyne (117/30-35, 40-44). It is important to note that the gathered "kynges and knyghtes" choose the regents at the king's specific request: "'Therefore I pray you, counseyle me that may be beste and most worshyp" (117/38-39). Arthur then agrees to resign "all the rule unto thes two lordis and quene Gwenyvere" (118/1-2). It is slightly jarring to find acts of Parliament embedded in a romance text; yet Malory has chosen to locate and emphasize Parliamentary privilege and power at just that moment in the Arthurian narrative when Arthur traditionally makes the fatal mistake of choosing the treasonous Mordred as regent. Malory's Mordred is not yet present in the text; presumably he is too young to be a knight, much less a regent. However, anyone familiar with the alliterative poem or the tradition behind it would immediately notice the change, and that moment of intertextual awareness would serve to emphasize the wisdom of parliament's recommendations. During the disturbances which later wrack Arthur's kingdom, the role of "parlementes" differs substantially from this early and optimistic view, perhaps reflecting a change in Malory's attitude towards the institution.

At no point in the troubles which end Arthur's reign does he call a "parlemente" as he did before the Roman War, but Lancelot and Mordred do. When Arthur last left Britain to fight overseas, he allowed his "parlemente" to choose his regents; on this occasion, "Arthur made sir Mordred chyeff ruler of all Ingelonde, and also he put the quene undir hys governaunce," and the reason given for this is that "Mordred was kynge Arthurs son" (700/16-19). No parliamentary legitimation seems necessary for the (temporary) transfer of power from father to son, leaving aside the difficulties inherent in Arthur's acknowledgment of Mordred's illegitimate and incestuous paternity (Knight 138); in another of Malory's sources, the *Stanzaic Morte Arthur*, Mordred is chosen by the king's counselors as steward while Arthur goes to war against Lancelot (2508-23), the professed reason being the father-son relationship (2957). The *Stanzaic Morte Arthur* also includes reference to Mordred's calling a "parlement" in which he is proclaimed king by the people unanimously after giving them feasts and "grete giftes" (2962-81). When Malory's Mordred seizes power, he also summons "a parlemente, and called the lordys togydir, and there he made them to chose hym kynge," on the basis of forged letters reporting his father's death (707/14-17). Parliament's acceptance of Mordred in Malory, since his paternity is apparently (but mysteriously) well-known, appears to be a formality, as it would be for any heir apparent of a deceased monarch; the process legitimates the transfer of power. Similarly, when Lancelot calls a "parlement" upon his return to Benwick, it is for the express purpose of ordering his realm: he crowns Bors and his other close kin as kings of the various parts of his lands, and makes Ector de Maris "prynce of them all" (699/26-32). While the parliaments held by Arthur and Mordred have their basis in Malory's sources, Lancelot's does not. For Malory, any transference of political power must be ratified and witnessed by a parliament; therefore, if Mordred's usurpation has parliamentary authority, Lancelot's division of his kingdom must also be shown to be legitimate and authorized.

It has been said of the medieval English Parliament that it differed from a royal council in that the king wanted discussion from his council and agreement from his parliament, usually on matters concerning taxation (Barnes 5). Certainly the parliaments called by Mordred and Lancelot fit this model, but Arthur's earlier parliament does not; Arthur's parliament seems to make crucial decisions, based on the order in which Malory narrates the events. Parliament's independence in this passage seems to contradict both the later uses of parliament in Malory's text and medieval political theory. The answer may be found in the Caxton version of the Roman War, which is substantially different from the longer version found in the Winchester Manuscript. Caxton's printed version emphasizes royal control over parliament, insisting upon the ratifying role of parliament in regal decision-making. The origin of the decision to arrest all shipping is far more ambiguous in Caxton, and Arthur himself chooses the two regents, Baudwin and Constantine (171).

In discussing the differences between the two versions, Withrington notes that Arthur's kingdom in the manuscript is a "newly-established realm" suffering a "sense of fragility" which Arthur, young and relatively inexperienced, cannot dispel; Caxton's Arthur is a monarch who "has already proven triumphant is establishing the political unity and civil peace" necessary to perpetuate his reign (353). Although scholars debate whether Caxton or Malory revised the Roman War episode, the likeliest candidate remains Caxton, whose emendations in the Roman War tale tend to make the text "more positively courtly, more like the French texts he [Caxton] so clearly admired" (McCarthy, "Caxton" 146).[3] Caxton eliminates parliament's independence in this passage, creating a more consistent portrayal of the institution between the Roman War and the final destruction of the realm. Unfortunately, this harmonization eclipses whatever point Malory might have been making by marking a decline in both parliamentary prestige and political discourse. Consistency may not have been what Malory was originally trying to portray; instead he may have wanted to show a historical process by which parliament was slowly subordinated to the will of a strong king. In both versions, by the end of Arthur's reign parliament has ceased to be an effective locus of political decision-making, and only the private council has any real influence over the course of events.

While "counceyle" is found throughout Malory's text, prominently in the Tristram and Grail books, the word occurs politically most often in the *Morte* proper. "Counceyle" occurs thirteen times in the section Vinaver called "Slander and Strife." The first four occurrences of the word come during the argument between Aggravayne and Gawayne concerning the queen's adultery with Lancelot: Aggravayne speaks "opynly, and nat in no counceyle, that manye knyghtes myght here" (673/14-16). Gawain twice states that he will not be of Aggravayne's counsel in this matter (673/22-24; 674/11-12); once he says that not by his "counceyle" will Aggravayne inform the king, citing the possibility of a dangerous factional split in the Round Table (673/33-36). Bors uses "counseyle" in the same manner when he urges Lancelot not to visit the queen on the night Aggravayne sets his trap (675/23), and twice when he urges Lancelot to rescue the queen and to "take the woo wyth the weall" (680/13-20). Gawain again uses the word when he asks Arthur not to be overhasty in condemning the queen (682/23) and when he rejects the idea of vengeance for Aggravayne's death, as Aggravayne and his men would "nat do be my counceyle" (683/12-16). Lancelot uses the word "counceyle" when he urges the knights at the queen's door to leave (677/36-38); good advice which, regrettably, they ignore.

The scene in which Bors counsels Lancelot following his escape from Aggravayne is greatly expanded from its French counterpart. While the Lancelot of the *Mort Artu* simply gathers Bors and a handful of sergeants and flees Camelot, Malory's Lancelot essentially calls a council, to see (as Bors says) "who that woll holde with" him (679/18-20). Once the various knights of his own kin group and the survivors of Lamorak and Tristram's groups are gathered, Lancelot informs them of the night's events and, significantly, asks them, "'Wherefore, my fayre lordy[s], my kyn and my fryndis,' seyde sir Launcelot, 'what woll ye do'" (680/27-28)? They answer "with one voyce" that they will do as he does, upon which Lancelot puts a "case unto" them, asking what they would do if the queen were sentenced to be burnt. They again agree, "with one voice," to do as Lancelot thinks best. Much the same circumstances occur after Lancelot returns Guinevere to Camelot; upon his return to Joyous Garde, he asks his followers what should be done, and they answer "all holé togydirs with one voyce" that they will do whatever Lancelot decides (698/15-17). The entire event seems very reminiscent of Arthur's earlier royal council, especially in its emphasis on unanimity and lack of substantial debate.

Carole Rawcliffe has written about baronial councils in late medieval England, arguing that most nobles had councils of their own which mirrored and often influenced royal councils (105-06). While most councils by the late fifteenth century were dominated by lawyers and bureaucrats, a nobleman's chief vassals and kinsmen would still play an important role (94). Clearly, Lancelot is able to call upon Bors and his other kinsmen (and the kinsmen of other deceased knights) to act as a council in his time of need. Just as clearly, Gawain has a baronial council of his own, consisting of his brothers (possibly excepting Gareth) and those "well-wyllers" who accompany Aggravayne on his ill-fated mission to the queen's chambers. Gawain's council seems smaller and focused more exclusively on his immediate kin, and Gawain himself does not seem entirely in control of it, but his faction does have the king's ear. However, Gawain's council may also be larger than it at first appears (recall those unnamed knights present while Aggravayne slanders Lancelot and the queen, and their ambiguous role in the text), yet it lacks one crucial element present in Lancelot's council, unanimity. The unanimous consent of the noble knights who choose to follow Lancelot helps to legitimate the risky and ambiguous course of action he adopts. The abstention of Gawain, Gareth and Gaheris from participating in Aggravayne's "counsayle" emphasizes the essential ignobility of his plans. If three-fifths of Arthur's council had disapproved of his answer to the Roman ambassadors, the story of the war with Lucius would by necessity have a very different moral.

Gawain's behavior when Aggravayne begins to openly slander the lovers is argumentative and ineffectual: "Brothir, sir Aggravayne, I pray you and charge you, meve no such maters no more afore me, for wyte you well, I woll nat be of youre counceyle" (673/22-24); and again, "'And I wolde that ye leffte [all thys,] and make you nat so bysy...'" (673/29-30). When Arthur enters the room at the height of the quarrel, Gawain orders Aggravayne to "stynte [his] stryfe," but Aggravayne pointedly refuses; Gawain responds by leaving the room and contenting himself with "makynge grete dole" (674/9-16). These are hardly effective demonstrations of his power as head of his affinity. Gawain seems incapable of controlling his fractious younger brothers, and rather than standing his ground and providing Arthur with an immediate (and possibly more effective) counterpoint to Aggravayne's contention, Gawain, lamenting all the while, abandons the field to the slanderers. Radelescu argues that Gawain's brothers "should have joined the conspiracy of silence, which was the guarantee of stability in King Arthur's court" (75). While Gawain escapes from criticism by washing his hands of his affinity's actions, Malory's text does not entirely support this assertion. Gawain fails on two counts: he cannot control his own followers, and he fails to provide Arthur with "counceyle" of any kind until the queen is already condemned to burn at the stake. He allows the divisiveness to continue when he should be imposing unanimity and silence.

By contrast, Bors is the perfect counselor to Lancelot. Lumiansky noted that Malory manipulated his sources to show how Bors becomes the "patient bearer of protective responsibility for Lancelot" (5). It would be more accurate to say that Bors stands to Lancelot as Gawain stands to Arthur; more than merely "protective," Bors is the loyal lieutenant and chief counsellor to his kinsman. At first he offers sound advice, that Lancelot should not visit the queen. When that advice is rejected, he prepares himself for the worst and is ready to counsel Lancelot further. He adjusts for the difference between his opinion and that of his leader by subordinating his own position to that of Lancelot, preventing any potential discord with a loyalty foreign to Aggravayne. When Lancelot returns from the battle against Aggravayne's allies, he is surprised to find Bors ready for action: "'Jesu mercy!' seyde Launcelot, 'why be ye all armed?'" (678/29-30). Bors replies that he and "all that ben of youre blood and youre well-wyllars" had bad dreams which caused some to wake up in a sweat and others to unconsciously grab their swords; subsequently they armed and gathered in Lancelot's quarters (678/31-37). In the OF *Mort Artu*, it is Bors who asks Lancelot why he returns armed when he left to visit the queen unarmed, and only after Hector wanders in and interrupts the two knights does anyone think to gather some followers and leave Camelot (121/11:117-19). In the *Stanzaic Morte* Bors and Lancelot's other followers are also forewarned by dreams, but seem less organized: Lancelot gives orders to gather his followers and see that "they be armed and redy dight" (1184). Lancelot neither asks why Bors is armed nor has he forgotten his kinsman's earlier warning: "For it is sooth that thou me told" (1885). Malory, by contrast, makes it clear that Bors is both prescient and extremely capable in preparing for whatever befalls his lord, even when Lancelot is not. Bors not only provides good counsel, but he can also organize Lancelot's many followers on short notice and have everything ready for his lord's departure. He succeeds where Gawain fails.

If both Lancelot and Gawain can be shown to have active, organized councils similar to those discussed by Rawcliffe, the reader might wonder what has happened to the royal councils and parliament so useful to Arthur in his preparations for the Roman War. In the Vulgate, Arthur is continually counselled by Mordred, King Yon, and other nameless barons; it is a council of barons who sentence the queen to death, albeit with direct orders from Arthur himself (122/12:120-21). The *Stanzaic Morte Arthur* agrees that the barons are predominantly responsible for the death sentence: Arthur "and all his knightes keen / Took their counsel" and decide that Guinevere should be burnt that same day (1919-25). Malory inserts a reference to "the law in tho dayes," which had no recourse but death for those "founden gylty of treson," and he states that "there was made grete ordynaunce in thys ire" (682/12-17). Arthur states that he is unable to commute this sentence despite being "sore amoved" (682/9-11). The "ordynanunce" itself is never said to issue directly from any source, king or council; Malory has obscured the issue, but he does not categorically state that Arthur is without the support of his counselors in making the decision. Even if the latter were the case, Malory has merely replaced the authority of the king's councillors with the authority of an impersonal, but equally incontrovertible, law.

E. D. Kennedy has discussed the narrative necessity of "the law" in this passage, which allows Malory to retain the shape of the Arthurian legend while ameliorating Arthur's role in determining the queen's fate (225-27). Pochoda, by contrast, believes that Malory's Arthur bears full responsibility for the decision (134-35). In fact, Arthur only commands the queen to be burnt after hearing "previs and experyenses" (proofs and events) which make his judgement inevitable. While this may not be trial by combat, it is a trial, with Mordred giving Arthur his side of the case "frome the begynnyng to the endynge" (682/4) and Gawain arguing against a hasty conclusion. The language of "counceyle" reappears in Gawain's long speech, as he argues for a "respite" until Lancelot can also be present and answer the charges against him (682/23-26). Gawain goes so far as to argue for a change of venue, from the "law" to trial by combat (682/38-41). This is not simply a trial, however, as the link between treason and adultery suggests. Even as Gawain and Mordred argue over the guilt or innocence of Lancelot and Guinevere, they also offer alternative visions concerning the political consequences of both the crime and any potential punishments. For whatever reason, Gawain's counsel is ignored, and he again absents himself from further debate (684/1-2).

Gawain, Mordred, Gareth and Gaheris are all demonstrably present when Arthur makes his judgement; Gareth and Gaheris are ordered to attend the burning of the queen after Gawain refuses, and they do not have to be summoned to receive their orders. Malory excises reference to other councillors such as the Vulgate's Yon in favor of repeated emphasis on the Orkney clan as Arthur's primary counsel-givers. As the Orkney faction begins to lose members to the conflict, Malory's Arthur becomes both increasingly isolated and far too dependent on Gawain. All but one of Gawain's brothers and sons are dead by the time Lancelot brings Guinevere to Joyous Garde. Malory has systematically eliminated all mention of Yon, Ywain, or the other royal counsellors present in his sources. Gawain thus has a powerful hold over Arthur, and not merely an emotional hold; without Gawain and his remaining "frendis," Arthur's political position is tenuous at best.

The "counceyle" of the Orkney brothers usually turns out to be bad advice. Aggravayne and Mordred's "prevy hate unto the quene," masquerading as concern for Arthur's reputation, leads inexorably to the utter destruction of Arthur's realm and, presumably, a great deal of suffering throughout his kingdom. The brothers continually agitate for conflict, Aggravayne and Mordred because of their "prevy hate" and Gawain because of his overwhelming grief following the deaths of Gareth and

Gaheris. Yet these are not private feuds dealt with far from innocent bystanders, as were the earlier battles between Gawain's kin and Pellinore's family. Every attempt at seeking redress for real or imagined slights in the *Morte* leads directly and inexorably to war between armies and nations.[4] Gawain's advice, ironically rejected when good, is heeded when bad, or "over hasty," to borrow his own phrase. Given more than one course of action, Arthur invariably seems to choose the most disastrous route. Arthur follows Gawain's advice to pursue the war in Benwick against his own best judgement: "'I woll do as ye advyse me; and yet mesemyth,' seyde kynge Arthur, 'hys fayre proffers were nat so good to be reffused'" (701/40- 42). When Lancelot tells Arthur that "lyars ye have lystened, and that hath caused grete debate betwyxte you and me" (694/26-27), Malory is invoking the reputation of kings as fair and benevolent but often led astray by bad or evil council.

Gawain and his brothers are often shown misleading the king, deliberately or otherwise. The Malorian emphasis on Aggravayne's envy, as opposed to the apparently genuine concern felt by his Vulgate equivalent, makes Aggravayne far more culpable in the fall of Arthur; Malory overtly states that Aggravyne "caused" the "morte Arthur" at the end of *The Book of Sir Launcelot and Guinevere* (669/33-34), whereas the Vulgate's Agravain has to be threatened with physical violence by Arthur before disobeying Gawain's order to keep silent (109-10). It is Aggravayne's deliberate machinations that lead to the fall of Arthur; his advice and counsel prompt the entire situation. Constantly the reader is reminded that Aggravayne and Mordred are trouble-makers: Lancelot's last comment before leaving England in exile is a prediction that "Mordred woll make trouble, for he ys passyng envyous and applyeth hym muche to trouble" (699/11-13). Gawain himself declares that Aggravayne will agree "unto all unhappynes" (673/28-29). Gawain's own inability to effectively counsel Arthur allows the situation to run its course. After the death of Gareth, Gawain gives up counselling and begins forcing his opinions upon king and court:

> 'My kynge, my lorde, and myne uncle,' seyde sir Gawayne, 'wyte you well, now I shall make you a promyse whych I shall holde be my knyghthode, that from thys day forewarde I shall never fayle sir Launcelot untyll that one of us have slayne the othir. And therefore I requyre you, my lorde and kynge, dresse you unto the warres, for wyte you well, I woll be revenged uppon sir Launcelot; and therefore, as ye woll have my servyse and my love, now haste you thereto and assay youre frendis.' (686/44-687/7)

The formality of Gawain's "promyse" limits his king's political options with its combination of rhetoric and threat. The course of the following conflict is one of Arthur considering a truce and Gawain refusing to allow it; Arthur is firmly under the control of "evil counseyle." Good counsel can prevail over a reluctant lord, but a good lord cannot prevail over evil counsel.

The king who follows evil advice is a recurrent topos in medieval English literature, as Dan Embree has shown in connection with complaint poems such as

Richard the Redeless. Embree calls the topos "The King's Ignorance" and finds it wherever poets need to blame someone for the corruption and despair around them: since the king as God's representative must be innocent, he is rhetorically considered "a victim of his own court's machinations and deceptions" and blame is ascribed to a variety of officials, but "especially those popular and enduring targets of medieval satire, corrupt and frivolous courtiers" (123). Embree writes that the topos of the King's Ignorance is usually found in the poetry of the middle or upper middle class, people with "property or position to protect and therefore with interests vested in civil order, in incorruptible legal proceedings"; furthermore, they exhibit "a fear of unchecked or capricious royal power only a little less than its fear of the unchecked or capricious power of the mob" (125). Malory's famous passage lamenting "the greate defaughte of us Englysshemen," the tendency to continually reject the familiar in favor of the new, is evidence enough of his interest in the capricious power of the people. Guinevere's trial, and Arthur's role therein as both victim and judge, shows an interest in "incorruptible legal proceedings." Malory shows a keen interest in the ability of "unchecked" factional power to eclipse the royal will. These factions are not necessarily painted as "corrupt and frivolous" so much as they are simply divisive, too stubborn to see that their own best interests and those of the king are not always convergent.

None of this alleviates Lancelot or Guinevere, or the capricious and disloyal people, of their roles in the disaster. Yet despite the tenuous nature of Lancelot's assertion of his and Guinevere's innocence, Malory's text supports Lancelot's statement that Arthur's troubles rest first and foremost on the king's inadequate and envious counsel. Lancelot's assertion that Arthur has listened to "lyars" and that their counsel "hat caused grete debate betwyxte" the two men can itself be seen as counsel (694/26-27), an attempt to re-establish the factional and internal nature of the conflict before it turns into a war between kingdoms (Kelly 113). Lancelot asserts that the matter should be settled within the Round Table society without recourse to the scorched earth policy Arthur and Gawain eventually adopt in France (700/20-22). A similar passage occurs earlier when Lancelot notes that there is little point in seeking "accordemente" while Gawain is "so myschevously sett" (689/23-26); if it were not for Gawain's constant insistence on war and vengeance, Lancelot claims that he would have Arthur's "good grace." During the battle at Joyous Garde, Lancelot's claim finds support when he saves Arthur from Bors and has an opportunity to speak to the king privately; the scene ends with Arthur lamenting that the war ever began and "thynkyng of the grete curtesy that was in sir Launcelot more than in ony other man" (691/21-30). With no mediators providing the king with evil council standing between them, Lancelot and Arthur would be quickly accorded. Unfortunately, "counceyle" in Arthur's court, and between the knights of the Round Table, has been completely replaced by "langayge"; mere noise, as Mark Lambert has argued (176-94). In Malory's usage, “langayge” is a largely negative term implying hostility, disagreement and empty rhetoric.

Of the five uses of “langayge” in the *Morte* proper, none is found in an unambiguously neutral context. Three occur in direct speech, all directed at Lancelot’s efforts to justify himself: once by Arthur (688/7) and twice by Gawain (696/28-29; 697/32). In Gawain’s mouth, it becomes the medieval equivalent of telling Lancelot to shut up and go away: “‘Make thou no more langayge,’ seyde sir Gawayne, ‘but delyvir the quene from the, and pyke the lyghtly oute of thys courte!’” The fourth instance of the word occurs when Lancelot’s men are encouraging him to raise the siege of Benwick, and Lancelot tells them to wait until all other options are gone; “Than they hylde their langayge...” (702/23). The last use is also narratorial, and refers to Gawain’s many taunts, crafted to lure Lancelot out from behind the walls and into combat (705/28). In all instances but one, “langayge” is meant pejoratively or refers to language meant for purposes beyond strictly honest communication. Beside “langayge,” Gawain also offers “babelynge” as a description of Lancelot’s efforts at maintaining or re-establishing peaceful relations (703/32-33). “Langayge” and “babelynge” can be seen as the opposite of “counseyle,” the words shared by enemies rather than allies; “langayge” refers to lies, taunts, and advice which might be considered inappropriate or untimely. It also has some suggestion of repetitiveness: both Gawain’s taunts and Lancelot’s excuses are overtly shown to be oft-repeated.

Lancelot’s speeches before Arthur’s court have been examined for a variety of themes and motifs: their unusual loquaciousness, their ineffectiveness in healing the rifts between the factions, the extent to which they are either true or false, their relationship to the shame/guilt dichotomy first adapted from anthropology by Derek Brewer (23-35). Mark Lambert’s principle contention, building on Brewer’s idea, is that Lancelot is not a lying hypocrite engaged in desperate self-justification; rather, he is a knight for whom public shame is more important than private guilt (Lambert 176-94). As Kelly has argued, the shame/guilt dichotomy adequately explains Lancelot’s behavior to a certain point, but once Lancelot attempts to rectify the situation by building chantries for the souls of his victims, the “shame” ethic no longer applies (126-27). The shame/guilt hypothesis is an interesting one, and certainly valid in its own way, but it has drawn critical attention away from the actual function and purpose of Lancelot’s speeches. There are undeniably other elements at work, but they are neither the primary reasons nor the most obvious: Lancelot’s speeches are politically motivated and given in a political context. The speeches have three main themes: his “grete proffers” to do religious penance for the death of Gareth and Gaheris, lament and praise for the realm that made him great and which he in turn strengthened, and blatant self-justification accompanied by attempts to deflect criticism and balance his recent deeds against the less contentious exploits of his youth.

The "grete proffers" are offered for the repose of the brothers' souls and to alleviate Lancelot's guilty conscience, which does seem to trouble him (Kelly 116); but always at the edges of his offer to walk barefoot from Sandwich founding religious houses every ten miles is the "everlastyng warre" which seems inevitable between himself and Gawain (and their respective realms), and which he suspects is the only possible outcome of the death of Gareth (696/5-7). Lancelot finishes urging Gawain to accept his offers by saying that the penance "were fayrar and more holyar and more perfyte to their soulis than ye, my moste noble kynge, and you, sir Gawayne, to warre uppon me, for thereby ye gete none avayle" (696/23-25). Lancelot cannot seem to help but boast even while promising religious humility, yet the statement does show that he wishes to avoid a costly war, even one which he is positive he can win.

Continually Lancelot tries to deflect the debate from the deaths of Gareth and Gaheris, and the guilt of the lovers, to previous services he has performed for Arthur and Gawain: his many rescues of Guinevere which necessitate and justify the latest and bloodiest (694/27-33), times in which he rescued Gawain and other Round Table knights or the realm itself (695/3-35), incidents in which "the hole Rounde Table hath bene encreced more in worshyp" by his efforts (697/16-19). Lancelot's references to his past deeds are not mere boasting, nor are they offered simply to make Gawain feel guilty for ever doubting him. His references to the "dyverce placis" and "dyvers tymes" in which he has rendered "bettir servyse than ony othir knyghtes have done" to Arthur serve to remind the king that, very often, Arthur's realm has only survived "many daungers" by Lancelot's might (695/3-11). One thinks of Lancelot's emergence during the Roman War, in which the close political ties between Ban's kin and Arthur were affirmed following the conquest of Claudas' lands. Furthermore, when he recalls the rescue of Gawain from Carados, Lancelot praises the deceased villain as "a full noble knyght and a passynge stronge man," exactly the sort of knight he professes to love (695/17-25). Nevertheless, Lancelot killed this noble knight in order to rescue Gawain, an act which must be seen politically as a choice Lancelot made: Carados "myght well be called a noble knyght whan he be fyne fors pulled you oute of youre sadyll and bounde you overthwarte afore hym to hys sadyll-bow. And there, my lorde sir Gawayne, I rescowed you and slew hym afore youre syght" (695/23-25). It is a firm reminder that there were other knights, strong and capable, throughout Arthur's realm, and that Lancelot removed them as political and social threats. Furthermore, he chose one set of knights (in this case, Gawain and his brother, Gaheris, to whom the speech also refers) over another potential set of "full noble" allies and companions (Carados and his brother, Tarquin). Lancelot subtly asks the king to imagine what would have happened had he and his kin joined the fellowship of Carados and Tarquin.

Finally, Lancelot's eloquent speech praising Arthur's kingdom, spoken exclusively to Bors in the OF *Mort Artu*, becomes a rhetorical *tour de force* before Arthur's entire court:

> 'Moste nobelyst Crysten realme, whom I have loved aboven all othir realmys! And in the I have gotyn a grete parte of my worshyp, and now that I shall departe in thys wyse, truly me repentis that ever I cam in thys realme, that I shulde be thus shamefully banysshyd, undeserved and causeles! But fortune ys so varyaunte, and the wheele so mutable, that there ys no constaunte abydynge. And that may be preved by many olde cronycles, as of noble Ector of Troy and Alysaunder, the myghty conquerroure, and many mo other: whan they were moste in her royalté, they alyght passynge lowe.' (697/8-16)

Malory alters the speech significantly, and not just in making it a public rather than a private lament. Lancelot makes an allusion to Fortune's Wheel, an image associated with Arthur's fall in Malory, the *Alliterative Morte Arthure* and the *Mort Artu*. By associating the inscrutable image of Fortune's Wheel with Lancelot as well as Arthur, Malory draws a strong parallel between the two men; the attentions of Fortune make them seem equal. Only great leaders of men rise and fall on Fortune's Wheel. The references to Hector of Troy and Alexander the Great, both traditionally counted with Arthur among the Nine Worthies, further serve to equate Lancelot with royalty and greatness, with political power. Alexander and Hector are the first of the "kinges" Arthur sees in his dream in Malory's source (*AMA* 3408-09); since Malory suppresses the explication of Arthur's dream in his version of the scene (711/19-33), Lancelot's association with both Fortune's Wheel and the Nine Worthies is more complete than Arthur's in that it has greater textual representation. Lancelot's praise for Arthur's realm is predicated on his having won most of his "worshyp" within it, and he makes it clear that this "worshyp" was reciprocal, with his deeds reflecting well upon the realm which they directly benefitted.

Once Lancelot has left Arthur's court for the final time, he holds another council at Joyous Garde and receives the solemn allegiance of "an hondred knyghtes" of the Round Table (699/16). Their stated reason for abandoning Arthur and following Lancelot is illuminating:

> Than spake all the knyghtes at onys: 'Have he shame that woll leve you! For we all undirstonde, in thys realme [woll be no] quyett, but ever debate and stryff, now the felyshyp of the Rounde Table ys brokyn. For by the noble felyship of the Rounde Table was kynge Arthur upborne, and by their nobeles the kynge and all the realme was ever in quyet and reste. And a grete part,' they sayde all, 'was because of youre moste nobeles, sir Lancelot.' (698/44-699/6)

The Round Table, with its martial prowess and its wise "counseyle," was largely responsible for the peace and quiet of Arthur's realm; once the Round Table is divided internally, Arthur cannot long survive. The faction united in the service of Lancelot removes itself from the site of continual "debate and stryff." Lancelot, the knight most responsible for Arthur's political longevity, becomes Arthur's only reasonable replacement and successor, even if he must inherit that longevity and peace elsewhere. The knights make “their avowis they wolde never leve hym for weale ne for woo” (699/17-18), a new and abbreviated version of the Pentecostal Oath taken by Round Table knights which avoids the semantic problems discussed by Wheeler in favor of strict and simple oaths of personal loyalty.[5] Shortly afterwards, Lancelot calls the “parlemente” at which he divides political power in his long neglected realm between his immediate kin and those Round Table knights who have chosen to follow him into exile. By showing a well-ordered series of lands organized under a strong central leadership and based on a loyal coterie of knights, and balancing this image against that of Arthur’s realm, wracked with strife and about to suffer usurpation and civil war, Malory depicts a transfer of political legitimacy from Arthur’s England to Lancelot’s France, in much the same way that Arthur’s England was traditionally seen (by the English at least) as the legitimate political heir to Rome.[6] The spirit of “counseyle” still exists at Lancelot’s court while England descends into chaos; when Mordred violently and ineffectually threatens the Archbishop of Canterbury, it is a low point in English political debate and a sign that tyranny rather than adherence to “counseyle” is firmly in the ascendent (708/10-11).

It is time for a few tentative conclusions. “Counseyle” is given no inherent political valuation in and of itself; unanimity in council is the highest political good. No council in which characters disagree before arriving at a final decision ever turns out well. In contrast to the later debates that wrack Arthur’s court, the parliament he holds before the Roman War is unanimous in its conclusions, with every participant agreeing with the first speaker’s desire to go to war (114/9-115/26). Kelly has noted, referring to the failure of Lancelot’s attempts to restore peace by returning the Queen, that “Malory strongly endorses” Lydgate’s comment upon the Greeks arguing before Troy: “Lo what meschef lyeth in variaunce / Amonge lordis, whan þei nat accorde” (Lydgate, *Troy Book* 3:2342-43, Kelly 123-24). All unanimity is not created equal: the unanimous support created by Mordred’s threats and bribes does not achieve the same degree of validity as that achieved by Lancelot or Arthur. The latter rulers show a willingness to follow council which should not be considered less noble simply because their counsellors always tell them what they want to hear. Counsel and diplomacy can both be undermined by “langayge” (excessive rhetorical speech-making or taunting), which can obscure issues and lead to further division. Malory may be sending a signal to be alert whenever his taciturn knights suddenly start making long speeches of self-justification. It might not be unfair to describe the *Morte* as anti-debate literature, the opposite of the many medieval texts in which dispute leads to wisdom and resolution. Gawain’s response to Lancelot’s late attempts to avoid battle is telling: “... leve thy babelynge and com off, and lat us ease oure hartis” (703/32-33). A great deal of bloodshed could have been avoided if Lancelot had simply faced Gawain in single combat when first challenged. Grieving hearts cannot be eased by talk, at least not in a chivalric world, and problems are best solved by action decided upon quickly and with a minimum of "babelynge."

Felicity Riddy has considered the Roman War as an imperialist narrative, a memory of Henry V's Norman conquests, which were being eroded by royal indecision within Malory's own life; she notes that "the loss of the French territories in 1453 had been a personal disaster" for Malory's contemporaries (68-71). Riddy does not mention that the Malory now commonly accepted as the author was apparently an MP in 1445, the long Parliamentary session in which the Commons refused to produce any new funds despite the breakdown of negotiations with the French (Field, *Life* 88-89,Butt 530-31). Malory could have been deeply influenced by witnessing a Parliament, indeed an entire kingdom, paralyzed by factional strife and divided councils. The fickleness of parliament, controlled throughout the period first by one faction and then another, also seems to have influenced Malory enough that he directly addresses the "grete defaughte of us Englysshemen" (708/34-41). It is not unlikely that a knight-prisoner, reflecting back upon his experiences in politics, might come to believe that parliament had unnecessarily hampered royal decision-making, that excessive debate in parliament was no match for the decision-making abilities of a royal council or a king. I would suggest that this is not proof that Malory was either a Yorkist or a Lancastrian sympathizer, but simply an old knight dying in prison and lamenting the loss of English empire and stability, and perhaps his own small role in the strife of the times.

University of Bristol

Notes

1. This type of council is the kind most commonly found in Middle English romance prior to Malory (excepting only the Alliterative Morte Arthure), as discussed by Geraldine Barnes, *Counsel and Strategy in Middle English Romance*. Of the examples she cites, few involve councils as a whole advising a king or ruler; most involve an individual or series of individuals who advise the romance's hero on his quest.

2. When not quoting directly from the text, I use "counceyle" because it is the most frequent variant.

3. The argument that Caxton significantly revised the Roman War episode was generally accepted until a posthumous paper by William Matthews was delivered at a meeting of the International Arthurian Society in Exeter in 1975; Matthews' theory that Malory was the author of his own revisions "circulated by word of mouth for over two decades as a sort of specter" strongly influencing many scholars (Kuskin 540). Support for Matthews' theory can be notably found in Lumiansky, "Sir Thomas Malory's Le Morte Darthur," *Speculum* 62 (1987): 878- 97; and Moorman, "Caxton's Morte Darthur," *Fifteenth-Century Studies* 12 (1986): 99-113. Recent authors have returned to the older view, including Withrington and Kuskin.

4. That the people blame Arthur's leadership for the war and factionalism is made explicit as the civil war between Mordred and Arthur is about to commence: "And muche

people drewe unto [Mordred]; for than was the comyn voyce amonge them that with kynge Arthur was never othir lyff but warre and stryff, and with sir Mordrede was grete joy and blysse." (708/27-30) Pochoda cites this passage as proof that the Round Table, having been "defined by its imposition of order in an unstable realm" is now held responsible for the instability that accompanies its internal divisions (Pochoda 133).

5. John Plummer and Bonnie Wheeler have both noted an essential breakdown in communication and language in Malory, Plummer from the beginning of the Grail Quest and Wheeler as early as the first meeting of the Round Table. Plummer points to the setting of the Grail Quest at Pentecost, and finds a parodic inversion of the ideals of "speech and fellowship" which Pentecost, in apostolic terms, represents; Camelot becomes a new Tower of Babel, a unity dissolving into mutual incomprehension (Plummer 154-56). He ignores an important detail marked by Wheeler, that Pentecost is the time of many events in the history of Arthur's court, not the least of which was the original Pentecostal Oath, "the most notable attempt by the Round Table community to codify behavior" (Wheeler 117). Wheeler rightly states that the Pentecost Oath is, from the very start, inadequate to its stated function. There is no hierarchy among its basic tenets which would allow a Round Table knight to make crucial decisions in the field; the Pentecostal Oath "reveals the gap between even the best-intentioned language and the reality it is meant to order" (Wheeler 118). Wheeler has a strong point; clearly the social strategies of Arthur and Merlin fall very short of their stated goals. Plummer, however, is dangerously literal; his interpretation of Gawain's reference to Lancelot's speeches as "babblynge" is to assume that to the vengeful knight, "Lancelot's language is so much unintelligible babble" (Plummer 164). Yet the problems that have arisen in Arthur's court are not the result solely of mere "noise," as Lambert and Plummer would have it; what Plummer calls "broken, lying, unheard, or unheeded language" is, in most cases, fully understood by all concerned. Gawain doesn't misunderstand Lancelot. He rejects Lancelot's "langayge and ... grete proffirs" (696/28-29). The entire court weeps at the generosity and humility of Lancelot's attempts at reconciliation (696/26-27), and Arthur himself on a later occasion remarks that Lancelot's "proffers were nat good to be reffused" (701/41-42). Other examples abound. Gawain does not misunderstand Aggravayne's intentions; he knows full well what his brother intends to do, but he disagrees with Aggravayne's methods. The same holds true for Gawain's disagreement with the king over Guinevere's sentence when the king ignores Gawain's pleas for a delay. Their conversation on the subject is a perfectly rational give and take, unencumbered by any hint of linguistic incomprehension. Arthur simply finds Mordred's interpretation of events more compelling. The reader may agree or disagree, but there is little support for any interpretation that effaces the ability of these characters to understand one another. One of the great glories of Malory's Morte Darthur is the dialogue. To subordinate Malory's text to an outside schemata based on biblical exegesis of the Pentecost and Babel stories is to do both the political nature and dramatic principle of the Morte Darthur a great disservice.

6. Lancelot's later career as a hermit, and the abandonment of their positions by his affinity, should not be taken to indicate the collapse of central authority in France. Bors and the others are said to have "stablysshed theyr londes, for, the book saith, so syr Launcelot commaunded them" before he died; their lands are clearly ordered and stable before they ride to the Holy Land (726/5-9). Constantine's inability to bring Lancelot's kin into his new court indicates a deep and lasting division between the affairs of England and France; although Constantine is said to rule "worshypfully" his realm is clearly not the equal of either Arthur's or Lancelot's (725/32-43).

Works Cited

Barnes, Geraldine. *Counsel and Strategy in Middle English Romance*. Cambridge: D. S. Brewer, 1993.

Benson, Larry D., ed. *King Arthur's Death: The Middle English Stanzaic Morte Arthur and Alliterative Morte Arthure*. Rev. Edward E. Foster. Kalamazoo: TEAMS, 1994.

Butt, Ronald. *A History of Parliament: The Middle Ages*. London: Constable, 1989.

Embree, Dan. "'The King's Ignorance': A Topos for Evil Times." *Medium Ævum* 54 (1984): 121-26.

Field, P. J. C., ed. *Le Morte Darthur: The Seventh and Eighth Tales by Thomas Malory*. London: Hodder and Stoughton, 1978.

—. The Life and Times of Sir Thomas Malory. *Arthurian Studies* 29. Cambridge: D. S. Brewer, 1993.

Griffiths, R. A. *King and Country: England and Wales in the Fifteenth Century*. London: Hambeldon, 1991.

Hanks, D. Thomas, Jr. "Foil and Forecast: Dinadan in The Book of Tristram." *Arthurian Yearbook* 1. Ed. Keith Busby. New York: Garland, 1991: 149-63.

Kelly, Robert L. "Penitence as a Remedy for War in Malory's 'Tale of the Death of Arthur.'" *Studies in Philology* 91 (1994): 111-35.

Kennedy, Edward Donald. "Malory's King Arthur and King Mark."*Mediaeval Studies* 37 (1975): 190-234.

Knight, Stephen. *Arthurian Literature and Society*. London: MacMillan, 1983.

Kuskin, William. "Caxton's Worthies Series: The Production of Literary Culture." *English Literary History* 66.3 (1999): 511-51.

Lambert, Mark. *Malory: Style and Vision in Le Morte Darthur*. Yale Studies in English 186. New Haven: Yale UP, 1975.

Lancelot-Grail: The Old French Arthurian Vulgate and Post-Vulgate in Translation. Norris Lacy, general ed. 5 vols. New York: Garland, 1993-6.

Lander, J. R. *Crown and Nobility 1450-1509*. Montreal: McGill-Queen's UP, 1976.

Lumiansky, R. M. "Malory's Steadfast Bors." *Tulane Studies in English* 8 (1958): 5-20.

Malory, Thomas. *Works*. Ed. Eugène Vinaver. 2nd ed. Oxford: Oxford UP, 1971.

—. *Le Morte D'Arthur*. Ed. Janet Lawlor. 2 vols. Harmondsworth: Penguin, 1969.

McCarthy, Terence. "Caxton and the Text of Malory's Book 2." *Modern Philology* 71 (1973): 144-52

—. "Reading the Morte Darthur." *Arthurian Studies* 20. Cambridge: D. S.Brewer, 1988

Plummer, John F. "Tunc se Coeperunt non Intelligere: The Image of Language in Malory's Last Books." *Studies in Malory*. Ed. James W. Spisak. Kalamazoo: Medieval Institute, 1985. 153-71.

Pochoda, Elizabeth. *Arthurian Propaganda: Le Morte Darthur as an Historical Ideal of Life*. Chapel Hill: U of North Carolina P, 1971.

Radulescu, Raluca. "John Vale's Book and Sir Thomas Malory's *Le Morte Darthur*: A Political Agenda." *Arthuriana* 9.4 (1999): 69-80.

Rawcliffe, Carole. "Baronial Councils in the Later Middle Ages." *Patronage, Pedigree and Power in Later Medieval England*. Ed. Charles Ross. Gloucester: Alan Sutton, 1979. 87-108.

Riddy, Felicity. "Contextualizing *Le Morte Darthur*: Empire and Civil War." *A Companion to Malory*. Eds. Elizabeth Archibald and A. S. G. Edwards. *Arthurian Studies* 37. Cambridge: D.S. Brewer, 1996. 55-74.

Wheeler, Bonnie. "Romance and Parataxis and Malory: The Case of Sir Gawain's Reputation." *Arthurian Studies* 12 (1993): 109-32.

Withrington, John. "Caxton, Malory, and the Roman War in the *Morte Darthur*." *Studies in Philology* 89 (1992): 350-66.

"Pinning Him to the Wall": The Poetics of Self-Destruction in the Court of Juan II*

Gregory S. Hutcheson

The *Cancionero* compiled by Juan Alfonso de Baena, poet-cum-scribe in the court of Juan II of Castile (1406-1454), contains the lyrical output of some sixty authors composing over the course of nearly three quarters of a century. The earliest works–those of the legendary Macías, the Archdeacon of Toro, or a young Villasandino–date from the mid-fourteenth century; many of these are still composed in Galician-Portuguese, the lyric language *par excellence* that was only just beginning to lose its grip on Castile's own lyric tradition. At the other extreme is a piece attributed to Juan de Mena, a commemorative work whose historical content ties it conclusively to the year 1449. But the focus of Baena's efforts seems to be more rigorously defined: of the nearly six hundred works he anthologizes, the bulk was penned by members of a rather exclusive poetic community that thrived at the turn of the fifteenth century, producing some of the most intriguing (and least studied) works in the Spanish literary canon.

Emerging as something of an elder statesman of the group is Alfonso Alvarez de Villasandino, whose verse comprises a good third of Baena's corpus. Villasandino was a professional poet in every sense of the term: he hired his talent out to cities and members of the aristocracy; composed commemorative pieces in some official capacity for the royal house of Castile; and in his later, more destitute years, devoted himself almost exclusively to the petitionary lyric for which modern scholarship has deemed him a consummate moocher.[1] But he kept company with the kings of Castile (he survived at least three of them), his wit was legendary and his versification impeccable, for which reason Baena is quick to crown him "king of the poets."[2] Equally renowned is Micer Francisco Imperial, scion of a Genoese merchant family; although represented by only eighteen works, Imperial is second only to Villasandino in sheer verbiage. Baena himself is third (with a total of eighty-one works), followed by the theologian Fray Diego de Valencia (with forty-three) and the petty aristocrat Fernán Manuel de Lando (with thirty-four).

It is the collective work of these five authors, totaling almost four hundred individual pieces, that constitutes the core of Baena's poetic universe. Together they represent the myriad of styles and voices available to late-medieval Spain, from the *metáforas obscuras* of intricate allegorical visions to the lilt of courtly love songs; from the deliberate pedantry of theological and philosophical debate to the savagery of poetic invective. Villasandino and Fray Diego de Valencia in particular distinguish themselves for their expertise in invective, a genre cultivated avidly since the heyday of the Galician-Portuguese troubadours.[3] In one piece, Villasandino vilifies a lady of the court–this at the instance of a jilted knight, the rubric tells us–in terms so obscene that not a few modern editors of the CB refused to print them.[4] Elsewhere rote misogyny gives way to xenophobia or anti-Semitism–for example, Fray Diego's assault on the land of León (CB 502), or Villasandino's barbs against García Fernández de Gerena who, through his conversion to Islam and relocation to Granada, earned for himself all the "blessings" afforded by life in Islamic lands, including "more whiskers than you had before, more husbands as well, and fellowship with Satan himself"[5]–all of this, scholars seem to agree, in the spirit of courtly entertainment.

Among the more curious of those works Baena anthologizes are the *recuestas*, poetic slugging matches in which rival poets take aim against each other in a vigorous exchange of response and counterresponse. We learn from both text and rubrics that these contests were generally planned in advance, that a third party served to judge the outcome, and that lofty personages (among whom the king himself) often made up the audience.[6] Once the stage was set, one poet stepped forth to challenge another (*travar recuesta*) by means of a short provocative piece of anywhere from one to five stanzas. These opening pieces often drew on the stock material of late-medieval debate poetry, posing questions on theology, poetic art, or the precepts of love (for example, whether will holds sway over reason [CB 399], or whether it is better to see one's ladylove and not speak to her or speak to her and not see her [CB 369].) They were just as often far more irreverent zingers, single stanzas intended to goad the rival poet ("picarle en lo vivo") by casting aspersions on his poetic talent, his physical appearance, even his sexual prowess. Whatever the case, the matter for debate quickly took back seat to alternating displays of wit whose only rule seemed to be adherence to the rhyme scheme and meter of the original piece. Since repetition of a word in rhyme position was strictly forbidden, poets soon found themselves straining both their imaginations and the lexicon to produce at least the semblance of a coherent response. Once the poetic system broke down completely, it fell to the judge to declare a winner.[7]

Baena provides documentation for dozens of *recuestas* staged by the most accomplished poets of his age,[8] although he styles himself as the undisputed champion of the sport; indeed, his name alone is identified explicitly with the *recuesta* in both the general prologue to the CB and the rubric introducing his own poetic works.[9] So too does Villasandino gain the advantage by virtue of his superior talents as versifier, a fact he is quick to throw in the face of his floundering rivals. His bout with Alfonso Sánchez de Jaén ends with the following coup-de-grâce: "your own clumsy efforts make you suitable for pigherding or tending sheep, or selling sweetbreads door-to-door; think no more about refined poetic art" (CB 126: 5-8). When Baena says of this particular piece that "it is well crafted and responds cleverly using the same consonants" (that is, following the rhyme of the original piece), he leaves little doubt that both participants and audience remain indelibly aware of poetic art no matter how low the blow or nonsensical the response.[10] Baena is invariably quick in his rubrics to point out poetic transgressions, whether faulty versification, failure to respect the rhyme, or failure to stay within the prescribed number of stanzas. And like Villasandino, he relishes every opportunity to turn his own wit to the denigration of another's poetic art, as in one delicious attack against Juan García: "you wouldn't merit for your efforts a thousand farts from a dark-brown she-ass" (CB 385: 18-20).

But poetry is only partially the point. In their efforts to earn the laurel, contestants engage in mutual defamation of the most personal (and oftentimes graphic) nature. For example, in one bout (CB 359-CB 363) Baena accuses rival poet Lando not only of cowardice but of incontinence: "Fernán Manuel, he who shits in the saddle out of fear shouldn't be so haughty; if they checked under your tailbone, they'd find such a stink as would give you away" (CB 361: 9- 12).[11] To which Lando responds with accusations of cuckoldry (and reference to one of the bawdier episodes of Juan Ruiz's *Libro de buen amor*): "Señor Juan Alfonso, [you are a] painter of friezes just as Pitas Payas was in the tale; while you go strutting through the town, others are busy screwing your wife" (CB 362: 9-12).[12] Elsewhere Lando is sodomized by a "snub-nosed shepherd" (CB 363: 1-4), Baena pelted with eggplants (CB 418: 3-4), and Villasandino made the target of a volley of cheap shots at the expense of his advanced years and physical decrepitude. (Says Baena in his preamble to one bout carried out in the presence of the king: "My lord, that putrid old sack of phlegm has just now arrived; I've readied for him his medicine, a brew of bile and vinegar, venom and spite..." [CB 364:1-4].) Invective, it would seem, is as essential to the *recuesta* as is poetic art, or so Baena gives us to understand in the *full* text of the rubric to CB 126 (cited only in part above): "[Villasandino's response] is well crafted and responds cleverly using the same consonants, while skewering Alfonso Sánchez in the liver and pinning him to the wall" ("picando en el fígado al dicho [Alfonso] Sanchez e pegándolo a la pared").[13]

The no-holds-barred nature of the *recuesta* has led most scholars to view it as poetic debate run amok, and indeed, few go beyond giving it a grudging footnote in their discussions of the far more conventional *preguntas y respuestas* ("questions and answers") genre of the same period. This genre, argues John G. Cummins, derives indirectly (via the Galician-Portuguese and Catalan schools) from Occitan poetic sport such as the *joc-partit* and the *tenso*. In the *joc-partit*, two contestants debate a matter of love, appealing to a third party for a decision. In the *tenso*, discussion is freer, falling at times into "bantering abuse" (9). Both types of debate are carried out in alternating stanzas and require rhyme imitation in the response, although they allow for a change of rhyme scheme after each volley. Castilian poets make a minor break with Occitan models in that they exchange complete poems rather than single stanzas; otherwise, argues Cummins, their *preguntas y respuestas* imitate slavishly the rules and themes established by the troubadours of previous centuries (13-14). What Cummins fails to recognize, however, is the degree to which Baena and his contemporaries practice the *recuesta* as a separate activity, one whose mark of distinction is the maintaining of a single rhyme scheme throughout the debate. Neither does he recognize that the "bantering abuse" only occasionally in evidence in the *tenso* is of the essence in the *recuesta*, where high points are scored for "striking where it hurts" ("picando en lo vivo").[14]

What is more, a quick survey reveals that "slanging-matches" such as the *recuesta* are far from exceptional, and indeed, are something of a universal within the realm of oral culture. In *Homo Ludens: A Study of the Play Element in Culture*, J. Huizinga documents similar phenomena in ancient Greece and pre-Islamic Arabia (66-68). Ilse Lichtenstadter describes in detail those contests among the Arabs in which a poet was called upon during battle to exchange taunts with the poets of rival tribes. These contests were formalized under the Umayyad caliphate into a genre known as the *naqa'id*, whereby poets would recall ancient rivalries in an exchange of vehement verse (20).[15] So too do Old Germanic and Old Norse sagas make reference to ceremonies of mutual bragging and derision, the *gelpen* of Middle High German. The French *gab*, notes Huizinga, was a similar event that served as a prelude to combat or as part of a banquet (68-71). To these examples we might add several of more recent vintage: the *payadas*, bragging matches characteristic of the gaucho culture of nineteenth-century Argentina; poetic contests between *bertsolari*, improvisational poets in the Basque tradition; and, closer to home, the games of verbal assault (such as "the dirty dozens") still prevalent in inner-city culture.[16] In virtually all these cases, insult is bound up in what can only be termed a poetics: the emphasis is on originality of expression within a predetermined framework (such as a particular cadence or the formula "You momma"), and indeed, the majority of bouts are carried out in verse or song.

Implied as well is the power of the word as purveyor of injury, or, by extension, the power of the poet in his role as guarantor of national identity. This was indeed true in what Huizinga deems "archaic" and Morton W. Bloomfield and Charles W. Dunn deem "primitive" societies. Here the poet

> can sing popular songs and tales for the common man as he works or relaxes. He can encourage the warriors by singing their praises, or the praises of their ancestors, and by hurling curses and satires at the enemy. For the priests, he can sing charms and incantations, help them in their rites, or aid them if they perform ecstatic dances or visions. He can encourage the king, sing his praises, act as a conduit of criticism (usually muted but clear) from his subjects; he can recite the names of the tribal ancestors, remember the praise-names of neighboring chieftains; he can entertain the people with riddles and stories, console them with proverbs and gnomes, protect them with words, move them with history, and provide them with practical knowledge. (20)

In sum, the poet is a repository of the collective consciousness whose words can cut as readily as the sword in defense of the nation. The assaultive power of the word is not lost among Arab poets of the classical period: Lichtenstadter refers to the story of the father who orders his son to lie down lest the "arrows" of the hostile poet's verse hit and hurt him.[17] Nor is it lost in Occitan lyric, where poetic invective (such as the *sirventes*) is forever likened to armed battle. In fourteenth-century Iberia, a figure such as the Rabbi Sem Tob is almost surely drawing on sources from both the East and the West when he warns Pedro I of Castile to beware the word (albeit the written word in this case): "There is no lance that passes through armor so readily as the word; the arrow flies only so far, but the letter reaches from Burgos to Egypt" (vv. 1809-16).

Baena's likening of his own tongue to an instrument of destruction (whether spear, crossbow, or razor) would suggest that Castilian poets of the fifteenth century believed themselves to be equally endowed. And yet separating Baena from his poetic forebears are the cataclysmic events of the mid-fourteenth century, beginning with Enrique of Trastámara's usurping of the throne from his half-brother Pedro in 1369. Enrique's supporters–in the main old Christians who resented the heavy hand of Jews in Castilian politics–embarked on what amounts to a cultural revolution, the recentering of Castilian society on the conservative values of the Christian aristocracy. Foremost on the agenda of these early Trastamarans was the need to iron out the wrinkles of their own cultural identity. In a simultaneous act of denial and self-creation, they strove to differentiate themselves from the Arab and Jewish peoples with whom their forebears had lived in intimate contact for well over six centuries. They stocked their consciousness with a bank of archaic symbols and values imported from greater Europe; armed with the mythologies of knighthood and nobility, they attempted to rewrite history and themselves in the process.[18]

The autonomous power of the word could not help but languish within this environment of cultural imperialism and self-definition. Literature as a whole, once brilliant for its defiance of conventional forms, was whitewashed in the image of France and its energy funneled into the exclusive pursuit of feeding the Trastamaran ego. Chronicle, narrative, epic, didactic treatises–virtually every literary form known to the Spain of Juan Ruiz imploded in a violent reaction to difference, only to be resurrected in the desperately conservative body of literature that would most characterize the court of Juan II. Lyric poetry was far from the exception; it too found itself literally locked into the conceptual framework imposed by the demands of a reactionary aristocracy. The poet of Baena's *Cancionero* is scarcely the *vates*–"the possessed, the God-smitten" (as per Huizinga). He is, rather, incidental to the workings of destiny, reduced to command performances and the endless repetition of slogans of nobility, orthodoxy, and power, this despite the claims of Baena's prologue–more formulaic than dogmatic–that the poet's art is "infused with the grace of God" (7).[19]

Not surprisingly, the ranks of the poets in Trastamaran Spain were readily filled by those who found themselves most estranged from the hegemonic order, whether disenfranchised members of the petty nobility, hangers-on at court, or the so-called Conversos–Jews who had converted to Christianity in the wake of the violent anti-Semitic uprisings of 1391.[20] One such poet was Baena himself, who makes little secret of his Jewish extraction and even labels himself "judino" in the prologue to his *Cancionero*.[21] Charles Fraker identifies half a dozen others of the Baena poets as Conversos, including Lando, reading in the works of each a residual Jewish mind-set characteristic of the recent convert.[22] Francisco Márquez Villanueva goes so far as to claim that Villasandino was the sole exception to the rule among court entertainers of his age: "he was not, like virtually every practitioner of the trade, a publicly-known Jew or *converso*" (388). Even so, he competed with the best of them not only in *recuestas*, but in the institutionalized begging that constitutes a full third of the CB corpus–petitionary lyric in which the poet composes from an authentic position of desire, powerlessness, and rejection.[23]

Such figures, already marginalized by their own design, were ripe candidates for participation in the *recuesta*, bearers of ready-made tags that could be converted instantly into the butt of an opponent's joke. We have already seen how Baena capitalizes on Villasandino's old age in his verbal assaults against the poet; so too does Villasandino draw on Baena's self-styled boorishness when he calls him an ass reeking of garlic and cheap wine (CB 365: 1-2). Delving further into the arsenal of the CB poets, we encounter a plethora of terms of abuse drawn from the deep-seated anxieties of fifteenth-century Castilian society, explicit references to a Jewish culture and identity that for many was still a little too close to home.[24] Fray Diego de Valencia alleges that his patron Simuel Dios-ayuda's generosity runs "against Jewish nature" (CB 511: 5- 8)–a backhanded compliment that taps into the stereotype of the rapacious Jew.[25] Pedro Ferruz, probably a Converso himself, complains drolly that the intoning of ritual prayers by the rabbis of neighboring synagogues is disturbing his sleep (CB 302). Far less indulgent is the parodic last will and testament composed by Villasandino for the backsliding Converso Alfonso Fernández Samuel–buried, claims the poet, with a crucifix at his feet, the Koran resting on his chest, and the Torah as a pillow (CB 142). Elsewhere Villasandino tags him with the parodic surname *Salta atrás* 'Leap Back' and invokes the size of his nose as proof positive of his apostasy (CB 140: 15- 16).[26] He deploys equally derisive terms against another Converso, whom he names pejoratively "Davihuelo" (little David). Here apostasy is aligned with sexual inadequacy when the poet alleges that Davihuelo's wife is an avid adulteress who "[receives] on her 'shield' frequent thrusts by low and vulgar people" (CB 183: 22-24).[27]

Baena represents something of a curiosity within this rising tide of anti-Semitism. While he certainly engages freely in attacks against fellow Conversos,[28] at the same time he not only invites but conspires in the construction of his own body as Jewish. He makes bald reference to his own *gorda nariz* 'imposing nose' (CB 444: 5-6), to which Juan García appends *ojos de berengena* 'eggplant eyes' (CB 384: 4-5) and Juan de Guzmán a taste for *adefina* (CB 404: 9-10), the rustic stew that had become by the fifteenth century a virtual marker of

Jewish identity.[29] Elsewhere he is accused of that rote opportunism central to the stereotype of the Jewish/Converso bureaucrat: "Although you've always made much of your prowess in battle," Lando chides him, "[your sword is] blackened with the ink used to add up this year's revenues" (CB 374: 5-8). Even more pointed are the charges of sexual dysfunction, drawn undoubtedly from the growing conviction that Jews lay at the root of Castile's social and moral disorder. Not only is Baena cuckolded by his wife (this in Lando, as we have seen), but he is implicated in a series of sodomitic encounters, including one with a Jew who fills Baena's *rabo* 'tail' with his potent *regadío* (CB 418: 6-9)[30] All told, Baena's body emerges from the *recuestas* as the irremediable site of Jewishness, whether understood as cultural difference or in the far more explosive terms of sexual aberration.

It is within the context of this construction of Jewish alterity and the simultaneous expansion of aristocratic self-awareness that the *recuesta* begins to make sense. In contrast to the poetic contests of primitive societies, where the tribe's own status was bound up in the triumph or defeat of its representative poet, here the audience (in the main members of the aristocracy) could witness from a safe distance the enactment of alterity. In this the *recuesta* bears a striking resemblance to those deliberately demeaning activities to which marginals were subjected throughout the late Middle Ages, for example, the forced participation of Jews in royal entries, of prostitutes and lackeys in footraces, or of vagabonds in mule races (the latter event predecessor to the Sienese *palio*).[31] The public exposure of these peoples "had a function," notes cultural historian Bronislaw Geremek, "since it reinforced the honor of the community organizing the exhibition and served to humiliate the community that the city considered its enemy" (371). In like manner, the *recuesta* guarantees the honor of the Trastamaran court through a spectacle of humiliation–two poets duking it out until one pins the other to the wall like some specimen of the dark side of Spanish identity. The *recuesta* in this sense participates fully in what Mary Elizabeth Perry reads as a political imperative of late-medieval and early-modern Spain, the forging of national identity through the creation of "counteridentities against which Christians could unify and define themselves" (45). It is no coincidence that those very discourses deployed in the *recuestas* (ethnicity, gender, sexuality) lie at the core of early-modern Spain's engagement with new minorities of its own making (Moriscos, Conversos, crypto-Jews).

How might we explain, however, the irony of the *recuesta*, that is, the *ready* collaboration of Conversos–Baena in particular–in a show of virtuosity that is tantamount to self-destruction? Márquez Villanueva suggests one possibility: that the Converso poet, much like the court jester, hoped to achieve through ribaldry and self-deprecation a certain "unbridled expression and the liberty to speak the bitter truth" (399). "This kind of language," Márquez Villanueva notes, "was in itself an exercise at the brink of disaster, a challenge to probe the uncertain limits of the permissible, for this clowning could turn at any moment into a deadly serious affair" (395).

And yet the material of the *recuestas* never turns on its audience, even in its most unbridled moments. The butt of its humor is never the status quo, but rather remains the marginalized, the disenfranchised, or those fallen from grace.[32] I cannot help but feel that the motivation for Conversos such as Baena is far more subtle, much more akin to the articulation of Jewish "self-hatred" as proposed by Sander Gilman in his landmark study. Gilman defines the first step toward self-hatred as the conflict that arises when an outsider attempts to join the ranks of a reference group:

> The first sign–be like us, you will become one of us–implies accepting one's own difference. But the more one attempts to identify with those who have labeled one as different, the more one accepts the values, social structures, and attitudes of this determining group, the farther away from true acceptability one seems to be. For as one approaches the norms set by the reference group, the approbation of the group recedes. (2-3)

"The fragmentation of identity that results," Gilman concludes, "is the articulation of self-hatred" (3).

What is the *recuesta* but the effort of one outsider to measure his level of acceptability against another. It is a game of "your difference is greater than mine," or, at its most psychologically complex, a projection of one's own alterity onto another in a play to eradicate it in oneself. Gilman notes the tragic irony of such efforts, the impossibility of creating a complete break with this new Other: "For even as one distances oneself from this aspect of oneself, there is always the voice of the power group saying, Under the skin you are really like them anyhow" (3). And so access to the dominant order is held ever beyond the reach of the Converso poet. The winner in the *recuesta* is just as much the loser, for he is still a Converso, and with it everything that constitutes the alterity of the Converso.

It is just this irony that was entirely lost on Baena, the self-proclaimed champion of the sport. But it would not be lost on a later generation of Converso poets, among whom Antón de Montoro, who engages in his own poetics of self-destruction just as Spain is hammering out the powers and purview of the Inquisition.[33] As Montoro protests in one piece addressed to no less than Isabel the Catholic, during his seventy years of playing the model Christian–professing tenets such as the Incarnation and the Trinity, engaging in dramatic shows of piety, even gorging himself on vats of bacon–"I've been unable to shake the tag 'Old bugger, Jew'" (#98). "Let this persecution cease," he implores in a closing remark dripping with sarcasm, "at least until Christmastide, when a warm fire would feel nice."[34]

Montoro's complaint is the product of an age of cynicism, of frank disillusionment for those Conversos who had been banking throughout the fifteenth century on the privileges of conversion. The *recuesta*, by contrast, emerges in an earlier age, in an age of innocence when Conversos still held fast to the illusion of access to the dominant order and Baena could naively offer the fruits of his labor for the diversion of the king and his boon companions. Even so, it taps inevitably into the ideological and psychological turmoil simmering beneath the appearance of a unified Trastamaran state. It cannot help but style itself as a spectacle of difference, Spain's emblematic confrontation with alterity. And in its bid to pin the poet (the Converso, the Jew) to the wall, it already presages the more violent turns of history as Spain enters its modern age.

University of Louisville

Notes

* A far more primitive version of this essay was presented under the auspices of the Division on Spanish Medieval Language and Literature at the annual meeting of the Modern Languages Association (San Diego, 1994). I have Anne J. Cruz to thank for her enthusiastic reading of that original essay and for her many suggestions for improvement. Ramon Cerdà and Wendy Pfeffer provided further insights into the Basque and the Occitan contexts respectively. So too am I indebted to José Labrador and the two anonymous readers for *Disputatio* for recommendations that helped bring my bibliography up to date. Finally, I wish to acknowledge Francisco Márquez Villanueva, who first introduced me to the matter of Baena. To him I dedicate this essay.

1. Menéndez y Pelayo is even more piquant when he notes: "That cynical *juglar* sold his wit the way whores sell their bodies" (l).

2. This in the rubric to CB 1.

3. The Galician-Portuguese school, which held sway in the lyric tradition of Christian Spain until well into the fourteenth century, is notorious for its *cantigas d'escarnho e de mal dizer*–songs of scorn and malediction–studied most recently (and most provocatively) by Blackmore, Liu.

4. Among the slights: "My lady, I'd be no more than a toad if I didn't plug up your ass with my balls and in five good thrusts give your pussy a soaking" ("Señora, en fin de razones, / yo me ternía por sapo / si el culo non vos atapo / con aquestos mis cojones; / e si a los çinco empuxones / non vos remojare el papo") (CB 104: 33-37). Azáceta was the first to print an unexpurgated version of the work, this with the *caveat* that it is a "tremendously vulgar piece, undeserving of appearing in print." Fray Diego de Valencia is substantially less vulgar when he lashes out against "a woman from León who was wicked and a whore" (CB 499). See López Quero and Urbán Fernández for a complete (although uncritical) survey of sexual terminology in the CB.

5. "...ganaste más barvas que trager solías, / ganaste maridos que acá non avías, / ganaste privança do demo mayor" (CB 107: 14-16). Dutton and González Cuenca dispute use of the term *maridos* 'husbands' in this piece, reading it as a scribal error for *maridas* 'wives.' The truth is that either term could function as a marker for Islamic sexual perversion, since both sodomy and polygamy were believed to be common practice among Muslims and were equally reprehensible to Christians (Perry 40). Literary attacks on Muslims, Jews, and Conversos (recent converts from Judaism) are so frequent as to be

topical. For a general consideration of poetic invective in medieval Spain, see Scholberg, Madero. On attacks against Jews/Conversos in particular, see Cantera Burgos, Scholberg (303-60), Madero (117-32).

6. The term *recuesta* also applies to fanciful poetic disputations, for example, CB 343, contrived by Pedro González de Uceda as a "*recuesta* waged by the colors of a handkerchief (green, black, and red), arguing which of them was best." Here Sir Love is called upon to render judgment (deciding ultimately in favor of black as the most humble of colors). See also CB 242 by Imperial, in which Chastity, Humility, Patience, and Loyalty engage in an allegorical debate (judged by the figure of Philosophy in favor of all four); CB 98, where Villasandino intervenes as judge in the competition (termed *recuesta* in the poem itself) between the nuns of Toledo and the nuns of Sevilla. *Recuesta* is also understood in the broader sense of any poetic complaint (whether inviting dialogue or not), as in the charges Villasandino launches against his fellow poets (CB 96, CB 200); Gómez Pérez Patiño's *contemptus mundi* (CB 353); Fray Diego de Valencia's satirical take on palace life (CB 515); or Fernán Sánchez Calavera's grievance against Love (CB 533).

7. Those *recuestas* documented among Baena's own works give the fairest indication of this procedure. In an introductory piece, Baena addresses to the king his intention to do battle "against two discerning and accomplished *trobadores*" (CB 357: 6-7). In the following piece, he identifies his opponents as Villasandino and Fernán Manuel de Lando and designates Don Fadrique and Alvaro de Luna (the king's uncle and favorite respectively) as judges. Following are several bouts of up to three exchanges apiece, at the end of which the rubric reports the decision of these judges, for example, "[Alfonso Alvarez] did not respond; the field was won by Juan Alfonso."

8. The most notable bouts include Alfonso Sánchez de Jaén vs. Villasandino (CB 123-CB 131); Baena vs. Villasandino (CB 364-CB 368); Baena vs. Lando (CB 359-CB363; CB 369-CB 377, including Fray Diego de Valencia's decision); Baena vs. Juan de Guzmán (CB 399-CB 411); Baena vs. Rodrigo de Harana (CB 429-CB 439); Juan García de Vinuesa vs. Baena (CB 382-CB 389). As for whether the *recuestas* were improvisational or not, this is a matter best left open to discussion. It seems unlikely that the longer works (of up to five eight-verse stanzas followed by a four-verse *finida*, or closing remark) were composed on the spot. Furthermore, there is the occasional reference to the *recuestas* as read rather than performed texts, for example, in Baena's *xaque*, or parting shot, after a volley of four-stanza pieces with Juan García: "Juan García, good friend, I believe you're all washed up, especially if those who understand what I'm saying *read well the above...*" (CB 388: 1-4, emphasis mine). The shorter pieces, on the other hand–most comprised of a single eight-verse stanza plus *finida*–readily lend themselves to improvisation.

9. Baena is the only poet listed as an author of *recuestas* in the table of contents appended to his general prologue to the collection (10). What is more, the rubric introducing his own works (133 recto of the manuscript) begins "Johan Alfonso de Baena: Requestas," written in substantially larger lettering spanning the width of the folio.

10. As Márquez Villanueva points out, "much in these *requestas* means next to nothing in a logical context, and only serves as support for several unexpected flashes of daring expression swimming in a sea of nonsense" (392). In other words, meaning gives way to sheer poetic virtuosity.

11. Incontinence is of course a universal topos for fear in battle, as Douglas notes (1), one given a new twist in Castile in popular reworkings of the epic poem of the Cid. The ballad "Acabó de yantar" recounts how the Cid's sons-in-law, the "redoubtable" Infantes

of Carrión, flee the Cid's court when a wild lion escapes from its cage. One of the Infantes becomes the butt of toilet humor when afterwards he is dragged from the latrines, where he had taken refuge: "See, my lord, here he comes; but stand to the side, because you'd need a censer to be able to stand next him" (Menéndez Pidal 184).

12. In the *fabliau*-styled tale as recounted by Juan Ruiz, Pitas Payas paints a sheep on his wife's privates in efforts to insure her fidelity while he is away on business. During his two-year absence, the young woman takes on a lover and the image of the sheep is eventually rubbed off by the friction of their constant lovemaking. Just before her husband's return, she has the lover repaint the image, but in his haste he paints a ram. So it is that the effort to conceal the adulterous act becomes ironically the exposure of that same act, the rams horns unambiguous publication of Pitas Payas's status as *cornudo* 'cuckold.' Lando adds a new level of punning when he calls Baena a painter of *ataurique*, that is, ornamental moldings used by the Moors. My translation reads quite simply "frieze," but Lando surely intends more when he deploys a syncopated form of the term (*taurique*) immediately evocative of *toro* 'bull' in its prefixal form *tauro-*.

13. Here the *recuesta* is envisaged as swordplay, elsewhere as a full-scale tournament, as in the expression "the field was won by X" ("fynco el campo por X"). So too are chess metaphors employed, as in the rubric to CB 389: "Checkmate (*mate*) by Juan Alfonso de Baena, because Juan García didn't provide a counter-response in the allotted time."

14. So too had Menéndez y Pelayo failed to recognize the peculiarities of the *recuesta* when he deemed it the Spanish analogue to the *tenso* (xlvi). Only Labrador, in a brief aside to his study of the *pregunta* in the CB, takes care to distinguish the *recuesta* as a separate category whose primary objective is verbal assault (28-29).

15. Evidently, once such rivalries were forgotten, the genre collapsed into the poetic sparring matches that would become standard fare in the courts of Islamic Spain. Whether the *recuesta* owes anything of its conventional aspect to the *naqa'id* is a matter that bears further investigation.

16. The tradition of the *payadas* is memorialized most notably in Argentinian poet José Hernández's epic *Martín Fierro*, first published in 1879; for a general consideration, see De La Fuente. See Aulestia for an overview of *bertsolaritza*, the Basque tradition of improvised poetry, which seems to be experiencing a veritable renaissance in recent years; on poetic contests in particular, see 41-42. On the "dirty dozens," see Allan and Brundage. Here the goal is to insult a rival's mother, this in a display of wit prefaced by the expression "You momma...," for example, "You momma wash her hair with Babo" or "Momma's pussy so big, airplane park in it" (150). Rap as well, at least in its primitive state, embraces many of the elements of the universal tradition of poetic contests.

17. "[T]he wounds inflicted through poetic curse and by the *hijà*, 'taunt,' of the Arab poet (as in the Biblical story of Balak's demand to curse the Children of Israel which God turned into a blessing in Bileam's mouth) were felt as real ones by those who were hit" (22).

18. For general accounts of Spain's late medieval period, see O'Callaghan (part 5), Reilly (ch. 7). Far more penetrating is the recent work of David Nirenberg, whose *Communities of Violence* argues for violence against minorities as a predicating factor in the maintaining of the sociopolitical status quo. Many of the conclusions he draws for fourteenth-century Valencia might be applied equally well to the court of Juan II, in which, as I shall argue, figurative violence against racial and social minorities undergirds the formation of class consciousness. See also Perry, who makes the argument that Spain's

budding national identity is bound up in the demonization and rejection of minorities such Conversos and Moriscos (Muslims converted to Christianity).

19. In this the material of the CB constitutes what I have called elsewhere "literature of collusion," a wholesale collaboration in the workings of orthodoxy and aristocratic privilege ("Marginality and Empowerment in Baena's *Cancionero*"). With regard to the *preguntas y respuestas* genre in particular, Cummins notes (perhaps unfairly): "A comparison with the poems of the *Recueil Général des Jeux-Partis* illuminates the poverty of invention of the Castilian poets; for some of them,...the repetition of such hackneyed themes presumably had some charm" (14). See Boase for a full-length study of the anachronisms of fifteenth-century Castilian poetry.

20. Four-thousand Jews were killed in Seville alone. So too did the coercive preaching of the Dominican Vicente de Ferrer bring about another wave of conversions in the first decades of the fifteenth century. The rise of the Converso class has a complex history, studied most comprehensively (albeit polemically) by B. Netanyahu in his monumental *The Origins of the Inquisition in Fifteenth Century Spain*. See also Y. Baer's now classic *A History of the Jews in Christian Spain* (vol. 2) and, more recently, Freund and Ruiz, Roth.

21. Although Avalle Arce, following Josef Müller, argues for transcribing the term as *yndino* 'unworthy.' Few scholars today seem quite as invested as Avalle Arce in demonstrating the non- Jewishness of Baena, and in fact most assume his Converso status as a matter of public record. See Cantera Burgos (81ff.), Márquez Villanueva (390ff.), Bahler and Gyékényesi Gatto (181-82), and most recently Cabrera, whose archival research on the demographics of Baena (the poet's place of origin) reveals a remarkably high percentage of Conversos (almost one quarter of the total population) throughout the fifteenth century.

22. Others studied by Fraker: Fernán Sánchez Calavera, Gonzalo Martínez de Medina, Nicolás de Valencia, and García Alvarez de Alarcón, the first two of whom, together with Lando, engage in vigorous debates on the sticking points of conversion, especially the doctrines of the Incarnation and the Trinity. From Baena's exchange with Alvar Ruiz de Toro we might deduce that the latter was also a Converso (Scholberg, *Sátira e invectiva* 307). To these Cantera Burgos adds Don Mosé (surgeon to Enrique III and almost surely a Jew) and Pedro Ferruz. So too does he suggest Fray Diego de Valencia's possible Jewish extraction, this based on the poet's manifest knowledge of Hebrew language and custom: in one show of virtuosity, an invective launched against Juan de España (CB 501), Fray Diego employs no fewer than two dozen Hebrew terms, most in rhyme position.

23. Says Villasandino in terms intended to elicit sympathy (and a little pocket change) from his addressee (Juan II's mother Catalina): "I have old age for my beloved; full of quarrel is she, a loathsome vessel covered with rust" (CB 63: 9-12). Cantera Burgos is not so quick to accept Villasandino's characteristic anti-Semiticism as evidence of his Old Christian status, making the perfectly valid point that his would not be the first case of a convert who lashes out against his former coreligionists (89).

24. See Cantera Burgos for a comprehensive survey of such references.

25. The charge of avarice is obviously a commonplace in anti-Semitic discourse, certainly manifest in Spanish letters since the twelfth-century epic *Cantar de mio Cid*. Here the Cid bilks the Jewish moneylenders Rachel and Vidas out of a small fortune, leaving in hock a chest containing nothing but sand. His recourse to deception is justified by both necessity as he marches into exile and the suggestion that the Jews themselves

would have stopped at nothing to get their hands on the Cid's estate. See Nepaulsingh for the most recent consideration of this episode and relevant bibliography.

26. Madero notes that the miniatures of Alfonso el Sabio's *Cantigas de Santa María* (thirteenth century) had already incorporated the hooked nose as an essential element of representations of the Jew (121-22).

27. Amer notes that the likening of the sexual act to thrusts of the spear at a shield is a metaphor that enjoyed broad cultivation in Arabic erotological works, yet more evidence of the import of Arabic tropes and forms in the Spanish lyric tradition.

28. Including Lando, Davihuelo, and one Juan Agraz, this in a lengthy invective not included in the CB. "There is no Converso so perverse," claims Baena as he narrates his rival's activities as traitor, pimp, thief, cuckold, and apostate. (See Scholberg, *Sátira e invectiva* 307-08.)

29. Eggplant (*berenjena*), a staple of the Mediterranean diet, would become by the sixteenth century an icon for Semitic culture (whether Arabic or Jewish), and so a fit subject for the satire of Cervantes when he names the pseudo-author of his *Don Quijote de la Mancha* Cidi Hamete Benengeli. So too does *adefina* recur as a theme in anti-Converso literature throughout the period, contrasting with *tocino* 'bacon,' whose ample consumption is the mark of the Old Christian. See Domínguez Ortiz (23-24) for a consideration of diet as cultural marker in early-modern Spain. Baena further confesses to an aversion *pez de vileza* (CB 405: 11-12), that is, the shellfish proscribed by Jewish dietary laws.

30. *Regadío* is a problematic term in the translation, although its literal sense–"land cultivated by means of irrigation"–gives fair indication of the poet's intended meaning. The stereotype of the sodomitic Jew had become topical by the fifteenth century, emerging most readily in the formulaic charge *puto judío* 'bugger Jew.' See my "Desperately Seeking Sodom" for more on the meanings and manipulations of sodomy as sociopolitical discourse in fifteenth-century Spain.

31. Nirenberg has uncovered in fourteenth-century Aragon a variation on these activities, the ritual stoning of Jews on Holy Thursday, noting that use of the term *jochs* 'games, jokes, plays' in the documentation underscores the "ritual, even ludic aspect of the violence" (211).

32. Cf. later pieces such as the *Coplas de Mingo Revulgo* or the *Coplas del Provincial,* both of which launch derisive attacks against the court of Enrique IV, although always from the safe ground of anonymity. See Rodríguez-Puértolas, *Poesía crítica y satírica*, for the text and a study of both.

33. Strong arguments have been made for a blood relationship between Baena and Montoro, whose father, Fernando Alonso de Baena Ventura, may very well have been Baena's brother. (See Márquez Villanueva 396 n18.)

34. Far more reckless than Montoro were the *chocarreros* 'shockers,' who would become a familiar social type in inquisitorial Spain. According to Stephen Gilman:

> . . . in addition to merely telling jokes, [they] frequently provoked laughter by playing verbally with [their] own suspicious self-image and making fun of the pretentious self-images of others. It was a dangerous game. Not only were these self-appointed wits frequently denounced to the Inquisition for their scandalous remarks, but also, as in the case of poor Francesillo de Zúñiga (perhaps the only professional fool ever to die by assassination), physical violence was a probability. Nevertheless, the aggressive negation which motivated such

> behavior could not be repressed by certain kinds of temperaments: those who were themselves irrepressible. (97)

Works Cited

Allan, Keith and Kate Burridge. *Euphemism and Dysphemism: Language Used As Shield and Weapon*. New York and Oxford: Oxford UP, 1991.

Amer, Sahar. "Lesbian Sex and the Military: From the Medieval Arabic Tradition to French Literature." *Same Sex Love and Desire Among Women in the Middle Ages*. Ed. Francesca Canadé Sautman and Pamela Sheingorn. New York: Palgrave, 2001.

Aulestia, Gorka. *Improvisational Poetry from the Basque Country*. Trans. Lisa Corcostegui and Linda White. Reno: U of Nevada P, 1989.

Avalle Arce, Juan Bautista. "Sobre Juan Alfonso de Baena." *Revista de Filología Hispánica*. 8.1-2 (January-June 1946): 141-47.

Baena, Juan Alfonso de. *Cancionero de Baena. Reproduced in Facsimile from the Unique Manuscript in the Bibliothèque Nacionale*. Ed. Henry R. Lang. New York: The Hispanic Society of America, 1926.

—. *Cancionero*. Ed. José María Azáceta. 3 vols. Madrid: Consejo Superior de Investigaciones Científicas, 1966.

—. *Cancionero de Juan Alfonso de Baena*. Ed. Brian Dutton and Joaquín González Cuenca. Madrid: Visor Libros, 1993.

Baer, Yitzhak. *A History of the Jews in Christian Spain*. 1961. Philadelphia: Jewish Publication Society of America, 1978.

Bahler, Ingrid, and Katherine Gyékényesi Gatto. *Of Kings and Poets: Cancionero Poetry of the Trastámaran Courts*. New York: Peter Lang, 1992.

Blackmore, Josiah. "The Poets of Sodom." *Queer Iberia: Sexualities, Cultures, and Crossings from the Middle Ages to the Renaissance*. Ed. Josiah Blackmore and Gregory S. Hutcheson. Durham, N.C.: Duke UP, 1999. 195-221.

Bloomfield, Morton W. and Charles W. Dunn. *The Role of the Poet in Early Societies*. Cambridge: D. S. Brewer, 1989.

Boase, Roger. *The Troubadour Revival: A Study of Social Change and Traditionalism in Late Medieval Spain*. London, Henley and Boston: Routledge & Kegan Paul, 1978.

Cabrera, Emilio. "Los conversos de Baena en el siglo XV." Serrano Reyes and Juan Fernández Jiménez. In press.

Cantera Burgos, Francisco. "El *CB*: Judíos y conversos en él." *Sefarad* 27.1 (1967): 71-111.

Cummins, John G. "The Survival in the Spanish *Cancioneros* of the Form and Themes of Provençal and Old French Poetic Debates." *Bulletin of Hispanic Studies* 42 (1965): 9-17.

De La Fuente, Alfredo. *El payador en la cultura nacional*. Buenos Aires: Corregidor, 1986.

Domínguez Ortiz, Antonio. *Los judeoconversos en España y América*. Madrid: ISTMO, [1971].

Douglas, Mary. *Purity and Danger: An Analysis of the Concepts of Pollution and Taboo*. 1966. London and Boston: Routledge and Paul Kegan, 1980.

Freund, Scarlett and Teófilo F. Ruiz. "Jews, Conversos, and the Inquisition in Spain, 1301-1492: The Ambiguities of History." *Jewish-Christian Encounters over the*

Centuries. Ed. Marvin Perry and Frederick Schweitzer. New York: Peter Lang, 1994. 169-95.

Fraker, Charles. *Studies on the* Cancionero de Baena. *Studies in the Romance Languages and Literatures* 61. Chapel Hill: U of North Carolina P, 1966.

Geremek, Bronislaw. "The Marginal Man." *Medieval Callings*. Ed. Jacques Le Goff. 1987. Chicago, IL: U of Chicago P, 1990.

Gilman, Sander. *Jewish Self-Hatred: Anti-Semitism and the Hidden Language of the Jews*. Baltimore: The Johns Hopkins UP, 1986.

Gilman, Stephen. "A Generation of *Conversos*." *Romance Philology* 33.1 (August 1979): 87- 101.

Huizinga, J. *Homo Ludens: A Study of the Play Element in Culture*. 1949. London and Boston: Routledge and Paul Kegan, 1980.

Hutcheson, Gregory S. "Desperately Seeking Sodom: Queerness in the Chronicles of Alvaro de Luna." *Queer Iberia: Sexualities, Cultures, and Crossings from the Middle Ages to the Renaissance*. Ed. Josiah Blackmore and Gregory S. Hutcheson. Durham, N.C.: Duke UP, 1999. 222-49.

—. "Marginality and Empowerment in Baena's *Cancionero*." Diss. Harvard University, 1993.

Labrador Herraiz, José J. *Poesía dialogada medieval: la «pregunta» en el «Cancionero de Baena»*. Madrid: Maisal, 1974.

Lichtenstadter, Ilse. *Introduction to Classical Arabic Literature. With Selections from Representative Works in English Translation*. 1974. New York: Schocken Books, 1976.

Liu, Benjamin. "'Affined to Love the Moor': Sexual Alliance and Cultural Mixing in the *Cantigas d'escarnho e de mal dizer*." *Queer Iberia: Sexualities, Cultures, and Crossings from the Middle Ages to the Renaissance*. Ed. Josiah Blackmore and Gregory S. Hutcheson. Durham, N.C.: Duke UP, 1999. 48-72.

López Quero, Salvador, and Angel C. Urbán Fernández. "Léxico sexual en el *Cancionero de Baena*." Serrano Reyes and Juan Fernández Jiménez. In press.

Madero, Marta. *Manos violentas, palabras vedadas: la injuria en Castilla y León, siglos XIII-XV*. Madrid: Taurus Humanidades, 1992.

Márquez Villanueva, Francisco. "Jewish 'Fools' of the Spanish Fifteenth Century." *Hispanic Review* 5.4 (Autumn 1982): 385-409.

Menéndez Pidal, Ramón. *Flor nueva de romances viejos*. 1938. 21st ed. Buenos Aires: Austral, 1983.

Menéndez y Pelayo, Marcelino. *Antología de poetas líricos castellanos desde la formación del idioma hasta nuestros días*. Vol. 4. 1890-1906. Madrid: Librería de Perlado, Páez y C.ª, 1918.

Montoro, Antón de. *Poesía completa*. Ed. Marithelma Costa. Cleveland: Cleveland State U, 1990.

Nepaulsingh, Colbert I. "Rachel and Vidas and Monocultural Criticism." *La Corónica* 25.1 (Fall 1999): 229-37.

Netanyahu, B. *The Origins of the Inquisition in Fifteenth Century Spain*. New York: Random House, 1995.

Nirenberg, David. *Communities of Violence: Persecution of Minorities in the Middle Ages*. Princeton, NJ: Princeton UP, 1998.

O'Callaghan, Joseph F. *A History of Medieval Spain*. Ithaca: Cornell UP, 1975.

Perry, Mary Elizabeth. "The Politics of Race, Ethnicity and Gender in the Making of the Spanish State." *Culture and the State in Spain*. Ed. Tom Lewis and Francisco J. Sánchez. New York: Garland, 1999. 34-54.

Reilly, Bernard F. *The Medieval Spains*. Cambridge: Cambridge UP, 1993.

Rodríguez-Puértolas, Julio. *Poesía crítica y satírica del siglo XV*. Madrid: Castalia, 1984.

Roth, Norman. *Conversos, Inquisition, and the Expulsion of the Jews from Spain*. Madison: U of Wisconsin P, 1995.

Scholberg, Kenneth R. *La poesía zahiriente del siglo XV*. La Coruña: Esquio, 1980.

—. *Sátira e invectiva en la España medieval*. Madrid: Gredos, 1971.

Sem Tob, Don. *Glosas de sabiduría o Proverbios morales y otras rimas*. Ed. Agustín García Calvo. Madrid: Alianza Editorial, 1985.

Serrano Reyes, Jesús L., and Juan Fernández Jiménez, eds. *Juan Alfonso de Baena y su Cancionero*. Proc. of the Primer Congreso del *Cancionero de Baena*, Feb. 1999, Baena, Spain. In press.

The Love Debate Tradition in the Reception of Gower's *Confessio Amantis* in the Iberian Peninsula

Francisco Javier Grande Quejigo and Bernardo Santano Moreno

Throughout the Castilian Middle Ages one can observe traces of the scholastic *disputatio* in works of a clear literary nature. This is the case of the thirteenth-century debates in couplets which follow various amorous traditions; for example, in the incomplete *Elena y María*, in which the form of the debate includes the learned amorous tradition of the eulogy of the cleric against the knight, the dispute takes place in the courtly context of the Court of Love.[1] This scholastic device is thus open to the world of the troubadour and to the culture of the Court. The other thirteenth-century debate, the *Razón de amor con los denuestos del agua y el vino*, maintains the technique of the *disputatio* in a more clearly scholastic context. With a miscellaneous juxtaposed two-part structure of goliardic tradition,[2] the poet is able to assimilate various troubadourist and courtly traditions of "fins amours" and to incorporate them in the models of the Medieval Latin tradition. In both cases, the literature in the Romance language is able to adapt contents of a scholastic nature to courtly forms (*Elena y María*) and courtly contents to scholastic forms (*Razón de amor*).

This capacity of cultural transference, in which the Romance language adopts the cultural manifestations that belong to Latin, is a basic characteristic of the medieval cleric, as demonstrated by Francisco Rico in his indispensable *La clerecía del mester.*[3] In addition, throughout the thirteenth century, there was a progressive tendency in the Court to adopt previous knowledge from different sources in order to deepen and improve the education of the Castilian noble. Not only did the translated literature of the thirteenth century and the works of Alfonso the Wise respond to the purpose of the education of nobles, but other works connected to the university and scholastic techniques of the time, such as the *Libro de Alexandre* or the *Libro de Apolonio*, in whose dialogues there are clear traces of the *disputatio*, also seemed to respond to an incipient tradition of the 'mirror of princes'.[4]

The relationship of the vernacular use of the forms and contents belonging to the Medieval Latin scholastic culture is represented in its forms by the presence of the *disputatio* as an instrument of pedagogic transmission of knowledge, and in its contents by materials pertaining to the erudition transmitted through Latin. This relationship is consolidated throughout the fourteenth century in the double direction that can be identified in the thirteenth-century debates. Works such as those by don Juan Manuel, in which a question-answer courtly model is used, enabled the noble to approach a type of knowledge (from different sources) in which there is a progressive imposition of the learned norm. In this respect, the increasing difficulty in the expression of the different parts of the *Conde Lucanor*, initially conceived as a collection of exempla framed as a doctrinal treatise, shows the courtly concern about approaching the scholastic techniques of learned prestige.[5] On the other hand, the Arcipreste de Hita, in his *Libro de buen amor*, used models connected to the scholastic and goliardic world in order to perform his educational task, and incorporated into his learned model a series of typically popular advice, habits and linguistic elements. Again, as in the thirteenth century, the culture in the vernacular became assimilated with the Medieval Latin culture, although in the fourteenth-century exempla there is a predominance of didactic formulas conveyed through the dialogues of two characters. The fusion of the miscellaneous scholastic model of the *Libro del buen amor* and the courtly one of the *Conde Lucanor* took place towards the end of the fourteenth century in Canciller López de Ayala's *Rimado de Palacio*. The fourteenth-century Castilian Court continued to practice the old tradition of cultural mediation that can be detected in the thirteenth century in order to promote the education of nobles.

After this initial excursus, which was necessary in order to pose the purpose of this article, we will try to explain an interesting cultural phenomenon that took place in the area of the medieval translations in the Iberian Peninsula. As Peter Russell points out,[6] the translations found in fourteenth- and fifteenth-century Castile are of Latin texts (progressively classical texts) and some Romance texts, mainly French. There is only one case of a work translated from English: John Gower's *Confessio Amantis*. The mid-fifteenth-century translation into Castilian Spanish was made by Juan de Cuenca via a previous mid-fifteenth-century Portuguese translation by Robert Payn, an Englishman and a canon of Lisbon Cathedral. The Castilian text, *Confisyon del amante*, is preserved in Ms. g-ii-19 of the Royal Library of El Escorial, and the Portuguese text, which has been recently discovered by Prof. Antonio Cortijo (University of California-Santa Barbara) is preserved in Ms. 3088 of the Biblioteca del Palacio Real (Madrid) under the title of *Livro do amante*. A comparative analysis of the Portuguese and Castilian prose texts and the original English poem by John Gower shows that the translators made an enormous effort not only to transmit the contents of the original to their respective languages, but also to adapt those contents to the mid-fifteenth-century Portuguese and Castilian cultures and audiences. In this sense, both translations incorporate many changes, but perhaps these are more prominent in the Castilian text. Juan de Cuenca omits passages of different length. Sometimes these omissions do not seriously affect the essential meaning of the original text, but there are occasions on which we can detect a clear intention to censure the contents of certain passages. There is also a large number of additions intended to clarify some cultural aspects, but there are instances in which Cuenca introduces fragments of an unquestionable didactic or moral nature. Finally, several *exempla* are also adapted by the translator on the basis of other versions which circulated in the Castile of his times. Considering the particular characteristics of these translations, the question still remains as to which literary traditions favoured the translation and circulation of Gower's work in mid-fifteenth-century Portugal and Castile. We believe that the comparison between *Confisyon del amante*, the *Libro de buen amor* and the *Conde Lucanor* can explain the success of the translation of Gower's work.

The Arcipreste de Hita's book adds to the model of love debate present in the *Razón de amor* a thematic element which coincides with that of *Confisyon del amante*: the Ovidian tradition of dispute with Love.[7] Hita's Ovidian element is augmented by adding the paraphrasis of a work of clear Ovidian influence in the Middle Ages: the paraphrasis of the elegiac comedy *Pamphilus de amore*, and by using the model of love autobiography as a moral exemplum and the didactic *exemplum ex contrario*, also connected to the love autobiography tradition.[8] In this way, Hita joins the medieval tradition of teaching through the Ovidian model. We observe that this tendency succeeds in the Middle Ages in works such as the various Medieval Latin elegiac comedies, the *Roman de la Rose*, Andreas Capelanus' *De amore*, etc. From such works, both the Ovidian conception of love and its connection to moralization and allegory will be transmitted to other later works such as *Confessio Amantis* and the Castilian lyric. On the other hand, Ovid had been extensively used in works of a doctrinal character, as in the works of Alfonso the Wise.[9]

If the *Libro de buen amor* and *Confisyon del amante* share the use of Ovidian themes in order to moralise, Gower's work and don Juan Manuel's *Conde Lucanor* share the use of the exemplum technique which is typical of the education of nobles. Thus, a mid-fifteenth-century member of the nobility could find in the *Confessio Amantis* a model in which learned Ovidian topics were used in order to moralize in a modern and attractive way. In the dialogues between Genius and *Amans* there is a confluence of the traditional technique of the education of nobles used by don Juan Manuel and the scholastic dialogue between master and disciple of the *Libro de buen amor*. Gower's work offered a type of teaching that included a number of exempla of moral behaviour set in the Ovidian story of love. This was one of the newest didactic elements in fourteenth-century Romance culture (the dynamic model of the *Libro de buen amor*[10]) together with the contents and best known expository forms of the traditional education of nobles which started with the thirteenth-century books of exempla. This becomes clearer when analysing the last two books of the *Confessio* dedicated to two characters whose biographies were used in the Castilian Middle Ages as an example for rulers and as a means for the transmission of encyclopaedic contents connected to the development of *courtesy* as understood by Alfonso X.[11] We refer to Alexander the Great, protagonist of the *Libro de Alexandre* and the IV part of Afonso X's *General Estoria,*[12] an example of the behaviour and education of the Medieval noble-king in its positive aspects, and a negative example of the pride of knowledge and power; and also the figure of the Christian king Apolonius, to whom the thirteenth-century "mester de clerecía"—"craft of the clergy", school of learned poets—dedicated the *Libro de Apolonio*, and to whom

Alfonso's compilers dedicated the V part of the *General Estoria*, unfortunately now lost.[13]

It is not strange, therefore, that the translations of Gower's *Confessio Amantis* would succeed because of their combination of new and traditional tendencies for the education of nobles. Curiously enough, a fifteenth-century Portuguese library provides evidence of the success of moral education through Ovidian themes, full of exempla and digressions to be used in the education of nobles. This library is King Duarte's, where we find *O amante* (the Portuguese version of Gower's work, also referred to as *Livro do amante*), the *Libro de buen amor* and the *Conde Lucanor.*[14] This should not be considered a case of mere chance, but an example of the interest of the receptor; in the case of these three books we can clearly identify a similar didactic and educational purpose.

The analysis of *Confisyon del amante* shows the use of didactic techniques which are similar to those of the other works found on the shelves of King Duarte's library. A narration presented in a frame is the common device of the three books, and this is also the basic technique used in the model of education of nobles. The *Libro de buen amor* inserts its doctrine in a love autobiography in the Ovidian tradition, which coincides with the frame of a confession of love used in the *Confessio*, also in the Ovidian tradition. The main sources are different. Gower's work is connected to the *Roman de la Rose* tradition (Genius, the priest of love, is the same character in both works) and Juan Ruiz, archpriest of Hita, is closer to the elegiac comedy.[15] However, in both cases, the Ovidian love frame is used to set a series of exempla and digressions of educational value. This is the way in which the archpriest explains the beginning of the dispute between him and *don Amor* (Love), and also in the different argumentations of his characters' disputes. The dejected lover expresses his complaint with different exempla:

> De cómo enflaquezes las gentes e las dapñas
> Muchos libros ay d'esto, de cómo las engañas
> Con tus muchos doñeos e con tus malas mañas;
> Siempre tiras la fuerça, dízenlo en fazañas. (stanza 188)[16]
>
> Los que te non provaron, en buen día nasçieron;
> Folgaron sin cuidado, nunca estristeçieron;
> Desque a ti fallaron, todo su bien perdieron,
> Fueles como a las ranas, quando el rey pidieron. (s. 198)[17]
>
> Contesçe cada día a tus amigos contigo,
> Como contesçió al topo que quiso ser amigo
> De la rana pintada quando lo levó consigo;
> Entiende bien la fabla e por qué te lo digo. (s. 407)

Love answers with an argument supported by an example in order to demonstrate his initial theory:

El Amor, con mesura, diome respuesta luego;
Diz: Arçipreste, sañudo non seyas, yo te ruego,
Non digas mal de Amor en verdat nin en juego,
Que a las vezes poco agua faze abaxar grand fuego. (s. 423)

Dezirte he la fazaña de los dos perezosos
Que querián casamiento e andavan acuziossos,
Amos por una dueña estava[n] codiçiossos,
Eran muy bien apuestos e verás quán fermosos: (s. 457)

The archpriest not only inserts his exempla in the dialogues between the characters, in the same way as Gower introduces his exempla in the dialogue between Genius and *Amans*, but also justifies the exemplum with a previous doctrinal exposition and concludes with a final moral explanation.[18] Thus, the archpriest coincides with Gower's intention and didactic practice, inserted in the Ovidian frame of a love confession, which stems from a traditional dispute between *don Amor* and *doña Venus* (Love and Venus). In the allegorical vision in the first book of the *Confessio* (which is similar to the archpriest's dream starting in stanza 181), Genius says that he will talk about matters beyond the cases of love:

> Fijo, para te fazer preguntas en tu confision yo soy asy asynado por mandado de Benus, la diesa, cuyo clerigo yo so de parte de amor. Pero a mj conviene por algunas rrazones no sola mente por te preguntar de las cosas de amor, mas de otras cosas mucho mas tocantes a los viçios...
> (*Confisyon del amante*, Ms. g-ii-19, fols. 36r.b.-37v.a.)[19]

And for this purpose Genius will use the exemplum technique:

> Por ende, fijo mjo, para mjentes a vna estoria que te yo agora dire, por la qual tu seras avisado de guardar tu vista que no pases fuera de rregla.
> (*Confisyon*, fol. 38v.a.)[20]

The Priest of Venus shows how love can also be used in order to present a moral exemplification on other themes:

> Fijo, tu deues de saber que asy en amor, commo en todas las otras cosas, sy presunçion en el onbre por qualquiera guysa cahe, no avra poder de quedar en njngun lugar. E, por ende, te consejo que te guardes della. E para ello sabras vna estoria que Ovidio rrecuenta, la qual a nuestra materia asaz allegada sera, de que sy quisyeres podras enxenplo tomar.
> (*Confisyon*, fols. 63r.b.-63v.a.)[21]

And he even includes, in an explicit way, examples that are not related to love:

> Agora escucha vna verdadera estoria, en la qual, avnque de amor non sea, fallaras en ella grant sentençya e enxenplo para fuyr deste viçio de vanjdad.
> (*Confisyon*, fol. 70r.a.)[22]

Cases of love are used in the *Confessio* in order to transmit a type of teaching that from the particular—

> E quien los enxenplos viejos quisyere oyr, podra bien entender que tal amor no estara mucho en su ser, çerca de la qual materia agora oyras vn enxenplo.
> (*Confisyon*, fol. 225v.b.)[23]

—the author may achieve a more general moralisation:

> Agora, padre, yo vos rruego, en enseñança de mj, me queraes contar algunt enxenplo, porque aqueste arrebatamyento de mj pueda lançar, τ el seso de buen consejo seguyr.
>
> Fijo, por ynformaçion de tu paçiençia, segunt la dotrina de los enxenplos antigos, mjra en lo que agora te dire.
> (*Confisyon*, fol. 144v.a.)[24]

Gower and the archpriest coincide in the use of exempla for the purpose of argumentation, but they both differ in the functions assigned to them in the dialogues. In the *Libro de buen amor*, the exempla are presented in a *disputatio* structure in which each opponent uses the exemplum to support a personal dialectic position. On the other hand, in the *Confessio*, the exempla are presented only by Genius, the priest of Venus, who assumes the functional role of the teacher before the disciple-*Amans*. The reason for this is that the dialogues of Gower's characters are inserted in a confessional frame and, therefore, Gower articulates a prolix question-answer structure between a disciple (*Amans*) and a teacher (Genius):

> Mucho vos agradesco, padre, esto que dicho aves, porque ello es enseñamyento de noble dotrina. Por ende, sy de soberuja ay alguna cosa demandadme que yo presto soy para rreçebjr qualquiera cosa de que me querays ynformar.
>
> Fijo mjo, vn viçio de soberuya avn esta por dezjr, el qual es semejante al falcon altanero porque asy buela en el deleyte de sus viçios e non quiere conoçer rrazon de onbre fasta que se trastorna e cahe debaxo. Este viçio es llamado vanagloria, del qual, fijo mjo, yo te prometo tratar en tal manera que tu seas en el enseñado e asy avisado que del te sepas bien guardar.
> (*Confisyon*, fols. 68v.a.-68v.b.)[25]

This is the same question-answer structure for the education of nobles used in the *Conde Lucanor*:

> Acaesció una vez que el conde Lucanor estava fablando en su poridat con Patronio, su consegero, et díxol:
>
> [...] Et vós dezitme et consejadme lo que vos paresce en este fecho.
> Señor conde Lucanor —dixo Patronio—, bien entiendo que el mío consejo non vos faze grant mengua, pero vuestra voluntad es que vos diga lo que en esto entiendo et vos conseje sobre ello, fazerlo he luego. Primeramente, vos digo que esto que aquel que cuydades que es vuestro amigo os dixo, que non lo fizo sinon por vos provar. Et paresce que vos conteció con él commo conteció a un rey con un su privado.
> El conde Lucanor le rogó quel dixiese cómmo fuera aquello.[26]

The assimilation of this traditional model for the education of nobles is more evident in the excursuses of books VI and VII of the *Confisyon del amante*:

> Padre, esto que me aves dicho, vos tengo en mucho grado, porque por ello de aqui adelante me guardare de espeçies de fechiseria. Mas, padre, allende de aquesto que al mj fecho de amor pertenesçe, otra cosa vos querria supljcar, que me mostrasedes la manera commo, por Aristotiles, a Alixandre fue enseñado de todas las cosas que perteneçen al rregimyento de vn rrey, por quanto mj coraçon desea mucho de las tales cosas. E pienso que, oyendo fablar de cosas estrañas que mjs padeçimjentos seran aljujados.
> (*Confisyon*, fol. 286v.a.-286v.b.)[27]
>
> [...] Por te declarar la escolastica dotrina que el grant filosofo Aristotil mostro al rrey Alixandre, segun que tu me lo has rrogado, fijo mjo, dixo Genyus, yo en parte soy en ello turbado, porque no es concordante a la materia de amor, de que Benus me mando tratar en tu confisyon. Mas, porque tu dises que oyendo de tales cosas de sabiduria te sera grant consolaçion e aliujamyento de tu pena, parte de la su dotrina te quiero dar a entender, segun que lo aprendi. Ca por aver verdadero conoçimyento de sabiduria, asy en amor commo en todas las cosas, mucho deue onbre trauajar. Por ende, fijo mjo, avnque esto non sea escripto en el rregistro de Benus, tu sabras parte de lo que Calistro e Aristotiles escriujeron al rrey Alixandre.
> (*Confisyon*, fol. 287r.a.-287r.b.)[28]

As we can see in the quotations above, in the *Confessio* there is a clear reference to the *auctoritas* of classical Antiquity as regards the practice of the education of nobles. In this respect, Gower differs from don Juan Manuel, who is closer to Arabic and Romance sources. In this didactic technique, as well as in the use of narrative frames for the introduction of exempla, we can see Gower using scholastic and traditional formulas. The scholastic Ovidian and Aristotelian traditions, more intense in the fourteenth century, coexist with the traditional figures of Alexander and Apolonius, which belong more to the thirteenth century. This is the way in which the three basic models of Castilian clerical education appear.

Ovid's presence in both the *Libro de buen amor* and the *Confessio* is the result of the influence of the same basic model: the medieval *Ars amandi*. In both books we find an extensive number of learned references that are part of the fourteenth-century scholastic world, and there is constant allusion to the written sources. Therefore, the archpriest's multiple sources and materials are well-known by the critics.[29] The same is true of Gower, who refers to his encyclopaedic work with a beautiful metaphor at the beginning of his prologue.[30]

> E asy commo el panar por la avejas de diversas flores es apañado, bien asy este mjsmo auctor de desuariadas estorias de coronjcas e dichos de poetas e filosofos, con grande estudio conpilo e fizo aqueste libro...
> (*Confisyon*, fol. Ir.b.)[31]

In the thirteenth century, the basic model for clerical education was the figure of Alexander taught by Aristotle. Book VII of the *Confessio* is dedicated to this character, the same as the *Libro de Alexandre* dedicates to him its first narrative part (stanzas 7-88).[32] The most exemplary clerical hero, prototype of the Christian prince, was Apolonius of Tyre. It is not strange that the *Confessio* closes with the story of this model hero who comprises the Christian use of knowledge (the authentic clergy) and a paradigmatic example of good human love within the limits of marital chastity. Gower uses this story as a conclusion to combine an amorous theme and his intention to educate a king:

> Para agora bien mjentes e mjra a los onbres que bien bjuen e su fundamento es bueno, quantos bienes e onores an de dios. Ca, porque este rrey se fundo sobre onestad de casamjento, logro para syenpre su amor e onesta mente ovo fijos de su muger. E de allj adelante, biuyo mucho a su voluntad. E, por enxenplo e rremenbrança de los que bien aman, esta su vida fue puesta en coronyca, por tal que ellos fuesen çiertos que su amor a la fyn se pareçeria.
>
> Sy quisyeres mjrar a lo contrario, fallaras quel rrey Antioco, con su soberuya e contra naturaleza acostunbrada, vso de su amor por mal deleyte, rreçibio despues penytençia, aviendo por vengança supita mente mal acabamyento. Por esto, fijo mjo, puedes bien entender quanto es bueno amar bien o mal, e que cosa es amor bueno o no, e el amor que es en buena manera, o no, e commo el gualardon dello sola mente proçede del buen seruyçio...
> (*Confisyon*, fols. 394r.a.-394v.a.)[33]

The final setting of the love frame indicates how the English poet has used, together with the traditional question-answer scheme, the more modern and pedagogical *exemplum ex contrario*, also found in the *Libro de buen amor*. In fact, the authorities used to show how Gower includes the three most traditional medieval figures assigning them different educational functions. Apolonio is the clearest case of the use of the imitative exemplum for his moral values. Alexander, the most valued hero of the Middle Ages, combines the model character of the ruler together with the *exemplum ex contrario* of his pride. When Gower uses him as an example of Aristotelian education, he is only using his character as a cleric-king to illustrate his audience.

Ovid, on the contrary, in his personality as an expert lover, is the basic excipient of the *ex contrario* moral teaching of the elegiac comedy and other works of the period, such as the second part of the allegorical *Roman de la Rose*. It is important to notice how this moral technique (dangerous to a certain extent) affects the *Libro de Buen amor* and the *Confessio*. The archpriest points out his intention to teach good love, although he offers (without recommending it) the possibility of choosing the wrong form of love:

> Onde yo, de mi poquilla çiençia de mucha e grand rudeza, ent[end]iendo quántos bienes faze perder al alma e al cuerpo e los males muchos que les apareja e trae el amor loco del pecado del mundo, escogiendo e amando con buena voluntad salvaçión e gloria del Paraíso para mi ánima, fiz esta chica escriptura en memoria de bien e conpuse este nuevo libro en que son escriptas algunas maneras e maestrías e sotilezas engañosas del loco amor del mundo, que usan algunos para pecar. Las quales, leyéndolas e oyéndolas omne o m[u]ger de buen entendimiento que se quiera salvar, descogerá e obrarlo ha. E podrá dezir con el salmista: *Viam veritatis e cetera* . Otrosí los de poco entendimiento non se perderán; ca leyendo e coidando el mal que fazen o tienen en la voluntad de fazer e [...] los porfiosos de sus malas maestrías, e descobrimiento publicado de sus muchas engañosas maneras que usan para pecar e engañar las mujeres, acordarán la memoria e non despreçiarán su fama; ca mucho es cruel quien su fama menospreçia: el Derecho lo dize. E querrán más amar a sí mesmos que al pecado; que la ordenada caridad, de sí mesmo comiença: el Decreto lo dize. E desecharán e aborrescerán las maneras e maestrías malas del loco amor que faze perder las almas e caer en saña de Dios, apocando la vida e dando fama e deshonra e muchos daños a los cuerpos.
>
> Enpero. Porque es umanal cosa el pecar, si algunos, lo que non los consejo, quisieren usar del loco amor, aquí fallarán algunas maneras para ello. E ansí este mi libro a todo omne o muger, al cuerdo e al non cuerdo, al que entendiere bien e escogiere salvaçión e obrare bien amando a Dios, otrosí al que quisiere el amor loco, en la carrera que andudiere puede cada uno bien dezir: *Intellectum tibi dabo e cetera.* (Prose prologue)[34]

The *Confessio*, in its narrative closing, also offers the same duality between good love and bad love found in the archpriest's book. This is the ending in Gower's exemplary story of Apolonius:

> Por esto, fijo mjo, puedes bien entender quanto es bueno amar bien o mal, e que cosa es amor bueno o no, e el amor que es en buena manera, o no, e commo el gualardon dello sola mente proçede del buen seruyçio; que, avnque Fortuna no sea en sy estable, ella a las veses es fauorable a aquellos que son en amor verdaderos. Mas es de aver pesar del amor que es vsado contra natura, porque es cosa que trahe a los onbres a mal acabamyento, segun que de suso me oyste desyr.
>
> Por ende, fijo mjo, yo te consejo que no vses de otro amor, saluo donde amor e rrason amos a buena fyn son acordados.
> *Confisyon*, fols. 394r.a.-394v.a.)[35]

This piece of advice in favour of good is not a frivolous comment. Gower's moralising intention, from the ambiguous and dangerous technique of analysing cases of love, is explicit. For Genius, love has not been an obstacle to achieve a correct moral education. It has been an excuse to teach *Amans* a correct moral behaviour using positive and negative examples:

> Ca, en el comyenço de aquesta tu confisyon, te promety que no enbargante que yo allegado fuese a la diesa Benus, por onrra de mj orden saçerdotal, yo de mj ofiçio te enseñaria tal dotrina, por la qual te ovieses de ynclјnar mas a virtudes que a viçios
>
> [...] Por ende, fijo mjo, lo que de nantes te dixe, agora te lo torno a rretifycar otra vez, que te levantes antes que caygas, en tal guysa que te puedas leuantar quando quisyeres. Ca Amor, que syenpre fue çiego, hase çiegos a todos aquellos que lo syruen. E, sy tu antes desto estovieste en este caso, tienpo es que te arrepientas dello e sometas tu coraçon a aquella ley que por rrason es gouernada e no por voluntad. E, por enseñança de aquesto que te digo, asaz de enxenplos te he contado, por los quales puedes entender que toda delectaçion dura muy poco.
>
> Agora, fijo myo, parte de lo que te queria dezjr tienes conçebido en la tu voluntad. E, sy tu creyeres la mj dotrina o no, de aqui adelante se pareçera τ sera sabido. Ca yo non te puedo mas dezjr, saluo enseñarte el camyno derecho. A tu escoger sea, sy qujsyeres beujr o morir.
> (*Confisyon*, fols. 395v.a.-396v.a.)[36]

Amans must choose between good and bad, the two moral possibilities. However, Genius is not equivocal when addressing the real receptor of his message, the king:

> Mas buen consejo traspasa todas cosas e espeçial mente en aquel que entiende de ser rrey, asy commo de todos los onbres general mente cada vno en su cabo tiene de judgar vn rreyno, conviene a saber, sy el mal rregyr de su juyzjo sera causa de perderse a sy mesmo. Ca aquel que no a poder de rregyr a sy mesmo, las piedras preçiosas e las caxcas de los atarmuses todo le esta en vn valor, porque, avnque touyese todo el mundo a su mandado, tanto que su coraçon no quiera guardar njn lo guyar commo deue, engaña a sy mesmo τ todos sus fechos son vanos.
> (*Confisyon*, fols. 396r.a.-396r.b.)[37]

After this strict sermon, it seems inevitable that *Amans* should choose the good path taught by Genius through his exempla *ex contrario*. However, the Ovidian tradition that has been used requires *Amans* to choose the dangers of mad love in order to learn the lesson:

> Estonçes entre mj y el my clerigo ovo vna habla de grant posybylidat e muy prolixa. Ca, no enbargante que mj rrazon no entendiese bien, lo que me el consejaua todo hera verdad y por mj grant bien. Pero la mj voluntad del su rrasonar fiso pequeña cuenta,

porque en cosa de tamaño seso al que con rrazon es afyncado, vienele dello poco plazer njn folgança. Porque donde Amor es señor del coraçon del onbre τ rrazon no a lugar en el, commo cosas muy contrarias que no tienden a vn fyn. Asy que, sobre aquesto, yo τ mj clerigo estamos desabenydos.
(*Confisyon*, fols. 397r.b.-397v.a.)[38]

Amans chooses the path of bad love since, as he says, "Nature techeth me the weie/ To love" (VIII, ll.2232-3) as in the case of animals. Similarly, the archpriest of Hita decides to choose mad love because of his natural determination in love:

Como dize Aristótiles, cosa es verdadera,
El mundo por dos cosas trabaja: la primera,
Por aver mantenençia; la otra cosa era
Por aver juntamiento con fenbra plazentera. (s. 71)

Que diz verdat el sabio clarame[n]te se prueva:
Omnes, aves, animalias, toda bestia de cueva
Quieren segund natura conpaña siempre nueva,
E quanto más el omne que toda cosa que.s mueva. (s. 73)

E yo, como só omne como otro, pecador,
Ove de las mugeres a las vezes grand amor;
Provar omne las cosas non es por ende peor,
E saber bien e mal, e usar lo mejor. (s. 76)

This obligatory dedication to bad love forces the author to morally punish his character in the plot of his book with the intention to use him as an example for having chosen bad love. The archpriest of Hita fails in all his amorous stories except for four. In the first one, the story of *don Melón y doña Endrina*, the exemplary value of the warning against deception in love is obvious. The moral reproval is presented, not in the argument, but in the poet's sermon:

Assí, señoras dueñas, entended el romançe:
Guardatvos de amor loco, non vos prenda ni alcançe;
Abrid vuestras orejas: el coraçón se lançe
En amor de Dios linpio; loco amor no'l trançe. (s. 904)

Entiende bien mi estoria de la fija del endrino:
Díxela por te dar ensienplo, mas non porque a mí vino;
Guárdate de falsa vieja, de riso de mal vezino,
Sola con omne non te fíes nin te llegues al espino. (s. 910)

In the second story, the archpriest takes advantage of a young and inexperienced lady, who has been deceived or is under the spell of doña Urraca. The punishment follows immediately. After obtaining her love, she dies, and the lover's health weakens as a punishment for the mad love he has enjoyed:

> Como es natural cosa el nasçer e el morir,
> Ovo, por mal pecado, la dueña a fallir:
> Murió a pocos días, ¡non lo puedo dezir!
> ¡Dios perdone su alma e quiérala resçebir!
>
> Con el triste quebranto e con el grand pesar,
> Yo caí en la cama e coidé peligrar;
> Pasaron bien dos días que me non pud levantar;
> Dixe yo: "¡Qué buen manjar, sinon por el escotar!". (s. 943-944)

The archpriest's third amorous success takes place in four wild adventures in which he is successful in a series of burlesque and parodic amorous stories with some ugly, rustic women who abuse the long-suffering lover. Mockery is the mark of moral reproval here and, at the same time, we notice a tendency to use humour as part of the technique of the exemplum *ex contrario*. The same characteristic can be found in Genius's final moralization, far from the previous amorous exempla:

> Fijo mjo, dexando todas las burlas aparte, yo por tu amor te quiero agora dezjr la verdad. (*Confisyon*, fol. 395r.b.)[39]

The archpriest of Hita insists on explaining the reasons for the use of mockery in his exposition, but this should not be misunderstood with the true moral intention of his book:

> E porque de buen seso non puede omne reír,
> Avré algunas bulras aquí a enxerir:
> Cada que las oyeres non quieras comedir
> Salvo en la manera del trobar e dezir. (s. 45)
>
> De la santidat mucha es bien grand liçionario,
> Mas de juego e de burla es chico brevïario;
> Por ende fago punto e çierro mi almario:
> Séavos chica fabla, solaz e letüario. (s.1632)

In his last amorous success, the archpriest wins the love of a nun, doña Garoza; but he only gets from her a pure and spiritual love, far from his initial sinful intention:

> Resçibióme la dueña por su buen servidor;
> Siempre le fui mandado e leal amador;
> Mucho de bien me fizo con Dios en linpio amor:

En quanto ella fue biva, Dios fue mi guïador.

Con mucha oraçión a Dios por mí rogava,
Con la su abstinençia mucho me ayudava;
La su vida muy limpia en Dios se deleitava:
En locura del mundo nunca se trabajava. (s. 1503-1504)

Doña Garoza will die soon (in stanza 1506), after two months of love.

As in the case of the archpriest's Ovidian tradition, the protagonist of the *Confisyon del amante* is morally punished at the end of the book. Gower chooses to ridicule his old age... and impotence:

> Ca tanto que esta diesa Benus paro mjentes a mj rrostro, por manera de escarnyo me dixo en esta guysa:
>
> Bien sabes tu que yo soy aquella Benus que, sola mente busco mys deleytes dondequier que los puedo aver. E, avnque tu trauajes de ganar mj amor, ya so bien çierta que en tu persona pocos deleytes fallare, porque deleytaçion en Amor e cabellos canos, en la camara donde mj coraçon es vsado de aver plaser, no an lugar njn son en vno concordantes. E puesto que tu des agora a entender que tienes coraçon de onbre nuevo e lo muestres de fuera por el tu donayre, bien se muestra que el viejo rroçin no es potro. Ca de ti e de otros muchos, que ya tenes muchos años furtados, fyngiendo ser onbres muy nuevos, y, al tienpo de la prueua, sy verdad quieres dezyr, no dexares de faser alguna falta y quedar con mengua, porque de vna cosa te çertifico que de los que querrien y no pueden, muy pocos son amados. E, por ende, antes que tu en Amor fagas tales prueva quales entiendas con ellas no poder salir, mejor te seria de fader tu juego, maña, τ que te retraigas fermosa mente. Ca puesto que tu pudieses llenar al tu amor, sy no eres bastante para conpljr lo que ha Amor pertenesçe, non se te seguyra dello onrra njn pro, mas, mengoso padeçimyento. Por ende, rrecoje tu coraçon a ti mesmo, por tal que, por tu vano trauajo, mj corte non quede engañada. Ca, avnque tu voluntad sea asaz buena, al cunple al aradro, de lo qual tu eres menguado, segun yo entiendo. Asy que, antes que comyençes cosa que no puedas acabar, cunplete de aver conoçimyento del flaco estado en que eres puesto, por tal que no seas semejante al onbre que se trauaja de tratar mercaduria e non tiene con que la pagar.
>
> Fijo mjo, sy tu quieres mjrar en lo que te he dicho todo pertenesçe a ti, antes que a otro onbre njnguno. E acuerdesete que tu fecho es ya tornado en fue, asy commo la yerua se torna en feno. Por ende, mjenbresete todavia commo ya heres viejo e del poder que soljas aver eres ya mucho falto.
> (*Confisyon*, fols.399v.b.-401v.a.)[40]

The model of exemplum *ex contrario* of the lover educated in the Ovidian tradition has yet another parallelism between the archpriest of Hita and Gower. We are referring to the character of fictitious autobiography adopted for the amorous protagonist. This is the case of the archpriest's multiple poetic I's[41] and of *Amans's* personality, which is revealed in the allegorical ending before the goddess Venus:

> E ella, mjrando a my rrostro, a manera de burla, me pregunto por mj nonbre. Señora, dixe yo, a my llaman Ioan Goer. (*Confisyon*, fols.399v.b.)[42]

The parallelisms that have been pointed out indicate how the *Confessio* and the *Libro de buen amor* are connected to a common moral literary tradition based on the Ovidian model of *exemplum ex contrario*. In both works we find the allegorical model of the *Ars amandi*, in which the teaching is illustrated with different exempla taken from the *Metamorphoses*, the *Epistolæ Heroidum* or the medieval elegiac comedy. This tradition is present not only in such distant works as Gower's and the archpriest of Hita's. As we can see in the allegorical dream vision which closes the *Confessio*, the French *Roman de la Rose*, especially in Jean de Meun's amplification, also shows this tradition and possibly, together with the medieval Latin sources, it is the common bridge between the English and the Peninsular literatures.

The *exemplum ex contrario* shows the taste for the educational model and contents used by Gower, which were also known and valued by the fourteenth- and fifteenth-century Portuguese and Castilian Courts. Both were intimately connected in their courtly culture as shown by the existence of a common learned lyric in Galician-Portuguese until the end of the fourteenth century and in Castilian throughout the fifteenth century.[43] However, its educational use is not shown in an atmosphere in which the receptor of the education is the nobility. In this respect, although the presence of authorities is known in the cultural circuit of the nobility —Alfonso X used them with profusion for his historical and encyclopaedic works—, it is not a characteristic of common use, since the basic scheme of the education of nobles consists of an oral exposition in dialogue form between the teacher (or advisor) and the disciple. This teaching technique appears with profusion in *Confisyon del amante*; and it happens to such an extent that what should have been a clerical structure of *disputatio* between the Priest of Venus and *Amans* becomes, through their dialogues, a question-answer structure typical of the education of nobles. The examples of Aristotle and Alexander perfectly show this system of education of nobles in which the contents of the learned writings are transferred to the noble through the oral explanations of a teacher who has had a scholastic education:

> ...por tanto lo que dello aprendi por tu correbçion te entiendo mostrar, segunt en los libros es contenjdo, avnque yo, de la forma del tal escreuyr, non sea del todo sabidor; pero parte de la materia, segun que la oy, te quiero declarar, porque adelante lo ayas en memoria. (*Confisyon*, fols. 286v.b.-287r.a.)[44]

From the similarities we have found in the three books that were part of king Duarte's library, it is obvious that the theme and didactic structure of the

Confessio have a correspondence with the academic educational tradition which tries to apply its most attractive techniques —the Ovidian tradition— to the education of nobles. The three books coincide in the use of exempla showing their academic sources. These sources are often translated in *Confisyon del amante* using the terms *clérigo* (clerk) and *clerecía* (clergy) as the written source of many exempla,[45] and there is also a need to translate those written sources to the vernacular:

> En las palabras de Ihesu Xristo, quien oviere sabor de leer, fallara en el Evangeljo que El mjsmo da testimonjo en commo este viçio es mucho de temer. E, commoquier que toda la clerezya e toda la lengua latina esto lean e canten en diversas yglesias, pero por mayor conoçimyento de la verdad, la qual es bien de saber, yo, en nuestro lenguaje, te la declarare conpljda mente, segun que en la santa Escriptura se falla. (*Confisyon*, fols. 271r.b.-271v.a.)[46]

The thematic interests of this clergy are similar to those of the late fourteenth-century Castilian nobility. In this respect, a clear example is the confessional frame used by Gower, which coincides with the one used in another fourteenth-century Castilian miscellaneous book of moral value: Pedro López de Ayala's *Rimado de palacio*, also composed for the education of nobles. Likewise, the use of a religious imagery for the development of the amorous theme is one of the most common forms of expression in the lyric; therefore, the love liturgy is well known and highly valued by the peninsular courtiers.[47] The contents and the form of the *Confessio* coincide with the tastes of the fifteenth-century court culture. This is more obvious when we observe that Juan de Cuenca does not limit himself to producing a close translation. He introduces profound moral and cultural modifications in order to adapt Gower's book to the educational needs of his audience.[48] On the other hand, it has already been studied how the Portuguese and Castilian translations were the result of a cultural concern in both Courts, where there was an intensive translation activity of Latin works.[49] Therefore, it seems evident that the translation of Gower's book responds to a cultural demand for a work with the characteristics of the *Confessio* in the fifteenth-century Peninsular Courts.

The comparison of the Castilian translation of the *Confessio* with the Castilian cultural tradition, stemming from the amorous dialogues, shows the coincidence in materials and in tastes among the fifteenth-century Castilian nobility and Gower's model for the education of King Richard II. The coincidence between the Court's demand and what the *Confessio* had to offer can explain its success in both its Portuguese and Castilian translation.

The educational model of the *Confessio* satisfied the fifteenth-century need for a learned education of a type of nobility that not only had to be moral and good rulers of their possessions, but also had to have a certain cultural veneer in which the different authorities from Antiquity should be known while maintaining, at the same time, the scholastic educational and nobiliary traditions.

Throughout the fifteenth century, the Court demanded a better knowledge of the classics and, during that century, the number of translations demanded by the nobles increased considerably. Thus, Gower offered the traditional contents and formulas for the education of the nobility within a classical encyclopaedism that satisfied the needs of education of the new Court culture. This would explain the reasons for the double translation of Gower's *Confessio Amantis*, the first and only case of interest in an English work in the Iberian Middle Ages.

University of Extremadura

Notes

1. See Ramón Menéndez Pidal, "*Elena y María* (Disputa del clérigo y el caballero). Poesía leonesa inédita del siglo XIII", in *Textos medievales españoles. Ediciones críticas y estudios. Obras completas de R. Menéndez Pidal, XII*, Madrid, Espasa Calpe, 1976, pp. 119-159.

2. It consists of an initial love vision and a later dispute between 'water' and 'wine', both belonging to a long goliardic tradition. For the goliardic traditions see Enzo Franchini, *El manuscrito, la lengua y el ser literario de la "Razón de amor"* (Madrid, CSIC, 1993); for the juxtaposed structure see Jesús de Burgos Tovar, "Razón de amor con los denuestos del agua y el vino" (in *El comentario de textos 4: la poesía medieval* , Madrid, Castalia, 1983, pp. 53-83) and Francisco Javier Grande Quejigo, *"Los Denuestos del Agua y el vino:* significados desde su contexto cultural" (in *XVI Jornadas de Viticultura y Enología de Tierra de Barros*, Badajoz, Dirección General de Comercio e Industrias Agrarias de la Consejería de Agricultura y Comercio de la Junta de Extremadura, 1995, pp. 905-926).

3. *Hispanic Rewiew*, 53 (1985) pp. 1-23 and 127-150.

4. In this respect, see the theses of the editors of both works (Jesús Cañas Murillo, ed., *Libro de Alexandre*, Cátedra, 1995, 2nd ed; and Manuel Alvar, *Libro de Apolonio. Estudios, ediciones, Concordancias*, 3 vols, Madrid, Fundación Juan March-Castalia, 1976). We also have to take into consideration Patrizia Caraffi, "*Clerecía, alegoría, escriptura*. Sull'identificazione con l'eroe *nel Libro de Alexandre*", *Medioevo Romanzo* 13 (1988), pp. 237-252 ; Mary Jane Kelley, "Mixed Messages in the *Libro de Apolonio*", *Journal of Interdisciplinary Literary Studies* , 2 (1990), pp. 1-11 , Jamile Trueba Lawand "El *Libro de Apolonio*, modelo del caballero virtuoso", *Romance Notes*, 36 (1996), pp. 261-264 and Francisco Javier Grande Quejigo, "Huellas textuales indirectas sobre la difusión oral de la literatura en el *Libro de Alexandre*", *Anuario de Estudios Filológicos* 20 (1997), pp. 169-190, "Huellas textuales indirectas sobre la difusión escrita de la literatura en el *Libro de Alexandre*", *Anuario de Estudios Filológicos*, 21 (1998), pp. 119-139.

5. See an updated *status questionis* and an extensive bibliography in Guillermo Serés, *Don Juan Manuel, El conde Lucanor*, Barcelona, Crítica, 1994.

6. Peter Russell, *Traducciones y traductores en la Peninsula Ibérica (1400-1550)*, Barcelona, Universidad Autónoma de Barcelona, 1984.

7. The Ovidian element in Juan Ruiz, Arcipreste de Hita, has been analysed by Francisco Rico in his masterful "Sobre el origen de la autobiografía en el *Libro de buen amor*", *Anuario de Estudios Medievales*, 4 (1967), pp. 301-325.

8. In this respect, apart from Francisco Rico's article, cited before, Alberto Blecua's introduction to his edition of the *Libro de buen amor* (Madrid, Cátedra, 1992) is also fundamental.

9. See Benito Brancaforte, *Las "Metamorfosis" y las "Herodias" de Ovidio en la "General estoria" de Alfonso el Sabio*, Madison, Hispanic Seminary of Medieval Studies, 1990.

10. In which, incidentally, there are many exempla in its contents.

11. Alfonso X, in his *Partidas*, when defining the concept of 'Court', presents the following cultural picture: "E los que desto se guardaren, e usaren de las palabras buenas e apuestas, llamáranlos buenos e enseñados; e otrosí llamáranlos corteses porque las bondades e los otros buenos enseñamientos a que llaman cortesía, siempre los fallaron e los preçiaron en las cortes" (in M.J. Lacarra & F. López Estrada, *Orígenes de la prosa*, Madrid, Júcar, 1993, p. 163).

12. See Alfonso X, *General estoria IV. La historia novelada de Alejandro Magno. Edición acompañada del original latino de la "Historia de preliis" (recensión J2)*, Tomás González Rolán & Pilar Saquero Suárez-Somonte, eds., Madrid, Universidad Complutense, 1982.

13. See Carmen Monedero's introduction to her edition of the *Libro de Apolonio* (Madrid, Castalia, 1987). Her statements on p. 60 suggest that Alfonso X and Gower used the same sources.

14. See João José Alves Dias, ed., *Livro dos conselhos de El-Rei D. Duarte (Livro da Cartuxa)* (Lisboa, ed. Estampa, 1982), pp. 206-208.

15. Francisco Rico, however, defends the idea that the *Roman* could have had a more direct influence in Juan Ruiz than has been admitted. See "'Por aver mantenencia'. El aristotelismo heterodoxo en el *Libro de buen amor*", *El Crotalón*, II,1985, pp.169-198; rpt. in *Homenaje a José Antonio Maravall*, Madrid, CSIC, 1986, pp. 271-297.

16. The quotations are taken from Alberto Blecua's edition, *op. cit.*

17. A series of fables follow in order to exemplify the different deadly sins for which love is responsible. The closing fable is the one introduced by stanza 407.

18. Stanzas 181-187 can be an example of the justification of the exemplum. Here Love is accused of fickleness.

19. The quotations of Juan de Cuenca's *Confisyon del amante* are from Bernardo Santano's transcription of Ms. g-ii-19 of the Royal Library of El Escorial. The passage quoted above corresponds to the following lines in Gower's English text:

> My Sone, I am assigned hiere
> Be Venus the godesse above,
> Whos Prest I am touchende of love.
> Bot natheles for certein skile
> I mot algate and nedes wile
> Noght only make my spekynges
> Of love, bot of othre thinges,
> That touchen to the cause of vice. (*C.A.* Book I, ll.234-41)

All quotations of the *Confessio Amantis* are taken from G.C. Macaulay, *The English Works of John Gower*, Vols. I & II, Oxford: O.U.P., 1900, rpt. 1969.

20. These are the lines that correspond to this fragment in Gower's text:

> Mi Sone, herkne now forthi
> A tale, to be war therby
> Thin yhe forto kepe and warde,

So that it passe noght his warde. (*C.A.* Book I, ll.329-32)

21. Although the Castilian translation is somewhat free, these would be the lines that correspond to this fragment in Gower's text:

Mi Sone, thou schalt understonde,
In love and othre thinges alle
If that Surquiderie falle,
It may to him noght wel betide
Which useth thilke vice of Pride,
Which torneth wisdom to wenynge
And Sothfastnesse into lesynge
Thurgh fol ymaginacion.
And for thin enformacion,
That thou this vice as I the rede
Eschuic schalt, a tale I rede,
Which fell whilom be daies olde,
So as the clerk Ovide tolde. (*C.A.* Book I, ll. 2262-74)

22. *Confessio Amantis*:

Now herkne a tale that is soth:
Thogh it be noght of loves kinde,
A gret ensample thou schalt finde
This veine gloire forto fle,
Which is so full of vanite. (Book I, ll. 2780-84)

23. *Confessio Amantis*:

And who that wolde ensamples telle,
Be olde daies as thei felle,
Than mihte a man wel understonde
Such love mai noght longe stonde.
Now herkne, Sone, and thou schalt hiere
A gret ensample of this matiere. (Book V, ll. 2637-42)

24. *Confessio Amantis*:

Now goode fader, I you preie,
That forto wisse me the more,
Som good ensample upon this lore
Ye wolden telle of that is write,
That I the betre mihte wite
How I Folhaste scholde eschuie,
And the wisdom of conseil suie.
Mi Sone, that thou miht enforme
Thi pacience upon the forme
Of old essamples, as thei felle,
Now understond what I schal telle. (Book III, ll. 1746-56)

25. *Confessio Amantis*:

I thonke you, my fader diere,
This scole is of a gentil lore;
And if ther be oght elles more
Of Pride, which I schal eschuie,
Now axeth forth, and I wol suie
What thing that ye me wole enforme.

Mi Sone, yit in other forme
Ther is a vice of Prides lore,
Which lich an hauk whan he wol sore,
Fleith upon heihte in his delices
After the likynge of his vices,
And wol no mannes resoun knowe,
Till he doun falle and overthrowe.
This vice veine gloire is hote,
Wherof, my Sone, I thee behote
To trete and speke in such a wise,
That thou thee myht the betre avise. (Book I, ll. -2664-80)

26. Don Juan Manuel, *El conde Lucanor* (G. Serés, ed., Barcelona, Crítica, 1994), 14-15.

27. *Confessio Amantis*:

Mi goode fader, grant mercy,
For evere I schal be war therby:
Of love what me so befalle,
Such Sorcerie aboven alle
Fro this dai forth I schal eschuie,
That so ne wol I noght poursuie
Mi lust of love forto seche.
Bot this I wolde you beseche,
Beside that me stant of love,
As I you herde speke above
Hou Alisandre was betawht
To Aristotle, and so wel tawht
Of al that to a king belongeth,
Wherof min herte sore longeth
To wite what it wolde mene.
For be reson I wolde wene
That if I herde of thinges strange,
Yit for a time it scholde change
Mi peine, and lisse me somdiel. (Book VI, ll.2401-19)

28. *Confessio Amantis*:

...I the Scole schal declare
Of Aristotle and ek the fare
Of Alisandre, hou he was tauht,
I am somdel therof destrauht;
For it is noght to the matiere
Of love, why we sitten hiere
To schryve, so as Venus bad.
Bot natheles, for it is glad,
So as thou seist, for thin aprise
To hiere of suche thinges wise,
Wherof thou myht the time lisse,
So as I can, I schal the wisse:
For wisdom is at every throwe
Above alle other thing to knowe

In loves cause and elleswhere.
Forthi, my Sone, unto thin Ere,
Though it be noght in the registre
Of Venus, yit of that Calistre
And Aristotle whylom write
To Alisandre, thou schalt wite. (Book VII, ll. 3-22)

29. A very useful summary can be found in Margherita Morreale's *Historia de la Literatura Española*, Madrid, Cátedra, 1990, I, pp. 211-222.

30. For a study of the learned metaphor of the 'bee', see João Dionísio, "Uma abelha no prólogo. Sobre um desejo formulado no inicio do *Leal conselleiro* de don Duarte", *Revista da Biblioteca Nacional*,10 (1995), pp. 7-22.

31. In the Castilian text, this reference appears as part of the main text, but in Gower's book this comment is made in a marginal note in Latin:

> ...Iohannes Gower... tamquam fauum ex variis floribus recollectum, presentem libellum ex variis cronicis, historiis, poetarum philosophorumque dictis...estudiosissime compilauit.

G.C. Macaulay, *op. cit.*, pp. 3-4.

32. This is according to the structure of the book as analysed by Jesús Cañas in his edition of *Alexandre* (Madrid, Cátedra, 1995, 2nd ed.).

33. *Confessio Amantis*:

Lo, what it is to be wel grounded:
For he hath ferst his love founded
Honesteliche as forto wedde,
Honesteliche his love he spedde
And hadde children with his wif,
And as him liste he ladde his lif;
And in ensample his lif was write,
That alle lovers myhten wite
How ate laste it schal be sene
Of love what thei wolden mene.
For se now on that other side,
Antiochus with al his Pride,
Which sette his love unkindely,
His ende he hadde al sodeinly,
Set ayein kinde upon vengance,
And for his lust hath his penance.
Lo thus, mi Sone, myht thou liere
What is to love in good manere,
And what to love in other wise:
The mede arist of the servise; (Book VIII, ll.1993-2012)

34. Alberto Blecua's edition (Madrid, Cátedra, 1992), pp. 9-10.

35. *Confessio Amantis*:

Lo thus, mi Sone, myht thou liere
What is to love in good manere,
And what to love in other wise:
The mede arist of the servise;
Fortune, thogh sche be noght stable,
Yit at som time is favorable

To hem that ben of love trewe.
Bot certes it is forto rewe
To se love ayein kinde falle,
For that makth sore a man to falle,
As thou myht of tofore rede.
Forthi, my Sone, I wolde rede
To lete al other love aweie,
Bot if it be thurgh such a weie
As love and reson wolde acorde. (Book VIII, ll.2009-2023)

36. *Confessio Amantis*:

For I behihte thee that yifte
Ferst whan thou come under my schrifte,
That thogh I toward Venus were,
Yit spak I suche wordes there,
That for the Presthod which I have,
Min ordre and min astat to save,
I seide I wolde of myn office
To vertu more than to vice
Encline, and teche thee mi lore.
[...]
And thus, my Sone, I wolde sein,
As I seide er, that thou aryse,
Er that thou falle in such a wise
That thou ne myht thiself rekevere;
For love, which that blind was evere,
Makth alle his servantz blinde also.
My Sone, and if thou have be so,
Yit is it time to withdrawe,
And set thin herte under that lawe,
The which of reson is governed
And noght of will. And to be lerned,
Ensamples thou hast many on
Of now and ek of time gon,
That every lust is bot a while;
And who that wole himself beguile,
He may the rathere be deceived.
Mi Sone, now thou hast conceived
Somwhat of that I wolde mene;
Hierafterward it schal be sene
If that thou lieve upon mi lore;
For I can do to thee nomore
Bot teche thee the rihte weie:
Now ches if thou wolt live or deie. (Book VIII, ll. 2075-83/ 2126-48)

37. *Confessio Amantis*:

For conseil passeth alle thing
To him which thenkth to ben a king;
And every man for his partie
A kingdom hath to justefie,

That is to sein his oghne dom.
If he misreule that kingdom,
He lest himself, and that is more
Than if he loste Schip and Ore
And al the worldes good withal:
For what man that in special
Hath noght himself, he hath noght elles,
Nomor the perles than the schelles;
Al is to him of o value:
Thogh he hadde at his retenue
The wyde world ryht as he wolde,
Whan he his herte hath noght withholde
Toward himself, al is in vein. (Book VIII, ll. 2109-25)

38. *Confessio Amantis*:
Tho was betwen mi Prest and me
Debat and gret perplexete:
Mi resoun understod him wel,
And knew it was sothe everydel
That he hath seid, bot noght forthi
Mi will hath nothing set therby.
For techinge of so wis a port
Is unto love of no desport;
Yit myhte nevere man beholde
Reson, wher love was withholde,
Thei be noght of o governance.
And thus we fellen in distance, (Book VIII, ll.2189-200)

39. *Confessio Amantis*:
Mi Sone, unto the trouthe wende
Now wol I for the love of thee,
And lete alle othre truffles be. (Book VIII, ll. 2060-2)

40. *Confessio Amantis*:
For whan sche hath me wel beholde,
Halvynge of scorn, sche seide thus:
"Thou wost wel that I am Venus,
Which al only my lustes seche;
And wel I wot, thogh thou beseche
Mi love, lustes ben ther none,
Whiche I mai take in thi persone;
For loves lust and lockes hore
In chambre acorden neveremore,
And thogh thou feigne a yong corage,
It scheweth wel be the visage
That olde grisel is no fole:
There ben fulmanye yeres stole
With thee and with suche othre mo,
That outward feignen youthe so
And ben withinne of pore assay.
Min herte wolde and I ne may

Is noght beloved nou adayes;
Er thou make eny suche assaies
To love, and faile upon the fet,
Betre is to make a beau retret;
For thogh thou myhtest love atteigne,
Yit were it bot an ydel peine,
Whan that thou art noght sufficant
To holde love his covenant.
Forthi tak hom thin herte ayein,
That thou travaile noght in vein,
Wherof my Court may be deceived.
I wot and have it wel conceived,
Hou that thi will is good ynowh;
Bot mor behoveth to the plowh,
Wherof the lacketh, as I trowe:
So sitte it wel that thou beknowe
Thi fieble astat, er thou beginne
Thing wher thou miht non ende winne.
What bargain scholde a man assaie,
Whan that him lacketh forto paie?
Mi Sone, if thou be wel bethoght,
This toucheth thee; foryet it noght:
The thing is torned into was;
That which was whilom grene gras,
Is welked hey at time now.
Forthi mi conseil is that thou
Remembre wel hou thou art old". (Book VIII, ll.-2396-2439)

41. See Francisco Rico, "Sobre el origen de la autobiografía..." and Alfonso Rey, "Juan Ruiz, don Melón de la Huerta y el yo poético medieval", *Bulletin of Hispanic Studies* LVI (1979), pp. 103-116.

42. *Confessio Amantis*:

Sche caste hire chiere upon mi face,
And as it were halvinge a game
Sche axeth me what is mi name.
"Ma dame", I seide, "John Gower". (Book VIII, ll. 2318-21)

43. We can also add the importance of the Castilian models in the Portuguese Court from the end of the fourteenth century and throughout the fifteenth century. This is the case of historiography through the Count of Barcelos's Portuguese version of Alfonso X's chronicle or Fernando Lopes's chronicles, which follow Pedro López de Ayala's model.

44. *Confessio Amantis*:

Yit thenke I forto specefie,
In boke as it is comprehended,
Wherof thou mihtest ben amended.
For thogh I be noght al cunnynge
Upon the forme of this wrytynge,
Som part therof yit have I herd,
In this matiere hou it hath ferd. (Book VI, ll. 2434-40)

45. There are may references to *Ovidio, el grande clerigo* ("the grete Clerk Ovide").

46. *Confessio Amantis*:

Of Cristes word, who wole it rede,
Hou that this vice is forto drede
In thevangile it telleth plein,
Which mot algate be certein,
For Crist himself it berth witnesse.
And thogh the clerk and the clergesse
In latin tunge it rede and singe,
Yit for the more knoulechinge
Of trouthe, which is good to wite,
I schal declare as it is write
In Engleissh, for thus it began. (Book VI, ll. 975-85)

47. See E. Michael Gerli, "La *religión del amor* y el antifeminismo en las letras castellanas del siglo XV", *Hispanic Review*, 49 (1981), pp. 65-86.

48. See Bernardo Santano Moreno, *Estudio sobre "Confessio Amantis" de John Gower y su versión castellana, "Confisyon del Amante" de Juan de Cuenca*, Cáceres, Universidad de Extremadura, 1990.

49. See Bernardo Santano Moreno, *op. cit.*, and Peter Russell, *op. cit.*

The European *Querelle des femmes*

Gisela Bock and Margarete Zimmermann

I *Querelle des femmes* and *Querelle du féminisme*

For a long time I have hesitated to write a book on woman. The subject is irritating, especially to women; and it is not new. Enough ink has been spilled in the quarrelling over feminism, now practically over, and perhaps we should say no more about it. It is still talked about, however, for the voluminous nonsense uttered during the last century seems to have done little to illuminate the problem. After all– is there a problem? And if so, what is it?[1]

Simone de Beauvoir begins her essay *Le Deuxième Sexe* (*The Second Sex*, 1949) with these words and it is surely no accident that she speaks of the *querelle du féminisme* in her programmatic introduction. With the term *querelle* she evokes, firstly, the long tradition of late medieval and early modern gender quarrels in texts and images which ever since the last turn of the century, and originating in France, has been known as the *querelle des femmes*. In a broader sense and more adequately it has been termed the *querelle des sexes* which until recently mainly referred to the French participants in this debate.[2] From the late 19th century onwards the respective Italian quarrel is called "polemics on the female sex".[3] With the word "feminism" Beauvoir takes up a term coined for the modern tendencies of the women's movement in late-19th-century France. It's definition was from the beginning a matter of debate and the term "feminism" spread internationally since the turn of the last century but was only explicitly and comprehensively appropriated by feminists of the "second wave". Thirdly, Beauvoir links *féminisme*, so to speak *ante litteram*, to the important debate of the "women's question" which dominated the 19th and continued far into the 20th century. In her historical survey, Beauvoir looks back to the old quarrel, the *vieille querelle*, but without defining any historical breaks or specific moments in this gender debate. Beauvoir's use of the *querelle des femmes* is symptomatic in more than one respect since it reveals the considerable casualness with which the concept is applied although its content and historical dimension, including the history of the word, continue to be undefined.

The term is ambiguous even in its linguistic appearance: in the nominal phrase, *querelle des femmes* can be a *genetivus subjectivus* (women's quarrel or quarrel of the sexes) as well as a *genetivus objectivus* (quarrel over the women or sexes). Thus, women can be both subjects and objects of the debate. And since Christine de Pizan's time, whose voice was the first (known) female voice to intervene in the quarrel, women's utterances have indeed increased, in spite of the fact that male voices – speaking for or against women – were to dominate for a long time. In German, the term is usually translated as "Debatte um die Frauen" (debate over women), "Frauenstreit" (women's quarrel) or "Geschlechterstreit" (gender quarrel).[4] In English, it is known as the "quarrel of the sexes", sometimes also as "war" or even "civil war".[5]

More recently, the French term has been used in all three languages (but not in Italian), a development resulting from Joan Kelly's widely received article "Early Feminist Theory and the *Querelle des femmes*, 1400-1789" (1982).[6] In any case, one should not overlook the complex history of the lexeme combination *querelle des femmes*: the meaning of *querelle* itself undergoes historical change.

Neither dictionaries nor reference works from various disciplines are able to provide a way out of the terminological chaos. The *querelle des femmes* is such a comprehensive phenomenon of European cultural history that it cannot be adequately described by a single discipline; and we still lack reliable women and gender history handbooks providing us with overviews or basic introductions. The different *querelle* varieties can perhaps be best perceived as a recurrent characteristic of French literature, as Augustin Simon Irailh attempts to show in his wide-ranging synthesis *Querelles littéraires* (1761) which in spite of its title does not throw any light on the literary variants of the *querelle des femmes*.[7] We want to sketch the historical outlines of the *querelle des femmes* in order to give the term a more reliable scientific footing and to encourage further research, since, as Marc Bloch has put it, "the best way to avoid being fooled by a word is to analyse its history."[8] At the same time we want to contextualise the *querelle des femmes* historically in two ways. On the one hand, the forms and content of the *querelle des femmes* differ according to its context, particularly in terms of place and time, and especially in its various national contexts. On the other hand, the academic use of the term also needs to be historicized since it too possesses an inherent dynamic and a history within which any (serious) recourse to the *querelle des femmes* has to situate itself. We intend to counteract the occasional carelessness with which it is often applied, thus restoring the dignity to an important gender-historical term. Furthermore, we intend to provide an insight into the international and multidisciplinary offshoots of this debate[9] although we can only hint at the Europe-wide circulation and effect of some texts such as, e.g., the treatise *Declamatio de nobilitate et praecellentia foeminei sexus (Declamation on the Nobility and Excellence of the Female Sex)* by Heinrich Cornelius Agrippa von Nettesheim, written in 1509 and published in Latin in 1529, in German in 1540;[10] or the *Disputatio nova contra mulieres, qua probatur eas homines non esse (A New Argument Against Women)* (1595) which was distributed all over Europe and which denied women their status as human beings, thus provoking numerous counter-publications. Four years later Giuseppe Passi's pamphlet *I donneschi diffetti (Women's Failings)* was published in Italy, bringing the Italian *querelle* to a head.[11] Particularly close relations of exchange and influence occurred within Romance-language areas, and in Italy learned Jews also participated in the debate in their hybrid Hebrew-Italian language.[12]

We intend first and foremost to illustrate the meaning and importance of the term *querelle des femmes*, to provide an insight into its many points of reference, and to mark out a field of research – hoping that in future the discussion may expand and that neighbouring disciplines, in addition to history and literary studies, may add their own contributions.[13]

II The History of the Word

The *querelle des femmes* was a specifically European and as it seems a Europe-wide phenomenon,[14] but the term is associated most of all with France, in particular with the late-medieval and early modern sources. In Martin Le Franc's *Le Champion des Dames (Defender of Women)* (1440-1442), a long-winded allegory in the tradition of the *Romance of the Rose* (13th century) as well as Christine de Pizan's *City of Ladies* (1404/5), one finds – to the best of our knowledge – the first use of the term. Not however, as *querelle des femmes* but as "*querelle des dames*". Even in the dedicatory epistle, addressed to the Duke of Burgundy, Philip the Good is spoken of as the defender of the "querelle des dames" and his partisanship for "*la querelle des dames*" is emphasized several times.[15] In general, one can say that the text is intended as a powerful defense of the female sex, instigated by Cupid, the God of Love – here Martin Le Franc draws on Christine de Pizan's *Epistre au Dieu d'Amours (Letter from Cupid)* (1399)[16] – who sends the defender of women, *Franc Vouloir (Free Will)* onto the gender-battlefield against the slanderous *Malebouche (Badmouth)*. It is *Franc Vouloir's* task to fight for the *querelle des dames* which in this instance is also a *querelle d'amours*. The battle resembles a court procedure: the plaintiff *Malebouche* and the council for the defense, *Franc Vouloir*, engage in long verbal battles which take place within a fictitious court. *Querelle* signifies "request, matter of concern" as well as (legal) "complaint" in this as well as in other relevant texts.[17] Women only appear as objects of the quarrel in this context, as objects of speech who hand their concerns over to male advocates.[18] In this respect, Martin Le Franc falls behind Christine de Pizan, who lets the women speak for themselves in her *City of Ladies*. Her text-persona, Christine, together with the eloquent allegories of virtue, Justice, Reason and Honesty, develops a new concept of femininity and destroys the allegedly sacrosanct power of traditional ideas with the help of trenchant dialogues.

A short survey of the term *querelle's* changing semantics illuminates the most important phases in the term's history and development.[19] Its Latin etymon is *querel(l)a* and signifies an expression of pain as well as displeasure: a charge in the sense of grievance or complaint. In Old French, *querelle* dates back to the 12th century and encompasses the semantic fields of "contradiction" and (legal) "complaint, charge", later also "dispute", "matter of concern", "case", and "cause". The lexeme's use in the sense of "grievance, complaint" becomes rarer even during the Old French period. From 1535 onwards – i.e. from that period onwards in which the *querelle des femmes* reaches a new peak after the quarrel over the *Romance of the Rose* sparked off by Christine de Pizan around 1400[20] –

the meaning of *querelle* as dispute, squabble, or controversy begins to dominate. From the 17th century onwards *querelle* in the sense of lament virtually disappears and the usages "dispute", "fight", "disagreement", and "legal complaint" (the latter's use diminishes during the 18th century) gain ascendancy. The semantic element "gender controversy" dominates in the voluminous apology of the male sex by the Southern French lawyer Gratien Du Pont in his *Controverses des sexes masculin et féminin (Controversies of the Male and Female Sex)* (1534), a text which also conveys the impression of a concentration within the discursive field of *querelle* texts as well as an acceleration of the debate at this point in time.[21] Twenty years later the philogynously inclined Guillaume Postel takes up the cause of "[...] la commune querelle dont on charge à tort le sexe féminin".[22] From 1541 onwards the debate broadens out to include the *querelle d'amours*. It begins with the poem *L'Amye de court (The Courtly Friend)* (1541) by Bertrand de la Borderie to which other authors react with "counter-poems" (*La Contr'amye de court, The Counter-Courtly Friend)*.[23]

Two hundred years after Christine de Pizan, women once again participate in the discussion, e.g. with Marie de Romieu's *Brief discours que l'excellence de la femme surpasse celle de l'homme (Brief Discourse On Women's Excellence Surpassing That of Men)* (1581),[24] with Catherine des Roches[25] and in particular with Marie de Gournay's *Egalité des hommes et des femmes (Men and Women's Equality)* (1622/23) and *Grief des femmes (Women's Grief)* (1626).[26] A new quality is thus added to the debate which is enriched by new aspects, particularly concerning the debate over marriage. Femininity now no longer refers to the generic "woman", she is no longer merely an object of speech or only present in the shape of the unattainable ideal of the *famous women*. Femininity manifests itself as a mocking, indignant, angry feminine voice in a debate which has again become a dialogue of the sexes.

It is during the same period that women in Italy join the debate, in particular in Venice with Moderata Fonte's text *Il merito delle donne (The Merits of Women)* (1600).[27] It was not Moderata Fonte – she died in 1592 – but Lucrezia Marinelli with her text *Le nobilità et eccellenze delle donne et i diffetti, e mancamenti de gli huomini (The Nobility and Excellent Qualities of Women and the Failings and Faults of Men)* (1600)[28] who reacted to the above-mentioned diatribe against women by Giuseppe Passi (1599) which itself was a reaction to earlier texts. As late as the mid-17th century the last text by the nun Arcangela Tarabotti (*Che le donne siano della spetie degli huomini. Difesa delle Donne*, 1651) *(That Woman is of the Same Species As Man. Defense of Women)*, is written as a polemical response to the Italian translation (1647) of that anonymous *Disputatio nova* which had provoked such a controversy in Germany in 1595. But in this as in other texts Tarabotti goes far beyond a simple riposte and develops a new vision of women's liberty.[29]

In England, the first female voice to enter the discussion can be found in 1589: using the pseudonym Jane Anger it polemicizes against a misogynous pamphlet. Polemic and pamphlet were both characteristics of the English *querelle* in the 16th and 17th centuries, as well as the use of pseudonyms, in particular in the case of the more aggressive treatises and titles *(Esther hath hang'd Haman*, 1617; *The Women's Sharp Revenge*, 1640) or the satirical "pamphlet war" between *Hic Mulier:, or, the Man-Woman* and *Haec Vir:, or, The Womanish Man* (both 1620).[30] Attempts have recently been made to uncover the true authorship or at least the author's sex hidden behind the pseudonyms, the satirical and fictitious names (e.g. Jane Anger, Mary Tattlewell, Joane Hit-him-home) or the anonymous authors – in 16th-century France numerous anonymous writers existed as well – and some assumptions have had to be revised accordingly.[31] The English gender quarrel is characterized by an impressive variety as regards form and content.[32] And while some work has been done regarding the Spanish context, other areas, in particular Middle and Eastern Europe, still remain largely unresearched.[33]

When we return to the *querelle des femmes'* primary history of the word, we have to observe that the term becomes rarer in French sources from the first half of the 16th century onwards. In particular the titles, to whose programmatic role and transformations Adriana Chemello has drawn attention,[34] in French often use words such as "controversy", "debate", "defence", "apology", occasionally also "war" or terms derived from inferiority and superiority *topoi.*[35] It is probably since the late 17th century at the latest that the lexeme *querelle* begins to carry negative connotations and is therefore more and more often replaced by "controversy", "fight" or "war".[36] Titles such as "della eccellenza et dignità delle donne" (*On the Excellence and Dignity of Women*), "la nobilità delle donne" (*Women's Nobility*), "difesa delle donne" (*Defense of Women*), "dell'eccellentia de l'huomo sopra quella de la donna" (*Of Man's Excellence Which is Superior to that of Woman*) dominate in Italian and while the titles may not contain the word "querellarsi" (to quarrel) the texts themselves do.[37] In Germany, one can find "Defensio sexus muliebris" (*Defense of the Female Sex*) (1595), "certamen masculo-foemineum" (*Male-Female Fight*) (1602 and 1606), "Disputatio" (*Dispute*) (1629), "Ehren-Preiß" (*In Praise of Honour*) (1663), "Lob-Rede" (*Eulogy*) (1716), and in 1639, Christiana Mariana von Ziegler's satirical ode "Das männliche Geschlecht, besungen im Namen einiger Frauenzimmer" (*The Male Sex, Celebrated in the Name of Some Women*) appeared.[38] In the succeeding period occasional references to the *querelle* – e.g. when Joseph von Eichendorff writes of the "equally old and curious dispute" in 1847[39] – cannot hide the fact that the term *querelle* recedes into the background.

In the early modern period the *querelle des femmes* was not the only *querelle* and controversy and dialogue were popular forms of representation. In 1516, Erasmus of Rotterdam's *Querela Pacis* ("The Complaint of Peace who was disowned and destroyed by all peoples") appeared and was re-published several times and translated into many languages.[40] Paintings by Pieter Breughel demonstrate the dispute between fasting and gluttony. 17th-century German

Pietism produced an impressive array of disputational texts.[41] Numerous scholars participated in the European *Querelle des Anciens et des Modernes* which already had a long pre-history at its height towards the end of the 17th century. It focused on the question of precedence of ancient versus modern art, science and statecraft. The term *querelle* can be found in this context from 1687 onwards, used for that "bourgeois war in academia" (1760), "dispute over scientific precedence of old and new" (1780) or the "Battle of the Books" (1704), and in 1761 the full phrase *Querelle des Anciens et des Modernes* can be found in the above-mentioned text by Abbé Irailh. In a manner similar to the *querelle des femmes* one can now draw the conclusion that this "bourgeois war" was not only present in the Renaissance but that the Middle Ages were also "characterized by querelle-like disputes".[42] The connections between the *Querelle des Anciens et des Modernes and* the *querelle des femmes* are still largely unresearched. It plays an important part in some catalogues of women, but now between *anciennes et modernes*, i.e. between female representatives.[43] Authors who defended the moderns in the one dispute often took the part of women in the other debate which was also concerned with superiority and precedence; they considered the growing influence of women on society a sign of general progress. Furthermore, the *Querelle des Anciens et des Modernes* became more and more not only a matter of aristocratic concern but also took place in the salons where – at least in France – women began to play an important role from the 16th century onwards. Dorothea Christiane Leporin (her married name was Erxleben) considered the condemnation of women's study a result of the *praejudicium antiquitatis* (prejudice in favour of the ancients) evinced by the defenders of the *Anciens*.[44]

A further parallel between the ancient-versus-moderns dispute and the *querelle* can be seen in the fact that both terms entered the academic terminology of the humanities and were used for the respective phenomena outside French-language areas. The term *Querelle des Anciens et des Modernes* was used in French research in 1856[45] and from 1900 onwards the term *querelle des femmes* also sees a kind of renaissance, namely in Abel Lefranc's and Emile Telle's literary studies.[46] It is no accident that the *querelle des femmes* becomes topical around the turn of the century: it is a period in which the new term "feminism" is very popular in France and is soon appropriated elsewhere. It sparks off an intensive and multivocal debate concerning its definition.[47] A parallel attempt can be observed to provide this contemporary phenomenon with a deeper historical perspective by searching for proto-feminist forms and predecessors of feminist thought which is then, depending on the chosen model of periodisation, attributed to Christine de Pizan during the Middle Ages, to Margaret of Navarre in the 16th century, to Marie de Gournay in the 17th century, to the *précieuses* during the *siècle classique* or later to the women in the context of the French Revolution.[48] We will meet with similar periodisation models for the *querelle des femmes.*

German-language studies also clearly convey this sense of period-relatedness, a reflection of early feminism or of the first women's movement, as the scholar of

Romance languages Kurt König put it: "Old-fashioned habits and deeply-engrained prejudices [...] formed a thick fog through which the sun of woman's emancipation from a degrading position could only break through very slowly. To analyse more closely the first fights of the later Middle Ages in the light of the women's movement should prove to be of considerable interest."[49] Julia Kalbfleisch, again a Romance language specialist, conveyed the period-relatedness in a less emotional but rather more sober philologist's manner. She received her doctorate in Bern with her edition of the *Triumphe des Dames (Triumph of Women)* by Olivier de la Marche (ca. 1492), which amongst other texts also draws on Christine de Pizan's work, during a period in which German universities were still closed to women. She dedicated her publication to her aunt Henriette Goldschmidt, the Jewess from Leipzig who was an important figure in the classic early stages of the German women's movement.[50]

Since the 1970s one can observe a second intensified recourse to the French *querelle* in the context of the "second wave" women's movement. But now it is regarded as a historical phenomenon *sui generis* and not only considered a predecessor of modern feminism. It was during this period that Maï té Albistur's and Daniel Armogathe's, Ian Maclean's, and Marc Angenot's studies appeared,[51] as well as Joan Kelly's influential essay which, just as Elisabeth Gössmann's simultaneous publication, presented the *querelle* as a European phenomenon. In the 1990s, texts from Italy, France, and England which are normally attributed to the *querelle* were analysed under titles such as *Renaissance Woman* or *Renaissance Feminism*,[52] and Linda Timmermans' ground-breaking study on women's culture of the 17th century continues the research into the French *querelle*.[53] Helen Solterer has provided new material concerning its medieval dimension, the development of a "disputational figure of a woman" and the "dialectic between masterful writing and women's response".[54] At the same time one can observe a renewed interest in the *querelle* in gender-historical studies from various disciplines, indicating that knowledge of the *querelle* has not fallen into oblivion and that it is constantly updated from various perspectives.[55]

III Topics, Historical Breaks, and Literary Forms

The tasks of defining the *querelle des femmes* and finding adequate periodisation models for it are obviously closely related. The longer one is concerned with the *querelle* the clearer it becomes that in its different shapes and media one cannot reduce it to a "quarrel over women". The concept of the *querelle des femmes/des Sexes* draws on the original sources' terminology but as a kind of technical term it is a more comprehensive creation of the 20th century and as such refers to a far more complex phenomenon: an all-encompassing gender debate in which not only women but – and that has been insufficiently realised – men are an issue as well. It is a quarrel *in* words and images but also *about* words and images.[56] Words and images are not only two different media but at a time in which reading and writing was largely restricted to the religiously educated, images were considered as the "layman's book", "scriptura laicorum", a formula which was already dated at the time.[57] The quarrel focuses on the definition of an *imaginaire*,[58] an imaginary space of masculinity and femininity, of gender hierarchies and of positions which the writers take up concerning the particular topics of the discussion.

Emphasis in terms of importance, content and form can change from period to period. The early manifestations of the quarrel often focus on marriage, one of the pressing problems of the late Middle Ages and the early modern period: *An uxor sit ducenda* (*Should One Take a Wife*) was a question much discussed by Italian men, and in Germany it could appear as *Ob einem manne sey zu nemen ein eelichs weyb oder nit (Should a Man Take a Wife or Not)* (Albrecht von Eyb, 1472). In the answer to this question male misogamy (hatred of marriage) is expressed as misogyny (hatred of women) and philogyny (love of women) as philogamy (love of marriage).[59] Christine de Pizan's praise of women was directed against the misogamists and misogynists of her time, the anonymous text *Les quinze joies de mariage (The Fifteen Joys of Marriage)* deplored the loss of male liberty in marriage, and a century later Erasmus of Rotterdam presented the misogamist virgin in his *Virgo misogamos (The Misogamist Virgin)* (1523), who desperately wants to enter a convent but inspired by love she thinks better of it at the last moment.[60] Philogynous texts questioned why women were punished more strictly for adultery than men oder why a husband had to be bought (by a dowry); misogamists and misogynists, e.g. in England, answered the question by stating that women tend to squeeze money out of their husbands.[61]

In Germany this aspect of the *querelle* has been largely ignored (interest has focused on voices which argued in favor of women's intelligence and reason) although the *querelle du mariage* played an important role here: the wide-ranging marriage debate during the Reformation, in particular in its sensational and scandalous early phases – public betrothals of monks and nuns, closures of monasteries and convents, an epidemic of marriages in Germany to which even French reformers travelled who wished to marry – must be read as an integral part of the European *querelle des sexes* and the same goes for the marriage debates of the Counter-Reformation. Martin Luther's *Vom ehelichen Leben (The Estate of Married Life)* (1522) speaks quite in the manner of a *querelle* text by turning against the traditional misogamist attitude: "what we would speak most of is the fact that the estate of marriage has universally fallen into such awful disrepute. There are many pagan books which treat of nothing but the depravity of womankind and the unhappiness of the estate of marriage [...]. So they [young men listening to the advice of a Roman official] concluded that woman is a necessary evil, and that no household can be without such an evil. [...] For this reason young men should be on their guard when they read pagan books and hear the common complaints about marriage, lest they inhale poison. For the estate of marriage does not sell well with the devil, because it is God's good will and work. This is why the devil has contrived to have so much shouted and written in the world against the institution of marriage [...]. The world says of marriage, 'Brief is the joy, lasting the bitterness.'" It is no coincidence that the marriage debate, in which Luther's voice is only one of many and in which religious-reforming as well as humanist voices can be heard, took place during a period in which the "married couple as working couple" had become very important.[62] Similarly relevant for the *querelle* are Luther's *Ursach und Antwort, daß Jungfrauen Klöster göttlich verlassen mögen (Cause and Answer that Virgins May Leave Convents in God)* (1523), as well as the closing of convents and the concomitant ferocious controversies (with a different dynamic for monasteries and convents respectively), and in particular the disputational literature in the shape of innumerable broadsides. As much as the marriage of reforming priests and the marriage-versus-virginity controversy were central elements of the European *querelle des femmes*, conversely they were just as crucial for the Reformation and at least for the main part of the people they were more important than Luther's 95 theses.[63] In 17th-century France it was the *précieuses* who were to delevop a feminine critique of marriage ("on se marie pour haï r et pour souffrir", "one marries in order to hate and to suffer"),[64] and in England, after various pamphlet wars, it was Mary Astell (ca. 1700) who said that the man marries because "he wants one to manage his Family, an Housekeeper, a necessary Evil, one whose Interest it will be not to wrong him, and in whom therefore he can put greater confidence than in any he can hire for Money. One who may breed his Children, taking all the care and trouble of their Education, to preserve his Name and Family. [...] In a word, one whom he can intirely Govern, and [...] who must be his for Life, and therefore cannot quit his Service let him treat her how he will." After considerable reflection she concluded: "never consent to be a Wife."[65]

When Mary Astell wrote her famous sentence "If all men are born free, how is it that all women are born slaves?" in her treatise on marriage, the debate on women's ability to rule had already been under way for a long time. In France it was Christine de Pizan who made it an issue and, as Susan Groag Bell has shown, tapestries with images from Christine's *City of Ladies* served as representation of and justification for women's power to rule.[66] The Salic Law would soon also be discussed. In England the question come up during Mary Tudor's and her half-sister Elizabeth's accession to the throne.[67] In Germany one could also hear statements on this topic: "That several women speak against [*against the sentence* that woman is under man's rule], the Holy Book giving them the name that they should be called wo-man so that they deserve to have power and to rule as well as men, and they assume power, such is a sacrilege" and "one can make the experience that there are few women who want to follow their husbands and submit to their rule, but that most of them are proud, forward, stubborn and obstinate, they do not want to be ruled" but rule themselves.[68] In the 17th and particularly in the 18th centuries the debate about female education and learning, as well as the argument over fashion and personal hygiene move centre-stage.[69] But "long-term issues" exist as well: gender anthropologies, the relation of gender and morality, gender and intellect, and power relations between men and women which, among other aspects, focus on the superiority or inferiority of women or on the equality of the sexes. In the course of the centuries comprehensive compilations of argumentative strategies and exempla develop out of these controversies to which subsequent authors can revert but which are then also significantly changed and displaced. All these debates illustrate how crucial gender relations were during this period.

It has proved to be of little value to argue that the *querelle* only has a rhetorical, imitative-topical and "static" character which is emphasized by literary studies "in general", and to suppose that the *querelle* is merely a subject for the history of ideas and its relevance to "social history" insignificant, as has been recently claimed.[70] In principle one must indeed assume a rhetorical shape for many utterances. This does not, however, in any way exclude references to social and political topics. Yet such topical references need to be uncovered for each individual text: to historicize them in the sense of providing a historical context is one of the main tasks of *querelle* research and it is from their literary, intellectual, and social contexts that the most important analyses have been developed. Secondly, the notion of the "static" character of the *querelle* and its tendency towards fixed "topoi" has itself become a *topos* which recent developments in literary studies have questioned.[71] Such a discourse betrays an ahistorical perspective since it judges texts of earlier periods on the basis of a modern aesthetic, thus failing to appreciate the importance that *imitatio* had for literature and art of an era which was a "period of emulation",[72] as well as underestimating the enormous relevance of rhetoric and the variations and different functions which mark one and the same argument or exemplum and can lend it entirely different meanings.[73] Thirdly, this type of argument overlooks the differences in quality among the *querelle* texts. One can, e.g., distinguish between primarily emulative texts and those which set new standards by enlarging the existing set of arguments or by introducing new perspectives which in their turn influence the larger debate, are themselves imitated and establish new traditions.[74] Finally one would wish that the harsh (and judgemental) distinction between "social history" and the "history of ideas", i.e. a topical (and partly specifically German) academic debate were not introduced into gender history (in particular in the sense of seemingly more important "lower class"-phenomena and the allegedly "elitist" *querelle* literature). In France as well as in other countries the *querelle* was by no means restricted to the (female) élites; as can be seen from the *Bibliothèque bleue (*editions of popular literature printed on cheap "blue" paper*)* and in particular from the relevant images.[75] Yet it will be the history of culture and mentalities, historical reflection of language and gender-specific approaches to a new "intellectual history" which will result in a more productive dialogue with the male and female participants in the *querelle* rather than a restricted notion of social history.

Where can one locate historical breaks and specific moments within the *querelle des femmes*? That it originated when Eve passed Adam an apple – the modern recourse to the term began with this aperçu – flattens out the historical specificity of the phenomenon in an inadmissable manner and thus requires no serious discussion.[76] It is quite a different matter when an author of the 16th century lets "la querelle de l'homme contre la femme" (*the quarrel of man against woman*) begin with Adam and Eve.[77] This reference to the Book of Genesis – the creation of the sexes and the Fall of Man – expresses the fundamental relevance of the gender dispute in this period as well as the enormous importance of the Book of Genesis for the *querelle*. It was a "foundation text" and its interpretation was already a matter of debate at the time.[78] Modern appropriations of the *querelle* term tended to focus on the early modern period yet the authors of these studies were always aware of the *querelle's* late-medieval origins.[79] Others date the *querelle* considerably later, e.g. Carolyn Lougee, Natalie Zemon Davis and Arlette Farge (16th century). Joan Kelly, however, dates its beginning with Christine de Pizan, as does Gerda Lerner.[80] A late-medieval beginning is also proposed in more recent studies; Constance Jordan sees it as a general medieval phenomenon and the relevant literature of the high and late Renaissance only "in some respects" as its continuation and expansion.[81] A certain but not accidental uncertainty lies in the frequent use of the category "Renaissance" since it is dated differently for the countries which are relevant here – the earliest occurrence was in Italy, then in France. It is often used (and partly with good reason) to bridge the historiographic distinction between the Middle Ages and the early modern period (the "early Renaissance" is also the "late Middle Ages"). Thirdly, it is still controversial whether the "Renaissance" can at all serve as a period-marker (there have been many occurrences of a "renaissance" and "renaissance" for many refers to a style more than to a historical period). Finally, there is a problem in that at least in an English-language research context the term "Renaissance" is also used as a period-marker for countries for which other terms would be more appropriate.[82]

Doubtlessly, the beginnings of the *querelle* lie in the Later Middle Ages, at the latest in the 14th century, in some respects even in the 13th cenutry when the misogynous texts were created or circulated in France to which Christine de Pizan reacted. In England, Geoffrey Chaucer (1340-1400) played an important role (in particular with *The Wife of Bath* in *The Canterbury Tales*)[83] and early beginnings can also be found in the Ibero-Romance areas where the 15th century sees a certain accumulation of relevant texts; numerous works also appear in Italy during the 14th and 15th centuries. Especially 15th-century sources frequently refer to the importance of writing and the relevance of written forms of "memoria"; recent research into the Later Middle Ages also emphasizes the importance of writing processes.[84] In this context the fight over a (written) definition of an imaginary space of male-female gender attributes which simultaneously implies inscribing oneself into the archives of collective memory gains a special importance. We can also observe an increased "discursivation" of femininity in this period[85] which one can prove, e.g. for France, with texts whose genres are called "Louenge/Blastenge/Miroir des Femmes" (*Praise/Reproach/Lookingglass for Women*): texts whose genesis and effects still remain largely unresearched.[86] In addition – Helen Solterer has drawn attention to this fact[87] – the legal issue of verbal injury attained a hitherto unknown importance in the late Middle Ages, a development which also influenced the *querelle*.

From the earliest phase of the *querelle* only male voices have survived – misogynous ones at that – and in terms of quantity and effect they continue to dominate even after 1500.[88] Although they are no less relevant in our context than texts by women, the latter's appearance on the scene is an essential factor in the debate's development which as a result expands and intensifies. In France this occurs around 1400 with the first intervention by a woman, the Franco-Italian writer Christine de Pizan whose three texts in particular, the *Epistre au Dieu d'Amour (Letter from Cupid)* (1399), her disputational texts directed against the *Romance of the Rose* (1400-1402) and especially her *Livre de la Cité des Dames (The Book of the City of Ladies*, 1404/5),[89] spark off the actual *querelle*, understood as a combative dialogue of the sexes. Since that period the female *querelle* authors take up the part of the women while some of the male authors argue for the women and some against them. In the Ibero-Romance area occasional 15th-century female voices existed; not surprisingly, they are to be found in a religious and monastic context.[90] In Italy, the first female voices speak out around the middle of the 15th century (even earlier if one also includes those works as *querelle* texts which were not directly written as gender polemics but belong to a religious and humanist context) – with greater self-confidence they did so from 1600 onwards, as Adriana Chemello has demonstrated.[91] The first contribution by an English woman dates from 1578, and she was soon followed by an author who called herself "Jane Anger". If we apply Moira Ferguson's classification (reactive, reasoned or analytical, and personal polemic)[92] to Germany, we can observe that "reasoned" polemics can only be found at a later date. But if we agree to consider the Reformation (or at least some of its parts) as an integral and specifically German or rather German-language element of the *querelle des femmes* then women who vehemently defended convents and virginity as legitimate forms of female existence – Caritas Pirckheimer is only one of many – as well as women such as Katharina Zell, who was instrumental in developing an ideal of marriage which enhanced the status of women, and the notion of priesthood for all believers and other relevant topics, can be included as *querelle* authors.[93]

How about the end of the *querelle*? Maclean already lets it cease in its "traditional" form as early as 1630 since in his opinion it was then superseded by a new "feminist" literature based on moral arguments.[94] Lerner locates its end around 1700 in one instance. She then emphasizes that not only the French salons of the 17th century as well as the English and German ones of the 18th century form part of the *querelle*, and thus names 1800 as its end in another instance, not without mentioning its continuities in the 19th century, in particular in the context of the debate about female education and the continued tradition of catalogues of famous women which now occurred in modern forms.[95] Frequently we come across a renewal of the *querelle* located at the turn of the 17th century.[96] Often its end is set with the French Revolution, e.g. in Joan Kelly's work, and the historian Geneviève Fraisse argues that "[t]he gender conflict which at first appears to be timeless, if not eternal, has in fact a long history. The to and fro of contradictory discourses on the preeminence of men compared to women and vice versa since the late Middle Ages is known as 'quarrel' (*querelle*). It is an endless verbal battle with equally fruitful and poor, equally apt and stupid arguments [...]. This quarrel ends with the Revolution; but it is not the gender debate which ceases but one of its manners of expression. The quarrel is now brought to court; with the beginning of a public political discussion it is now carried out in another place."[97]

Geneviève Fraisse makes two important distinctions: on the one hand she distinguishes a limited phenomenon which can be situated historically, related to a long-gone past; and a gender conflict which characterizes all periods or at least the early modern one; on the other hand she differentiates between an older, pre-political and a newer, political or politicized contest. When she argues against a de-historicization of the *querelle* she also raises the question of "politics" and gender history. Doubtlessly the French Revolution is of momentous importance here and marks a historical break, not only for France. Nevertheless some further aspects should be taken into account. On the one hand in this context as in others, especially as regards gender history, the borders marking off periods, between continuity and discontinuity, should not be drawn too sharply. On the other hand the political element was quite visible in the old *querelle* as we have seen; conversely, research into the genesis of the women's movement in the 19th century has shown clearly that for a long time political aspects were not its main focus but rather that social questions were more important and the movement itself was considered a genuinely social development.[98] Finally we need to take into consideration that the French Revolution did not only end an older dispute but that it actually opened the "woman's question", the renewed question *Qu'est-ce qu'une femme (What Is Woman?)* so dominant in the 19th century.[99] It is in this sense but also in the sense of a polemical quarrel that Claire Moses refers to the dramatic and public contest in the 1850s and 1860s between Juliette Lamber-Adam and Jenny d'Héricourt on the one hand and Jules Michelet and Pierre-Joseph Proudhon on the other – the dispute was between a new misogynous variant versus anti-misogyny or philogyny – as the *querelle des femmes* of the Second Empire.[100] Sometimes the term is also used for the classic phase of the women's movement.[101] And in a broader sense others see today's gender controversies as "a new *querelle des femmes*".[102]

Thus, locating the *querelle* historically cannot be separated from its definition: should we define it in accordance with the larger social and political context in which it took place or rather according to its content and its continuity or change, or rather according to its literary form? The latter criterion leads us to the question of a *querelle* corpus which is frought with considerable difficulties and again takes us back into a far-away past. Does a verbal or visual *querelle* genre exist? Can one list characteristics with which we can determine whether a text or an image forms part of this context? On the one hand not every discourse on women – in whatever media – should be considered a *querelle* text or image, since their determination as such texts requires certain verbal or visual signals as well as an unmistakable *querelle* context. On the other hand and as holds true for other historical problems: borders can be flexible and distinctions need not imply separations.

The determining criterion is unquestionably the feature of quarreling, polemic, controversy, debate, verbal action and reaction. *Querrelle* characteristics can manifest themselves on different levels. In a significant manner, the over-all *querelle* is constituted by the numerous single *querelles*, beginning with Christine de Pizan's reaction to the *Romance of the Rose*, through the reactions to Agrippa von Nettesheim's text (written in 1509), to the numerous German reactions to the anonymous *Disputatio nova* (ca. 1595), in Italy the reaction to Giuseppe Passi (1599) and the translation of the *Disputatio nova* into Italian (1647), to the English series of "pamphlet wars" of the first half of the 17th century or the texts such as *Woman not Inferior to Man* (1739), *Man Superior to Woman* (1740) and *Woman's Superior Excellence over Man* (1740) which responded to each other. Mary Wollstonecraft also wrote in the context of this culture of dispute, although she was already influenced by the new language of the French (and American) Revolution: in her *Vindication of the Rights of Woman* (1792) she violently attacked Jean Jacques Rousseau, in spite of her admiration for him, because of his notions of women. Furthermore that text was a counterpart to her *Vindication of the Rights of Man* (1790) with which she reacted to Edmund Burke's critique of the French Revolution even before Thomas Paine had published his similarly entitled text.[103]

It is in this sense that Moira Ferguson has used the term "polemics" as an analytical category.[104] The dispute can be lead in open or – as Sara Matthews Grieco has shown with the example of Georgette de Montenay, who distanced herself from the emblematic tradition – a more subtle polemic. The debate can be carried out in one individual text – hence the considerable importance of dialogue for the *querelle*.[105] Frequently, dispute and polemic are expressed in ironic, parodic, paradoxical or sarcastic forms, forms which characterized other literary genres of the same period, such as, e.g., historiography.[106] We also need to consider more than has been the case that the relation of action and reaction, attack and defense, of statement and response can be very complex: all actions, in those cases briefly mentioned as well as in all others, may just as well already be reactions themselves. Giuseppe Passi did not only instigate a new phase of the Italian *querelle* but himself reacted to numerous earlier texts. Agrippa von Nettesheim, whose text became rapidly and widely known and was so important for the development of the *querelle* that Maclean rightly counts it as one of the "seminal works", inspired many later authors and his own text was re-written accordingly. Agrippa did not only react to earlier *querelle* texts (in particular to Italian and Latin ones), he also took up some passages himself (the term "plagiarism" which is frequently invoked is inappropriate for that period since it is anachronistic). Especially a passage in which he describes woman's inferior social position, denounces "male tyranny" and opposes "natural" woman's "liberty" to it – it was occasionally read as the first provable call for social change, namely through female education – was taken over from Mario Equicolas *De mulieribus* (*Of Women*) (ca. 1501).[107]

One can differentiate "primary" and "secondary" *querelle* texts and images. Primary verbal and visual utterances are those which refer directly to the *querelle des femmes* in their title, main content and with regard to their readership. Primary *querelle* texts mostly draw on the epistolary genre, treatises, dialogues, and polemic and are often, at least in part, encyclopaedias, exempla-collections and catalogues (of women and men). These texts and/or images are often characterised by highly marked intertextuality and referential features. Analysing the (frequently very slow) movements and restructurings within the canon of quoted or re-written authorities gives us valuable insights into developments within the *querelle*, which in this respect is far from static. Those texts and images which integrate their references to the *querelle* into other, larger contexts, and in which the *querelle* plays a subordinate role can be classified as secondary *querelle* texts. Notwithstanding their status as literary "classics", Baldassar Castiglione's *Il cortegiano* (1528) and Ludovico Ariosto's *Orlando Furioso* (1532) can be counted as secondary *querelle* texts.[108]

It should have become clear that the distinction between primary and secondary *querelle* texts does not aim at a hierarchical judgement concerning a text's historical meaningfulness or distribution but rather at the problem of explicit centrality opposed to implicit and partial references to this gender controversy. From the distance of several centuries it is not always easy to make the right distinction. In addition this distinction may produce varied results according to its context, depending on whether the distinction refers to the genesis or the effect of a text. It is, for instance, probable that the anonymous *Disputatio nova* (1595) was not primarily written in relation to the *querelle* but for a larger religious purpose, in order to prove the Anabaptists wrong; in terms of the work's effect it clearly became a primary *querelle* text.[109] Our distinction is thus not an invitation to classify schematically and hastily; rather it requires, if it is to be precise and profitable, the uncovering of hidden traces and patient reconstruction of historical contexts which may be difficult to perceive nowadays.[110]

Imitatio, the imitation of model texts through copying and re-writing, certainly a characteristic of many if not all *querelle* texts, used often to be measured by the standard of originality, was thus deplored and seen as indicative of the texts' insignificance. But it is that procedure, the constant taking-up of current debates and more or less well-known texts – or to put it more generally: the impressive intertextuality of the *querelle* literature – that shows the *querelle's* true historical meaning. Not only literary history but also social history and the history of mentalities often deal with frequently not very "original" even repetitive, serial documents heavily marked by *topoi* which furthermore – in particular as regards a popular audience which did not only read but which also had texts read to them aloud and absorbed the *querelle* imagery in its own manner – were received more widely than others. The *querelle's* disputational character, its intertextuality and the distinction between "primary" and "secondary" texts suggest that this gender debate was not restricted to one single, sharply delineated genre and subject but that it tended to transcend its boundaries, could express itself in many forms and – in accordance with the cultural omnipresence of gender relations – could spread to many other areas and subjects. Its intertextuality and distribution should therefore be read as an expression of a Europe-wide cultural circulation and communication of gender questions and thus as a significant phenomenon of gender as well as of social history and the history of mentalities, ideas, and culture.

Translated by Gesa Stedman

Institut für Geschichtswissenschaft, Institut für Romanische Philologie, Freie Universitaet Berlin

Notes

1. Beauvoir, Simone de: The Second Sex, translated by H. M. Parshley, New York 1968 (French original 1949), p.xiii. All other English translations, unless otherwise indicated, by Gesa Stedman. The editors would like to thank Joan DeJean and Claudia Ulbrich for important references. We would also like to thank the participants of the conference on "Superiority and Inferiority in the European *querelle des femmes*" (European University Institute, Florence 1989): Adriana Chemello, Françine Daenens, Maria Luisa Doglio, Elisabeth Gössmann, Constance Jordan, Madeleine Lazard, Ian Maclean, Sara Matthews Grieco, Marie-Françoise Piéjus, Hilda Smith, Heide Wunder, Marina Zancan.

2. Abel Lefranc introduced the term as a genre-marker in 1904: Le Tiers-Livre du "Pantagruel" et la Querelle des femmes. In: Revue des Etudes rabelaisiennes, vol. 2, 1904; repr. in id.: Grands Ecrivains Français de la Renaissance, Paris 1914, repr. Paris 1969, pp. 251-303, and in id.: Œuvres de François Rabelais. Le Tiers-Livre, Paris 1931; Telle, Emil: L'Œuvre de Marguerite d'Angoulême, Reine de Navarre, et la Querelle des Femmes. Toulouse 1936, repr. Geneva 1969. "Querelle des sexes" or "quarrel of the sexes" can e.g. be found in Dow, Blanche Hinman: The Varying Attitude Toward Women in French

Literature of the Fifteenth Century: The Opening Years. New York 1936, p. 48, and in Screech, Michael A.: Rabelais, de Billon and Erasmus. A Reexamination of Rabelais's Attitude to Women. In: Bibliothèque d'Humanisme et Renaissance, vol. 13, 1951, pp. 241-65, here p. 241.

3. Marchesi, G. Battista: Le polemiche sul sesso femminile ne' sec. XVI e XVII. In: Giornale storico della letteratura italiana, vol. 25, 1895, pp. 362-369; likewise Spini, Giorgio: Ricerca dei libertini. La teoria dell'impostura delle religioni nel Seicento italiano. Casellina 1983, p. 220ff. French authors also call the Italian polemic *querelle des femmes*, e.g. Anitchkoff, Eugène: Le "Roland furieux" et la Querelle des Femmes au XVIe siècle. In: Revue du XVIe siècle, vol. 19, 1932/33, pp. 262-72.

4. Fietze, Katharina: Frauenbildung in der *Querelle des Femmes*. In: Kleinau, Elke/Opitz, Claudia (eds.): Geschichte der Mädchen- und Frauenbildung, vol. 1, Frankfurt a. M., New York 1996, pp. 237-251 ("Debatte um die Frauen"); Steinbrügge, Lieselotte: Vom Aufstieg und Fall der gelehrten Frau. Einige Aspekte der "Querelle des femmes" im XVIII. Jahrhundert. In: *lendemains*, vol. 25/26, 1982, pp. 157-167 (on page 157 the *querelle des femmes* is referred to as "woman's quarrel" and the "question of the equality of the sexes"); Metken, Sigrid: Der Kampf um die Hose. Geschlechterstreit und die Macht im Haus. Die Geschichte eines Symbols. Frankfurt a. M. 1996. Wunder, Heide: "Er ist die Sonn', sie ist der Mond". Frauen in der Frühen Neuzeit. München 1992, p. 63: Die *Querelle* als "Streit um die Natur der Frau". Likewise in American publications: Wiesner, Merry E.: Women and Gender in Early Modern Europe. Cambridge 1993, pp. 15-21. The *querelle* as male dispute concerning women: Honegger, Claudia: Die Ordnung der Geschlechter. Frankfurt a. M. 1991, p. 45f, 75, 140 (Germany ca. 1800). Cf. also Davis, Natalie Z.: Women on top. In: id.: Society and culture in early modern France. London 1975, pp. 124-151.

5. See above, note 2. Cf. Moxey, Keith: Peasants, Warriors, and Wives. Popular Imagery in the Reformation. Chicago, London 1989, chap. 5 ("The Battle of the Sexes and the World Upside Down"); Nadelhaft, Jerome: The Englishwoman's Sexual Civil War: Feminist Attitudes Towards Men, Women, and Marriage. In: Journal of the History of Ideas, vol. 43, 1982, pp. 555-79; Beaumont-Maillet, Laure: La Guerre des sexes. XVe-XIXe siècles. Paris 1984; Travitsky, Betty: The Lady Doth Protest: Protest in the Popular Writings of Renaissance Englishwomen. In: English Literary Renaissance, vol. 14, 1984, pp. 255-283.

6. Kelly, Joan: Early Feminist Theory and the *Querelle des Femmes*, 1400-1789. In: Signs, vol. 8, 1982, pp. 4-28, and in id.: Women, History and Theory, Chicago 1984, pp. 65-109. The term *Querelle des femmes* plays no part in Zancan, Marina (ed.): Nel cerchio della luna: Figure di donne nel XVI secolo. Padua 1983, a study which is of great importance for the Italian context.

7. The exception is the controversy between "Jean de Meun and the women of Philip the Fair's court" for which Irailh draws on Charles Sorel's *La Bibliothèque Françoise*, 2nd ed. Paris 1667, p. 247. Cf. Irailh, Augustin Simon: Querelles littéraires ou mémoires pour servir à l'histoire des révolutions de la République des Lettres, depuis Homère jusqu'à nos jours. 2 vols., Paris 1761, vol. 1, pp. 94-105 (repr. Geneva 1967, pp. 33-36).

8. Quoted in: Raulff, Ulrich: Ein Historiker im 20. Jahrhundert: Marc Bloch. Frankfurt a. M. 1995, p. 118.

9. The text mentioned below in note 11, the *Disputatio nova*, may have been written in Poland. For the German context cf. in particular Gössmann, Elisabeth (ed.): Archiv für philosophie- und theologiegeschichtliche Frauenforschung, vol. 1-7, Munich 1984-1998;

Plume, Cornelia: Heroinen in der Geschlechterordnung. Weiblichkeitsprojektionen im Werk Daniel Caspers von Lohenstein und die *Querelle des Femmes*. Weimar 1996; Conrad, Anne: Zwischen Kloster und Welt. Ursulinen und Jesuitinnen in der katholischen Reformbewegung des 16./17. Jahrhunderts. Mainz 1991, in part. chap. 5; Wunder 1992 and Metken 1996 (as in note 4).

10. It was published in French in 1530, three Italian editions appeared between 1544 and 1549, it appeared in Polish in 1575, in Dutch in 1658. Cf. Jörg Jungmayr's edition and commentary of the German version from 1540: Vom Adel und Fürtreffen Weibliches geschlechts. In: Gössmann, Elisabeth (ed.): Ob die Weiber Menschen seyn, oder nicht? Munich 1988 (Archiv für philosophie- und theologiegeschichtliche Frauenforschung, vol. 4), pp. 53-96 (introduction: pp. 33-52). On Agrippa's influence in Italy but also on the influence of early Italian texts on Agrippa cf. Fahy, Conor: Three Early Renaissance Treatises on Women. In: Italian Studies, vol. 11, 1956, pp. 30-55. That article with its appendix containing a list of relevant Italian treatises from the 15th and 16th centuries was an important starting point for Italian research into the *querelle*. Cf. also Zambelli, Paola: Agrippa von Nettesheim in den neueren kritischen Studien und in den Handschriften. In: Archiv für Kulturgeschichte, vol. 51, 1969, pp. 264-295.

11. Passi, Giuseppe: I donneschi diffetti. Padua 1599 (and 1601, 1605, 1618); anon.: Disputatio nova contra mulieres, qua probatur eas homines non esse. Zerbst 1595, many further editions and a translation into Italian from 1647 (Che le donne non siano della spetie degli uomini). For the text as well as for Valens Acidalius who was often considered the author of the text, an allegation which he steadfastly denied (he died young in 1595), cf. Maclean, Ian: The Renaissance Notion of Woman. A Study in the Fortunes of Scholasticism and Medical Science in European Intellectual Life. Cambridge 1980, pp. 12-13; Fleischer, Manfred P.: Der Wirbel um Acidalius. In: id.: Späthumanismus in Schlesien. Munich 1984, pp. 190-212.

12. For Romance-language contexts cf. Brandenberger, Tobias: "*Malas hembras* und *virtuosas mujeres: Querelles* in der spätmittelalterlichen und frühneuzeitlichen Iberoromania". In: Bock, Gisela/Zimmermann, Margarete (eds.), Die europäische Querelle des Femmes. Geschlechterdebatten seit dem 15. Jahrhundert. *Querelles. Jahrbuch für Frauenforschung*, vol. 2 1997, pp. 183-202, Chemello, Adriana: "Weibliche Freiheit und venezianische Freiheit. Moderata Fonte und die Traktatliteratur über Frauen im 16. Jahrhundert." In: op. cit., pp. 239-268, Hassauer, Friederike: "*Die Seele ist nicht Mann, nicht Weib*. Stationen der *Querelles des Femmes* in Spanien und Lateinamerika vom 16. zum 18. Jahrhundert." In: op. cit., pp. 203-238, Lauer, Esther: "'Bellezza' und 'ornamenti' im italienischen Geschlechterstreit um 1600." In: op. cit., pp. 269-291 and Pieper, Julia: "*Désir et Vertu*. Bildung und weibliche Identiät im Werk der Dames des Roches." In: op. cit., pp. 57-77. Cf. also De Benedetti Stow, Sandra: Due poesie bilingue inedite contro le donne di Semu'èl Da Castiglione (1553). In: Italia: Studi e ricerche sulla cultura e sulla letteratura degli ebrei d'Italia. vol. II, no. 1-2, Jerusalem 1980, pp. 7-64. Cf. also Adelman, Howard: Images of Women in Italian Jewish Literature in the late Middle Ages. In: Proceedings of the Tenth World Congress of Jewish Studies. Division B, vol. II, Jerusalem 1990, pp. 99-106; Baskin, Judith R.: Jewish Women in the Middle Ages. In: id. (ed.).: Jewish Women in Historical Perspective. Detroit 1991, pp. 94-114; Zinberg, Israel: A History of Jewish Literature, vol. 4: Italian Jewry in the Renaissance Era. Cincinatti, New York 1974, p. 97f.

13. Cf. in particular Maclean 1980 (as in note 11). For legal, theological and further historical approaches cf. e.g. Henning, Clara Maria: Canon Law and the Battle of the

Sexes. In: Ruether, Rosemary Radford (ed.): Religion and Sexism. Images of Woman in the Jewish and Christian Traditions. New York 1974, pp. 267-291; Vogel, Ursula: Political Philosophers and the Trouble With Polygamy: Patriarchal Reasoning in Modern Natural Law. In: History of Political Thought, vol. 12, 1991, pp. 229-252; Buchholz, Stephan: Recht, Religion und Ehe. Orientierungswandel und gelehrte Kontroversen im Übergang vom 17. zum 18. Jahrhundert. Frankfurt a. M. 1988; Gierl, Martin: Pietismus und Aufklärung. Theologische Polemik und der gelehrte Kommunikationswandel am Ende des 17. Jahrhunderts. Göttingen 1997; Harth, Erica: Cartesian Women. Versions and Subversions of Rational Discourse in the Old Regime. Ithaca, London 1992; Lloyd, Geneviève: The Man of Reason: "Male" and "Female" in Western Philosophy. London 1993 (revised edition of the 1984 edition; German transl.: Das Patriarchat der Vernunft. Bielefeld 1985); Harvey, Elizabeth/Okruhlik, Kathleen (eds.): Women and Reason. Ann Arbor 1992.

14. *Querelle* authors seem to have been aware of this fact. Wilhelm Ignatius Schütz (Ehren-Preiß Deß Hochlöblichen Frauen-Zimmers, 1663) addresses the "European woman" and Johannes Gorgias (Gestürtzter Ehren-Preiß des hochlöblichen Frauen-Zimmers, 1666) speaks to the "honourable-European male sex": Gössmann, Elisabeth (ed.): Das wohlgelahrte Frauenzimmer. Munich 1984 (Archiv für philosophie- und theologiegeschichtliche Frauenforschung, vol. 1), p. 55, 72. For the Spanish versions in colonized Latin America cf. Sor Juana Inés de la Cruz: The Answer/La Respuesta. Including a Selection of Poems. Critical Edition and Translation. Ed. by Electa Arenal and Amanda Powell, New York 1994 (bilingual edition); cf. also Hassauer 1997 (as in note 12) and the contributions on Sor Juana, María de Zayas y Sotomayor and Rebeca Correa in: Potthast-Jutkeit, Barbara/Stoll, André (eds.): La Creatividad femenina y las trampas del poder. Kassel 1998.

15. Le Franc, Martin: Le Champion des Dames. Paris 1530 (first print: Lyon, ca. 1488), table of contents (s. p.), dedication (p. a ii verso), also p. 6, 13 verso, 14, 18 verso, 39ff, 49 verso, 408 verso. Modern editions of parts of the texts were published by Gaston Paris (in: Romania, vol. 16, 1887, pp. 383-437, with commentary), Artur Piaget (Lausanne 1968) and Don Arthur Fischer (dissertation Florida State University 1981). Cf. also Barbey, Léon: Martin Le Franc, prévôt de Lausanne, avocat de l'amour et de la femme au XVe siècle. Fribourg 1985. On the French history of the term cf. Zimmermann, Margarete: Vom Streit der Geschlechter. Die französische und italienische *Querelle des Femmes* des 15.-17. Jahrhunderts. In: Baumgärtel, Bettina/Neysters, Silvia (eds.): Die Galerie der Starken Frauen. Die Heldin in der französischen und italienischen Kunst des 17. Jahrhunderts. Munich 1995, pp. 14-33.

16. In Christine's text Cupid takes up the cause of women from all ranks seeking help, who complain of seriously disturbed gender relations and ask him for succour. In this short verse poem written at the beginning of her literary career she prefigures all important topics and strategies which she then expands in her texts against the *Romance of the Rose* and in the *City of Ladies*. However, in the *Letter* she still hands the female protest over to Cupid, i.e. to a male "advocate". The English translation by Thomas Hoccleve can be found in Fenster, Thelma S. (ed.): *Poems of Cupid, God of Love*. Leiden 1990.

17. For the importance of legal terminology for late Medieval literature cf. Becker, Karin: Amors Urteilssprüche. Recht und Liebe in der französischen Literatur des Spätmittelalters. Bonn 1991. Cf. also Bouchet, Jean: Le Jugement poetic de l'honneur

femenin et séjour des illustres et claires dames. Poitiers 1536: "la querelle de l'homme contre la femme" (p. a verso).

18. The illustrator of the edition of *Le Champion des Dames* (Paris 1530) "modernises" this position and adapts it to the level the *querelle* had attained in the 16th century: the wood-cut on page 125 shows a man and a woman as the audience of a male-female lance fight.

19. Some information can be found in Zévaco, D.: Querelle. In: Revue de philologie française, no. 30, 1917/18, pp. 36-40.

20. A useful overview can be found in König, Kurt: Die literarische Ehrenrettung der Frau in Frankreich während der ersten Hälfte des XVI. Jahrhunderts, Dresden 1909.

21. Du Pont, Gratien: Controverses des sexes masculin et fémenin. Toulouse 1534: "querelle [du 'sexe masculin'] contre cil [= le sexe fémenin]", the "bonne querrel" of the men against women, "les controverses des susditz sexes" (s. p.). Cf. Oulmont, Charles: Gratien Du Pont Sieur de Drusac et les femmes. In: Revue des Etudes rabelaisiennes, vol. 4, 1906, pp. 1-28, 135-153.

22. Postel, Guillaume: Les très-merveilleuses victoires des femmes du nouveau monde. Padua 1553, quoted in: Albistur, Maïté/Armogathe, Daniel: Histoire du féminisme français. Paris 1977, vol. 1, p. 144. For Postel's text cf. Kuntz, Marion L.: The Virgin of Venice and Concepts of the Millenium in Venice. In: Brink, Jean R. et al. (eds.): The Politics of Gender in Early Modern Europe. Kirksville 1989, pp. 111-130.

23. At the centre of this debate which is closely linked to Castiglione's notion of woman as the "donna di palazzo", developed in the third book of *Il cortegiano* (1528, French translation: 1537, English translation: 1561, German translation: 1565), we find the rules of women's conduct in the context of the "sociotope" constituted by the royal court. For the *querelle de l'amye* which has not been sufficiently researched yet cf. Telle 1936/1969 (as in note 2), chap. V; Screech, Michael A.: An Interpretation of the Querelle des Amyes. In: Bibliothèque d'Humanisme et Renaissance, vol. 21, 1959, pp. 103-130.

24. Romieu, Marie de: Brief discours que l'excellence de la femme surpasse celle de l'homme. In: id.: Les premières œuvres poétiques. Ed. by André Winandy, Geneva, Paris 1972, here pp. 12-25.

25. For an analysis of her texts cf. Pieper 1997 (as in note 12).

26. Latest editions: Paris 1989 (introd. by Milagros Palma); Venesoen, Constant (ed.): Geneva 1993. Important texts can also be found in: Gournay, Marie de: Fragments d'un discours féminin. Ed. by Elyane Dezon-Jones, Paris 1988. Cf. e.g. Ilsley, Marjorie H.: A Daughter of the Renaissance: Marie le Jars de Gounray. Her Life and Works, The Hague 1963 (for the *querelle* cf. p. 201); Maclean, Ian: Marie de Gournay et la préhistoire du discours féminin. In: Haase Dubosc, Danielle/Viennot, Eliane (eds.): Femmes et pouvoirs sous l'ancien régime. Paris 1991, pp. 120-134.

27. Cf. Lauer and Chemello 1997 (as in note 12).

28. No modern edition of the complete original exists. Adriana Chemello is preparing a critical edition which will comment on the textual structure, based on numerous quotations and borrowings. For the English translation see below, note 29.

29. The first new edition since the text's original publication: Tarabotti, Arcangela: Che le donne siano della spezie degli uomini – Women Are No Less Rational Than Men. Ed. and introd. by Letizia Panizza, London 1994. For the other texts by Tarabotti, cf. also Medioli, Francesca: L'"Inferno monacale" di Arcangela Tarabotti. Turin 1990. On Tarabotti's position on the situation of women in her time cf. Bock, Gisela: Frauenräume und Frauenehre: Frühneuzeitliche Armenfürsorge in Italien. In: Hausen, Karin/Wunder,

Heide (eds.): Frauengeschichte – Geschlechtergeschichte. Frankfurt a. M. 1992, pp. 25-49; Hunecke, Volker: Kindbett oder Kloster: Lebenswege venezianischer Patrizierinnen im 17. und 18. Jahrhundert. In: Geschichte und Gesellschaft, vol. 18, 1992, pp. 446-76. Cf. also Zimmermann, Margarete: Die italienische 'Querelle des Femmes': Feministische Traktate von Moderata Fonte und Lucrezia Marinelli. In: Schneider, Gisela (ed.): Frauenforum (= Trierer Beiträge, special issue 8). Trier 1994, pp. 53-61, and for further references see Chemello 1997 (as in note 12), and the introduction to Moderata Fonte: The Worth of Women. Ed. and transl. by Virginia Cox. Chicago, London 1997, and to Lucrezia Marinella: The Nobility and Excellence of Women and the Defects and Vices of Men. Ed. and transl. by Anne Durhill. Introduction by Letizia Panizza. Chicago, London 1999.

30. Editions of this and further pamphlets can be found in Henderson, Katherine Usher/McManus, Barbara F. (eds.): Half Humankind. Contexts and Texts of the Controversy about Women in England, 1540-1640. Urbana, Chicago 1985; Shepherd, Simon (ed.): The Women's Sharp Revenge: Five Women's Pamphlets from the Renaissance. New York 1985. Cf. also the following works: Smith, Hilda: Reason's Disciples. Seventeenth-Century English Feminists. Chicago 1982; Jordan, Constance: Renaissance Feminism. Literary Texts and Political Models. Ithaca 1990 (England, Italy, France); Benson, Pamela Joseph: The Invention of the Renaissance Woman. The Challenge of Female Independence in the Literature and Thought of Italy and England. University Park 1992. For English *querelle* texts cf. also Haselkorn, Anne M./Travitsky, Betty S. (eds.): The Renaissance Englishwoman in Print. Counterbalancing the Canon. Amherst 1990; Harvey, Elizabeth D.: Ventriloquized Voices. Feminist Theory and English Renaissance Texts. London 1992; Lewalski, Barbara Kiefer: Writing Women in Jacobean England. Cambridge, Mass. 1993; Woodbridge, Linda: Women and the English Renaissance. Literature and the Nature of Womankind, 1540-1620. Urbana 1984; Beilin, Elaine V.: Redeeming Eve. Women Writers of the English Renaissance. Princeton 1987; Rogers, Katherine M.: Feminism in Eighteenth-Century England. Brighton 1982.

31. In France, anonymous texts, probably mainly written by women, can be found as well as mistaken attributions, as e.g. in the case of the text *Le Triomphe des Dames* (1599), attributed to a certain Pierre de Brinon which was definitely written by a woman. For the discussion of the anonymous English writers' sex cf. Henderson/McManus (eds.) 1985 (as in note 30), pp. 20-24; Shepherd (ed.) 1985 (as in note 30), e.g. p. 160f. Elisabeth Gössmann estimates the share of women writers of *querelle* texts to have been twenty per cent: id. (ed.) 1988 (as in note 9), p. 32. No one has yet attempted to quantify the relation of philogynous and misogynous *querelle* texts in Europe.

32. Cf. Ferguson, Moira: Feminist Polemic: British Women's Writings in English from the Late Renaissance to the French Revolution. In: Women's Studies International Forum 9, 1986, pp. 451-464.

33. Cf. Brandenberger and Hassauer 1997 (as in note 12) for analyses of the equivalent Spanish texts of the same period.

34. Cf. Chemello 1997 (as in note 12).

35. Cf. the telling lists of titles in Albistur/Armogathe 1977 (as in note 22), pp. 114-118 (1502-1599: "La querelle des femmes au XVIe siècle") and pp. 192-194 (1660-1700: "Le féminisme à l'âge classique"). Cf. also Nicolas de Cholières: La guerre des mâles contre les femelles (1588).

36. Joan DeJean draws attention to this in the context of the *Querelle des Anciens et des Modernes*: Did the Seventeenth Century Invent our Fin de Siècle? Or, the Creation of

the Enlightenment That We May at Last Be Leaving Behind. In: Critical Inquiry, vol. 22, no. 4, 1996, pp. 790-816, in part. p. 794f.

37. Cf. the Italian lists of titles in Fahy 1956 (as in note 10); Zancan 1983 (as in note 6), pp. 237-64; Capra, Galeazzo Flavio: Della eccellenza e dignità delle donne. Ed. by Maria Luisa Doglio, Rome 1988, pp. 113-125. An example for "querellarsi" can be found in Chemello 1997 (as in note 12). Cf. also below, note 50.

38. Wunder, Heide: "Das andere Geschlecht". Geschlechterperspektiven in der Frühen Neuzeit. In: Henke-Bockschatz, Gerhard (ed.): Geschichte und historisches Lernen. Jochen Huhn zum 65. Geburtstag. Kassel 1995, pp. 229-245. Cf. Maclean 1980 (see above, note 11), p. 74: *certamen* as "war of the sexes" (here the issue is the "differentiae sexus" in the dynastic lines of succession and the accession to the throne in Italy, France, Spain and Germany): Gössmann (ed.): Archiv, vol. 1, 2, 4 (as in note 9).

39. Eichendorff, Joseph von: Die deutsche Salon-Poesie der Frauen, in: Historisch-politische Blätter für das katholische Deutschland, vol. 19, 1847, pp. 463-480, here p. 464.

40. Erasmus von Rotterdam: Ausgewählte Schriften. Ed. by Werner Welzig, 8 vols., Darmstadt 1968, vol. 5, pp. 359-451.

41. Gierl 1997 (as in note 13).

42. Kapitza, Peter K.: Ein bürgerlicher Krieg in der gelehrten Welt. Zur Geschichte der Querelle des Anciens et des Modernes in Deutschland. Munich 1980, pp. 9-16, 25. More specific information on the titles mentioned above can also be found here. For Irailh s. above, note 7 and Kapitza 1980, p. 10, 447. Cf. also Gössmann, Elisabeth: Antiqui und Moderni im Mittelalter, Munich 1974.

43. E.g. in Jean de la Forge: Le Cercle des Femmes Sçavantes. Paris 1663.

44. Kapitza 1980, p. 430f, 374. Cf. also Kortum, Hans: Charles Perrault und Nicolas Boileau. Der Antike-Streit im Zeitalter der klassischen französischen Literatur. Berlin 1966, e.g. p. 14; Adam, Antoine: Baroque et préciosité. In: Revue des sciences humaines, vol. 1949, pp. 208-224, here p. 213; Leporin, Dorothea Christiane: Gründliche Untersuchung der Ursachen, die das Weibliche Geschlecht vom Studiren abhalten [...]. Berlin 1742.

45. Buck, August: Die "Querelle des anciens et des modernes" im italienischen Selbstverständnis der Renaissance und des Barocks. In: Sitzungsberichte der wissenschaftlichen Gesellschaft an der Johann Wolfgang Goethe-Universität Frankfurt, vol. 11, no. 1, Wiesbaden 1973, p. 5; Kapitza 1980 (as in note 42), p. 9, 16, 447, 485. In addition cf. DeJean 1996 (as in note 36) and Le Goff, Jacques: Geschichte und Gedächtnis. Frankfurt a. M. 1992, in part. pp. 56-61.

46. See above, note 2.

47. Numerous texts published around 1900 carry the word "feminism" in their titles, in particular texts by the conservative writer Théodore Joran, whose constant outpourings include almost yearly statements on this topic. English examples are the following: Richards, Samuel Alfred: Feminist Writers of the Seventeenth Century, London 1914; Richardson, Lula McDowell: The Forerunners of Feminism in French Literature of the Renaissance from Christine de Pisan to Marie de Gournay. Baltimore, Paris 1929, repr. Ann Arbor 1979. From a modern perspective cf. Bard, Christine: Les Filles de Marianne. Histoire des féminismes 1914-1940, Paris 1995, pp. 21-23; Zimmermann, Margarete: Christine de Pizan und die Feminismus-Debatten des frühen XX. Jahrhunderts. In: Kroll, Renate/Zimmermann, Margarete (eds.): Feministische Literaturwissenschaft in der Romanistik. Stuttgart, Weimar 1995, pp. 156-185.

48. The "classic" studies by the pupil of Abel Lefranc, Georges Ascoli, emerged in this context: Essay sur l'histoire des idées féministes en France du XVIe siècle à la Révolution. In: Revue de Synthèse historique, vol. 13, 1906, pp. 25-57, 99-106, 161-184; Léon Abensour: Histoire générale du féminisme. Des origines à nos jours, Paris 1921; id.: La Femme et le féminisme avant la Révolution. Paris 1923. He had also identified an earlier form of "feminism" in Milano: Un mouvement féministe au XIIIe siècle. In: La Nouvelle Revue, vol. 20, 1911, pp. 111-116; more recently cf. Muraro, Luisa: Guglielma e Maifreda. Storia di un'eresia femminista, Milano 1985 (German translation: Freiburg 1987). The question remains, however, whether the importance of the gender controversy *querelle* is not unsuitably played down if one reverts to the term *querelle des femmes* when identifying such a historical depth for "feminism". Cf. DeJean (as in note 36), p. 794: "Thus, *querelle*, a relatively lightweight term, is used to designate intellectual controversies as sustained and as momentous as the centuries-long conflict over women's rights and status known as the *Querelle des femmes*."

49. König 1909 (as in note 20), p. 2.

50. Kalbfleisch, Julia, née Benas: Le Triumphe des Dames von Olivier de la Marche. Ausgabe nach den Handschriften (Diss. phil., Bern 1899). Rostock 1901. In the glossary Kalbfleisch also refers to the occurrence of "querre, querir" in the sense of "beseech, look for, desire" (p. 118). Yet neither "querelle" nor "feminism" are mentioned. Henriette Goldschmidt is not considered an eminent figure in today's gender historiography. She is known rather for her alleged opposition to women's right to vote and the sentence considered "typical" for her: "Our programme must be moderate and not precipitate" (Gerhard, Ute: Unerhört. Die Geschichte der deutschen Frauenbewegung. Reinbek 1990, p. 124). But neither the oppositional attitude nor the quotation are from the woman from Leipzig but from a woman from Berlin who had the same name. She was a board-member of the Berlin society "Frauenwohl" (*Women's Welfare*) which is counted as part of the "radical" wing of the movement. Cf. Kemp, Annerose: Henriette Goldschmidt. Vom Frauenrecht zur Kindererziehung. In: Ephraim Carlebach Stiftung (ed.): Judaica Lipsiensia. Zur Geschichte der Juden in Leipzig. Leipzig 1994, pp. 33-53.

51. Albistur/Armogathe 1977 (as in note 22); Maclean, Ian: Woman Triumphant. Feminism in French Literature, 1610-1652. Oxford 1977; Angenot, Marc: Les Champions des femmes. Examen du discours sur la supériorité des femmes, 1400-1800. Montréal 1977. For similar studies on English developments s. above, note 30.

52. Kelly (as in note 6); Gössmann (as in note 9); Jordan and Benson (as in note 30). Many European *querelle* texts as well as other relevant works were already compiled by Ruth Kelso (891 for Europe for the period 1400-1600), in whose influential study the "war of the sexes" was only one consideration among many others: Kelso, Ruth: Doctrine for the Lady of the Renaissance. Urbana 1978 (first edition 1956), p. 2 and list of titles pp. 326-424. Kelso had conceived her study as an appendix for an earlier work: The Doctrine of the English Gentleman in the Sixteenth Century. Gloucester, Mass. 1964 (first edition 1929). The following studies focus on more than one country: Wilson, Katharine M. (ed.): Women Writers of the Renaissance and Reformation. Athens, London 1987 (Italy, France, Germany, The Netherlands, Spain, Hungary, England); Ferguson, Margaret W. et al. (eds.): Rewriting the Renaissance. The Discourses of Sexual Difference in Early Modern Europe. Chicago, London 1986.

53. Timmermans, Linda: L'Accès des femmes à la culture (1598-1715). Un débat d'idées de Saint François de Sales à la Marquise de Lambert. Paris 1993 (Bibliothèque

Littéraire de la Renaissance, series 3, vol. 26). Cf. also Steinbrügge, Lieselotte: The Moral Sex. Woman's Nature in the French Enlightenment. Oxford, New York 1995.

54. Solterer, Helen: The Master and Minerva. Disputing Women in French Medieval Culture. Berkeley, Los Angeles, London 1995, p. 18.

55. Cf. e.g. Garrard, Mary D.: Artemisia Gentileschi. The Image of the Female Hero in Italian Baroque Art. Princeton 1989, p. 10 and chap. 2; King, Margaret L.: Women of the Renaissance, Chicago, London 1991, p. 187; Duby, Georges/Perrot, Michelle (eds.): A History of Women in the West, vol. 3 Renaissance and Enlightenment Paradoxes. Natalie Zemon Davis and Arlette Farge (eds.): Introduction. Cambridge, Mass./London 1993; Fraisse, Geneviève: Der Bruch der Französischen Revolution und die Geschichte der Frauen. In: id.: Geschlecht und Moderne. Archäologien der Gleichberechtigung. Frankfurt a. M. 1995, pp. 77-95; Opitz, Claudia: Die Ehre des weiblichen Geschlechts. Jeanne d'Arc in der frühneuzeitlichen "querelle des femmes". In: Roeckelein, Hedwig et al. (eds.): Jeanne d'Arc oder: Wie Geschichte eine Figur konstruiert. Freiburg 1996, pp. 111-136.

56. For analyses of the *querelle's* iconographic tradition, see Groag Bell, Susan: "Verlorene Wandteppiche und politische Symbolik. Die *Cité des Dames* der Margarete von Österreich." In: Bock/Zimmermann (as in note 12), pp. 39-56, Matthews Grieco, Sara: "Georgette de Montenay: Eine andere Stimme in der Emblematik des 16. Jahrhunderts." In: op. cit., pp. 78-146 and Baumgärtel, Bettina: "Zum Bilderstreit um die Frau im 17. Jahrhundert. Inszenierungen französischer Regentinnen." In: op. cit., pp. 147-182.

57. Cf. Lawrence, Duggan G.: Was Art Really the "book of the illiterate"? In: Word and Image, vol. 5, 1989, pp. 227-51; Schnitzler, Norbert: Ikonoklasmus – Bildersturm: Theologischer Bilderstreit und ikonoklastisches Handeln während des 15. und 16. Jahrhunderts. Munich 1996, p. 20; Schreiner, Klaus: Maria – Jungfrau, Mutter, Herrscherin. Munich 1994, p. 252f. Iconographic gender research has come up with numerous findings during the past few decades; cf. e.g. Signori, Gabriele: Wörter, Sachen und Bilder. Oder: Die Mehrdeutigkeit des scheinbar Eindeutigen. In: Löther, Andrea et al. (eds.): Mundus in imagine. Bildersprache und Lebenswelten im Mittelalter. Festgabe für Klaus Schreiner. Munich 1996, pp. 11-34 (and additional important contributions to the same volume); King, John N.: The Godly Woman in Elizabethan Iconography. In: Renaissance Quarterly, vol. 38, 1985, pp. 41-84; Dresen-Coenders, Lène (ed.): Tussen heks en heilige. Nijmwegen 1985 (engl. translation: Saints and She-Devils: Images of Women in the 15th and 16th Centuries. London 1987); Zarri, Gabriela: Ursula and Catherine: The Marriage of Virgins in the Sixteenth Century. In: Matter, E. Ann/Coakley, John (eds.): Creative Women in Medieval and Early Modern Italy. A Religious and Artistic Renaissance. Philadelphia 1994, pp. 237-78; Simons, Patricia: Women in Frames: the Gaze, the Eye, the Profile in Renaissance Portraiture. In: History Workshop, vol. 25, 1988, pp. 4-30; Franits, Wayne E.: Paragons of Virtue: Women and Domesticity in Seventeenth-Century Dutch Art. Cambridge 1993; Junkerman, Anne Christine: Bellissima donna. An Interdisciplinary Study of Venetian Sensuous Half-length Images of the Early Sixteenth Century. Diss. University of Berkeley, 1988; Garrard 1989 (as in note 55); Moxey 1989 (as in note 5); Metken 1996 (as in note 4).

58. For this term see Le Goff, Jacques: L'Imaginaire médieval. Paris 1985, and the critical discussion of Le Goff's concept of the *imaginaire* in Oexle, Otto Gerhard: Das Andere, die Unterschiede, das Ganze. Jacques Le Goffs Bild des europäischen Mittelalters. In: Francia. Forschungen zur westeuropäischen Geschichte, vol. 17/1, 1990, pp. 141-158.

59. In *De re uxoria* (1415/16, German translation Berlin 1933) the Venetian Francesco Barbaro argues for marriage as the most praiseworthy way of life, while his grandson Ermolao Barbaro argues against it in *De coelibatu* (ca. 1472): only without the distraction provided by a wife and children can one devote oneself to studying and to state affairs. Cf. Della Casa, Giovanni: Se si debba prendere moglie [= An uxor sit ducenda, 1537]. Galateo. Ed. by Arnaldo di Benedetto, Turin 1991 (bilingual edition). On the subject of marriage in texts by women cf. Zimmermann, Margarete: Gamologien und Geschlechtertänze. Ehereflexionen in Texten französischer und italienischer Autorinnen des 15.-17. Jahrhunderts. In: Rüdiger Schnell (ed.): Text und Geschlecht. Mann und Frau in Eheschriften der frühen Neuzeit. Frankfurt a. M. 1997, pp. 303-327; for the same topic in texts by men: Walter, Eric: Le complexe d'Abélard ou le célibat des gens de lettres. In: Dix-huitième Siècle, vol. 12, 1980, pp. 126-152.

60. For the problem of marriage and liberty in the *Quinze joyes de mariage* cf. Zimmermann, Margarete: Vom Hausbuch zur Novelle. Didaktische und erzählende Prosa im Frankreich des späten Mittelalters. Düsseldorf 1989, pp. 79-232. Schneider, Elisabeth: Das Bild der Frau im Werk des Erasmus von Rotterdam. Basel, Stuttgart 1955, p. 54.

61. See below, *Discoveries*. For diatribes against women cf. Wilson, Katharina M./Makowski, Elizabeth M.: Wykked Wyves and the Woes of Marriage. Misogamous Literature from Juvenal to Chaucer. Albany 1991. Tobias Brandenberger 1997 (as in note 12) has shown how the marriage debate in the Iberian region forms part of a more comprehensive gender debate.

62. Brandt, Walther I. (ed.): Luther's Works, vol. 45. General editor: Helmut T. Lehmann. Philadelphia 1962 (quotations: pp. 36-38). Luther also polemicized against the misogynous tradition in other texts; cf. e.g. id.: Sämtliche Schriften. Groß Osingen 1987, vol. 14, p. 415f. Cf. Wunder 1992 (as in note 4): on the married couple as working couple see chap. 3 and 4; on the *querelle* in the context of the marriage debate: p. 63, 73f; Chrisman, Miriam Usher: Lay Culture, Learned Culture, 1480-1599. New Haven 1982, p. 104f, 111f; Harrington, Joel F.: Reordering Marriage and Society in Reformation Germany. Cambridge 1995.

63. Telle 1937 (as in note 2), pp. 329-335; Moeller, Bernd: Die Brautwerbung Martin Bucers für Wolfgang Capito. Zur Sozialgeschichte des evangelischen Pfarrerstandes. In: Grenzmann, Ludger et al. (eds.): Philologie als Kulturwissenschaft. Festschrift für Karl Stackmann zum 65. Geburtstag. Göttingen 1987, pp. 306-325; Roper, Lyndal: Das fromme Haus. Frauen und Moral in der Reformation. Frankfurt a. M. 1995. A treasure trove still awaiting thorough analysis is the collection compiled by Köhler, Hans Joachim (ed.): Flugschriften des frühen 16. Jahrhunderts (1501-1530). Microfiche-collection. Leiden 1978-1987 (ca. 2000 broadsides).

64. Quoted in: Albistur/Armogathe 1977 (as in note 22), p. 202. On the critique of marriage by the *précieuses* cf. Maclean 1977 (as in note 51), pp. 114-118; Baader, Renate: Dames de Lettres. Autorinnen des preziösen, hocharistokratischen und "modernen" Salons (1649-1698): Mlle de Scudéry – Mlle de Montpensier – Mme d'Aulnoy. Stuttgart 1986, pp. 95-131; Büff, Renate: Ruelle und Realität. Preziöse Liebes- und Ehekonzeptionen und ihre Hintergründe. Heidelberg 1979 (Studia Romanica, vol. 35).

65. In: Hill, Bridget (ed.): The First English Feminist: *Reflections Upon Marriage* and Other Writings. Aldershot 1986, p. 105f, 127. Cf. Perry, Ruth: The Celebrated Mary Astell: An Early Feminist. Chicago 1986.

66. Cf. Groag Bell 1997 (as in note 56).

67. John Knox: First Blast of the Trumpet against the Monstruous regiment of women (1558), and the answer by John Aylmer: An Harborowe for faithfull and trewe Subjectes against the late blowne Blaste, concerning the Government of Women (1559). Cf. Jordan, Constance: Woman's Rule in Sixteenth-Century British Political Thought. In: Renaissance Quarterly, vol. 40, 1987, pp. 262-72; Jordan 1990 (as in note 30), in part. chap. 2; Maclean 1980 (as in note 11), pp. 60-63, 73-75. For France cf. Maclean 1977 (as in note 51); pp. 16, 58-62, 192f; Hanley, Sara: La loi salique. In: Christine Faurié (ed.): Encyclopédie politique et historique des femmes. Paris 1997, pp. 11-30.

68. "Das aber hiewider sagen [*gegen den Satz, daß* das Weib under des Mannes macht sey], die heylige Schrift gebe jnen den Nammen, das sie Männin heissen, darumb jnen die Herrschafft und regierung gleich so wohl als dem Manne gebüre, faren derhalben zu unnd understehen sich des Regiments, [...] solches ist ein frevel"; "die erfahrunge gibts, das man wenig Weiber findet, die jhren Ehemännern gehorsam und unterthänig sein wollen, sondern sein des mehrern teils stoltz, fräch, hartnäckig und eigensinning, wollen sich nicht regieren lassen". Spangenberg, Cyriacus: Ehespiegel. Straßburg 1563, quoted in: Fischer, Hubertus: Ehe, Eros und das Recht zu reden. Anmerkungen zum protestantischen Ehebild in Texten des 16. Jahrhunderts. In: Müller, Maria E. (ed.): Eheglück und Liebesjoch. Bilder von Liebe, Ehe und Familie in der Literatur des 15. und 16. Jahrhunderts. Berlin 1988, p. 220f. We are grateful to Jutta Eming for her help with this translation.

69. See Lauer 1997 (as in note 12).

70. Opitz, Claudia: Streit der Frauen? Die frühneuzeitliche "Querelle des femmes" aus sozial- und frauengeschichtlicher Sicht. In: Historische Mitteilungen, vol. 8, no. 1, 1995, pp. 15-27 (on France). Likewise Fietze 1996 (as in note 4). On Claudia Opitz' suggestion to divide the *querelle* material into three groups – "the querelle of the courtly ladies and salons ladies", "the scholars' querelle" and "the querelle of everyday life" see Hassauer 1997 (as in note 12).

71. Cf. e.g. Jordan 1990, Benson 1992 (as in note 30) and the contributions to Bock/Zimmermann 1997 (as in note 12).

72. Cf. the fundamental study by De Rentiis, Dina: Die Zeit der Nachfolge. Zur Interdependenz von *imitatio Christi* und *imitatio auctorum* im 12.-16. Jahrhundert. Tübingen 1996.

73. Cf. the recent research into exempla undertaken from a perspective inspired by literary history and the history of mentalities: Bremond, Claude/Le Goff, Jacques: L'Exemplum. Turnhout 1982; von Moos, Peter: Geschichte der Topik. Das rhetorische Exemplum von der Antike zur Neuzeit und die *historiae* im *Policraticus* des Johannes von Salisbury. Hildesheim 1988; also Struever, Nancy C.: The Language of History in the Renaissance. Princeton 1970; Kessler, Eckhard: Petrarca und die Geschichte. Geschichtsschreibung, Rhetorik, Philosophie im Übergang vom Mittelalter zur Neuzeit. Munich 1978; Wunder 1992 (as in note 4); p. 267.

74. Ian Maclean suggests the term "seminal works" for theses texts and counts amongst them e.g. Heinrich Cornelius Agrippa's *Declamatio de nobilitate et praecellentia foeminei sexus*. Maclean 1977 (as in note 51), p. 25f.

75. Cf. e.g. Di Nardi, Maria: La donna nella 'Bibliothèque bleue' ovvero le perversioni di un mito. In: Bollème, Geneviève (ed.): La 'Bibiothèque bleue' nel seicento o della letteratura per il popolo. Bari, Paris 1981, pp. 91-110; Farge, Arlette (ed.): Le Miroir des femmes. Paris 1982 (in the "Bibliothèque bleue" edited by Daniel Roche); Hufton,

Olwen: The Prospect Before Her. A History of Women in Western Europe. vol. 1: 1500-1800, London 1995, pp. 49-51; Wunder 1992 (as in note 4), p. 74.

76. Lefranc 1914 (first edition 1904, as in note 2), p. 253: "C'est, du reste, une vieille querelle, aussi ancienne que le monde, puisqu'elle commença à l'aurore de l'humanité, au moment où notre première mère tend la pomme à notre premier père, et elle durera sans doute jusqu'à la fin des âges." ("It is incidentally an old quarrel, as old as the world, since it began when humankind first saw the light of day, when our progenitrix first gave the apple to our progenitor, and it will doubtlessly continue till the end of all time.") This is of course no historical analysis but itself a (*querelle*) *topos*.

77. Bouchet 1536 (as in note 17), p. a verso.

78. Hufton 1995 (as in note 75), p. 29 and chap. 1 ("Constructing Woman"); Lerner, Gerda: The Creation of Feminist Consciousness from the Middle Ages to Eighteen-seventy, in particular chap. 7 ("One Thousand Years of Feminist Bible Criticism"). Cf. also Turner, James Grantham: One Flesh: Paradisal Marriage and Sexual Relations in the Age of Milton. Oxford 1987, in part. chap. 3: "'The State of Eve': Female Ontogeny and the Politics of Marriage" (pp. 96-123). The interpretation to be found on postcards today – "When God created man she was only practising" – was of course already known at the time. Bible exegesis and the interpretation of the Book of Genesis was part of the controversy during the 19th century; one example among many: Schwarzkopf, Jutta: Women in the Chartist Movement. New York 1991, in part. chap. 4.

79. Lefranc 1914 (first edition 1904, as in note 2), pp. 251-69 ("avant le XVIe siècle"); Ascoli 1906 (as in note 48), p. 99; Telle 1936/1969 (as in note 2), chap. 1 and 2; Dow 1936 (as in note 2).

80. Davis/Farge 1994 (as in note 55), p. 12f; Lougee, Carolyn C.: Le Paradis des Femmes. Women, Salons and Social Stratification in 17th-Century France. Princeton 1976, p. 3, 174; Kelly 1982 (as in note 6); Lerner 1993 (as in note 78), p. 176, 278ff; Maclean 1977 (as in note 51), p. VIII, 35, 63, 208, 266f.

81. Jordan 1990 (as in note 30), p. 2, 86-94, 100-105, 191. She uses the term exclusively for France. The (late) Middle Ages as the beginning of the *querelle* also in Angenot 1977 and Maclean 1977 (as in note 51), p. 25; Jardine, Alice A.: Gynesis. Configurations of Woman and Modernity. Ithaca, London 1985, pp. 93-96 (here the *querelle's* beginning is even situated in the 10th and 11th centuries); Solterer 1995 (as in note 54); Zimmermann 1995 (as in note 15).

82. As e.g. in the important work by Wiesner, Merry E.: Working Women in Renaissance Germany. New Brunswick 1986; cf. Wiesner 1993 (as in note 4), p. 15 ("The Renaissance Debate About Women").

83. Cf. Wilson/Makowski 1991 (as in note 61).

84. Several research groups are currently working on oral and written culture since the Middle Ages: Freiburg ("Übergänge und Spannungsfelder zwischen Mündlichkeit und Schriftlichkeit"), Münster ("Träger, Felder, Formen pragmatischer Schriftlichkeit im Mittelalter"), Zürich ("Schriftlichkeit, Kommunikationskultur und Herrschaftspraktiken im Spätmittelalter").

85. Cf. Jardine 1985 (as in note 81); Solterer 1995 (as in note 54).

86. Cf. Wulff, A.: Die frauenfeindlichen Dichtungen in den romanischen Literaturen des Mittelalters bis zum Ende des 13. Jahrhunderts. Halle 1914; Pagano, Mario (ed.): *Dit des Cornetes*. Poemetto misogino antico francese del XIII secolo. Naples 1982, in part. "Introduzione" (pp. 7-24). A useful selection of texts from the 12th-15th centuries:

Blamires, Alcuin (ed.): Woman Defamed and Woman Defended. An Anthology of Medieval Texts. Oxford 1992. Cf. also: Grundriß der Romanischen Literaturen des Mittelalters, vol. VIII, 1: La littérature française aux XIVe et XVe siècles. Heidelberg 1988, p. 158f: "Pour et contre les femmes".

87. Solterer 1995 (as in note 54), p. 12ff.

88. A profound account of this problem which focuses on the male voices can be found in Fletcher, Anthony: Gender, Sex and Subordination in England 1500-1800. New Haven, London 1995. Fletcher argues that at the beginning of that period men felt threatened by women's self-assertion and thus looked for literary and social ways of stabilising gender hierarchies.– Women's voices did exist during the early phase of the *querelle*, yet normally they are not counted as *querelle* texts; cf. e.g. Lerner 1993 (as in note 78), in part. chap. 3.

89. See above, note 16. The most important texts of the dispute over the *Romance of the Rose*: Hicks, Eric (ed.): Le Débat sur le *Roman de la Rose*, Paris 1977. Christine de Pizan: Le Livre de la Cité des Dames. Ed. by Maureen Cheney Curnow. 2 vols., Diss. Vanderbilt University, 1975 (an edition of the Middle French original); a new Middle French edition by Earl Jeffrey Richards with an Italian translation by Patrizia Caraffi has recently been published (Rome 1997). English translations: The Book of the City of Ladies. Translated by Earl Jeffrey Richards. Revised edition, New York 1988; The book of the city of ladies. Translated and with an introduction and notes by Rosalind Brown-Grant. London 1999. Afterwards Christine wrote *Le Livre des Trois Vertus* (or *Livre du Trésor de la Cité des Dames*). German transl. by Claudia Probst: Pizan, Christine de: Der Schatz der Stadt der Frauen. Weibliche Lebensklugheit in der Welt des Spätmittelalters. Ed. by Claudia Opitz, Freiburg 1996. Engl. transl. by Charity Cannon Willard: Pizan, Christine de: A Medieval Woman's Mirror of Honor. The Treasury of the City of Ladies. Ed. with an introd. by Madeleine Pelner Cosman. New York 1989.

90. See Brandenberger 1997 (as in note 12).

91. Cf. Chemello 1997 (as in note 12) and Arslan, Antonia et al. (eds.): Le Stanze Ritrovate. Antologia di Scrittrici Venete dal Quattrocento al Novecento. Mirano-Venezia 1991; Niccoli, Ottavia (ed.): Rinascimento al femminile. Bari 1991; Migiel, Marylin/Schiesari, Juliana (eds.): Refiguring Women. Perspectives on Gender and the Italian Renaissance. Ithaca 1991; Wilson (ed.) 1987 (as in note 52); Panizza (ed.) 1997 (as in note 29). Mainly Italian authors are currently being translated into English and are published in the series *The Other Voice in Early Modern Europe*. Ed. by Margaret King and Albert Rabil (University of Chicago Press). So far texts by Agrippa von Nettesheim, Cecilia Ferrazzi, Antonia Pulci, Moderata Fonte, Tullia d'Aragona, Laura Cereta, Anna Maria van Schurman and Lucrezia Marinelli have been published.

92. Cf. Ferguson 1986 (as in note 32).

93. Cf. Ulbrich, Claudia: Frauen in der Reformation. In: Boskowska-Leimgruber, Nada (ed.): Die Frühe Neuzeit in der Geschichtswissenschaft: Forschungstendenzen und Forschungserträge. Paderborn 1997; Classen, Albrecht: Frauen in der deutschen Reformation: Neufunde von Texten und Autorinnen sowie deren Neubewertung. In: Schmidt, Paul Gerhard (ed.): Die Frau in der Renaissance. Wiesbaden 1994; Wunder 1992 (as in note 4), in part. chap. 3; Archiv für Reformationsgeschichte, vol. 63, 1972 (special issue "Frauen und Reformation"); Zimmerli-Witschi, Alice: Frauen in der Reformationszeit. Zurich 1981; Roper 1995 (as in note 63), pp. 183-208; Halbach, Silke: Argula von Grumbach als Verfasserin reformatorischer Flugschriften. Frankfurt a. M. 1992; Bainton, Roland H.: Women of the Reformation in Germany and Italy. Minneapolis

1971; id.: Women of the Reformation from Spain to Scandinavia. Minneapolis 1973; Marschall, Sherrin (ed.): Women in Reformation and Counter-Reformation Europe. Bloomington 1989; Roper, Lyndal: Sexualutopien in der deutschen Reformation. In: id.: Ödipus und der Teufel. Körper und Psyche in der Frühen Neuzeit. Frankfurt a. M. 1995, pp. 78-108; Kobelt-Groch, Marion: Aufsässige Töchter Gottes. Frauen im Bauernkrieg und in den Täuferbewegungen. Frankfurt a. M. 1993.

94. Maclean 1977 (as in note 51), p. VIII, 25, 35, 63, 208, 266f.

95. Lerner 1993 (as in note 78), p. 176, 179f, 235, 278ff, 303ff, 31ff, 317. For the latter aspect cf. also Smith, Bonnie G.: The Contribution of Women to Modern Historiography in Great Britain, France, and the United States, 1750-1940. In: American Historical Review, vol. 89, 1984, p. 709-731; Davis, Natalie Z.: Gender and Genre: Women as Historical Writers, 1400-1820. In: Labalme, Patricia H. (ed.): Beyond Their Sex. Learned Women in the European Past. New York 1984.

96. Honegger (as in note 4); Albistur/Armogathe 1977 (as in note 22), vol. 1, pp. 266-272.

97. Fraisse 1995 (as in note 55), p. 93f; cf. also Fraisse, Geneviève: La Raison des femmes. Paris 1992, in part. part one, chap. 1.

98. Cf. Rendall, Jane: The Origins of Feminism, 1780-1860. Women in Britain, France and the United States. Basingstoke, London 1985.

99. Badinter, Elisabeth (ed.): Qu'est-ce qu'une femme? Paris 1989. Cf. id. (ed.): Paroles d'hommes. Paris 1989.

100. Moses, Claire: French Feminism in the 19th Century. Albany 1984, chap. 7 ("*La Querelle des femmes* of the Second Empire").

101. E.g. Harper, Paula Hays: Votes for Women? A Graphic Episode in the Battle of the Sexes. In: Millon, Henry A./Nochlin, Linda (eds.): Art and Architecture in the Service of Politics. Cambridge, Mass. 1978, pp. 150-161.

102. After surveying the historical *querelle des femmes* Alice A. Jardine claims its tradition for modern feminism and sees "a new kind of *querelle des femmes*: a strangely new and urgent emphasis on uses of woman as part of a strategy of radical reading and writing – the urgently explicit and unavoidable attempts of modernity to think the unnameable (God or Woman?) before it thinks 'us'. Who?" (as in note 81, p. 102). Friederike Hassauer closes her contribution to Bock/Zimmermann 1997 (as in note 12) in a similar manner.

103. Both texts were recently published together for the first time: Wollstonecraft, Mary: A Vindication of the Rights of Men, with A Vindication of the Rights of Woman and Hints. Ed. by Sylvana Tomaselli, Cambridge 1995 (on the research situation: pp. XXXIII-XXXVII). Olympe de Gouges has also recently been considered from the perspective of the preceding *querelle des femmes*: Harth 1992 (as in note 13), p. 2, 13, 116, 163, 213-234.

104. See Ferguson 1986 (as in note 32).

105. Cf. e.g Chemello 1997 (as in note 12). Further texts are e.g.: Erasmus von Rotterdam: Colloquia familiaria [1526]. Vertraute Gespräche. Stuttgart 1976 (bilingual ed.), pp. 3-17: "Abbatis et Eruditae. Der Abt und die gelehrte Frau" (in the above-mentioned edition, see note 36: vol. 6, pp. 252-265).

106. Maclean, Ian: Parody, Pastiche and the Self-Consciousness of Women in France, 1600-1660. Contribution to the conference on "Inferiority and Superiority: The 'Querelle des femmes' in Renaissance Europe" (European University Institute, Florence, 1989). On irony and sarcasm in the historiographical writings of that period cf. Struever 1970 (as in

note 73); Bock, Gisela: Machiavelli als Geschichtsschreiber. In: Quellen und Forschungen aus italienischen Archiven und Bibliotheken, vol. 66, 1986, pp. 153-191.

107. Fahy 1956 (as in note 10), p. 38f: Maclean 1980 (as in note 11), p. 80; Agrippa, Ed. by Jungmayr (as in note 10), p. 93. for the concept of "seminal works" see above, note 74.

108. Cf. Benson 1992 (as in note 30), Chemello 1997 (as in note 12), and Kolsky, Stephen D.: Women Through Men's Eyes: The Third Book of *Il Cortegiano*. In: O'Neill, Tom (ed.): The Shared Horizon. Melbourne Essays in Italian Language and Literature in Memory of Colin McCornick. Dublin 1990, pp. 41-91.

109. Cf. Fleischer 1981 (as in note 11) and Maclean 1980 (as in note 11), p. 12f.

110. For examples of this kind of work cf. Brandenberger 1997 (as in note 12), Chemello 1997 (as in note 12), Matthews Grieco 1997 (as in note 56) and Pieper 1997 (as in note 12).

Muslime und Christen im *Grafen Rudolf* und in der *Kreuzfahrt Landgraf Ludwigs des Frommen von Thüringen*: Zu Toleranz und Religiösem Disput zur Zeit der Kreuzzüge

Maria Dorninger

English Summary

The era of the Crusades is usually regarded as a period of increasing intolerance of other religions. The concept of a *bellum iustum* in the sense of a defensive war legitimizes the conflict from a Christian point of view and influences the images found in epic literature. Moreover, this necessitates highlighting the differences between the two faiths. Arguments and discourse strategies may have been shaped by contacts with the other religion or drawn from dispute literature. The presentation of the Muslims and of the opposition to their religious beliefs cannot be separated from the depictions of tolerance that can be found even in Crusade literature.

Therefore, the tolerance depicted in these two Crusade epics and its counterpoint of religious argument are of special interest. Both are evident in the remarks of individuals and in the interactions between members of the two different religions.

In both epics there seems to be little difference between Christians and Muslims with regard to their cultural achievements, behaviour in warfare, respect for treaties, and attitudes toward knighthood. Allusions can even be found in which Christians are justified in fighting on the side of the Muslims. However, the real proving ground for tolerance is at the religious level, where the central accusation of polytheism discredits the other faith. Originating in polemical dispute literature, this censure renders religious consensus impossible and provides a rationalization for military combat. Thus, while remaining true to their genre, the epics promote a more or less polemical model, although more accurate information about Islam was known and available. Nevertheless, from the Christian point of view, the anguish caused by religious divisions affecting deep human relationships with respected members of the other culture becomes the starting point for a more enlightened attitude and an impetus for new dialogue with the other religion.

* * *

wer was der [...] *die sigenunft gewan*
daz er er der helle porten brach
unt der Adames ungemach erwante? daz tet diu Trinitat!
der sich einen selben dritten hat
ebenglich unt ebenher,
sich, der enstirbet nimmer mer
durh man noch wibes schulde.[...]
Do sprach der von Tenabri (ze Gyburc)*: „den einen möhten doch die dri*
vor dem tode han bewart.[1]

In dieser Auseinandersetzung zwischen der zur Christin gewordenen muslimischen Königin Gyburc und ihrem in seinem alten Glauben verharrenden Vater wird deutlich, welche Rolle Religion innerhalb der familiären Beziehungen einnehmen kann, oder auch in weiterer Folge zwischen unterschiedlichen Völkern. Nach Klaus Schreiner kann Religion als ‚eine alle Lebensbereiche durchdringende Deutungs-macht' definiert werden.[2] So kann bei Angehörigen unterschiedlicher Religionen zuerst Uninformiertheit gegeben sein, die bei einem größeren Informationsgrad jedoch nicht unbedingt zu einem größeren Verständnis des anderen führen muss. Eine Hilfestellung dazu kann das Gespräch über Religion, das Religionsgespräch, bieten, wie im Falle Gyburcs und ihres Vaters. Dennoch sind Verständnis-schwierigkeiten nicht immer ausräumbar. So ist die Komplexheit des christlichen Trinitätsgedanken dem muslimischen Vater nicht nachvollziehbar wie auch, dass Christus durch diese nicht vom Tode gerettet worden sei. Das Gespräch wird jedoch weiter geführt und weist in diesem Sinne trotz aller möglichen Einwände im Hinblick auf den Wunsch eines *persuadere*, das die Begriffe des Überredens wie auch Überzeugens beinhaltet, auf den Willen hin, mit dem anderen im Gespräch zu bleiben, sich zu informieren, möglicherweise auch darauf, die Haltung des anderen ernsthaft kennen zu lernen.

Die Information vom anderen bzw. der anderen Religion, die auch in Form religiöser Dialoge stattfinden kann, soll daher im Folgenden im Vordergrund stehen. Mit dem Aufkommen der Kreuzzüge gewinnt die Auseinandersetzung mit den außerchristlichen Religionen an Bedeutung, die einerseits in der Darstellung der Nichtchristen und ihrer vermuteten wie erforschten Glaubensinhalte in einer Spezialliteratur ihren Niederschlag finden kann. Informationen dieser Art können jedoch auch in epischen Werken Gestalt gewinnen, die von schriftlich fixierten Auseinandersetzungen und religiösen Gesprächen profitieren und die bisweilen - je nach Intention - deren oder zumindest ausgewählte Schlussfolgerungen einbeziehen. In diesem Sinne soll im Zentrum der Erörterungen die Darstellung des anderen in vulgärsprachliche Werken stehen. Die beiden anonym überlieferten Werke (der noch im 12. Jahrhundert verfasste) ‚Graf Rudolf' und die ‚Kreuzfahrt des Landgrafen Ludwig des Frommen von Thüringen' (aus dem Beginn des 14. Jahrhunderts) haben ihre Schauplätze im Heiligen Land. Die genannten Werke stehen in Verbindung mit der Kreuzzugsthematik und können in geringerem bzw. größerem Ausmaße der Kreuzzugsepik zugerechnet werden. Vor ihrer näheren Betrachtung, erscheint es jedoch als angemessen, noch einige Begriffe und Hintergründe zu klären, wie die Begriffe der Kreuzzugsliteratur, der Toleranz oder Termini der Disputliteratur.

I. 1 Zur Definition von Kreuzzugsliteratur

Im engeren Sinne gehören zur Kreuzzugliteratur Werke, die sich mit der Kreuzzugsthematik auseinandersetzen. Unter Kreuzzug wird dabei nach der Definition von Ulrich Müller ein Krieg im Sinne eines Augustinischen ‚bellum de auctore'[3] verstanden. Dieser Krieg schließt nach dem Verständnis Urbans II. den Krieg zur Befreiung und Verteidigung von Glaubensgenossen ein,[4] der somit die Kriegszüge oder bewaffneten Pilgerreisen[5] ins Heilige Land umfasst wie sich auch gegen Mauren, Slawen und Ketzer richten kann.[6]

Als Papst Urban II. im November 1095 auf dem Konzil von Clermont zum ersten Kreuzzug aufrief, blieb sein bewegender Hilferuf für die im Heiligen Land bedrängten Christen nicht ungehört, die misshandelt und deren heilige Stätten entweiht wurden. Gleichzeitig wurde den designierten Helfern Ablass und Vergebung ihrer Sünden gewährt und damit dieser Krieg zum *bellum iustum* der Christen erklärt.[7]

Die Zeit der Kreuzzüge, die damit eingeleitet wurde, ist wohl eine der faszinierendsten Epochen des Mittelalters, öffnet sich hier doch in besonderer Weise der Westen für die Kultur und Pracht des Orients. Gleichzeitig gilt diese Epoche jedoch auch als eine der verstärkten Intoleranz gegenüber anderen Religionsgemeinschaften, dem nun die meisten an den Kreuzzügen beteiligten *nationes* direkter begegnen konnten.

Bei der Begegnung und der Beschreibung dieser beiden Kulturen, der christlich-westlichen und der islamisch-orientalischen, wurde die jeweils andere Kultur und damit auch die Menschen wohl mit den Vorstellungen der jeweiligen internal(isierten) ‚mental map'[8] wahrgenommen, wie in den literarischen Darstellungen sichtbar werden kann. Dabei wird auch die Problematik der Integrierung des anderen in das in der wahrnehmenden Kultur vorhandene Weltbild sichtbar gemacht und Tendenzen von Toleranz und Intoleranz aus christlicher Perspektive wahrnehmbar, bzw. Strategien des religiösen Diskurses, die das Miteinander bestimmen können. Diese sollen hier aufgezeigt werden.

I.2 Zum Begriff der Toleranz

Ein religiöser Diskurs ist daher auch im Zusammenhang mit dem Begriff der Toleranz bzw. *ex negativo* der Intoleranz zu sehen, die den Verlauf oder das Ergebnis des Diskurses maßgeblich mitbestimmen und diesen prägen. Der Begriff der Toleranz wiederum zeigt seine eigene Problematik und Historie. So weist die Geschichte des Begriffes auf seine Relativität wie das Bemühen von Menschen Beziehungen untereinander auch normativ zu gestalten.[9]

Ursprünglich in der klassischen Bedeutung bezieht sich das Verb ‚*tolerare*' wie auch sein Substantiv auf das schlichte Ertragen von äußeren Widrigkeiten wie Unrecht, Folter, Gewalttätigkeit, Schmerz, Schicksalsschlägen, Naturkatastrophen, militärischen Niederlagen und Ähnlichem, indem es immer um ein Ausharren des Menschen geht, oder um den Gleichmut des Menschen (nach Seneca) in diesen Begebenheiten, jedoch nicht um das Erdulden von Menschen, die anders denken.[10] Wegweisend (für die Begriffsbedeutung) wurde die Bibelübersetzung der *Vetus latina*, die die Bezeichnungen ‚*patientia*, *sustinentia*, *sufferentia*' und ‚*tolerantia*' als Synonyme verwendete.[11] Bereits bei Cyprian wurde die *tolerantia* mit sozialethischem Inhalt gefüllt und auf die Einheit der christlichen Gemeinde bezogen, wobei jedoch auch die religiöse Konkurrenz, die Juden, zu ertragen seien (‚*in Judaeis tolerandis*'). Durch die Haltung der *tolerantia* ist es jedoch auch möglich, in Ungläubigen eine Neigung für den Glauben der Christen zu bewirken.

Prägend für die Vorstellung der Toleranz im Mittelalter wurde jedoch der Kirchenvater Augustinus. *Tolerantia* wird nun eine soziale Grundtugend, wieder jedoch vor allem auf die christlichen Gemeinden, wie die Gesamtkirche bezogen. So soll der Mensch nicht nur *tolerantia* üben, sondern bedarf gleichzeitig infolge seines sündhaften Wesen selbst der Toleranz seiner Mitmenschen. Das Verhalten der Toleranz, das auch von der christlichen ‚*caritas*' geprägt ist, dient der kirchlichen Friedenswahrung innerhalb der Gemeinde, jedoch soll sich dieses Verhalten nach Augustinus auch nach außen richten. Es ist anzuwenden gegenüber Häretikern und Schismatikern wie auch den Heiden und den Juden, wobei diese jedoch nur in ihrer körperlichen und sozialen Existenz toleriert werden sollen, also von außen.[12]

Die Toleranz gegenüber dem Judentum, das die Wertschätzung und das Wohlwollen der Christen verdient, gründet sich dabei auf seine theologische Bedeutung für das Christentum als ‚Träger und Verwalter der alttestamentlichen Schriften für die christliche Kirche' wie auch für seine Funktion als Zeuge für die Wahrheit des Evangeliums, das sich aus den von den Christen nicht erfundenen Büchern des Alten Bundes erschließt. Das duldsame Verhalten der Kirche kann sich ihnen gegenüber auf biblische Argumente stützen. Zudem wird Israel sich am Ende der Tage bekehren und gerettet werden.[13]

Ähnlich wie bei den Juden, spricht sich auch Augustinus gegen eine Bekehrung durch Gewalt bei den Heiden aus und lehnt daher Zwangsmaßnahmen ab, dennoch distanziert er sich nicht von staatlichen Maßnahmen, die heidnische Kulte verbieten bzw. heidnische Tempel zerstören. Am rigorosesten ist Augustinus Einstellung gegenüber Häretikern im Zusammenhang mit der Abspaltung der Donatisten, die gewaltsam gegen die katholische Kirche vorgingen. Die staatliche Gewalt gegen sie versucht Augustinus mit dem Gedanken eines ‚legitimen Zwang[es] zum Guten' zu rechtfertigen, der durch das biblische Gleichnis vom Gastmahl mit der in ihm enthaltenen Aufforderung (‚*compelle intrare*' bzw. ‚*Cogite intrare'*, Lk 14, 16-24) gerechtfertigt werden konnte. Im Hinblick auf Häretiker konnte die Gewalt-anwendung als legitimes religiöses Verhalten auf die mit Gewalt verbundenen Provokationen der Donatisten gesehen werden.[14] Gleichzeitig wird jedoch das Gleichnis von Unkraut und Weizen (Mt 13,24-30) als ‚Plädoyer für Geduld und Toleranz' gegenüber falschen Brüdern Schismatikern und Ketzern gelesen.[15]

Dem christlichen Mittelalter waren diese Begriffsbestimmungen und Verhaltensforderungen nicht unbekannt und wurden nicht nur rezipiert, sondern auch weiterentwickelt. So konnte die Forderung nach Duldung/ Toleranz theologisch, pragmatisch doch auch naturrechtlich begründet werden, wobei jedoch aufgrund des Wahrheitsanspruches (nicht nur der christlichen Kirche) keine Ethik existierte, die anderen Kulturen oder Religionsformen eine vorbehaltlosen Anerkennung gewähr-te.[16] Ein Phänomen, das Ulrich Müller in seinem Artikel zur Toleranz auch bei anderen Weltreligionen wie dem Islam erkennen kann,[17] wobei nach der Definition von Franz-Xaver Kaufmann Religion als ‚eine alle Lebensbereiche durchdringende und sie zu regulierende Deutungsmacht'[18] definiert wird.

Eine vorbehaltlose Anerkennung einer anderen Religion als der christlichen wäre für das christliche Mittelalter nicht vorstellbar, daher muss vom Begriff der Toleranz und damit Duldung im Mittelalter der Begriff der Billigung (‚*approbatio*') getrennt werden. Die Möglichkeit zur Toleranz zeigt sich somit aus heutiger Sicht als eine eingeschränkte, jedoch als eine durchaus gegebene,[19] wobei es jedoch auch die Vorstellung von einem Recht auf ‚eine glaubensunabhängige Menschlichkeit' gibt.[20] Nach Klaus Schreiner gilt es bei dem Begriff Toleranz und seiner Verwirk-lichung (und dies gilt auch für die Gegenwart und die Vergangenheit) ebenso zu beachten, dass für ihn die ‚Differenzen und Distanzen zwischen ethischem Anspruch und tatsächlichem Verhalten [...] typisch [sind].' Gleichzeitig bedarf die Toleranz einer Grenzziehung, so dass bei der Beschäftigung mit Toleranz auch von einer ‚Geschichte sich stetig verändernder Grenzziehungen' gesprochen werden muss.[21]

I.3 Disput, Disputatio, Debatte und Religionsgespräch

Für die Art des Diskurses mit einer anderen Religion sind unterschiedliche Bezeichnungen möglich, wie Disputatio, Disput, Debatte oder auch Religionsgespräch, die sich jedoch in ihren Bedeutungen überschneiden können und bisweilen auch synonym verwendet werden.

Der Begriff ‚Disput' leitet sich vom lateinischen Verb *disputare* ab, das im kaufmännischen Sinn soviel wie ‚*überschätzen, abschätzen, berechnen*' bedeutet bzw. auch ‚*durch Reden, Sprechen mit Anderen, erwägen, genau untersuchen, erörtern*' oder ‚*über eine Sache abhandeln, sprechen*'. In diesem Sinne bedeutet das Abstraktum ‚*disputatio*' dann auch im eigentlichen Sinn 1) eine ‚*Überrechnung, einen Überschlag*' und 2) ‚*eine Untersuchung durch ein Gespräch wie auch eine Abhandlung*'.[22] Die ‚Disputation' zeigt sich somit als ‚*eine streitrede über einen wissenschaftlichen gegenstand*' wie auch als ‚*eine gelehrte streitschrift (dissertation)*'.[23] Bereits im Französischen wird das aus dem Lateinischen stam-mende Wort in der Bedeutung ‚*streiten*' verwendet und prägt so ab dem 17. Jahrhundert das Substantiv Disput in seinen Bedeutungen ‚*Auseinandersetzung*' und ‚*Wortstreit*' im Deutschen.[24]

Ähnlich geht die ‚Debatte' auf das französische Wort ‚*debatter*' zurück, das im eigentlichen Sinne sich *(mit Worten) schlagen*' meint[25] und auch die Bedeutungen ‚*erörtern, verhandeln, eingehend besprechen; lebhaft diskutieren*' einschließt.[26] Die Debatte als Wortschlacht im eigentlichen Sinne wird somit als lebhafte Diskussion, Auseinandersetzung oder auch Streitgespräch gesehen, während unter Disput auch ein Streitgespräch jedoch mehr im Sinne eines kontrovers geführten Gespräches verstanden wird.[27]

Allgemeiner und sachlicher zeigt sich der Terminus ‚Gespräch'. Gemeinsam ist jedoch allen Termini, ob sie nun im Sinne einer schriftlichen oder mündlichen Auseinandersetzung verstanden werden, die Ausrichtung auf einen realen oder fiktiven Dialogpartner und damit die dialogische Intention und Struktur.

Der französische Begriff ‚Débat' meint im Mittelalter als Gattung im strengen Sinn ein didaktisches Streitgedicht in Dialogform oft zwischen zwei Personen bzw. auch personifizierten Opponenten meist vor einem Schiedsrichter, das auch religiöse, politisch-soziale, ethische Themen aufgreift.[28] S. Griffith unterscheidet formal innerhalb der Disput-Literatur vor allem Berichte von (historischen?) Dialogen, für die er auch den Begriff Debatten verwendet, dem Thema entsprechend zwischen einem Muslim (‚Muslim official'), der Fragen stellt und einem christlichen Kleriker (‚Christian churchman'), der darauf antwortet, bzw. in der Form eines Lehrer-Schüler-Gesprächs, wobei der Schüler den Part des Muslim übernimmt. Der Disput kann jedoch auch in Form eines Briefes geführt werden.[29] U. Mattejiet wiederum unterscheidet zwischen der Form des mündlichen (öffent-lichen) Streitgespräches als Disputation und der schriftlichen Auseinandersetzung in Form der Traktatliteratur, wobei er ebenso auf die Dialogform rekurriert, die jedoch nicht eine historische Gesprächssituation als Ausgangspunkt haben muss.[30]

Die Funktionen des Disputes können unterschiedlich sein. Die überlieferten syrischen Texte zeigen vor allem apologetischen Charakter. Sie waren für die Christen selbst bestimmt, um deren Glauben zu stärken und sie mit Argumenten auszustatten.[31] Die in Arabisch verfassten Schriften versuchten der Tatsache Rechnung zu tragen, dass viele Christen zum Islam konvertierten und hoben vor allem die Unterschiede der beiden Religionen hervor. Sie waren für die Zielgruppe der religiös Unsicheren bestimmt. Die griechischen und lateinischen Schriften wiederum hatten oft polemischen Charakter und dienten dazu, den Islam zu dis-kreditieren. Sie spielten daher oft eine Rolle im Zusammenhang mit militärischen Aktionen gegen die Muslime.[32]

Ähnliche Funktionen sieht auch J. Waardenburg für das Religionsgespräch, das in einfachster Definition als ‚*Diskussion*' oder ‚*Gespräch über Religion*' gedeutet werden kann und sich mit dem Disput überschneiden kann. Diese Gespräche können dazu dienen, die Identität und Überlegenheit der eigenen Religion auszudrücken und deren Wahrheit zu betonen, wobei auch als Ziel gesehen werden kann, andere für diese Wahrheit zu gewinnen oder durch die Anerkennung der anderen Religion ‚*bestimmte Gesamtinteressen*' in den Vordergrund zu stellen.[33]

Dispute bzw. Debatten über Religionen ereignen sich jedoch nicht nur direkt in den dieser Gattung entsprechenden Textsorten. Dieser Diskurs bzw. Anregungen davon zeigen sich auch innerhalb anderer literarischen Gattungen, so im epischen Bereich. Hier können (Streit-) Gespräche über Religion zwischen Personen unter-schiedlicher Bekenntnisse stattfinden.[34] Hauptpunkte, Prinzipien und Ergebnisse der engeren Disputliteratur, auch polemischen Charakters, können dabei aufgegriffen werden wie auch ein Werk insgesamt im Hinblick auf die Darstellung unter-schiedlicher kultureller und religiöser Gruppen Ergebnisse oder Anregungen dieser Diskurse widerspiegeln kann. Der Autor oder Verfasser als derjenige, der die Diskurse gruppiert,[35] führt in gewissem Sinne durch seine Rezipientenorientiertheit einen Dialog mit dem Leser/ Hörer. In der Ausführung dieser Thematik kann dabei die Intention des Verfassers sichtbar werden.

II. Sarazenen und Christen

Bei der Analyse der Darstellung der Sarazenen[36] in den epischen Werken werden im Hinblick auf den Bereich der Toleranz die in den Werken gestaltete Toleranz bzw. deren Grenzen betrachtet und folgende Gesichtspunkte einbezogen, die sich jedoch auch überschneiden können:[37]

1) die Betrachtung des Islams unter einem evtl. auch feindlichen Vorzeichen. Hier werden auch die religiösen Aspekte einbezogen werden, wie auch ob es zu einem religiösen Gespräch, einem Disput, zwischen Christen und Muslimen kommen kann und wie sich der Diskurs (Auseinandersetzung) mit dem Andersgläubigen oder der anderen Religion gestaltet.
2) die sozio-kulturellen Beziehungen zum individuellen Muslim und
3) sofern sichtbar, die Ebene von rechtlichen Beziehungen.

II.1 Der ‚Graf Rudolf'

Das mitteldeutsche Kreuzzugsepos wurde von Hans Fromm in die 90ger Jahre des 12. Jahrhunderts datiert.[38] Durch die Hervorhebung der Belagerung von Askalon erschiene es nicht unmöglich - so auch Fromm - die Handlung der Erzählung in der Zeit des ersten Kreuzzuges zu sehen.[39] Vermutlich hatte das Epos eine französische Vorlage, worauf vor allem die französischen Namen hinweisen,[40] jedoch zeigt es auch, wie Hans Fromm teilweise ausgeführt hat, Motive aus der *chanson de geste*, wie Bezüge zur *chanson* de Guillaume oder der *chanson de Roland* zeigen.[41] Aufgrund seiner fragmentarischen Überlieferung erweist sich das Epos als sperrig für Interpretationen, jedoch zeigen sich - soweit erhalten - sichtbar der Kampf der Christen gegen die Heiden, eine Minnehandlung und das Verhältnis zwischen Vasall und Herr als gewichtige Themata der Darstellung.[42] Zusätzlich zur Hand-lungsebene der Figuren gibt es eine Erzählerebene, wobei der Erzähler kom-mentierend, doch auch bewertend auftreten kann.[43] Die 14 Fragmente einer Hand-schrift überliefern an die 1400 Verse, deren unleserliche Teile von Wilhelm Grimm genial ergänzt wurden.[44] Dennoch lassen sich inhaltlich einige Handlungslinien erkennen.

Das Geschehen lässt sich kurz zusammenfassen:

Graf Rudolf von Flandern setzt gegen den Willen seines Vaters die Teilnahme an einem Kreuzzug nach Jerusalem durch, da ihn die bedrängte Lage der Christen im Heiligen Land bewegt. Nachdem er an der Belagerung von Askalon teil-genommen hat und ein hohes Amt bei dem christlichen König Gilot bekleidet, erfährt der Leser/Hörer, dass Rudolf die politische Seite gewechselt und sich in eine heidnische Prinzessin verliebt hat. Rudolf gerät in (christliche) Gefangenschaft, die Prinzessin entschließt sich zur Taufe. Rudolf gelingt es zu entfliehen. In Konstan-tinopel gibt es ein Wiedersehen. Mit der Darstellung eines Raubüberfalls auf der Flucht bzw. der geheimgehaltenen Reise der beiden in die Heimat Graf Rudolfs endet das Epos.

Ist der Text auch nur bruchstückhaft vorhanden, Hans Fromm vermutet,[45] dass nur ein Viertel der eigentlich Länge erhalten ist, so lassen sich mit der Einschränkung, dass hier kein vollständiger Text gegeben sei, doch Rückschlüsse auf die Beziehung zwischen Christen und Heiden im Sinne von Islamgläubigen zeigen.[46]

II.1.1 Die Beziehung zwischen Christen und Sarazenen bzw. Heiden

Die Handlung auf christlicher Seite wird vor allem von zwei Gestalten beherrscht, dem christlichen König Gilot und Graf Rudolf. Während sich das Verhalten des Königs zu den Sarazenen statisch zeigt, wird das von Rudolf differenzierter gezeichnet.

Die Einstellung des Königs zu den Feinden wird vom Erzähler dekuvriert, indem er dessen Kriegsführung beschreibt. Gilot verwüstet ungehemmt das feindliche Gebiet (eine durchaus übliche Vorgangsweise) und tötet auch Frau und Kinder der Gegner, die - so muss man vermuten - von ihm nicht ganz als vollwertige Menschen eingestuft werden, denn er tötet sie, als ob sie Vieh wären ‚*die sluc man alse rinder*‘ (GR 31,18-19 und 25-26).[47] Als die Sarazenen bei der Belagerung Askalons zu einer List greifen und da es an Kämpfern mangelt, die Frauen als solche verkleiden, durchschauen die Christen diese List nicht. Für den König gibt es nur zwei Lösungsmöglichkeiten: im menschlichen Bereich das Versagen der von ihm aufgestellten Wachen, das eine Bestrafung nach sich ziehen muss, oder im geistlich-metaphysischen Bereich die Hilfe des Antichristen[48] für die Sarazenen und damit die eindeutige religiöse Zuordnung des Gegners in den Bereich des Bösen (GR 36,15-26).

Die Handlung und damit auch die Figur Rudolfs ist dagegen dynamischer gestaltet und reflektiert vieles von den Hintergründen der Kreuzzugsbewegung.

Das erste der erhaltenen Fragmente führt in die Motivation eines Kreuzzuges ein und damit in den Beweggrund Rudolfs, in das Heilige Land zu ziehen. Die Darstellung gibt damit wohl auch die allgemeine Ansicht über die Ereignisse im Osten wieder. Der Papst schickt einen Brief, um zur Befreiung des Heiligen Grabes aufzurufen. Vom Inhalt dieser Botschaft wird Graf Rudolf zu seinem Entschluss zur Kreuzfahrt bewegt. Es geht hier nicht so sehr um die Befreiung des Heiligen Grabes, sondern um die im Heiligen Land gefangenen und die unzähligen erschlagenen Christen (GR 26,7-10), wodurch Rudolfs sozialreligiöses Empfinden angesprochen wird. Der Bote spricht an dieser Stelle im

Topos der Überbietung über das Leid der Christen: ‚*der cristenen was gevangen/ also unmaze vil ir slagen/ daz u nieman ne kann gesagen/ umme die not die man in tud*‘ (GR 26,7-10). Die Feinde bleiben ungenannt, sind aber für den Zuhörer leicht zu entschlüsseln. Im Gebet des jungen Grafen Rudolf, der seine Kreuzfahrt gegenüber seinem Vater durchsetzen muss, unter dessen *munt* er steht,[49] wird jedoch der Feind vorerst eindeutig einer geistlichen Domäne zugeordnet, nämlich der des ‚*tuvel*[s]‘ (GR 26, 20).[50] Dadurch werden die beiden Sphären der durch Augustinus tradierten und prominent gemachten Vorstellung von einer *civitas Dei* und der *civitas diaboli* und ihre Opposition zueinander sichtbar gemacht.[51] Gleichzeitig wird mithin das Motiv der bewaffneten Pilgerfahrt als *bellum iustum* deklariert.

Das Gebet des jungen Grafen war erfolgreich. Im Heiligen Land rät er dem christlichen König Gilot zu der Belagerung von Askalon, wobei als Motivation dafür auch die Vergeltung für das (den Christen) angetane Leid steht (GR 30,20-23). Während der König in der Gegend herumzieht, belagert Rudolf Askalon, wo er einen ebenbürtigen Gegner in dem Vassalen Girabobe, dem Berater des heidnischen Königs findet, dem der Erzähler das Attribut *wise* (GR 32,39) nicht vorenthält. Drei weitere Anführer in der Umgebung Girabobes werden mit Namen genannt: es sind Gaiol Gruwin, Agarrain und Agar (GR 33,33-35), wobei gerade die Namen der Letztgenannten die Gegner als Nachkommen Abrahams und Hagar, der Magd seiner Frau Sara, deklarieren, und sie so als Nachkommen Ismaels ausweisen,[52] eine Deutung, die sich schon in der Chronik Fredegars im 7. Jh. findet, wobei bereits von Isidor von Sevilla die Bezeichnung der Agarener als Sarazenen (die im Mittelalter geläufige Bezeichnung) als eine Korruption des Namens gedeutet wird, die eine Abkunft von Sara, der legitimen Frau Abrahams, suggeriert.[53]

Als nach einem Ausfall der Bewohner Askalons Rudolf die beiden Gefährten des im Kampf gefallenen Gaiol Gruwin gefangenhält, will Rudolf sie nur unter der Bedingung freigeben, dass sich die Stadt ergibt und ihre Gottheiten beseitigt (GR 34,15-16).[54] In dieser Forderung zeigen sich militärische Lösung und religiöser Missionierungswille kombiniert, wobei jedoch der militärische Wunsch an der ersten Stelle steht. Dies ist ebenso die einzige erhaltene Stelle, in der sich ein Hinweis auf einen Polytheismus bei den Sarazenen findet, die Rudolf vor allem ‚*heiden*’ (GR 35,35) nennt. Rudolf lässt sich nicht durch die hohe Menge des angebotenen Lösegeldes erweichen und lässt die beiden Gefangenen durch Erhängen töten.[55] Er kann zu diesem Zeitpunkt die militärische Tapferkeit seiner Gegner nicht soweit goutieren, als dass er diese deshalb verschonen könnte. Dennoch gibt es eine gewisse Wertschätzung Rudolfs der Einzelperson gegenüber, die vermutlich auch durch die langwährende Belagerung gefördert wird, denn Girabobe wird nicht nur vom Erzähler sondern auch von Rudolf selbst als ‚*der gute*‘ (GR 37,36/ 38,12) bezeichnet. Bei den Friedensverhandlungen hält man sich an die Vereinbarungen (GR 37,55-36,2). Rudolf wird als hohem und vorbildlichem Diener seines Königs (bei einem Fest) von diesem ein vornehmer heidnischer Knabe (GR 44,9-11) zur höfischen Erziehung übergeben und damit auch die Sarazenen als Kulturell-Lernende gezeigt, wobei der Knabe auch die gebräuchlichen Kampf-weisen erlernen soll.[56] Dieser Knabe wird später auch sein Knappe sein (GR 47,7). Rudolf wechselt die Seite, jedenfalls zeigt er ein Verhalten, das von dem christlichen König mit ‚*untruwe*' (GR 51,32) bezeichnet wird, und ist nun bei König Halap zu finden, dessen Tochter er liebt und mit der er liebend-respektvoll umgeht (GR 49,1-50,10). Rudolf geht auf die gleiche selbstverständliche Weise mit seiner heidnischen Umgebung um, wie er es vormals am christlichen Hof tat. Seinen Neffen Bonifaite vertraut er Halap an, bevor er eine heikle militärische Mission für ihn erfüllt (GR 53,9-11). Im Kampf gegen die Christen jedoch schlägt Rudolf nur mit dem flachen Schwert zu (GR 56,53-54). Als Rudolf aus seinem Gefängnis flieht, gelobt er Busse für seine Missetat (GR 60,48f), die wohl im Kampf gegen die Christen bestand.[57]

Die in dem Epos dargestellten Heiden werden durchaus positiv gezeichnet, der *gute* und *wise* Girabobe wird gleichsam als Ideal eines Beraters geschildert (GR 32,38-45) und erweist sich als gewitzt, indem er den Mangel an Kämpfern im belagerten Askalon durch verkleidete Frauen verbirgt (GR 35,39-46).[58] Auch König Halap, der Vater der Geliebten und Gattin Rudolfs wird als vornehm und ‚*wise*' (GR 54,55) beschrieben. Die Bitte König Gilots Rudolf als Gefangenen auszuliefern verweigert König Halap, er will Rudolf nicht wie einen ‚*hunt*'[59] (GR 52,50) behandelt wissen.

Überaus gelobt und als das ‚*aller beste wip*'(GR 59,2) wird vom Erzähler auch die heidnische Minnedame und Gemahlin Rudolfs geschildert, allerdings erst nach ihrem Taufentschluss. Sie lässt sich freiwillig taufen,[60] wenn man nicht annimmt, dass sie - wie es in der Szene mit dem christlichen König sichtbar werden könnte - erst durch die Taufe zum vollwertigen Menschen aufsteigt. Die vorher Namenlose heißt nun Irmengart (GR 59,9). Sie bekommt sozusagen erst als Christin einen Namen. Als Christin ist die Konvertitin geradezu ‚*keiserliche*' (GR 59,26) großzügig, verständlicherweise mit dem Hintergedanken, ihren Rudolf dadurch wiederzuerhalten.

Insgesamt werden die Heiden, die hier auffälligerweise in den erhaltenen Stellen nie Sarazenen genannt werden, vom menschlichen Verhalten positiver als die Christen gezeichnet. Sie sind klug, zuverlässig bei Vereinbarungen und auch im zwischenmenschlichen Bereich. Kulturell erscheinen die Heiden nicht überlegen gezeichnet. Ein negatives Bild wird eher von den Christen gezeigt, die sich auch anmaßend verhalten, so betrachtet sich König Gilot vermessen dem Kaiser als ebenbürtig. Graf Rudolf hat sich der Bedrängten wegen in das Heilige Land begeben. Als die Bedrängten werden jedoch in erster Linie die Heiden gezeigt, die hier nicht für eine Minnedame oder für Sold kämpfen, also keine Mietlinge sind. Insofern kann es nicht erstaunen, vielleicht auch durch die Zuneigung der heidnischen Prinzessin noch zusätzlich motiviert, dass Rudolf schließlich auf der Seite der Heiden zu finden ist. Auch die religiöse Problematik ist in den Hintergrund gedrängt, so wird auch in den erhaltenen Fragmenten kaum über Religionsunterschiede gesprochen bzw. gar nicht die sittliche Qualität einer Religion oder ihren Wahrheitsgehalt, jedoch scheint diese Dimension nicht ganz belanglos zu sein, denn erst nach der Taufe der heidnischen Prinzessin, gelingt die Flucht Rudolfs und es erfolgt sein Schuldbekenntnis, das einen neuen Anfang ermöglicht und ihn zu willentlichen und unwillentlichen Samaritern führt.[61] Auffällig dabei ist allerdings, dass der Erzähler die *untriuwe* Rudolfs wie auch sein Schuldbekenntnis nur zitiert, jedoch nicht kommentiert und auch in der ganzen Handlung an dem Edelmut Rudolfs festhält,[62] der somit auch Rudolfs Dienst auf sarazenischer Seite einschließt.

II.2 Die Kreuzfahrt des Landgrafen Ludwigs des Frommen von Thüringen

Auch der Autor der Kreuzfahrt Landgraf Ludwigs ist anonym. Vermutlich stammt er selbst aus dem Troppauer Lande, wohin seine ostmitteldeutsche Mundart weist. Wahrscheinlich war er am Hof zu Prag und hat im Auftrag von Herzog Bolko I. von Schweidnitz-Jauer am schlesischen Hof das Epos verfasst. Es umfasst etwa 8178 Reimpaarverse und wird von Naumann auf das Jahr 1301 datiert.[63] Wie der Titel verheißt, steht im Zentrum die Person Landgraf Ludwigs des Frommen von Thüringen und sein vorbildliches Verhalten als *miles Christianus*. Missfallen hat in der Forschung vor allem die historische Sorglosigkeit erweckt, die der Verfasser walten ließ.. So wird etwa Ludwig der Fromme ungeniert mit der Hl. Elisabeth vermählt oder auch Friedrich Barbarossa darf über seine ihm geschichtlich zubemessene Zeit hinaus leben. Dennoch erweist sich die Darstellung, die auch unterhalten will (LgL 15), interessant[64] im Hinblick auf ihr Bild, das sie von den Arabern zeigt.

Das Epos setzt ein mit einer kleinen Geschichte der Kreuzzüge bis zur Ankunft Ludwigs. Im weiteren Verlauf werden die wechselhaften Kämpfe zwischen Christen und Sarazenen beschrieben, wobei den Schauplatz die von den Christen belagerte Stadt Akkon und ihre Umgebung bilden. Nicht außer Acht gelassen werden vom Erzähler auch die Schwierigkeiten der Christen untereinander, die teilweise aufgrund innerer Zwistigkeiten Separatfrieden mit den Sarazenen schließen oder ein gemeinsames Vorgehen zu verhindern drohen, wie es vor allem die Spannungen zwischen den romanischen Rittern und denen aus den deutschen Landen zeigen. Das Epos endet mit dem Tod Ludwigs, der durch Überanstrengung und innere Verletzung verursacht worden sein soll, und der Überführung und Bestattung seiner Gebeine in seiner Heimat.

II.2.1 Die Beziehungen zwischen Christen und Sarazenen

Auch hier zeigen sich die Ebenen der Handlung und des Erzählers, der das Geschehen begleitet, kommentierend und erläuternd. Ungleich zum Grafen Rudolf wird in dieser Schrift vor allem die Bezeichnung Sarazenen für die Araber verwendet. Durch eine Darstellung der Ereignisse vom ersten bis zum dritten Kreuzzug, an dem Ludwig teilnimmt, wird der Leser/Hörer mit dem Beginn der Auseinandersetzung zwischen westlichen Christen und Heiden im Heiligen Land vertraut gemacht. Ludwig selbst wird vom Erzähler in das Epos eingeführt als Seligkeit der Christen und Feind der Heiden, der die Sarazenen zu ihrer ewigen Pein in die Hölle wirft, wodurch die Opposition Christ und Heide betont wird. Bei dem Zusammentreffen mit König Guido bei der Stadt Tyrus werden dem Landgrafen und seinem Bruder die Bedrängnisse der Christen geschildert. So wird das ‚*unmâzige leit*' (LgL 743) hervorgehoben, das Saladin, der König von Babilô, den Christen angetan hat, der viele Christen tötete und gefangen nahm, darunter auch den König selbst. Auch das Hl. Kreuz hatte er erbeutet.[65] Mit der Bezeichnung Saladins als König von Babilô wird eine weitere Konnotation zu dem dem Gottesstaat feindlichen Babylon hergestellt, das vor allem durch die Auslegung von Augustinus zum Symbol für den Staat der ‚*impiorum*', der Frevler, wird.[66] Der Katalog der tapferen Ritter im Heere Ludwigs ist eine gute Gelegenheit, um die innere Haltung des echten *miles christianus* zu präsentieren, der Gott liebt und auf sein Gebot hin, Gut und Leben in die Hand Gottes gibt, und sich um das ewige Heil sorgt (LgL 1123-1128). Sowohl vom Erzähler wie auch in den Reden von Ludwig selbst wird der religiöse Unterschied zwischen Christen und Heiden betont, so werden die christlichen Kämpfer im Sinne Bernhards von Clairvaux[67] bezeichnet als ‚*gotes soldier*' (LgL 6424) oder als ‚*gotes rîtterschaft*' (LgL 6430), die erwählt ist (LgL 7467). Im Gegensatz zu den Heiden bzw. Sarazenen kämpfen sie um ‚*himellône*' (LgL 4228), um die ‚*Christi êre*'(LgL 6152) und das ‚*lobe*' Gottes (LgL 4219). Daher sind nach den Worten des Erzählers die im Kampf gegen die Heiden sterben diejenigen, die ‚*die crône der sigenunft [] tragen/ mit den marterên glîche,/ gewîhte kunige in himelrîche/ in ir selbes blûte.*' (LgL 7275-7277) Märtyrern gleich sind also die Gefallenen, während die noch Lebenden für das ewige Leben kämpfen um die ‚*himelsgebe*' (LgL 7655). Der ‚*himelgot*' (LgL 7752), an den Ludwig glaubt, wird vom Landgrafen selbst in seiner letzten großen Rede als der ‚*wâre got*' (LgL 7767) bezeichnet und damit eindeutig Stellung hinsichtlich der Religion bezogen, der die Priorität gehört. Besonders eindrucksvoll wird das Eingreifen der himmlischen Mächte gestaltet. Der hl. Georg, zuletzt nur mehr Ludwig dem *wîse*[n] (LgL 4884) und einem visionär begabten Ordensbruder sichtbar, erscheint drei Mal weißgewandet mit rotem Kreuz und Banner, dies ebenfalls mit rotem Kreuze, auf weißem Pferde. Er kämpft an der Seite Ludwigs allein, mahnt zum Maßhalten beim Töten[68] oder führt eine unsichtbare Heerschar göttlicher Streiter, die die Übermacht der Feinde besiegt und das zahlenmäßig unterlegene christliche Heer zum Sieg führt.

Als Gegenbild zu den Christen werden die Sarazenen gestaltet. Wohl sind auch sie prächtige Ritter (‚*menlich/ rîch*' LgL 5110-5111, ‚*edel*[]' LgL 5153, ‚*wol geborn*' LgL 5153), an deren Tapferkeit es keinen Zweifel gibt, doch ist ihre Motivation völlig unterschiedlich, so heißt es auch von ihnen:

des quam manich stolzer Sarrazîn
uf solt, uf prîses gewin, sumelîche durch fruntschaf,t

etslîche twanc der minnen craft,
als sie dâ ir frundin
an ritterschaft zu dienste sîn
wolden, unverdrozzenlich
uf prîses bejac wâgen sich. (LgL 7075-7083)

So sind es weltliche Gründe, weltliche Ehre nach der die Sarazenen streben: Sold, weltliches Lob oder Ansehen, sie kämpfen aus Gründen der Freundschaft oder für ihre Minnedame, deshalb erhalten sie auch einen anderen Lohn als die Christen.[69] Das Heer Saladins wird mit einem Vergleich der Pracht des Heeres von Terramer, dem mächtigen heidnischen König und Vater Giburcs im „Willehalm“ Wolframs gleichgestellt (LgL 1793-1805), so sind auch diese Heiden ‚*geflorieret*‘ (LgL 1810, 1830).[70] Während die Christen *âne hochvart* LgL 4640 sind, wird *hochvart* gerade bei der ausführlicheren Darstellung einzelner Sarazenen besonders hervorgehoben (Saladîn LgL 3280, Levi LgL 2215)[71], jedoch sind sie edel (LgL 6671), stolz (LgL 7094), ritterlich (LgL 7283) und frech (LgL 6511). Sie haben auch Sitten, die nicht den Beifall eines Christen finden sollten: ‚*daz ist gemeine ir site,/ der Sarrazên, und grôzlich,/ daz sie uf die naht sich/ ubertrinken, dar zû unkûschen sie*‘ (LgL 6410-6414). Die Strafe folgt auf dem Fuß nach diesem Verhalten, die Schlagkraft der Sarazenen wird dadurch lahmgelegt und Graf Burchart gelingt ein Überfall auf ihre Belagerungswerke. Durch die Betonung des Irdischen auf Seiten der Sarazenen wird gleichzeitig gezeigt, wes Geistes Kind sie sind. Sie orientieren sich an der Welt. Als Gott verehren sie Mahomet, dessen Namen sie oft zu ihrem Schlachtruf wählen und der der Sarazenen ‚*abgot*‘ (LgL 7320) ist. Doch nicht allein an Mohammed, sondern noch an viele Götter glauben die Sarazenen, wobei die aus dem *Rolandslied* des Pfaffen Konrad und Wolframs ‚Willehalm‘ bekannte führende Trias des sarazenischen Polytheismus Tervagant, Mahomet, Apollo[72] durch die Vierheit Venus, Mars, Iovis und Iupiter[73] ersetzt wird (LgL 1345-1362), zu denen sich Mahomet gesellt (LgL 6916). So kann der Tod für einen Sarazenen nur einen ‚*zwîfaltigen tot*‘ (LgL 3212, 3179) bedeuten, nämlich den des Leibes und der Seele. Daher werden die Sarazenen, wenn sie getötet werden, geradezu in die Hölle geschickt (LgL 3023-3024, 4446). Dies ist eine Situation, die einen gläubigen Christen nicht sehr befriedigen kann, folglich klagt auch der Erzähler, der die Sarazenen durchaus als Menschen und Gottes Geschöpfe sieht:

sô hât mich jamer der Sarrazîn,
der dâ sô vil gevallen sîn
an ritterlîcher werke tât.
sie wâren ouch lûte, got sie hât
und sîn almehtige craft
als menschen geschaft.
mich mût doch mêr ir sêle nôt,
dan daz sie sîn geslagen tôt. (LgL 7286-7298)[74]

Auch die hervorgehobenen Heiden werden mit sehr positiven Zügen ausgestattet, wie die sarazenischen Edlen Achor und Assar, die von Ludwig getötet werden. Sie sind beide jung, auserwählt, von hoher Geburt und tapfer (LgL 7337-7347). Doch die Persönlichkeit Saladins übertrifft alle. Auch er zeichnet sich im Kampf aus (LgL 6706-6708). Freigebigkeit, Tatkraft, ‚*wîse*' nach seiner Lebensart, jedoch nach dem Ruhm der Welt strebend, männlich gesinnt, das war Saladin, wie ihn der Erzähler sieht (LgL 7057-7063). Ähnlich wie die Christen empfindet auch Saladin seine Religion bedroht und sieht Mohammed durch die Christen beschimpft und verunehrt (LgL 7066-7068). So ist auch dieser Krieg für Saladin ein Glaubenskrieg, nicht jedoch für den vornehmen Arfax, der um der *minne* willen kämpft.[75] Begierig darauf, Ludwig selbst kennen zu lernen, lässt Arfax sich sein Rittertum mitten im Kampf von Ludwig bestätigen und schenkt dem Landgrafen ein Pferd (LgL 6840-6859). Saladins ‚*hochvart*' (LgL 3280) wiederum hindert diesen jedoch nicht, seinen eigenen Vater um Rat zu bitten, oder die Tapferkeit Ludwigs zu respektieren, ja sie so zu verehren, dass er den verletzten Christen zu sich bitten will, um diesem die besten Ärzte der Sarazenen zu verschaffen. Seine ehrliche Absicht will Saladin mit Geiseln, die er den Christen stellt, bekräftigen. Saladin versucht so die religiösen und politischen Schranken zu überschreiten, die den ihm ebenbürtigen Gegner von ihm trennen. Von der politischen Seite betrachtet könnte dieses Angebot, falls Ludwig darauf eingehen würde, auch einen zukünftigen Seitenwechsel Ludwigs prognostizieren. Zudem erfolgte von der Seite Saladins kein Angebot, Ludwig die arabischen Ärzte ins christliche Lager zu senden. Ludwig jedoch argumentiert religiös (LgL 7736-7740), denn der Glaube ist es, der Ludwig lenkt und leitet. So wird beinahe unmittelbar an die lobende Darstellung von Assar und Achor vom Landgrafen erzählt, der sich auf die Heiden im Kampfe wirft, ‚*als er den gotes vinden haz/ um irn ungelouben trûc/ âne zal sie nider slûc*' (LgL 7350-7352). Der Unglaube der Heiden wird damit zum Movens für Ludwig.

Diese Szene, in der ein Bote dem bereits todkranken Ludwig das Angebot Saladins, Ludwig in seinem Lager pflegen zu lassen LgL 7679-7714, überbringt wie auch die darauf folgende Antwort Ludwigs wird als eine Art Religionsgespräch inszeniert. Diese Antwort erstaunt zunächst und zeigt sich im Gewande eines Glaubensbekenntnisses, das als letzte größere Rede Ludwigs und damit als sein Vermächtnis gelten kann. Dennoch scheint diese Rede auch eine tiefere Antwort auf Saladins Angebot zu sein, das somit auch eine Bedrohung Ludwigs verbergen könnte. Nicht zufällig wird vom Verfasser die Wehklage über die Verführung und den Lohn der schnöden Welt (LgL. 7619-7649), die die Bitterkeit arger Galle in sich trägt und deren Lohn zuletzt verhasst ist, dem Lob Saladins vorangestellt. Saladin wird in den der Klage folgenden Versen unter diesem Einfluss der Welt gezeigt, zu dem er Ludwig verleiten will. Ludwig erkennt jedoch die tiefere Dimension dieses Angebotes, das für ihn auch bedeuten würde, an der Allmacht seines Gottes zu zweifeln und so neben einem politischen auch zu einem religiösen Überläufer zu werden, da er mit der Heilkunst der heidnischen Ärzte, sich zugleich deren ‚Göttern' und ihrer Macht anvertrauen würde. Denn warum sonst hätte es der auserwählte Landgraf, dem der hl. Georg wiederholt zur Seite steht, nötig, persönliche Hilfe ausgerechnet bei seinem politischen und eigentlich religiösen Feind zu suchen. So antwortet Ludwig: ‚*wer* [...] [Saladin] *mîner ê/ wolt er versagen sînen goten,/ waz sô er mir hât enpoten,/ al sîn beger ich solde/ erfullen* [...]', LgL 7736-7740. Gibt es auch die Möglichkeit einer Achtung des anderen, einer menschlichen Begegnung, so kann dieser Feind dennoch nicht von seinem Glauben getrennt werden. Wenn auch Vernunftgründe für dieses Angebot sprechen könnten wie der Gestank im Lager und die dort herrschenden hygienischen Zustände, die eine Genesung durchaus erschweren können, so erweist sich dennoch die unterschiedliche Religion als Schranke. Mit dem Eingehen auf Saladins Angebot würde sich Ludwig den Sinn seines bisherigen Daseins im Kreuzzug zerstören. Ein Zurück erscheint ihm nicht möglich. Insofern antwortet Ludwig auch auf den verdeckten Vorwurf, warum ihn nicht sein christlicher Gott heile, während er durch die Hilfe arabischer Ärzte und damit auch Mohammeds geheilt werden könnte. Aus dieser Sicht erscheint die Antwort Ludwigs, die auf den ersten Blick etwas scharf, ja auch beleidigend erscheint, verständlich. Ludwig reagiert mit einem Glaubensbekenntnis, das ihn selbst in seiner Haltung bestärkt und zugleich das Trennende der Religion zwischen Sarazenen und Christen deutlich hervorhebt: den Polytheismus (LgL 7737) und die Bedeutung von *Machmet* (LgL 7745-7750). Ludwig vertraut seine Genesung dem ‚*wâren got*', dessen Willen sich im Himmel und auf Erden[76] und an Ludwig erfüllen soll (LgL 7766-7770). Für Mohammed, von dem sich Saladin betrügen lässt,[77] kann Ludwig dagegen nur harsche Worte finden ‚*der sêle sich sâlden roubet,/* [der] *an Machmeten geloubet,/ der der werlde ein affêre/ hie was und ein trugenêre,/ des er zur helle lîdet nôt*', LgL 7747-7751. Im Gegensatz dazu sollte Saladin an den Gott des Himmels und an Jesus Christus, den Sohn der Jungfrau glauben, dessen Geschöpf doch Saladin ist (LgL 7752-7754). Mit dieser dezidierten Erwähnung des Polytheismus grenzt sich Ludwig deutlich ab und zeigt, dass sein Gott nicht der Gott Saladins sein kann. Mit dem Hinweis auf die volle Gottheit Christi und seine Geburt als Mensch von einer Jungfrau weist er auf zentrale Artikel der christlichen Glaubenslehre hin, die für einen Sarazenen schwer zu akzeptieren sind und die religiöse Debatte zwischen Christen und Muslimen bestimmen.[78] Mit der Anerkennung dieser beiden Artikel ist zudem die Erlösungstat Christi wie auch der Glaube an die Trinität verbunden,[79] in deren Namen auch die Kreuzfahrer kämpfen (LgL 1607). Eine Harmonie auf religiösem Gebiet kann also trotz aller menschlichen Verbundenheit nicht stattfinden. Falls diese Utopie dennoch zustande kommen würde, würde sie auch politische Lösungen bringen. Sollte Saladin seinem Glauben absagen, würde sich Ludwig mit seinem Heer Saladin unterstellen (LgL 7755-7761).

Dennoch kann Ludwig Saladins und der Sarazenen menschlichen Qualitäten erkennen. Das Angebot Saladins zeigt Edelmut. Umso mehr spürt auch Ludwig schmerzlich die Trennung zwischen den beiden Völkern, die durch die unterschiedlichen Glaubensvorstellungen gegeben ist: *„sô ich des gelouben mit im* [Saladin] *bin/ gescheiden; sînhalp daz ist mir leit/*" (LgL 7742-7743) *„sus mûz er der heimliche mîn* [Saladin]*,/ ouch der sînen ich gescheiden sîn/ genzlich, daz ist mir leit*', LgL 7759-7761. Der Glaube bildet die unüberbrückbare Kluft, an der Saladin und Ludwig scheitern müssen, während die politischen Differenzen in den Hintergrund treten.

Das Verständnis der gegenseitigen festen religiösen Positionen und die gegenseitige Wertschätzung lässt Saladin milde auf die Anwort Ludwigs reagieren,[80] die auch als indirekte Aufforderung an Saladin, sich zu bekehren, aufgefasst werden kann. Saladin wie Einzelne auf heidnischer Seite scheint es eher möglich, das Trennende zu überwinden, indem der religiöse Aspekt ignoriert wird,[81] dennoch wird betont, dass beide Parteien, Christen wie Heiden, um ihres Glaubens willen kämpfen (LgL 7076-7078, 7350-7351),[82] in dem beide fest verankert sind. So zeigt sich, obwohl Saladin die Macht des christlichen Gottes erfasst, der Ludwig unterstützt und die heidnischen Götter zuschanden macht, ist der Sultan nicht bereit, Konsequenzen aus seiner Erkenntnis zu ziehen.[83]

In der Ritterlichkeit sind sich Heiden und Christen annähernd ebenbürtig. Jedoch wird bis auf eine Episode Einheit auf der sarazenischen Seite demonstriert, während die Christen andauernd um diese Einheit ringen müssen. Wiewohl der Reichtum der Sarazenen, ihr Mut, ihr Adel auch hervorgehoben und damit auch auf den Respekt vor der anderen Kultur und ihrer Errungenschaften hingewiesen wird, kann jedoch diese Präsentation auch dazu dienen, Ludwig und sein Charisma zu erhöhen, vor dem sich doch in gewissem Sinne Saladin und der vornehme Arfax beugen. Sie bleiben jedoch dem Irdischen verhaftet, streben nach dem Lohn der Welt, nach Minne, irdischem Gewinn, der auch im Materiellen liegt und der die Sarazenen in dieser speziellen Hinsicht den Juden gleichstellt, die sich ebenfalls dem Materiellen zuwenden, wiewohl sie jedoch den gleichen Gott wie die Christen verehren,[84] während die Sarazenen als Verehrer vieler Götter dargestellt sind.

Auch im Kampfverhalten, in der Kriegsführung ähneln sich Christen und Sarazenen und keiner steht dem anderen nach. Sowohl Saladin lässt die Christen niedermetzeln wie Vieh (LgL 3937-3939),[85] während auch die Christen unter den Heiden wüten.[86] Das Recht scheint sich jedoch nach dem Erzähler auf der Seite der Christen zu befinden. Die rechtliche legitime Position der Christen in diesen Kämpfen wird bereits zu Beginn des Epos betont, da Gottfried von Bouillon den Christen des Orients zu Hilfe (LgL 36) kommt. So werden die Kreuzfahrer hier auch nicht als Angreifer, sondern auch als Verteidiger dargestellt, die ‚*wern lûte unde lant*' (LgL 1882), das sie von Gott als Lehen empfangen haben.

IV. Fazit

Sowohl im Graf Rudolf als auch in der Kreuzfahrt Landgraf Ludwigs gestalten sich die persönlichen Beziehungen der Kreuzfahrer zu den Sarazenen positiv. Beide Seiten, soweit sie sich kennen gelernt haben, schätzen sich gegenseitig und schreiben einander positive Eigenschaften zu.[87] Besonders auffällig ist im Graf Rudolf der Seitenwechsel des Protagonisten. Sein Verhalten, christlicherseits als *untriuwe* gestempelt, findet jedoch seine Entsprechung in dem Verhalten der orientalischen Christen bzw. eingewanderten Franken. So schlossen christliche und muslimische Herrscher Bündnisse und Verträge miteinander, die auch von beiden Seiten nicht immer eingehalten wurden. Man kämpfte gegen gemeinsame Feinde, sowohl gegen christliche wie auch nichtchristliche. Dies führte dazu, dass die Fronten nicht immer klar waren.[88] Ähnlich erstaunlich ist die Begegnung am Rande des Kampfgeschehens zwischen Ludwig und Arfax. Hier werden mitten im Krieg Geschenke gemacht. Ähnliches berichtet Usâma Ibn Munqidh, der von den zahlreichen Begegnungen und Geschenken zwischen Sarazenen und Christen spricht, die sich auch manchmal mitten im Krieg ereignen. So wird, ähnlich wie in der Episode in der Kreuzfahrt Ludwigs, König Richard Löwenherz, der sein Pferd verloren hat, von einem Gegner wiederum ein solches zur Verfügung gestellt. Sogar mit Eis und Früchten kann sich Richard auf dem Markt des Heeres Saladins versorgen. Ähnlich dem Wunsch von Arfax Ludwig kennenzulernen, gibt es wiederholt Zeugnisse darüber, dass man den Gegner kennenlernen möchte, um diesen und dessen Wunden zu bestaunen.[89] In einen ähnlichen Zusammenhang kann auch die Großzügigkeit Saladins gesehen werden, der dem verletzen Ludwig als Labung u.a. ,*wilt, zam, edele vische,/ von Damassô edele phlumelîn,/ rein îs, den aller besten wîn/ und waz sô nutzes mohte hân*' (LgL 7810-7813) sendet.

Nahe den realen Fakten wiederum zeigt sich im Grafen Rudolf die Erwähnung, dass ein vornehmer heidnischer Knabe am Hofe König Gilots erzogen werden soll. Ähnliche Vorkommnisse weist auch Hans Prutz[90] nach, der die Erziehung von heidnischen Knaben edler Abstammung auch am Hof zu Jerusalem oder Antiochien wie auch Akkon erwähnt. Ein Beweggrund dafür war wohl auch die fränkische Kultur und Sprache dadurch kennenzulernen und zu erlernen.[91]

Im Grafen Rudolf gibt es eine Bekehrung, die Irmengarts. Häufig scheinen es Frauen zu sein, die auch aus Liebe zu ihrem Gemahl und/ oder aus Überzeugung die Religion wechseln, wie etwa Brechmundâ, die Gemahlin des heidnischen Königs Marsilie im Rolandslied (Vv. 8595-8640) oder Gyburc im Willehalm.[92] Ähnlich weist die Gestalt der Irmengart auf die von der Kirche nicht so gerne gesehenen Verbindungen zwischen Christen und Sarazenen hin.[93] Eine völlige Akzeptanz erfolgt jedoch durch die Taufe.

In der Kreuzfahrt Ludwigs gibt es zwar keine Bekehrung, geschweige denn eine Liebesbeziehung, dagegen eine Vielzahl an wunderbaren Begebenheiten durch das machtvolle Wirken des hl. Georg. Dieses stärkt den Glauben der Christen, wirkt jedoch nicht auf die Sarazenen, die sich in diesem Sinne als wider besseres Wissen verstockt erweisen.[94]

In den erhaltenen Versen von Graf Rudolf ist es der Graf, der den Bedrängten im Heiligen Land zu Hilfe kommen will und sich schließlich auf der Seite der Heiden wiederfindet. Durch diesen Seitenwechsel des Protagonisten, der vom Erzähler keineswegs negativ kommentiert wird, wird trotz des Schuldbekenntnisses von Rudolf auch der Anspruch des *bellum iustum* der Christen insgesamt etwas in Frage gestellt. Dass die Heiden Menschen sind und den Christen ebenbürtig, ergibt sich hier zwangsläufig aus der Liebesbeziehung. Für die Ehe selbst hatte Rudolf keine Taufe eingefordert. Diese erweist sich jedoch von der Konstruktion der Fabel als nötig, spätestens für den Teil, in dem die beiden nach Flandern reisen.

Im späteren Werk, in der Kreuzfahrt Landgraf Ludwigs, wird auf das von Gott den Christen gegebene Recht auf das Land hingewiesen, das die Kreuzfahrer verteidigen.[95] Doch trotz aller Erfolge sind es nicht so sehr in den Auseinandersetzungen die Heiden, die bedrängt werden, sondern die Übermacht des heidnischen Heeres ist den Christen immer vor Augen. Sie sind in die Rolle der Bedrängten gerückt, die nur durch göttliche Hilfe gerettet werden können. Insofern erweckt der Tod Ludwigs auch den Eindruck, dass kein Erfolg der Kreuzfahrer mehr möglich ist.[96] Ein Eindruck, der wohl aus der Perspektive des Verfassers stammt, der bereits den Verlust Akkons (1291), der letzten christlichen Bastion im Heiligen Land, vor Augen hat. Doch zeigt der Verfasser im Detail, dass auch gegenüber Angehörigen von Saladins Heer, die Unrecht erlitten haben, Genugtuung geleistet werden muss. Als Saladin Ludwig einen Leoparden schenkt, wird der Führer des Tieres von einem Franzosen aus Feindschaft gegen Ludwig erschlagen. Ludwig will den Übeltäter zur Strafe töten.[97]

Während Graf Rudolf im Hinblick auf das Recht eine tolerantere Haltung zeigt, wurde jedoch von dem langjährigen Kanzler von Jerusalem Wilhelm von Tyrus hinsichtlich der Toleranz ein noch ‚radikalerer' Standpunkt eingenommen. In seinem *Chronicon,* das er nach 15 Jahren 1184 abschließt,[98] gesteht er den Muslimen ein ‚Recht auf Heimat, Freiheit, Eigentum, und Familie' zu,[99] zudem das Recht, sich gegen ein von Christen erlittenes Unrecht in einem *bellum iustum* zur Wehr zu setzen.

In den Fragmenten des Grafen Rudolf nur schwach hervorgehoben, im Kreuzzug Ludwigs jedoch stärker betont, wird der Polytheismus der Sarazenen. Kenntnisse eines islamischen Monotheismus mussten jedoch zur Zeit der genannten Werke vorhanden sein. Bereits in dem nach 1140 ‚Dialogus inter Philosophum, Judaeum et Christianum' von Petrus Abaelard, bekennt sich der Ismaelit eindeutig zum Monotheismus.[100] Ähnlich weist auch Bischof Otto von Freising in seiner 1146/47 (2.Fassung 1157) entstandenen ‚Chronik'[101] auf den Eingottglauben der Sarazenen hin, die auch Christus anerkennen, jedoch nicht als Gott und Heiland. Doch sei der Verführer Mohammed für sie der Prophet des höchsten Gottes. Ähnlich wird auch von Gottfried von Viterbo eindeutig auf den Monotheismus der Sarazenen hingewiesen und auf Mohammed, der obwohl ein Betrüger, doch als Fürsprecher seinen Gläubigen gilt.[102] Für Wilhelm von Tyrus ist der Eingottglaube der Sarazenen nicht nur eine Selbstverständlichkeit, sondern er kann in ihm auch eine dem Christentum verwandte Religion erkennen.[103]

Nach Rainer Chr. Schwinges gab es im mittelalterlichen christlichen Abendland vor allem drei Sichtweisen des Islams. Er konnte 1) als eine autonome Weltreligion gesehen werden, die dem Judentum wie auch der christlichen Religion verwandt ist durch den Monotheismus und dem Gott der Väter, der identisch gesehen wird. Die Muslime jedoch wurden nicht als stark genug für den christlichen Glauben betrachtet.[104] Diese Ansicht fand sich vor allem bei den orientalischen Christen in der Ostkirche. Jedoch konnte 2) der Islam auch als Sekte gesehen werden, die von ‚Christentum und/ oder Judentum' ausging. Ihre Irrlehren bezogen sich besonders auf die Göttlichkeit Christi und auf das Trinitätsdogma. Diese Einschätzung war vor allem auf der iberischen Halbinsel unter den Christen zu finden, die unter islamischer Herrschaft lebten.[105] Eine weitere Auffassung des Islam sieht ihn 3) als Heidentum, in der Gestalt des Paganismus, der nach götzendienerischer Art den Monotheismus leugnet. Dieses Bild des Islams diente nach Schwinges immer einer ideologischen Absicht, der Gegner sollte dadurch abqualifiziert und kämpferisch widerlegt werden. In gleicher Weise konnte damit eine deutliche Abgrenzung vollzogen werden. Entstanden war dieses Bild im Orient, das im 9. Jahrhundert intensiv als Reichspolemik gegen den Islam von Byzanz eingesetzt wurde. Im selben Jahrhundert taucht es auch in Spanien auf und ist schließlich auch in Italien und jenseits der Alpen zu finden.[106]

Bereits Hrotsvith von Gandersheim hatte im 10. Jahrhundert die Sarazenen als Götzendiener bezeichnet und damit auch in die Richtung des Polytheismus gewiesen. Mit dem dahinterstehenden Konzept des Paganen wurde damit ebenso im schriftstellerischen Bereich auch ein kämpferischer Akzent gesetzt, der eine gemeinsame religiöse Grundlage für Christentum und Islam ausschloss.[107]

Bereits seit dem 7. Jahrhundert sind Religionsgespräche zwischen Christen und Moslems aus dem Orient überliefert, [108] die teilweise auf ein historisches Gespräch zurückgehen, die jedoch auch konstruiert sein können. Christlicherseits weisen sie vor allem apologetischen Charakter auf. In der arabischer Sprache entwickelte sich eine schärfer konzipierte literarische Polemik nach der Mitte des 9. Jahrhunderts. Mit ??????¢lî b. Rabbân al-Þabarî, der 855 starb, nimmt auf muslimischer Seite diese Polemik ihren Anfang, auf die von christlicher Seite geantwortet wird. In Byzanz entfaltete sich gegen den Islam bereits seit dem 9. Jahrhundert ein polemisches Schrifttum, während im lateinischen Westen der Islam vor allem mit dem Aufkommen der Kreuzzüge mehr ins Bewusstsein trat und eine reiche polemische Literatur entstand.[109] Christlich-islamische

Religionsgespräche fanden jedoch eigentlich nur in islamischen Gebieten statt, da es bis zur *Reconquista* in Spanien in den christlichen Gebieten praktisch keine Muslime gab.[110] Einfluss auf die Religionsgespräche nahm schließlich auch die scholastische Rezeption der Philosophie von Aristoteles, die über die Araber vermittelt wurde, wie sie auch im ‚Dialogus inter philosophum, Judaeum et Christianum' (um 1140) von Petrus Abaelardus zu finden ist.[111]

Auf dieses Konzept des Paganen wie auch in gewissem Sinne auf die dazugehörige Funktion verweist vor allem die ‚Kreuzfahrt des Landgrafen Ludwigs'. Wenn auch im menschlichen Bereich in den oben genannten vulgärsprachlichen Werken tolerantes Verhalten und die Zustimmung dazu gefunden werden kann und sich damit auch teilweise rechtliche Ansätze zur Toleranz finden – mag sich dahinter auch eine pragmatische Toleranz verbergen -,[112] scheint doch im religiösen Bereich eine Toleranz im Sinne der Akzeptanz eines religiösen Pluralismus nicht möglich. Die geringere oder größere Unfähigkeit dazu ist wohl bedingt durch die *mental map* der einzelnen Protagonisten zumindest bei Landgraf Ludwig nicht möglich. Die Unmöglichkeit dieses Unterfangens wird jedoch durch die Betonung des Polytheismus verstärkt, der als unlogische, rückständige, Glaubensposition erscheint, insbesondere durch seine Präsentation durch die Nennung römischer ‚Götter'.[113] Der andere ist zwar ‚fast so wie wir, aber [eben] ein Heide'.[114] Dieses ‚fast so wie wir', kann gerade im Hinblick auf den Landgrafen Ludwig beruhigend wirken. Die Stadt, das Land, das die Christen nicht halten können, bleibt dennoch in der Hand von Menschen, fast gibt es hier ein *arrangement* mit der Niederlage. Dennoch die Botschaft scheint eindeutig und im Sinne des Genre der Kreuzzugsdichtung. Eine vollkommene Akzeptanz und Integrierung findet nur und kann nur durch eine Taufe stattfinden, wie es im Grafen Rudolf angedeutet wird und in der letzten großen Rede Ludwigs, die er an Saladin richtet.[115]

Was bleibt jedoch ist der Schmerz, das Leiden an dem nicht möglichen tieferen Einverständnis mit dem anderen. Wo aber dieses Leiden daran vorhanden ist, bleibt die Hoffnung auf weiteres Gespräch und damit auf ein zukünftiges besseres Verständnis.

Institut fur Germanistik, Universitat Salzburg

Notes

1. Wer war es der [...] den Sieg behielt,/ das Höllentor sprengte/ und Adams Not enden ließ? Das war der dreieinige Gott!/ Der einer ist und drei,/ stets gleich und gleich erhaben,/ sieh, der wird kein zweites Mal sterben/ für die Sünden der Menschen [...] Der Herr von Tenabri aber erwiderte: „Den einen [Christus] hätten doch die Drei/ vor dem Tod erretten können?"', Wolfram von Eschenbach, Willehalm, Text der Ausgabe von Werner Schröder, völlig neubearbeitete Übersetzung, Vorwort und Register von Dieter Kartschoke (Berlin/ New York: de Gruyter, 1989), Wh. 218,25-29 und 219,1-2. Im Weiteren wird nach dieser Ausgabe mit der Abkürzung Wh. zitiert.

2. Klaus Schreiner, ‚"Tolerantia", Begriffs- und wirkungsgeschichtliche Studien zur Toleranzauffassung des Kirchenvaters Augustinus', in Toleranz im Mittelalter, hrsg. von Alexander Patschovsky und Harald Zimmermann (Sigmaringen: Thorbecke, 1998), 335-389 (S. 381).

3. Ulrich Müller, ‚Tendenzen und Formen. Versuch über mittelhochdeutsche Kreuzzugsdichtung', in ‚Getempert und gemischet', für Wolfgang Mohr zum 65. Geburtstag, hrsg. von Franz Hundsnurscher und Ulrich Müller (Göppingen: Kümmerle, 1972), 251-280 (S. 252). Siehe dazu auch Peter Hölzle, ‚Kreuzzug und Kreuzzugsdichtung. Das Problem ihrer Definition', in Festschrift für Kurt Herbert Halbach zum 70. Geburtstag, hrsg. von Rose Beate Schäfer-Maulbetsch, Manfred Günter Scholz und Günther Schweikle (Göppingen: Kümmerle, 1972), 55-72 (S. 70).

4. Siehe dazu auch die Definition von Claude Cahen, auf die sich auch Ulrich Müller bezieht, P. Hölzle, ‚Kreuzzug und Kreuzzugsdichtung', S. 58 und U. Müller, ‚Tendenzen und Formen', S. 252.

5. Zur Verbindung von Wallfahrt und Heidenkrieg siehe auch, Albrecht Noth, Heiliger Krieg und Heiliger Kampf in Islam und Christentum. Beiträge zur Vorgeschichte und Ge-schichte der Kreuzzüge (Bonn: Ludwig Röhrscheid, 1966), S. 128-130.

6. Vergleiche P. Hölzle, ‚Kreuzzug', S. 71.

7. Siehe dazu Steven Runciman, Geschichte der Kreuzzüge (München: dtv, 1997), S. 105-106.

8. Bernhard Jahn, Raumkonzepte in der Frühen Neuzeit. Zur Konstruktion von Wirklichkeit in Pilgerberichten, Amerikareisebeschreibungen und Prosaerzählungen (Fran-kfurt a.Main; Berlin; New York; Wien u.a., 1993), S. 13. Der Ausdruck der *mental map* stammt aus dem Bereich der kognitiven Kartographie und wird teilweise mit dem Begriff image synonym verwendet, wobei von Y.F. Tuan der Begriff *image* jede Art von Vorstellung einschließt. Ausgangspunkt für diese Auffassung der mental map oder des image ist nach Lowenthal ‚Every image and idea about the world is compounded, then, of personal experience, learning, imagination and memory. [...] All types of experience [...] come together to make up our individual picture of reality.', ebd. Somit spielen bei der Konstituierung einer mental map unterschiedliche Faktoren eine Rolle, die im geographischen, religiösen, politischen, sozialen oder auch ethnologischen Bereich liegen können. Das wahrnehmende Subjekt strukturiert. Nach Bernhard Jahn besteht eine mental map weniger aus falschen Daten, denn aus selektierten, ebd., S. 14. Ähnlich den Raumkonzepten muss ein Text auch nicht insgesamt eine *mental map* eines Verfassers widerspiegeln, der auch vermutlich gewisse Rücksichten gegenüber Auftraggebern und Gesellschaft nehmen muss. Doch kann seine *mental map* vielleicht in den Brüchen des Textes sichtbar werden. Zur Bedeutung der Textbrüche, siehe auch B. Jahn, ebd., S. 19.

9. Klaus Schreiner, Artikel ‚Toleranz', in Geschichtliche Grundlagen. Historisches Lexikon zur politisch-sozialen Sprache in Deutschland, hrsg. von Otto Brunner, Werner Conze und Reinhart Koselleck, Band 6 (Stuttgart: Klett-Cotta 1990), 445-605 (S. 446).

10. K. Schreiner, Artikel ‚Toleranz', S. 446-447.

11. K. Schreiner, Artikel ‚Toleranz', S. 446, siehe auch K. Schreiner, „‚Tolerantia"', S. 338.

12. K. Schreiner, „‚Tolerantia"', S. 367, siehe auch K. Schreiner, Artikel ‚Toleranz', S. 452.

13. Siehe dazu Paulus im Römerbrief, Rö 11,26. Die Bibel. Altes und Neues Testament. Einheitsübersetzung (Stuttgart: Katholische Bibelanstalt, 1980)

14. K. Schreiner, Artikel ‚Toleranz', S. 452-453, 462, siehe dazu auch: K. Schreiner, „‚Tolerantia'", S. 368. Zur Zeugenschaft der Juden, siehe ebd., S. 369.

15. K. Schreiner, „‚Tolerantia'", S. 343. Ähnlich wie Jesus Judas gegenüber Geduld zeigte, so gibt es keinen Grund, Bindungen persönlicher oder verwandtschaftlicher Art aufzugeben, wenn jemand einer anderen Glaubensrichtung angehört. Daher gibt es nach den päpstlichen Nuntien ‚ein Recht auf glaubensunabhängige Menschlichkeit', K. Schreiner, „‚Tolerantia'", S. 366.

16. K. Schreiner, „‚Tolerantia'", S. 381.

17. Ulrich Müller, ‚Toleranz zwischen Christen und Muslimen im Mittelalter? Zur Archäologie der Beziehungen zwischen dem christlich-lateinischen Okzident und dem islamischen Orient', in Kulturthema Toleranz. Zur Grundlegung einer interdisziplinären und interkulturellen Toleranzforschung, hrsg. von Alois Wierlacher (München: iudicium, 1996), 307-353 (S. 307-308).

18. Zitiert nach K. Schreiner, „‚Tolerantia'", S. 381.

19. Siehe dazu K. Schreiner, „‚Tolerantia'", S. 383.

20. K. Schreiner, „‚Tolerantia'", S. 366.

21. K. Schreiner, „‚Tolerantia'", S. 387.

22. Handwörterbuch der lateinischen Sprache, hrsg. von Reinhold Klotz, Bd. 1, 7. Auflage (Graz: Akademische Druck-und Verlagsanstalt, 1963), S. 1319.

23. Zur ‚Disputation' und ‚disputieren' siehe Jacob und Wilhelm Grimm, Deutsches Wörterbuch, Band 2 (Leipzig: Hirzel 1860), Sp. 1190-1191. Als Disputierer wird dort ‚ein streitsüchtiger, disputator, altercator' bezeichnet, ebd. Zur *disputatio* im philosophischen und theologischen Lehrbetrieb siehe auch L. Hödl, Artikel ‚Disputatio(n) [Philosophie und Theologie]', in Lexikon des Mittelalters, hrsg. von Robert Auty, Robert-Henri Bautier u.a., Bd. 3 (München; Zürich: Artemis, 1986), Sp.1116-1118.

24. Kluge, Etymologisches Wörterbuch der deutschen Sprache, bearbeitet von Elmar Seebold, 23., erweiterte Auflage (Berlin/ New York: de Gruyter, 1999), S. 185.

25. Kluge, Etymologisches Wörterbuch, S. 165.

26. Duden, Das große Wörterbuch der deutschen Sprache in zehn Bänden. 3., völlig neu bearbeitete und erweiterte Auflage, hrsg. vom Wissenschaftlichen Rat der Dudenredaktion, Band 2 (Mannheim; Leipzig; Wien; Zürich, 1999), S. 762.

27. Duden, Das große Wörterbuch, S. 762-763. Zu den Begriffen Debatte und Disput siehe auch Longman, Dictionary of Contemporary English, völlige Neubearbeitung, Lizenzausgabe (Berlin; München: Langenscheidt KG, 1987, 1. Auflage (London: Longman, 1978), S. 264, S. 295. 'debate' meint hier: '1) a meeting, esp. in public, in which a question is talked about by at least two people or groups, each expressing a different opinion [...] 2) the process of talking about a question in detail; DISCUSSION und 'dispute': '[...] (an) argument or quarrel, esp.an official one between one group or organization and another'.

28. Gero von Wilpert, Artikel ‚Débat', in Sachwörterbuch der Literatur, 7. erweiterte Auflage (Stuttgart: Alfred Kröner, 1989), Sp. 170, ebenso ders.: Artikel ‚Streitschrift', in ebd., 895-897. (Sp. 896) und Artikel ‚Synkrisis', ebd., Sp. 913-914. Bei der Synkrisis handelt es sich um ein direkt oder indirekt geführtes Streitgespräch in längerer oder kürzerer Form, in dem der Vorrang einer Position vor einer anderen dargestellt wird.

29. Sidney H. Griffith, ‚Disputes with Muslims in Syriac Christian Texts', in Religions-gespräche im Mittelalter (Vorträge des Wolfenbütteler Symposions vom 11.-15. Juni 1989 in der Herzog August Bibliothek), hrsg. von Bernard Lewis und Friedrich Niewöhner (Wiesbaden: Harrassowitz, 1992), 251-273 (S. 256).

30. U. Mattejiet, Artikel ‚Religionsgespräche, I. Einleitung,‘ in Lexikon des Mittelalters, Bd. 7, hrsg. von Robert Auty, Robert-Henri Bautier u.a. (München: LexMA, 1995), 691-692. (Sp. 691). Den Terminus ‚Polemik, bzw. Apologie' verwendet Georg Graf, wobei er unterscheidet zwischen einer ‚wissenschaftlichen Polemik', die von Gelehrten geführt wird und sich an Gelehrte richtet, und einer ‚populären Polemik', deren Zielpublikum weitere Kreise sind und die in einer allgemein verständlichen Form verfasst ist, Georg Graf, ‚Christliche Polemik gegen den Islam‘, Gelbe Hefte, 2, Heft 2 (1926), 825-842 (S. 827).

31. S. H. Griffith, 'Disputes with Muslims in Syriac Christian Texts', S. 256-257.

32. S. H. Griffith, 'Disputes with Muslims in Syriac Christian Texts', S. 272-273.

33. J. Waardenburg, ‚Religionsgespräche, I. Allgemein und II. Muslimisch-christlich‘, in Theologische Realenzyklopädie, hrsg. von Gerhard Müller in Gemeinschaft mit Horst Balz u.a. (Berlin; New York: Walter de Gruyter, 1997), 631-648 (S. 632). Nach J. Waardenburg sollten bei den Religionsgesprächen insofern auch die Vorgeschichte eines Gespräches, die sozialen Bedingungen der Situation der Teilnehmer wie auch die äußeren und inneren Machtverhältnisse, unter letzterer sind vor allem geistige und psychologische Faktoren zu verstehen, in Betracht gezogen werden. Ebenso sind die Motivationen der Teilnehmer, praktische Interessen und Intentionen wie auch die ‚Früchte des Gesprächs' zu beachten, ebd., S. 632-633.

34. Siehe dazu das ausführlich wiedergegebene Religionsgespräch in der Kaiserchronik zwischen dem Papst Silvester und Juden und Heiden (Kaiserchronik 8675-10385), vergleiche auch im ‚Willehalm' Wolframs von Eschenbach die Gespräche der christlichen Gyburc mit ihrem heidnischen/ muslimischen Vater, wie etwa Wh. 215,8-222,9.

35. Siehe dazu Michel Foucault, Die Ordnung des Diskurses. Mit einem Essay von Ralf Konersmann (Frankfurt a. Main: Fischer Taschenbuch, 2000), S. 20.

36. Siehe dazu und zur Etymologie der Bezeichnung auch Ekkehart Rotter: Abendland und Sarazenen (Berlin; New York: Walter de Gruyter, 1986), S. 68 und bes. S. 75.

37. Zu den Kriterien siehe auch Rainer C. Schwinges: ‚Wilhelm von Tyrus. Vom Um-gang mit Feindbildern im 12. Jahrhundert‘, in Spannungen und Widersprüche. Gedenkschrift für Frantisek Graus, hrsg. von Susanna Burghartz, Hans-Jörg Gilomen, Guy P. Marchal, Rainer C. Schwinges und Katharina Simon-Muscheid (Sigmaringen: Thorbecke, 1992), 155-172 (S. 160).

38. Fromm orientiert sich bei der Datierung auch an Beobachtungen von Volker Schupp im Zusammenhang mit Sprachformeln, die sich bei Heinrich von Veldeke finden, Hans Fromm, ‚Der Graf Rudolf‘, Beiträge zur Geschichte der Deutschen Sprache und Literatur, 119 (1997), 214-234 (S. 218-219). Zu den möglichen sprachlichen Beziehungen zu Heinrich von Veldeke siehe auch ebd., S. 233. Siehe dazu auch Volker Schupp, ‚Zur Datierung des „Grafen Rudolf“‘, ZDA, 97 (1968), 37-56 (S. 51-54).

39. Fromm, ‚Graf Rudolf‘, S. 223 Anm. 11.

40. Peter Ganz, ‚Einleitung‘, in Graf Rudolf, hrsg. von Peter F. Ganz (Berlin: Erich Schmidt, 1964), 10-22 (S. 11).

41. Fromm, ‚Graf Rudolf‘, S. 224-225, 232. Zur Nähe des Graf Rudolf in seiner unmittelbaren Darstellung der Ereignisse und im Hinblick auf seine Wirklichkeitsnähe zur *chanson d'Antioche*, Fromm, ebd., S. 232, 227. Jedoch betont Fromm die im Epos statt-findenden Innovationen, so ist es auch seine Absicht zu zeigen: wie aus der idealtypischen

Statik eine Dynamik des erfahrenen Weges wird, die im Aufbruch zum neuen Roman ist [...]', S. 225.

42. Zu dem Verhältnis zwischen Vasall und Herr siehe bes. Fromm, ,Graf Rudolf', S. 225.

43. Siehe dazu auch Fromm, der noch weiter differenziert und dabei beobachtet, dass der Erzähler die Handlung ,den Erlebnis- und Wertbereichen der höfischen Kultur Gesellschaft zu[ordnet].', Fromm, ,Graf Rudolf', S. 223.

44. Siehe Peter Ganz, ,Einleitung', S. 22.

45. Hans Fromm, ,Graf Rudolf', S. 216.

46. Auf die problematische Übersetzung des Terminus ,heide' hat auch U. Müller hingewiesen: Ulrich Müller, ,Toleranz zwischen Christen und Muslimen', S. 314. Zum lateinischen Begriff des Heiden (paganus), der bereits bei Tertullian nachgewiesen werden kann, siehe auch die Studie von B. Altaner, ,Paganus. Eine bedeutungsgeschichtliche Unter-suchung', ZKG 58 (1939), 130-141 (S. 141). Zum Begriff des Heiden siehe auch Rainer C. Schwinges, Kreuzzugsideologie und Toleranz. Studien zu Wilhelm von Tyrus (Stuttgart: Hiersemann, 1977), S. 90-91. Schwinges unterscheidet zwischen dem gentilen Heiden, der noch nicht glaubt, jedoch zur Bekehrung berufen ist, und dem paganen Heiden, der mit einer ,widergöttlich-heidnischen Idee' verbunden ist, der sich aktiv und institutionell organisiert gegen den christlichen Glauben richtet. - Die Zitierung des Grafen Rudolf richtet sich nach der Seitenzahl der Ausgabe von Peter Ganz und der Zählung der Verse auf der entsprechenden Seite, die Abkürzung GR steht dabei für „Graf Rudolf".

47. „beide wip unde kinder/ die sluc man alse rinder." Die Zitate erfolgen nach den Seitenzahlen und den entsprechenden Verszeilen, Graf Rudolf, hrsg. von Peter F. Ganz (Berlin: Erich Schmidt, 1964). Zur Brutalität des ersten Kreuzzuges, bei der bei der Einnahme von Jerusalem auch Frauen und Kinder der Feinde getötet wurden, siehe auch Fulcher von Chartres, ,Chronik', in The First Crusade. The Chronicle of Fulcher of Chartres and Other Source Materials, edited, with an introduction by Edward Peters (Philadelphia: Univ. of Pennsylvania Press, 1971), 23-91 (S. 77). Zur Eroberung von Jerusalem siehe auch Hannes Möhring, ,Die Kreuzfahrer, ihre muslimischen Untertanen und die heiligen Stätten', in Toleranz im Mittelalter, 129- 157 (S. 130-131).

48. Die Verbindung der Sarazenen mit dem Antichristen machte vor allem ihre Gefährlichkeit gegenüber den Christen, dem christlichen Glauben deutlich. Diese Konzeption war jedoch ursprünglich nur als Möglichkeit formuliert worden, Rainer C. Schwinges, Kreuzzugsideologie, S. 100-101, 103.

49. Zum Gebet Rudolfs siehe GR 26,13-27. Vgl. dazu auch die Glaubens- und Überzeugungskraft des *gemahels* bei Hartmann von Aue, das sich mit seiner Vorstellung gegenüber dem Willen der Eltern durchsetzt. Hartmann von Aue, Der arme Heinrich, hrsg. von Hermann Paul, 15. neu bearbeitet Auflage von Gesa Bonath (Tübingen: Niemeyer, 1984), Vv. 859-864.

50. Auch nach Bernhard von Clairvaux kämpfen die Ritter einen zweifachen Kampf ,adversus carnem et sanguinem, tum contra spiritualia nequitiae in caelestibus', Bernhard von Clairvaux. De laude novae militiae, in Sämtliche Werke. Lat./ Dt., hrsg. von Gerhard B. Winkler (Innsbruck: Tyrolia, 1990), S. 214. Siehe dazu auch Rudolf Hiestand, ,Der Kreuzfahrer und sein islamisches Gegenüber', in Das Ritterbild in Mittelalter und Renaissance, hrsg. vom Forschungsinstitut für Mittelalter und Renaissance (Düsseldorf: Droste, 1985), 51-68 (S. 51-52).

51. Vergleiche dazu auch die Konzeption des Gottesstaates bei Augustinus, Aurelius Augustinus: Der Gottesstaat. De civitate Dei. Lat./Dt., übersetzt von Carl Johann Perl, 2 Bände (Paderborn; München; Wien; Zürich: Ferdinand Schöningh, 1979), Bd. 1, S. 704 (civ. Dei XI,1).

52. Zur Bezeichnung Agarener oder Sarazenen siehe Rotter: Abendland und Sarazenen, S. 68-70 Nach Schupp könnte die Namen Agar und Agarain sich jedoch auch auf den Gebirgsnamen Ahaggar beziehen, V. Schupp, ‚Zur Datierung', S. 50.

53. Rotter: Abendland und Sarazenen, S. 72.

54. ‚*wollet ir die lant* lazen stan/ unde rumen die gote *ze eren*'.

55. Die Hinrichtung (GR 34,2-3) wird nicht weiter erwähnt, ergibt sich jedoch durch die ablehnende Haltung Rudolfs gegenüber Girabobe.

56. Nach Hiestand, ‚Der Kreuzfahrer', S. 60 veränderten die militärischen Kontakte von Muslimen und Christen auch die jeweilige Kampfweise der beiden Gegner.

57. Vermutlich hat Rudolf nicht nur einfach die Seite gewechselt, sondern auch den Sohn des Königs Gilot, dessen Erzieher er gewesen zu sein scheint (GR 46,9-10), heimlich an den Hof des heidnischen Königs gebracht (GR 51,33-35).

58. Ähnlich einfallsreich wie Girabobe erweist sich auch Gyburc im Willehalm. Auch sie, von heidnischer Abstammung, greift auf sich gestellt im belagerten Orange zu einer List gegen ihre heidnischen Verwandten, die sie militärisch bedrängen. Sie versucht Krieger vorzutäuschen, indem sie den Gefallenen Helme aufsetzen lässt und anordnet, diese als ob sie noch lebten zu bewegen. Ähnlich wie Girabobe verkleidet auch Gyburc ihre Mädchen mit Rüstungen als Kämpfer. Wolfram hat dieses Motiv vermutlich aus „Aliscans" übernommen, siehe dazu Eva Schäufele, Normabweichendes Rollenverhalten: Die kämpfende Frau in der deutschen Literatur des 12. und 13. Jahrhunderts (Göppingen: Kümmerle, 1979), S. 51. Jedoch ist hier dieses Motiv der Mädchen in Waffenrüstungen, die zahlreiche Kämpfer vortäuschen müssen auffallend, da diese List von Heiden bzw. von Personen, die von heidnischer Kultur geprägt sind, angewendet wird. Nach Hiestand, ‚Der Kreuzfahrer', S. 66 hatten auf muslimischer Seite besonders beim dritten Kreuzzug Frauen, die in Rüstungen am Kampf teilnahmen, Erstaunen erweckt. Der Verkehr mit Fremden in Gesellschaft ebenso wie die Teilnahme einer Frau am Kampf waren für Muslime unvorstellbar. Zum Eindruck der fränkischen Frauen auf die Muslime, siehe auch Aleya Khattab, Das Bild der Franken in der arabischen Literatur des Mittelalters. Ein Beitrag zum Dialog über die Kreuzzüge (Göppingen: Kümmerle, 1989), S. 33-34.

59. Mit dieser Bezeichnung hatte man im ersten Kreuzzug üblicherweise die Türken versehen, siehe dazu Fulcher, Historia Hierosolymitana II 3.1, S. 362, zitiert nach Hiestand, ‚Der Kreuzfahrer', S 55.

60. Die Stelle (GR 57,23-39) interpretiert Fromm als diplomatischen Versuch der heidnischen Prinzessin dem nicht ganz reinen Ansinnen des Königs zu entkommen, indem sie sich schließlich durch die Bitte um die Taufe rettet, siehe dazu GR 57,28-34.37-39): ‚sie wisete ime [dem König] die straze/ da her doch erste inne reit./ her vir los sine arbeit./ des ne darf man ire wizen nicht,/ wende ire manich herzelip/ von dem*e* was geschen des [Rudolf] sie da beit./ manige not sie mit ime irleit, [...] „herre, ir sult schaffen/ mit bischofen unde mit phaffe*n*/ daz ir mich lazet toufen."'

61. Zur Fluchtbeschreibung und ihrer Nähe zum Bibelgleichnis des barmherzigen Samariters siehe auch Wolfgang Mohr, ‚Zum frühhöfischen Menschenbild in „Graf Rudolf"', ZDA, 96 (1967), 97-109, (S. 105-107).

62. Nach Naumann ist Graf Rudolf gleichsam ein Vorläufer von Gahmuret, Hans Naumann, ‚Der wilde und der edle Heide. Versuch über die höfische Toleranz', in Vom

Werden des deutschen Geistes, Festgabe für Gustav Ehrismann (Berlin; Leipzig: de Gruyter & co, 1925), 80-101 (S. 89).

63. Siehe dazu R. Röhricht, ‚Das Gedicht von des Landgrafen Ludwig Kreuzfahrt nach Sprache und Composition. III. Erläuterungen nach seiner historischen Seite', ZfdPh, 8 (1877), 419-446 (S. 420-421) und Dietrich Huschenbett, Artikel ‚Die Kreuzfahrt Landgraf Ludwigs des Frommen', in Verfasserlexikon. Die deutsche Literatur des Mittelalters, Bd. 5, begründet von Wolfgang Stammler, fortgeführt von Karl Langosch, hrsg. von Kurt Ruh (Berlin; New York 1985), 372-376 (Sp. 372-373). Zudem gibt es literarische Beziehungen der Kreuzfahrt zum ‚Willehalm' Ulrichs von dem Türlin, zu ‚Alexander' und ‚Wilhelm von Wenden' von Ulrich von Etzenbach und zu ‚Herzog Ernst D'. Damit zeigt sich eine stilistische, doch auch thematische Verbindung zu Wolfram von Eschenbach, ebd., Sp. 374. – Die Zitierung der Textstellen erfolgt weiterhin mit der Abkürzung LgL und den entsprechenden Versen.

64. Bereits Kinzel hatte Rietel zitiert im Hinblick auf das Werk als ‚culturhistorische quelle, ein[en] interessante[n] beleg für anschauungen und stimmungen der zeit', Karl Kinzel, ‚Das Gedicht von des Landgrafen Ludwig Kreuzfahrt nach Sprache und Composition', ZfdPh, 8 (1877), 379-419 (S. 392). Zu den Quellen des anonymen Dichters siehe auch: R. Röhricht, ‚Das Gedicht von des Landgrafen Ludwig Kreuzfahrt', S. 437-438. - Die Dichtung kann auch als Erbauungsliteratur mit apologetischem Charakter aufgefasst werden.

65. Das Hl. Kreuz symbolisierte aus islamischer Sicht seit der zweiten Hälfte des 12. Jahrhunderts die Kreuzzüge. Insofern war seine Eroberung eines der Ziele des Jihad, Emmanuel Sivan, ‚Islam and the Crusades: Antagonism, Polemics, Dialogue', in Religionsgespräche im Mittelalter, hrsg. von Bernard Lewis und Friedrich Niewöhner (Wiesbaden: Harrassowitz, 1992), 207-215 (S. 212). Gleichzeitig erregte seine Verehrung durch die Christen Anstoß und wurde als Götzendienst betrachtet, Julia Gauss, ‚Toleranz und Intoleranz zwischen Christen und Muslimen in der Zeit vor den Kreuzzügen', Saeculum, 19 (1969), 362-389 (S. 381).

66. Augustinus, Der Gottesstaat, Bd. 2, S. 381-284 und S. 106-108. (civ. Dei XVIII,41 und XVI,4). Gleichzeitig kann mit dem Namen auch die Gestalt des Königs von Babylon im Ludus de Antichristo, der dort der König der Heidenheit ist, verbunden werden. Dieser belagert auch Jerusalem, Ludus de Antichristo, Lat./ Dt., übersetzt und Nachwort von Rolf Engelsing (Stuttgart: Reclam, 1968), Vv. 122-124.

67. Siehe dazu Bernhard von Clairvaux, De novae militiae, S. 215.

68. Dies erinnert an das Vergilzitat, das von Augustinus übernommen wurde: ‚Parcere subiectis et debellare superbos', (Aen. VI, 847-849), Augustinus, Der Gottesstaat, Bd. 1, S. 320 (civ. Dei V,12). Die Unterworfenen schonen und die Stolzen zu bekämpfen kann in diesem Sinne meinen, diejenigen, die schon besiegt sind zu verschonen und auch im Kampf Milde walten zu lassen.

69. Siehe dazu den Kaufvergleich in LgL 7409-7410: ‚Ungelîch sie kouften,/ die heiden und die getouften./'. Der Unterschied wirkt sich natürlich auch im Ausgang des Kampfes aus: ‚die fluht gâben die Sarrazîn.' (LgL 7411).

70. Vergleiche Wh. 76,19.

71. Mit der Bezeichnung eines Sarazenen als Levi wird zugleich eine Verbindung zu dem Judentum hergestellt, da Levi ein gebräuchlicher jüdischer Name ist. Der Name weist zugleich auf den gleichnamigen Ahnherrn des Stammes éâì, den Sohn Jakobs, hin, siehe dazu auch J. Schreiner, Artikel ‚Levi', in Lexikon für Theologie und Kirche, begründet von Michael Buchberger, 2. völlig neu bearbeitete Auflage, hrsg. von Josef Höfer und

Karl Rahner, Bd. 6 (Freiburg: Herder, 1961), 993-995. Während sonst das Judentum keine Rolle in der „Kreuzfahrt Landgraf Ludwigs" spielt, zeigt Wolfram jedoch eine wesentlich engere Beziehung zwischen Sarazenen und Judentum und stellt beide Religionen auf die gleiche Stufe, Wh. 162,29-30: ‚des waren gelouben ane,/ juden, heiden, publicane'.

72. Das Rolandslied des Pfaffen Konrad, hrsg. von Carl Wesle, 2. Aufl. Besorgt von Peter Wapnewski (Tübingen: Max Niemeyer, 1967), Vv. 8134-8137 und (Wh.17,20-21). Apollo kann auch mit Off 9,11 in Verbindung gebracht werden. Nach dem Blasen der fünften Posaune werden die Menschen von einem dämonischen Heer von Heuschrecken heimgesucht und gequält. Ihr König ist der Engel des Abgrunds; ‚er heißt auf hebräisch Abaddon, auf griechisch Apollyon'. Die Menschen, die nicht das Siegel Gottes tragen, die also (noch) nicht auf der Seite Gottes stehen, werfen sich vor ihren Dämonen und Götzen aus ‚Gold, Silber, Erz, Stein und Holz' nieder, Off 9,20b.

73. Iovis und Iupiter sind eigentlich identisch, werden hier jedoch als zwei heidnische Götter gesehen.

74. Vergleiche auch zu den Heiden als Gottes Geschöpfe LgL 7119 und 7754 (hier wird Saladin von Ludwig als Geschöpf Gottes bezeichnet) und diverse Stellen im „Willehalm" Wolframs von Eschenbach wie etwa Wh. 306,28; 307,1.

75. Zur Verbindung von Religiosität und Frau bei den Sarazenen, siehe auch die Stelle, in der der Vater Saladins Mohammed im Irrealis anruft, da er die Unmöglichkeit seines Ansinnens erkennt. Würde ihm wieder die Kraft gegeben, so würde er sich im Kampf für die Heiligkeit Mohammeds und die Ehre der Frauen einsetzen, LgL 6567-6568.

76. Vergleiche dazu die Formulierung des Pater-nosters in Mt 6,10: ‚dein Wille geschehe/ wie im Himmel, so auf der Erde'.

77. Zum betrügerischen Mohammed siehe auch Wh. 17,21.

78. Siehe dazu Julia Gauss, ‚Toleranz und Intoleranz', S. 380-381. Im Islam wird Christus allein als Prophet aufgefasst, siehe dazu auch Erdmann Fritsch, Islam und das Christentum im Mittelalter (Breslau: Müller & Seiffert, 1930), S. 102-104. Vergleiche dazu auch Otto von Freising, Chronica sive Historia de duabus civitatibus, hrsg. von Walther Lammers, übersetzt von Adolf Schmidtg (Darmstadt: Wissenschaftliche Buchgesellschaft, 1961), S. 510 (Chronik VII,7).

79. Die ‚hôhe[] trinitât' wird nur einmal in einer Rede Ludwigs erwähnt. Das Verständnis der Trinität war für Muslime äußerst schwierig, J. Gauss, Toleranz und Intoleranz, S. 379. Nach G. Graf können ausgehend von einer Trinität plus Christus als zusätzlichem Gott von den Muslimen sogar vier Gottheiten gezählt werden. Ein weiteres Problem bildet die göttliche Vaterschaft, denn bei einer Vaterschaft Gottes könnten Geist und Sohn nicht Gott sein. Ähnliche Probleme werden in Zusammenhang mit der Rolle Mariens bei der Geburt Christi angesprochen, die letztlich polemisch auch dahingehend aufgefasst werden konnte, dass Gott ein Akzidenz Mariens gewesen sei, wie denn überhaupt von muslimischer Seite sich die Frage erhob, ob überhaupt in der Zeit Gott, der Ewige, geboren werden kann, siehe dazu besonders Georg Graf, ‚Christliche Polemik', S. 825-842 (833-835). Vergleiche auch Griffith, ‚Disputes with Muslims in Syriac Texts', S. 254 (Taufe), S. 265, 268 (Trinität und Fleischwerdung Christi). Ebenso gab es den Vorwurf, wenn Vater, Sohn und Geist untrennbar miteinander verbunden seien, dann müssten sie ebenso bei der Inkarnation ungetrennt gewesen sein. Dieser Vernunftschluss war eines der größten Probleme in der christlichen Apologie, siehe J. Gauss, ebd.

80. ‚die rede ist in füge siten' (LgL 7780).

81. Eine Ausnahme scheint Konrad von Montferrat zu sein, dem nachgesagt wurde, eine Seperatvereinbarung mit dem Sultan geschlossen zu haben, LgL 2496-2502, siehe dazu auch Runciman, Geschichte der Kreuzzüge, S. 788.

82. Siehe dazu auch Hans Prutz, Kulturgeschichte der Kreuzzüge, Reprografischer Nachdruck der Ausgabe Berlin 1883 (Hildesheim: Georg Olms, 1964), S. 42-43, der auf ähnliche Erscheinungen bei Christen und Moslems hinweist. Er sieht die religiöse Begeisterung der Moslems ähnlich geartet wie die der Christen, sie haben eine ähnliche ritterliche Gesinnung und glauben ähnlich dem christlichen Kämpfer unmittelbar nach dem Tod in das Paradies einzugehen. Auch die Tempelritter finden ihr Vorbild in mohammedanischen Kriegergenossenschaften wie der der Rabiten.

83. ‚[...] unêre ir hât/ Machmet, sô lasterlîcher tât,/ und al ir gote der heidenschaft./ hêten sie helfe, gotlîche craft/ sie hûten ir volc als Ihêsus Crist, der ein wâre helfe den Cristen ist./ wes wir gedenken zu in,/ an dem schaden wir des sîn./' (LgL 6478-6584).

84. Vgl. dazu Gottfried von Viterbo, Pantheon, hrsg. von Joannis Pistorius Nidanus curante Burcardus Gotthelfus Struvius (Ratisbonae: Joannis Conradi Peezii, 1736), S. 239.

85. ‚sîn zorn an in alsô ergienc,/ daz er liez jâmerlîchen die/ nider morden als daz vie.' Ähnlich wird auch die verwegene Tapferkeit der Fußsoldaten beim Sturm Akkons beschrieben: ‚ez liez sich morden als daz vie,' (LgL 2931).

86. ‚ouch die fûzgênden man,/ sie hêten grôzen mort begân/ an orsen, ouch an den heiden hie' (LgL 2019-2021), oder die Christen schlagen die Heiden ‚âne erbarmde' (LgL 6958).

87. Hiestand, ‚Der Kreuzfahrer', S. 62. Prutz, Kulturgeschichte der Kreuzzüge, S. 57-58.

88. Schwinges, ‚Wilhelm von Tyrus', S. 157. Zu den politischen Verbindungen zwischen Christen und Muslimen siehe auch Prutz, Kulturgeschichte der Kreuzzüge, S. 70 und Emmanuel Sivan, ‚Islam and the Crusades', in Religionsgespräche im Mittelalter, 207-216 (S. 209).

89. Hiestand, ‚Der Kreuzfahrer', S. 63-64. Dort auch wird in der Anm. 59 auf den Ritter Philipp und den Ritter Pedrovant hingewiesen. Letzterer kann seinen Wunsch, den muslimischen Gegner kennenzulernen nicht mehr umsetzen, da er vorher von einem Löwen gefressen wird. Zu Richard Löwenherz siehe auch Prutz, Kulturgeschichte der Kreuzzüge, S. 68. Dort auch zu dem Austausch von Geschenken zwischen Richard Löwenherz, Philipp II. August von Frankreich und Saladin. Auch Turniere zwischen christlichen Streitern und Beduinen waren keine Seltenheit.

90. Prutz, Kulturgeschichte der Kreuzzüge, S. 63. Ebenso wurde auch die Schwertleite an islamischen Adeligen vollzogen, so hatte Richard Löwenherz den Sohn Seifeddins 1192 zu Acco das Schwert gegeben, ähnlich wird auch von Friedrich II. berichtet, dass er den Ritterschlag auch Sarazenen gab, ebd., S. 69. Siehe dazu auch E. Sivan, ‚Islam and the Crusades', S. 208.

91. Prutz, Kulturgeschichte der Kreuzzüge, S. 63.

92. Auch die dunkle Belakane in Wolframs Parzival hätte sich gerne taufen lassen, zumindest um Gahmuret halten zu können (Pz 57,6-8), doch da hatte Gahmuret sie schon verlassen, Wolfram von Eschenbach, Parzival, nach der Ausgabe von Karl Lachmann, übersetzt und mit Nachwort von Wolfgang Spiewok (Stuttgart: Reclam, 1996).

93. Prutz, Kulturgeschichte der Kreuzzüge, S. 63. So gab es den Plan die Schwester Königs Richard Löwenherz Johanna von Sizilien mit el-Adil, dem Sohn Saladins, zu vermählen. Weniger Rücksicht auf kirchlich-politische Einstellungen nahmen dagegen

niedrigere Kreise, ebd. Zu dem Heiratsplan siehe auch Runciman, Geschichte der Kreuzzüge, S. 832-833.

94. Zum Renegatentum, das anfangs nur sehr selten vorkam und nur meist aus praktischen Erwägungen entstand, siehe Prutz, S. 66. Im Rolandslied dagegen bekehren sich nach dem Sieg Karls Brechmundâ und ihr Volk., Rolandslied Vv. 8620-8631. – Hinsichtlich des hl. Georg und anderen Heiligen als Schlachthelfer siehe auch J. Gauss, ‚Toleranz und Intoleranz', S. 371-372.

95. Zum Heimatgefühl der Orientfranken, siehe Schwinges, ‚Wilhelm von Tyrus', S. 157-158.

96. In der Kreuzfahrt wird noch nicht vom Eintreffen Richard Löwenherz gesprochen, der Akkon 1191 einnimmt.

97. Siehe dazu, LgL 7814-7958.

98. Schwinges, Kreuzzugsideologie und Toleranz, S. 38.

99. Schwinges: ‚Wilhelm von Tyrus', S. 166-167. Zum Begriff der ‚informellen Toleranz' und Toleranz auch als dem Aushalten der Pluralität, Schwinges, ebd. S. 159.

100. Im Dialogus werden in revolutionärer Weise ‚[c]hristliche Heilsexklusivität, Auserwählungsbewußtsein und Bekehrungszwänge' ausgeschlossen, jedoch erscheint die Position des Christen als eine höherwertige. Die Vollkommenheit der christlichen Lehre, die für Abelard die ‚wahre Ethik' ist, ergibt sich aus einer ihrer Beziehung zur ‚beatitudo divina'. Die rationale Erschließung dieser Ethik ist nach Abelard möglich: Winfried Eberhard, ‚Ansätze zur Bewältigung ideologischer Pluralität im 12. Jahrhundert. Pierre Abélard und Anselm von Havelberg', HJ, 105 (1985), 353-387 (S. 361-362). ‚Zur Beurteilung der Heilsfunktion des natürlichen Sittengesetzes für die Heilsfähigkeit der Heiden ist jedoch auch die Rolle der vormosaischen Patriarchen (Abel, Noe, Abraham, Henoch etc.) und außermosaischer Gerechten (Job) im Dialogus zu beachten. Sie gehorchten nämlich, frei vom geschriebenen Gesetz, nur dem Naturgesetz der Gottesliebe und anerkannten Gott als den „Gott der Menschen" Sie wurden dadurch gerecht und gerettet ebenso wie der „Job gentilis", der bereits in der Zeit des mosaischen Gesetzes nur der lex naturalis gemäß der ratio naturalis folgte und der so beweist, daß die lex naturalis auch ohne Thora heilssuffizient war.', Eberhard, ebd., S. 364. Für Abelard ‚bleiben Glaube und Christentum Ziel von rationaler Erkenntnis und Ethik', ebd., S. 366. - 1141 veranlasst Peter von Cluny die Übersetzung des Koran, Prutz, Kulturgeschichte der Kreuzzüge, S. 74.

101. Im Zusammenhang mit dem Martyrium Erzbischofs Thiemo von Salzburg, Otto von Freising, Chronica, VII,7.

102. Siehe dazu die particula XXVIII der unvollständige Fassung E des Pantheon in der Hs IX,2 von St. Peter, Salzburg. Hier werden neben dem Leben des Propheten auch Prinzipien des Djihad und eine Darstellung der Sitten und Glaubensvorstellungen gegeben, wie etwa Polygamie, die Vorstellungen des islamischen Paradieses, der Ramadan, der Freitag als heiliger Tag. Gottfried behauptet viele Informationen auch mündlich erhalten zu haben. Die bisher unedierte Stelle von etwa 2770 Wörtern beabsichtige ich, in einem weiteren Artikel zu veröffentlichen.

103. Schwinges, ‚Wilhelm von Tyrus', S. 163. Wilhelm erkennt im Islam auch eine Lehre die zu Gottesfurcht und Frömmigkeit führt, doch verwirft er an sich den Islam, ebd.

104. Ähnlich auch Gottfried von Viterbo.

105. Siehe dazu auch den genauen Titel der Schrift von Petrus Venerabilis, ‚Adversus nefandam haeresim sive sectam saracenorum', S. 674. Nach Schwinges, ‚Wilhelm von Tyrus', S. 162 wurde diese Ansicht zunächst nur vereinzelt erst im 11.

Jahrhundert im Gebiet der lateinischen Kirche rezipiert. Zum Islam als Ketzertum siehe auch S.H. Griffith, ‚Disputes with Muslimes in Syriac Texts', S. 267 und J. Gauss, ‚Toleranz und Intoleranz', S. 378.

106. Schwinges, ‚Wilhelm von Tyrus', S. 162, zum Paganismus ebenfalls Schwinges, Kreuzzugsideologie und Toleranz 1977, S. 79-92. Bereits über Eusebius war das Wissen vermittelt worden, dass die Sarazenen die Venus verehrten. Durch einen Irrtum wird von Beda Venus mit Lucifer wiedergegeben und dadurch weiteren Assoziationen Tür und Tor geöffnet. Auch Mohammed wird aufgrund der im nachgesagten sexuellen Potenz in Verbindung mit Venus gebracht. Von Johannes Damascenus wird ebenso die Ka'ba in Beziehung mit Venus gesetzt, Rotter, Abendland und Sarazenen, S. 247-249. Zu den römischen Namen siehe auch Leo Jordan, ‚Wie man sich im Mittelalter die Heiden des Orients vorstellte', GRM, 5 (1913), 391-400 (S. 391).

107. R.C. Schwinges, Kreuzzugsideologie, S. 102-103.

108. Jacques Waardenburg weist auf die Bedeutung der christlichen Gelehrten für die Araber bzw. den Islam hin, die die Griechisch-hellenistische Wissenschaft und Philosophie den Arabern vermittelten. Von ihnen wurden Texte aus dem Syrischen wie auch aus dem Griechischen in das Arabische übersetzt. Zunächst waren die Christen den Arabern noch kulturell überlegen, Jacques Waardenburg, Artikel ‚Religionsgespräche', S. 642.

109. Siehe dazu Sidney H. Griffith, ‚Disputes with Muslims in Syriac Christian Texts', S. 257; Waardenburg, Artikel ‚Religionsgespräche', S. 643. Von dem Engländer Robert von Ketton wurde 1143 der Koran ins Lateinische übersetzt, ebd. Nach H. Prutz waren an diesem 1141 begonnenen Übersetzungsprojekt des Koran von Peter von Cluny neben dem Engländer Robert auch Peter von Toledo, Hermann aus Dalmatien und ein Sarazene namens Mohammed beteiligt. Zusätzlich wurde noch ein Leben Mohammeds und eine Darstellung der wesentlichen Punkte der islamischen Glaubenslehre, Hans Prutz, Kulturgeschichte der Kreuzzüge, S. 74. Peter von Cluny verfasste nun selbst eine Abhandlung in vier Büchern „Adversus nefandam sectam saracenorum", auf die nach Prutz die meisten polemischen Schriften des Mittelalters zurückgehen, ebd., S. 75. Zur Schrift selbst siehe Petrus Venerabilis, ‚Adversus nefandam sectam sarazenorum', in Patrologia Latina, ed. J.-P. Migne, vol. 189, (Paris, 1854), S. 660-720. –Im Verlauf des 9. Jahrhunderts machten sich die Sarazenen vor allem durch ständige Überfälle auch außerhalb der iberischen Halbinsel in Europa bemerkbar. In Sizilien setzten sie sich fest, die Küsten Südfrankreichs wurden von ihnen heimgesucht. Sie kamen aus dem Süden, aus den Alpentälern. Es gelang ihnen im burgundischen Fraxinetum für etwa ein Jahrhundert zu bleiben. Auch italisches Gebiet wurde angegriffen, wie etwa die Sabina, Latium oder auch Tuszien, bauten Raubburgen in der Campagna. Auch Rom blieb nicht verschont. Die Kirchen St. Peter und St. Paul wurden geplündert (846), selbst die Apostelgräber wurden nicht verschont. Erst im 916 konnten die Sarazenen vom italischen Stiefel vertrieben werden, Ferdinand Gregorovius, Geschichte der Stadt Rom im Mittelalter, vol. I,2, (München: dtv, 1988), S. 507-509, 549, 585, 587-588. Im burgundischen Gebiet hatten sie noch bis etwa 975 Fraxinetum als Stützpunkt. Siehe dazu auch Rainer Christoph Schwinges, Kreuzzugsideologie und Toleranz, S. 100. Bereits in dem ersten Viertel des 8. Jahrhundert stand zumindest der südliche Teil Sardiniens unter arabischem Einfluss, siehe dazu und zum Vorstoß der Sarazenen im selben Jahrhundert ins Frankenreich auch besonders Ekkehart Rotter, Abendland und Sarazenen, S. 205, 212-230.

110. Waardenburg, Artikel ‚Religionsgespräche', S. 643.

111. U. Mattejiet, Artikel ‚Religionsgespräche', S. 691. Als geradezu ein „Wagnis" bezeichnet Julia Gauss den Entschluss der frühscholastischen Theologie unter der Führung von Anselm von Canterbury mit der rationalen Glaubensbegründung zu argumentieren, Julia Gauss, ‚Toleranz und Intoleranz', S. 389.

112. Nach den Darstellungen von Klaus Schreiner ist die mittelalterliche Toleranz auch immer eine pragmatische, K. Schreiner, Artikel ‚Toleranz', S. 446-466.

113. Insbesondere die Nennung von Dreier-Gruppen heidnischer „Götter" hat die Funktion die muslimische Ablehnung der christlichen Trinität lächerlich zu machen, Geert H.M. Claassens, ‚Jacob van Maerlant on Muhammad and Islam', in Medieval Christian Perceptions of Islam, hrsg. von John Victor Tolan (New York; Londen: Garland, 1996), S. 211-242 (S. 213).

114. Hiestand, ‚Kreuzfahrer', S. 63.

115. In dieselbe Richtung weisen auch die Epen der *chanson de geste*.

La réception en langue vulgaire du "De falconibus" d'Albert le Grand

An Smets

English summary

During the Middle Ages, hunting was one of the favourite activities of the high society. The animals who helped the hunters were of great value and, as a consequence, were often taken care of by specialised people, with generally detailed zoological and medical knowledge. This knowledge is conserved in the medieval hunting treatises, which should be considered as real scientific works. Besides, a study of these treatises is not only useful for our knowledge about medieval science. Other fields, like lexicology, are also involved, especially when it is possible to compare a Latin text with its translations in one or more vernacular languages. Such a text is the "De falconibus", by Albertus Magnus († 1280). The treatise is divided into four sections: the differences between the birds of prey and the other birds, the different kinds of falcons, the way of preparing them for the hunt, and finally the cures for sick or wounded falcons. The accuracy of his observations clearly shows that Albertus Magnus was a real expert in this field. After some time, the "De falconibus" was inserted in the larger work *De animalibus* (book 23, chapter 40), but simultaneously the treatise also circulated as an autonomous work. By the end of the Middle Ages, several different translations appeared. Up to now, we know of two German versions. The first one, by Werner Ernesti, is based only on the therapeutical part, whereas the second one, composed by Heinrich Münsinger, deals with the whole Latin text and was written from a more practical point of view. There are also four French translations, dating from the end of the fourteenth until the sixteenth century. Like the German versions, these French texts, which were written independently from each other, show a clear evolution in the way they transmit the technical vocabulary. Finally, we also possess three Italian versions from the fifteenth century, of which two are again dealing with the therapeutical part only.

Introduction

Que la chasse était une des activités préférées de la noblesse médiévale est un fait généralement connu et accepté. Une place importante y était accordée aux animaux, surtout le chien et l'oiseau de proie, qui aidaient les hommes et qui en général avaient reçu un entraînement spécifique à cet effet. Ces animaux étaient donc d'une grande valeur et par conséquent, ils étaient souvent entourés d'un personnel spécialisé, qui, en rapport avec son travail, possédait des connaissances zoologiques et médicales développées. Les traces de ce savoir se trouvent dans les nombreux traités cynégétiques que le moyen âge nous a légués.[1] Cependant, cette littérature cynégétique n'est pas tellement connue, à quelques exceptions près.[2] Il ne faut pourtant pas mépriser ces traités ou les considérer naï vement comme des textes folkloriques où la magie et la science sont parfois mélangées. Ce sont par contre de véritables traités scientifiques. D'ailleurs, dans son *Didascalicon*, Hugues de Saint-Victor rangeait la chasse dans la branche mécanique de la philosophie (ou de la science), à côté de la médecine et de la navigation, parmi d'autres. Il soulignait ainsi la valeur scientifique que l'homme médiéval accordait à cette activité, que nous considérons actuellement comme un simple loisir.[3]

Pour le domaine latin, nous connaissons 29 traités différents,[4] conservés dans 67 manuscrits, et dont le premier remonte au Xe s.[5] Les premiers textes cynégétiques sont surtout d'ordre thérapeutique. En d'autres termes, ils sont presque exclusivement composés de recettes pour soigner les rapaces malades ou blessés. Plus tard, les auteurs donnent également des informations zoologiques, telle la description des différents oiseaux de chasse. Ainsi, les traités de fauconnerie latins atteignent leur sommet au XIIIe s. avec l'oeuvre magistrale de Frédéric II de Hohenstaufen, le *De arte venandi cum avibus*, qui fournit dans sa version complète (6 livres) une ornithologie générale et des renseignements très précis sur l'apprivoisement et l'affaitage des faucons. En même temps, et sans qu'il existe la moindre relation entre ces travaux contemporains, la fauconnerie fait son entrée dans la littérature encyclopédique, notamment chez Albert le Grand.

Le XIIIe s. ne voit pas seulement apparaître des chefs-d'oeuvre latins, mais aussi les premiers textes en langue vulgaire. Au début, il s'agit surtout de traductions, qui sont complétées par des ouvrages originaux à partir du second quart du XIVe s.[6] Parmi les textes en langue vulgaire, la tradition française se montre la plus riche : un dépouillement récent a abouti à un total de 44 textes (dont 11 traductions[7]) et 173 manuscrits.[8] Ce chiffre dépasse donc de loin les témoins latins, de même que les témoins dans les autres langues vulgaires:[9] pour l'instant 57 copies sont connues pour la péninsule ibérique, une quarantaine pour le domaine italien,[10] une trentaine pour l'allemand et un peu plus pour l'anglais (± 40).

L'étude des textes cynégétiques est certes utile pour une meilleure connaissance de la science médiévale, mais les résultats peuvent être utilisés dans différents domains.[11] Parmi ceux-ci, la lexicologie occupe une place très importante, surtout si on possède à côté du texte latin des traductions en une ou plusieurs langues vulgaires ou des traductions qui se situent sur une échelle temporelle assez grande. Ceci est entre autres le cas du "De falconibus" d'Albert le Grand. Avec ses traductions en allemand, en italien et en français, il est possible d'indiquer les divergences et les points communs entre les différentes versions et c'est ce que nous tentons de faire dans la présente contribution.

Albert le Grand, "De falconibus" et "De animalibus": le problème de la datation

Cependant, avant d'étudier plus en détail les traductions en langue vulgaire de cette oeuvre, il convient de s'arrêter un instant auprès du texte latin. Tout d'abord, l'auteur du traité est bien connu.[12] Albert le Grand ou Albertus Magnus, décédé en 1280, compte parmi les hommes les plus importants de la vie intellectuelle du XIIIe s. En effet, le dominicain allemand, professeur entre autres à Paris et à Cologne, nous laissa plus de cent ouvrages où, à côté de la philosophie et de la théologie, les sciences naturelles occupent une place importante.

Dans le *De animalibus,*[13] Albert le Grand décrit en vingt-six livres le monde animal, en se basant surtout sur la zoologie d'Aristote. Le vingt-troisième livre, consacré aux oiseaux, traite dans l'ordre alphabétique cent quatorze espèces différentes, d'*aquila* à *zeleucides*. Mais alors que la plupart de ces descriptions se limitent à quelques paragraphes, le quarantième chapitre, intitulé "De falconibus", est subdivisé lui-même en vingt-quatre chapitres et occupe ainsi presque la moitié du livre. A cause de l'ampleur de ce chapitre, plusieurs chercheurs ont pensé qu'il s'agit d'un traité qui à l'origine était indépendant mais qui a été ajouté plus tard à l'ouvrage complet du *De animalibus*.

Cette hypothèse est corroborée par le fait que le "De falconibus" est déjà cité dans le *Speculum naturale* de Vincent de Beauvais, ouvrage terminé vers 1257-1258, ce qui fait remonter la rédaction du "De falconibus" vers 1250[14] ou même plus tôt.[15] La question de la rédaction du *De animalibus* se révèle complexe, et les études ne convergent pas toujours.[16] K. Lindner,[17] qui a étudié ce problème en détail, croit que le "De falconibus" pourrait bien être la partie la plus ancienne du *De animalibus*, ouvrage composé pendant plusieurs années (ou même décennies) et terminé probablement dans les années soixante du XIIIe s.

La tradition manuscrite du "De falconibus" s'incline également en faveur d'une composition indépendante. En effet, le traité de fauconnerie se retrouve dans quatre manuscrits[18] qui ne contiennent pas d'autres parties du *De animalibus*. Finalement, ce traité connaissait déjà des traductions médiévales en allemand, en italien et en français, qui seront commentées ci-après.

Il existe donc plusieurs arguments en faveur d'une composition autonome du "De falconibus", située vers 1250. Toutefois, jusqu'à maintenant, aucune preuve indiscutable ne permet de trancher définitivement cette question.

Le contenu et les sources du "De falconibus"

Le "De falconibus" se divise en quatre parties, qui, à leur tour, se composent de plusieurs chapitres. Dans la première partie, l'auteur décrit en quoi les rapaces diffèrent des autres oiseaux. Ainsi, il passe en revue la forme de leur corps, leur couleur, leur manière de chasser et dernièrement leur voix. La deuxième partie est consacrée aux différentes espèces. Parmi les dix-sept décrites, dix sont nobles (le sacre, le gerfaut, le montagnard, le pèlerin, le faucon bossu, le faucon noir, le faucon blanc, le faucon rouge, le faucon aux pieds d'azur et l'émerillon).[19] Les trois espèces de laniers (blanche, noire et rouge) sont considérées comme non nobles. Enfin, il existe quatre espèces de faucons bâtards (croisement des faucons nobles et non nobles). Ensuite, le dix-septième chapitre constitue à lui-seul la troisième partie, qui traite de l'affaitage et du dressage du faucon. Finalement, la quatrième partie est d'ordre thérapeutique. En premier lieu y sont décrites les maladies des faucons (chap. XVIII-XIX), ensuite celles des autours (chap. XX) et des éperviers (chap. XXI) et finalement celles de tous les rapaces (chap. XXIII). Le vingt-deuxième chapitre parle de l'affaitage des autours et le vingt-quatrième et dernier mentionne encore deux autres espèces de faucons, à savoir le lapidaire et l'arboréal. Ce chapitre appartient donc plutôt à la seconde qu'à la dernière partie.

Les trois premières parties sont surtout le résultat des expériences et observations de l'auteur même, complétées par les contacts avec d'autres fauconniers.[20] Dans ces descriptions très détaillées, il s'est montré un bon observateur et connaisseur des rapaces. Par contre, la partie consacrée à la thérapeutique est basée sur plusieurs ouvrages antérieurs. Dans les titres des chapitres, Albert le Grand renvoie lui-même à l'empereur Frédéric II et à Guillelmus falconarius,[21] mais ces renvois se révèlent incorrects. De l'autre côté, la mention d'Aquila, Symachus et Theodotion dans le titre du vingt-troisième chapitre est exacte, parce que celui-ci reprend leur soi-disante *Epistola ad Ptolomeum regem*. Les autres sources de la quatrième partie sont *Dancus rex* (chap. XVIII), *Gerardus falconarius* (chap. XIX), l'anonyme *Tractatus de austuribus* (chap. XXI) et une compilation d'*Alexander medicus*, Adélard de Bath et *Gerardus Falconarius* (chap. XX).[22]

Les traductions médiévales allemandes du "De falconibus"

Grâce aux travaux de Kurt Lindner et Jan-Dirk Müller,[23] nous sommes bien renseignés sur ces traductions allemandes. Il en existe deux versions indépendantes du XVe s., la première étant de la main de Werner Ernesti, la seconde de Heinrich Münsinger. Dans les deux cas, le commanditaire a été le comte palatin Ludwig III, devenu ensuite électeur, à la cour de Heidelberg. Les traductions ne se limitent pas au traité sur les faucons, mais contiennent aussi les passages sur le chien et le cheval du *De animalibus*, donc tous les animaux qui sont associés au chevalier médiéval. Cette "compilation" se présente également dans le ms. Heidelberg, UB, Cpl 1326, fol. 1-19, le modèle probable d'Ernesti et peut-être aussi de Münsinger.

Le travail de Heinrich Münsinger a connu plus de succès que son prédécesseur : actuellement, nous en connaissons dix manuscripts,[24] contre un seul de l'ouvrage de Werner Ernesti.[25] Il existe plusieurs différences entre les deux versions. En premier lieu, la traduction du "De falconibus" se limite chez Ernesti aux chapitres 18 à 23, c'est-à-dire aux passages thérapeutiques.[26] Les différentes recettes y sont énumérées l'une après l'autre et étant donné la diversité des sources qu'Albert le Grand avait utilisées pour ces chapitres, il arrive que certaines recettes se répètent. Un autre aspect est que plusieurs termes latins, pas nécessairement les plus difficiles, restent sans traduction. Le lecteur se trouve alors devant un texte où les mots latins se trouvent à côté des termes allemands et il doit donc nécessairement connaître le latin pour pouvoir comprendre cette version "allemande". Dans une deuxième phase, le texte de Werner Ernesti est pourvu de gloses, qui en faciliteront la compréhension. Tout doucement, il se développe une terminologie spécifique en langue vulgaire, ce qui explique qu'environ 50 ans plus tard, on fait appel à Heinrich Münsinger pour rédiger une nouvelle traduction, indépendante de la première et presque exclusivement en langue vulgaire. Cette nouvelle version ne traite pas seulement de la thérapie, mais aussi de l'aspect ornithologique. Dans les différentes parties, Münsinger introduit en outre sa propre structure : par exemple, il met les recettes dans l'ordre *a capite ad calcem*, ce qui n'était pas le cas chez Albert le Grand et Werner Ernesti. La seconde traduction est ainsi plus tournée vers la pratique, alors que la première était surtout basée sur des sources écrites, aussi parce que son auteur n'avait personnellement pas de contact quotidien avec les rapaces.

Les traductions médiévales françaises du "De falconibus"

Du XIVe au XVIe s. furent exécutées quatre traductions françaises du "De falconibus", qui sont indépendantes les unes des autres. Elles sont toutes conservées à la BNF de Paris, sous les cotes fr. 1304 (XVIe s.), fr. 2003 (XVe s.; daté erronément de 1284 par K. Lindner[27]), fr. 25342 (XVe s.) et nouv.acq.fr. 18800 (fin XIVe - début XVe s.). Les quatre traductions sont de longueur inégale : le codex nouv.acq.fr. 18800 est le plus complet, contenant toute la traduction du texte latin, c'est-à-dire 24 chapitres, qu'on peut à leur tour subdiviser en paragraphes, basés sur les pieds-de-mouche dans le texte. Si on rapporte ensuite cette numérotation des paragraphes au texte latin et aux autres versions françaises, la comparaison des textes devient beaucoup plus facile. Premièrement, il s'en révèle que le ms. fr. 1304 est presqu'aussi développé que le codex nouv.acq.fr. 18800 : il n'y manque que sept paragraphes. En outre, il contient une petite histoire à la fin, racontant comment un autour aveugle est nourri par de jeunes autours. Ensuite, le ms. fr. 2003, le seul texte édité jusqu'à present,[28] contient une version complète mais fort abrégée. C'est-à-dire que tous les chapitres y sont présents, mais il manque plusieurs paragraphes et d'autres donnent plutôt un résumé qu'une traduction du texte latin. Finalement, le codex fr. 25342 ne contient que les chapitres XVIII et XIX. Le chapitre XVIII y est presque complet, à deux paragraphes près, alors qu'il manque plusieurs alinéas dans le chapitre XIX (7 sur 31).

Malheureusement, nous ne possédons pas de données sur les traducteurs ou commanditaires des différentes versions françaises. Toutefois, les manuscrits fr. 2003 et nouv.acq.fr. 18800 sont clairement exécutés avec plus de soin que les deux autres. Pour le ms. fr. 2003, cela se voit à la lettrine sur fonds d'or au folio 1, et aux dessins marginaux de cette page, avec des fleurs, des fruits et des feuilles. En outre, dans ces deux codex, les majuscules sont généralement rehaussées d'encre jaune et dans le ms. nouv.acq.fr. 18800, la division en paragraphes se fait par des pieds-de-mouche bleus et rouges. Avec l'emploi du vélin (à une époque où le papier était déjà beaucoup utilisé[29]), tous ces éléments indiquent que les manuscrits fr. 2003 et nouv.acq.fr. 18800 sont probablement des manuscrits de luxe, contrairement aux deux autres.

De l'autre côté, il est difficile à savoir quelle copie latine se trouve à la base de quelle copie française, parce qu'à première vue les copies latines se ressemblent beaucoup. L'histoire ajoutée de l'autour aveugle, que le traducteur attribue également à Albert le Grand, pourrait être un indice précieux, à condition bien sûr qu'on trouve le manuscrit latin qui présente également cette anecdote à cet endroit. Jusqu'à maintenant, ce n'était pas encore le cas ...

Comme pour les traductions allemandes, on constate aussi dans les différentes versions françaises une progression de l'emploi de la langue vulgaire. En effet, le traducteur du ms. nouv.acq.fr. 18800 (le manuscrit le plus ancien) ne possédait pas encore toutes les connaissances nécessaires pour bien traduire les recettes. Il utilise beaucoup de termes latins au lieu de leur équivalent français qui se trouve dans les versions postérieures, et à plusieurs reprises ces termes sont écrits de façon incorrecte (fautes de lecture qui trahissent une mauvaise compréhension des termes en question). Cela donne parfois des constructions bizarres comme "en jus fet de concussis rafano et de lubercis terre" (XVII.10). Dans les versions plus tardives, cela donne "en jus de rafain et de longs vers de terre" (ms. fr. 2003, XVe siècle) ou "en just fait de reffort et de vers de terre" (ms. fr. 1304, XVIe siècle). Sur un total de 231 ingrédients mentionnés dans le codex nouv.acq.fr. 18800, 45 - ou un sur cinq - ont gardé leur forme latine. Il s'ensuit que le lecteur doit nécessairement posséder quelques notions de latin botanique, sinon il aura du mal à bien comprendre certaines recettes! Ce problème diminue plus tard, parce que les codex du XVe s. contiennent respectivement un[30] et quatre termes latins et celui du XVIe s., plus développé, six.

Par contre, ce dernier codex remplace quinze fois le terme latin par un autre ingrédient, c'est le double des cas par rapport aux manuscrits nouv.acq.fr. 18800 (8 fois) et fr. 2003 (7 fois). En outre, il ne s'agit pas seulement des changements à l'intérieur d'une même catégorie (végétale, animale, minérale ou *preparata*), mais parfois le traducteur change une plante par un produit animalier, comme dans la recette XXIII.19, où la *char d'anel* remplace l'*anetum* du texte latin.[31] Une des explications possibles de cette divergence est que certains produits mentionnés par Albert le Grand n'étaient plus connus quelques siècles plus tard, soit parce qu'ils n'existaient plus, soit parce qu'ils avaient reçu un autre nom.

Les traductions médiévales italiennes du "De falconibus"

Finalement, il existe aussi trois traductions italiennes, dont deux partielles. La traduction complète date du XVe s. et est conservée dans le ms. Dresden, Sächsische Landesbibliothek, Ob 21, aux folios 107v - 153 v.[32] Des deux traductions partielles, l'une date de la fin du XIVe s. et l'autre du XVe s. Grâce à quelques chercheurs avisés, les textes ont pu être identifiés correctement, parce que les données dans les catalogues se révèlent incorrectes.[33] Dans les deux cas, il s'agit des traductions de la partie thérapeutique, respectivement les chapitres

20, 21 et 23 pour le manuscrit le plus ancien et les chapitres 21 et 22 avec la première partie du chapitre 23 pour l'autre.

Conclusion

Actuellement, nous connaissons neuf traductions médiévales du "De falconibus" d'Albertus Magnus: deux en allemand, quatre en français et trois en italien. Malgré les différences qui existent entre ces versions, il y aussi quelques points communs. En premier lieu, les renvois au texte-source et à son auteur son très rares : seul le ms. Paris, BNF, fr. 1304 mentionne explicitement le nom d'Albert le Grand, pas dans le corps du texte mais dans l'histoire ajoutée à la fin. Ce manuscrit est également le seul codex qui renvoie à l'ouvrage général *De animalibus*, trois fois au total. La première référence se trouve dans le douzième chapitre de la deuxième partie (= chap. XVI ms. nouv.acq.fr. 18800), où le scribe note "comme nous avons dit en notre livre, intitullé des anymables". *Anymables* doit dans ce contexte sans doute être considéré comme une erreur de copiste pour *anymalles*, puisque les autres renvois sont corrects. Le second exemple se trouve dans le dernier chapitre (= chap. IV.7 ou chap. 24, par. 4): "mais est encore assavoir en ce volume des anymalles". Dans ces deux cas, c'est le traducteur qui a ajouté la précision "des anymalles", parce que le texte latin mentionne pour la première citation "per ea quae in antehabitis istius scientiae libris conscripta sunt" et pour la deuxième "quod sicut in antehabitis libris dictum est." Le troisième renvoi, celui du passage ajouté, semble plus précis, parce que le traducteur mentionne clairement "Albert le Grand en son xxme livre des annimalles raconte comment ...". Toutefois, ce renvoi se révèle incorrect, parce que le passage original latin se trouve dans le huitième livre du *De animalibus* (second traité, chap. 6).[34] Il n'est pas clair pourquoi l'auteur renvoie au vingtième livre.[35]

En deuxième lieu, la partie thérapeutique est clairement la plus populaire. En effet, les traducteurs traduisent soit tout le "De falconibus", soit seulement la partie thérapeutique (entièrement ou quelques chapitres). En outre, il y a encore une autre ressemblance entre les différentes traductions au niveau des recettes. Dans le chapitre XIX, Albert le Grand suit fidèlement ses sources en inclut donc comme elles cinq recettes magiques dans le traité, toutefois en les laissant suivre par le commentaire "haec tamen ultima non ita rationabilia sunt sicut prima". Or, aucune des versions allemandes ou italiennes ne reprend ces recettes; elles sont également absentes des mss fr. 25342 et fr. 2003, à l'exception, pour ce dernier codex, d'une recette pour éviter que le faucon abandonne son maître. Dans ce cas, le remède se ressemble aux autres recettes, c'est-à-dire qu'il se constitue d'une combinaison de simples et ne contient pas de formule magique. Une telle "formulation de sorcière", parfois littéralement empruntée à l'Apocalypse, se trouve dans trois des cinq recettes magiques. Il est d'ailleurs à remarquer que dans le codex fr. 1304, qui contient également tous ces éléments magiques, moins un,[36] ces formulations sont restées en latin, alors que le traducteur du ms. nouv.acq.fr. 18800 a gardé une formule en latin et a traduit les deux autres.

Mais, avec ou sans recettes magiques, l'existence des traductions en trois langues différentes montre que le "De falconibus" d'Albert le Grand était bien apprécié dans différentes aires culturelles au moyen âge.[37]

Katholieke Universiteit Leuven

Notes

1. Pour une définition et des renseignements supplémentaires sur la littérature cynégétique, ou l'ensemble des traités relatifs à la chasse, voir B. van den Abeele, *La littérature cynégétique*, Turnhout 1996.

2. Dans le domaine latin, le *De arte venandi cum avibus* est à juste titre bien célèbre, alors que pour le domaine français, presque toute l'attention se fixe sur les trois chefs-d'oeuvre du XIVe s., à savoir le *Roman des deduis* de Gace de la Buigne, le *Livre de chasse* de Gaston Phébus et *Les livres du roy Modus et de la royne Ratio* d'Henri de Ferrières. Voici les éditions principales : Å. Blomqvist éd., *Gace de la Buigne. Le roman des deduis*, Karlshamn 1951; G. Tilander éd., *Les livres du Roy Modus et de la Royne Ratio,* Paris 1962 et G. Tilander éd., *Gaston Phébus, Livre de chasse (édité avec introduction, glossaire et reproduction des 87 miniatures du manuscrit 616 de la Bibliothèque nationale de Paris),* Karlshamn 1971.

3. Voir C.H. Buttimer éd., *Hugonis de Sancto Victore, Didascalicon. De studio Legendi. A Critical Text*, Washington 1939, 38-39 et 42-43. Une traduction anglaise se trouve dans *The* Didascalicon *of Hugh of St. Victor. A medieval guide to the arts*, translated from the Latin with an introduction and notes by Jerome Taylor, New York – London 1968; une traduction française dans Hugues de Saint-Victor, *L'art de lire.* Didascalicon. Introduction, traduction et notes par Michel Lemoine, Paris 1991. A ce sujet, voir également G. Eis, "Die Stellung der Jagd im mittelalterlichen System des Wissens", *Zeitschrift für Jagdwissenschaft*, 7 (1961), 25-28.

4. A la liste de 28 textes qui sont étudiés par B. van den Abeele, *La fauconnerie au Moyen Âge. Connaissance, affaitage et médecine des oiseaux de chasse*, Paris 1994, il faut ajouter une compilation de trois textes du XIIe s. (Rottenburg am Neckar, Diözesanbibliothek, H 38.

5. Le plus ancien traité connu est un réceptaire latin, conservé dans les pages de garde du ms. Vercelli, B. Capitolare, 144. Il a été édité par B. Bischoff, "Die älteste europäische Falkenmedizin (Mitte des zehnten Jahrhunderts)", dans *Anecdota novissima*, Stuttgart 1984, 171-82.

6. Van den Abeele, *La littérature cynégétique*, Turnhout 1996, 40.

7. Il s'agit surtout des traités du XIIe s. : la suite *Dancus rex, Guillelmus falconarius, Gerardus falconarius, Alexander medicus*, de même que le *De avibus tractatus* d'Adélard de Bath et la soi-disante lettre au roi Ptolomée par Aquila, Symachus et Theodotion. Il faut évidemment y ajouter les oeuvres majeures du XIIIe s., à savoir le *De arte venandi cum avibus* de Frédéric II et le "De falconibus" d'Albert le Grand, avec la traduction des traités orientaux de Moamin et Ghatrif, également réalisée à la cour de Frédéric II. La série de textes traduits se termine par *Le Debat du faucon et du levrier*, transposé du latin en français au XVe s. par Robert du Herlin.

8. A. Smets - B. van den Abeele, "Manuscrits et traités de chasse français du Moyen Âge. Recensement et perspectives de recherche", *Romania*, 116 3/4 (1998), 316-367.

9. Voir Smets - van den Abeele, "Manuscrits et traités", 44.

10. Ce sont les manuscrits connus à l'heure actuelle. Etant donné qu'il n'existe pas d'inventaire de manuscrits italiens, leur nombre réel pourrait être sensiblement supérieur.

11. Sur l'apport historique de l'étude des traités cynégétiques, voir van den Abeele, *La littérature cynégétique*, 75-84.

12. La bibliographie sur Albert le Grand est très riche, c'est pourquoi il faut se limiter à citer quelques travaux importants, comme G. Meyer - A. Zimmermann éd., *Albertus Magnus. Doctor universalis 1280-1980*, Mayence 1980 et J. A. Weisheipl éd., *Albertus Magnus and the Sciences. Commemorative Essays*, Toronto 1980.

13. Texte édité par H. Stadler éd., "De animalibus libri XXVI. Nach der Kölner Urschrift', *Beiträge zur Geschichte der Philosophie des Mittelalters*, 15-16 (1916-1920).

14. Voir van den Abeele, *Les traités de fauconnerie*, II, 338.

15. H. Werth, "Altfranzösische Jagdlehrbücher nebst Handschriftenbibliographie der abendländischen Jagdlitteratur überhaupt", dans *Zeitschrift für romanische Philologie*, 12 (1888), 181.

16. B. van den Abeele, *Les traités de fauconnerie latins au Moyen Age*, Louvain-la-Neuve 1991, II, 338. B. van den Abeele et K. Lindner (cf. note suivante) situent l'achèvement du *De animalibus* vers 1270, alors que G. Tilander écrit que le *De animalibus* fut terminé vers 1260. (Voir Tilander, "Albert le Grand", dans *Dictionnaire des lettres françaises. Le moyen âge*, Paris 1992, 35-37). De son côté, J. A. Weisheipl, dans *Albertus Magnus and the Sciences*, 573, date les dix premiers livres du *De animalibus* de 1260-1261, mais n'avance pas de datation pour les autres parties. Récemment, Pieter De Leemans a également consacré un article à la composition et la rédaction du *De animalibus* (P. De Leemans, "The Discovery and Use of Aristotle's *De Motu Animalium* by Albert the Great",dans J.A. Aertsen—A. Speer, ed., *Miscellanea Mediaevalia*, Band 27. *Geistesleben im 13. Jahrhundert,* Berlin—New York 2000, 170-88).

17. K. Lindner, *Von Falken, Hunden und Pferden : Deutsche Albertus-Magnus-Übersetzungen aus der ersten Hälfte des 15. Jahrhunderts,* Berlin 1962.

18. Ce sont les mss Milano, Biblioteca ambrosiana, B 91 sup. (XIIIe - XIVe s.); Oxford, Bodleian Library, Rawlinson D 483 (XVe s.) et Oriel College 28 (XVe s.) et Wien, Österreichische Nationalbibliothek, 5315 (milieu du XVe s.).

19. Les équivalents français de ces termes dans les différentes versions se ressemblent beaucoup, et on ne constate donc pas de véritable différence entre les siècles, comme c'est le cas dans le domaine de la *materia medica* (cf. infra).

20. Dans les chapitres VIII et IX, Albertus Magnus mentionne ce qu'il a appris d'un ermite fauconnier vivant dans les Alpes.

21. Traité de fauconnerie latin du XIIe s., qui est d'ordre thérapeutique. Voir Tilander éd., *Dancus rex, Guillelmus falconarius, Gerardus falconarius. Les plus anciens traités de fauconnerie de l'Occident publiés d'après tous les manuscrits connus*, Lund 1963.

22. Pour l'identification des sources, voir K. Lindner, *Von Falken*, 23-37 et van den Abeele, *Les traités de fauconnerie latins,* II, 341-43.

23. A côté de l'édition réalisée par K. Lindner (note 17), une étude beaucoup plus récente a paru : J.-D. Müller, "Naturkunde für den Hof. Die Albertus-Magnus-

Übersetzungen des Werner Ernesti und Heinrich Münsinger", dans *Wissen für den Hof. Der spätmittelalterliche Verschriftungsprozess am Beispiel Heidelberg im 15. Jahrhundert*, München 1994, 121-68. Le présent paragraphe est basé sur les écrits de K. Lindner et J.-D. Müller.

24. Voici la liste complète : Heidelberg, UB, Cpg 247, fol. 1-86 (ms. A, le plus important, ± 1460); Heidelberg, UB, Cpg 281, fol. 1-110v (B); Stuttgart, Württembergische LB, Cod. Cam. 4°52, fol. 1-116 (C); Stuttgart, Württembergische LB, Cod. HB XI, 51, p. 1-155 (D); Darmstadt, Hessische Landes- und Hochschulbibliothek, 448, fol. 1-117 (E); Halle, Marienbibliothek., 73, fol. 1-70 (F); Halle, Marienbibliothek., 74, fol. 1-44 (G); Vienne, ÖNB, Cod. Vindob. 5213, fol. 1-84v (H); Heidelberg, UB, Cpg 406, fol. 2-44 (J); Heidelberg, UB, Cpg 408, fol. 1v-46v (K) et *olim* Görlitz, Bibliothek der Oberlausitzischen Gesellschaft der Wissenschaften, A III.I.23, fol. 1-40 (L).

25. Heidelberg, UB, Cpg 406, daté 1404.

26. K. Lindner, *Von Falken*, 58, dit que le texte d'Ernesti contient les chapitres 18 à 33 de l'original, mais c'est impossible parce que le *De falconibus* contient seulement 24 chapitres. Toutefois, J.-D. Müller, "Naturkunde für den Hof", 133, a repris cette erreur.

27. La datation proposée par Lindner, *Von Falken*, 22, est incorrecte. Le codex daté de 1284 est le ms. Paris, BNF, fr. 12581, qui ne contient pas le traité d'Albertus Magnus, mais une traduction française du traité de fauconnerie du roi Dancus. Celle-ci a été éditée par H. Martin-Dairvault avec la traduction française d'Albert le Grand du ms. BNF, fr. 2003 (*Le livre du roi Dancus, texte français inédit du XIIIe siècle, suivi d'un traité de fauconnerie, également inédit, d'après Albert le Grand, avec un notice et des notes*, Paris 1883). Dans son introduction (XII), l'éditeur note que le texte du roi Dancus "n'est qu'une traduction de l'article d'Albert le Grand sur les faucons". C'est toutefois le cas contraire qui se présente. D'autres chercheurs y ont déjà attiré l'attention (voir J. Thiébaud, *Bibliographie des ouvrages français sur la chasse*, Paris 1934, 246). En effet, nous savons que l'original latin du traité du roi Dancus date du XIIe s. (cf. Tilander éd., *Dancus rex, Guillelmus falconarius, Gerardus falconarius*) et que celui-ci constitue une des sources pour la partie thérapeutique du "De falconibus". Faute de savoir plus sur le traité du roi Dancus, l'introduction de H. Martin-Dairvault est donc totalement incorrecte sur ce point. K. Lindner n'a pas constaté cette erreur et s'est donc basé sur des données fautives. En réalité, le ms. fr. 2003, qui contient le texte d'Albert le Grand et qui date selon lui de 1284, est de la fin du XVe s.

28. Martin-Dairvault éd., *Le livre du roi Dancus.*

Pour notre thèse de doctorat consacrée aux traductions françaises du "De falconibus", nous préparons une édition de chacune des quatre versions.

29. Cf. J. Lemaire, *Introduction à la codicologie*, Louvain-la-Neuve, 1989, 12.

30. Le seul terme latin dans le ms. fr. 2003 est *mastic*.

31. Une éventuelle explication pourrait se trouver dans l'équivalent (*anetum* -) *aneta* pour *anas*, et ensuite dans une confusion entre *asinus* et *anas*.

32. Pour plus d'informations, voir H. Werth, "Altfranzösische Jagdlehrbücher", 181-190.

33. Le ms. du XIVe s., conservé à Londres, Wellcome Historical Medical Library, 307, est mentionné par B. van den Abeele, *Les traités de fauconnerie*, II, 336. D'après le catalogue, il s'agit d'une version italienne de l'*Epistola ad Ptolomeum*, insérée dans le *Summa de modo medendi* de Gérard de Crémone. L'autre ms., conservé à la Biblioteca Nazionale Vittorio Emanuele de Rome, a été édité par G. Holmér, "Traduction en ancien

italien de quelques chapitres du *Liber de animalibus* d'Albert le Grand. Le manuscrit V.E.506", *Studia neophilologica*, 38 (1966), 211-56. D'après le catalogue, il s'agit d'un résumé en langue vulgaire du traité *Cura degli asturi* de Guglielmo ou Guillaume de Saliceto.

34. Stadler éd., "De animalibus libri XXVI", 618.

35. La numérotation des livres à l'intérieur du *De animalibus* n'a pas toujours été pareille. Ainsi, d'après l'édition de H. Stadler, le "De falconibus" figure dans le vingt-troisième livre du *De animalibus*, alors qu'il figure d'après l'autographe même dans le vingt-cinquième. Mais à première vue il n'est pas possible d'expliquer par ce fait le saut du huitième au vingtième livre. Pour la différence entre les deux numérotations, voir De Leemans, "The discovery and use".

36. La recette magique du paragraphe 25 a été remplacée par une autre, purement thérapeutique.

37. Cette contribution s'inscrit dans le projet "La traduction des traités biologiques médiévaux", lequel est subventionné par le Onderzoeksfonds / Research Fund K.U.Leuven (OT/01/06)